A COMPANION TO
NATURAL
BRITAIN

Discover the wildlife
around you

A COMPANION TO
NATURAL
BRITAIN

Discover the wildlife
around you

Foreword by
TONY SOPER

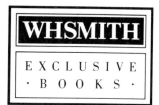

WHSMITH

EXCLUSIVE
· BOOKS ·

Produced exclusively for WH Smith Limited by
Marshall Cavendish Books Limited,
58 Old Compton Street,
London W1V 5PA

ISBN 1 85435 316 0

Printed in Hong Kong

This material was previously published in the Marshall Cavendish partwork *Country Companion*.

Contents

Foreword

An Englishman's home is his castle – but only so long as he's prepared to share it with a lot of lodgers. Some members of the extended household are welcomed; others, like the woodworm which makes a meal of the best furniture, or house mice, or bed bugs, are not. As people, we naturally see the pros and cons of these gatecrashers' lifestyles through human eyes. We see the mice as spoilers and destroyers of food, not as a tasty meal for the owl we cherish.

On the grand scale, the whole countryside can be viewed in this way, for in truth very little of it is devoid of the works of man. We have covered the land with the labours of centuries, to suit our own purposes. But that is not to say it is 'unnatural', because wild plants and animals adapt and adjust to the new opportunities which we place before them. As the dominant species, we hold it in our power to offer a place or deny refuge to any of the other creatures of the planet.

By concentrating on the man-made habitats in the landscape, this book gives a powerful insight into the lives of plants and animals which we, in effect, control. There are choices to exercise – to form our garden boundaries of plastic fencing, for example, or to grow a natural hedge which provides food, shelter and breeding sites for all manner of birds and other animals. Every development we undertake involves such choices; our decisions should balance the needs of other creatures with those of our own. The waterworks, swarming with starlings or wagtails, or the cemetery with lichens and moss-covered gravestones, can be just as exciting a place to watch wildlife as any 'natural' location.

Towards the end of the twentieth century 'natural' land is a pretty scarce commodity. Farmland – the rolling acres so often seen from car or train – is often perceived as natural. But farmland can be a much less inviting habitat to wildlife than the surburban jungles which include such quiet retreats as disused railway lines complete with tunnels for bats, or churchyards with their rare tranquility. The farm can provide a forbidding landscape of monotonous crops without the benefit of hedge or spinney, or with hedges brutally trimmed before the autumn harvesters can take their fill of berries, nuts and seeds. It is up to us to decide what kind of farmscape we want to provide just as much as what kind of housing estate or factory. And we are all realising, at last, that it matters, and there is reason for great hope that farms will become friendlier places for wildlife in the future.

That is a change in the right direction. For all man-made habitats, just like totally natural ones, enter upon a course of evolution from the moment they are initiated. The stone wall slabs, freshly cleaved from the quarry, take many years to become a graceful garden of mosses, lichens and creepers. The deserted railway line, given time, will become a foxy forest. Other habitats, like the golf course for example, are kept in a state of arrested development to suit a particular purpose of ours. But that is good news for the grassland flowers and the great crested newt which fit that particular niche, claiming the territory to flourish.

What is important is that we manage our supremely developed landscape in a way which is sympathetic to the needs of other creatures. It's all too easy to set aside nature reserves and then presume that the needs of wildlife have been catered for – a kind of 'them and us' world. How much better to strive for harmonious communities where man's works are shared enterprises.

It is much easier to think of doing things this way if you have some knowledge of the lifestyles and needs of other creatures, and *A Companion to Natural Britain* provides a good starting point for this kind of study. By describing a good selection of well-established and easily accessible environments a breadth of information is provided, with closer concentration on an individual species from each section – the barn owl and the bat in the churchyard, for example, to add deeper satisfaction.

To study wildlife in these semi-wild situations makes a lot of sense. The creatures are more used to the human comings and goings and less easily disturbed. It's much easier to watch birds in the local park where they will linger in the hope of food rather than panic at the first footfall. And from these semi-natural studies it's easier to progress to the really wild countryside – to compare the life of the harbour-side herring gull begging for food and nesting between the chimney pots with the remote coastal members of the same species; or to contrast the sedentary tame ducks of the village pond with the wild and wary mallards escaping the subarctic to winter on our estuaries.

Whether we like it or not we are in control of the landscape. Visiting truly wild country, coasts and mountain-tops is a marvellously refreshing experience. But if we all did it, all the time, the places would change and be destroyed. So it is good for this book to show the way to an understanding and enjoyment of the many wild creatures which share the developed sites of our everyday lives.

The Town House and Garden

Until about 100 years ago, most people lived and worked on the land. With industrialization, though, the picture changed completely and now most of us live and work in large towns and cities. Consequently, the countryside has largely become a recreational refuge from the pressures of urban life. But, excluded from the rural scene, many people have begun to take a greater interest in their homes and gardens, particularly deep within the bigger urban centres where many previously deprived housing areas are gaining a new lease of life.

NEAT TERRACES
(left) Modest brick-built terraced houses, like these, originally built for Victorian workers, are experiencing a new lease of life as the inner suburbs are repopulated and revitalized. Although their small front yards may be paved and contain little but the odd flowering shrub, their back gardens are usually more extensive, collectively forming a green oasis in the desert of brick and concrete, where wildlife can thrive. The fabric of the buildings creates a habitat, too, particularly for those creatures that live in association with man.

The idea of the elegant – or at least pleasant – town house and garden is not new. It inspired the ancient civilizations of Greece, Rome and Byzantium. But it is not one which has held much sway in British life in the many centuries between Roman Britain and Milton Keynes.

In medieval and Tudor Britain, towns were haphazard in layout and rural in character, distinguished initially from villages only by their markets. Some towns then developed more specialist functions, such as trade, defence or manufacture. But until the Industrial Revolution, trade remained the predominant function of towns, and merchants and tradespeople their main inhabitants. The upper classes were firmly rooted to their estates and the merchants aspired to the status of landed gentry. Town life therefore had little social standing, and town gardens, orchards and paddocks, though often extensive, remained firmly functional, devoted to the production of food and medicinal herbs.

CLASSICAL URBANITY

London, the seat of government and centre of intellectual life, was an exception to this rule. Especially throughout the 17th and 18th centuries, it offered a sophisticated, consciously classical urbanity, promoted particularly by Charles I and Charles II. Their main environmental contribution, however, was to the City's public spaces, such as the Covent Garden Piazza and St James's Park, and it was this almost European ideal of public urban space, rather than private gardens, which flourished subsequently in the gracious squares of Georgian London and Bath. Land prices were high and town houses were developed on ever narrower frontages; gardens, if any, were long and thin. Often, even grand houses backed onto a yard and mews rather than a garden.

Those interested in gardens for their own sake created them outside the town proper, as did the poet Alexander Pope in the early 18th century at his villa in Twickenham, Middlesex, thus per-

Many interesting reminders of grander bygone eras can be spotted in a street of town houses:

STANDARD GAS LAMPS come in various designs; those that remain are likely to be safely preserved.

COAL-HOLE COVERS feature an astonishing variety of designs, often extremely intricate.

PARISH BOUNDARY MARKERS usually take the form of bollards, which may be silver-coloured on a black base.

petuating the growth of the suburbs, that typic-ally British compromise between the illusion of country life and the reality of work in the town.

It was the Industrial Revolution which largely created the towns we inhabit today and erased forever the rural basis to British life. Dickens's

RISING STANDARDS *(above) Blocks of prestige flats, such as these, at the Barbican, in London, are designed with the total environment in mind, and, in striking contrast to the stark tower blocks of the 1950s and 60s, allow generous space for growing plants. This usually meets with an enthusiastic response from the tenants, creating an attractive and elegant synthesis of functional architecture and the flowing, organic lines of shrubs and flowers, which are allowed to spill over on to the common space.*

PERFECT PATIO *Those with the time, money and patience to spare can create what amounts to a replica in miniature of a classic grand garden, as this superb London patio garden illustrates.*

Coketown, black, noisy, and congested, epito-mized in fiction what Manchester presented in shocking reality The resulting cholera epidemics led directly to the creation of the Victorian public parks, but in the crowded inner areas it was the street, not the garden, which provided the only outdoor space for dwellings until well into the present century. What we think of now as town houses and gardens were at that time the rings of suburbs built by those escaping the horrors of the town proper.

GREENING THE CITY

Yet despite its chequered and low-key history in this country, the town garden is now in the ascendant. The British have never really taken to flats, keeping their feet on the ground in narrow-fronted houses. They have also always been great plant-growers, cramming their functional plots with herbs and flowers, or crowding windowsills and balconies with pots in the absence of a garden. The congestion and pollu-tion of industrialization eclipsed this passion; there was little space for gardens and few plants could survive the soot and shade. But the decline was temporary. Pollution was reduced by the Clean Air Acts, and many plants now benefit from the shelter and longer growing season of the urban micro-climate.

Meanwhile, the seemingly endless growth of the outer suburbs was checked, and there has been a movement back to inner city housing, which is generally being revitalized. On the one hand, the classical ideal of the town garden as an outdoor room, the setting for conversation, relaxation and natural beauty, has come into its own. On the other, the growing realization of the ecological importance of towns has led to the Greening the City movement, which at its most extreme sees the whole town as a potential garden or landscape, with roofs as alpine meadows, streets as ravines, houses as cliffs and balconies as terraces.

Around Town

**Indoors, spiders and beetles fight a losing battle against the
vacuum cleaner but are tolerated in the walled garden among the mosses,
ferns and flowers that attract other colourful insects.**

Human occupants of town houses are usually intolerant of the wildlife that shares their homes. The hammock webs of long-legged, fast-moving house spiders are regularly swept away. Spring-cleaning disturbs the silken cells of tiny, pink spiders which hunt, with groping stealth, across ceilings at night. Thousands of microscopic, scavenging mites are sucked into the vacuum cleaner with the dust.

Holes in curtains or carpets may have been chewed by the 'woolly bear' larvae of a small beetle, and stored woollen clothes are food and shelter for the caterpillars of clothes moths. Minute, round holes in antique furniture are the exit holes of furniture beetles, which, as 'wood-worms', have spent as long as four years eating their way through the wood.

In the kitchen, a variety of animals exploit careless food preparation and untidy storage. Agile cockroaches, waving their long antennae, scuttle behind the stove. Caterpillars of flour moths clog flour with sticky, silken threads, and several sorts of tiny brown beetles and their larvae gnaw at stored grain, nuts and spices. A pungent vinegary smell in the larder and tooth-marks on damaged food betray the activities of a house mouse. It is probably nesting beneath the floor boards, a space that may occasionally be home to quite harmless escaped pet snakes, such as North American garter snakes.

OUT OF DOORS

Few town houses are as teeming with wildlife as this might suggest, and it is only when we step outside the back door that we can really start nature-watching. Many town gardens are hemmed in and shadowed by tall buildings, but are often like an active green pool deep in a well of inanimate concrete and brick. Buildings are severe barriers to animals and plants, other than those that fly or glide, and most of the garden's unbidden guests have flown or parachuted in.

The majority of the weeds are those with plumed or feathery seeds that are readily transported by the wind, such as groundsel and rosebay willowherb. The garden plants attract bees, moths, winged aphids and other flying insects. Sparrows, blackbirds and other birds come for food and water, but there are no

mammals except the pipistrelle bat swooping overhead in the summer dusk, and the house mouse venturing out of a crevice in the masonry.

The walls and surrounds of the garden are a habitat in themselves. Grey-green, black and brown lichens splash stones with colour. On the damp paving slabs by the drain, cluster green, fleshy flaps of liverwort sprouting spore-forming structures like miniature parasols. Compact cushions of wall screw moss and glossy fronds of silky feather moss soften the surface of a wall. In a cool corner, leafy sprays of small ferns, such as wall-rue and maidenhair spleenwort, sprout from crevices, and the elegant fronds of male fern arch over the paving stones.

A lacy mesh of bluish-white cobweb on the wall surrounds the silk-lined lair of a shiny

TAWNY OWL
This versatile bird has adapted well to town life and is the only owl likely to be found in built-up areas. Its nocturnal hooting is a familiar sound even in city centres. In town, they feed mainly on house sparrows and brown rats but are also partial to earthworms. They generally nest in tree holes in parks, churchyards or large gardens but also build in chimneys. Although this is the commonest of our owls it is not found in Ireland.

TOWN HOUSE WILDLIFE

Jackdaws nest in chimneys, sparrows and swifts under the roof, and feral pigeons will colonize derelict buildings. Breeding or hibernating pipistrelles hang from the rafters, as may the papery nest of wasps. The beams may be infested with woodworm, the wood-boring larvae of the furniture beetle. Tortoiseshell and peacock butterflies will overwinter indoors but house spiders and their webs can be seen at all times. Clothes moths lurk in carpets as well as in the wardrobe.

Flies, cockroaches, ants and mice are unwelcome in the kitchen as they spoil or contaminate food. Both pharaoh's ant and the common cockroach were accidentally introduced from the tropics and need the warmth of heated buildings.

Many invertebrates relish the dark, damp undisturbed cellars and the conditions can be ideal for the wood-destroying dry rot fungus.

Outside, spiders and other invertebrates may fall prey to shrews and the snail-breaking song thrush.

KEY TO THE SPECIES
 1 *Feral pigeons*
 2 *Jackdaw*
 3 *Furniture beetle*
 4 *Pipistrelle bats*
 5 *House sparrow's nest*
 6 *Common wasps' nest*
 7 *Swift*
 8 *House sparrow*
 9 *Hibernating peacock butterfly*
10 *House spider*
11 *Clothes moth*
12 *Privet hawk-moth*
13 *Privet hawk-moth caterpillar*
14 *Garden spider*
15 *Bluebottle*
16 *Housefly*
17 *Pharoah's ant*
18 *Peacock butterfly*
19 *Song thrush*
20 *Zygiella x-notata spider*
21 *Green lacewing*
22 *Common cockroach*
23 *House mouse*
24 *Silver thread moss*
25 *Common shrew*
26 *Churchyard beetle*
27 *Woodlouse*
28 *Meta menardi spider*
29 *Dry rot fungus*

NESTING JACKDAW
(left) Jackdaws are noisy, sociable birds, often to be found where old buildings, such as churches and castles, provide nesting cavities. They are equally at home, though, nesting in chimney pots where their large twiggy nests may prove a nuisance to householders.

HOUSE SPIDER
(right) Found in houses in many countries, this familiar spider can survive for several months without food or water. Here it has trapped a fly and a crane fly. Females can live for four years but males have a shorter lifespan.

black spider, which rushes out to pounce on any woodlouse or other small animal entangled in her sticky web. Woodlice thrive in the garden, feeding on decaying plant material. They cluster in cool, dark, damp nooks and crannies as, being crustaceans, they breathe by means of gills, which need to remain moist. They may fall prey to another fierce spider, which is brownish-red with a pinky-grey abdomen and has long, curved fangs. It is an agile hunter specializing in woodlice.

A purple-leaved Myrobalan plum, gracing the garden in spring with its star-spangle of pale flowers, repays a closer look. Among the leaves, some of the bare twiglets prove to be immobile stick caterpillars, holding themselves rigid on their hind claspers. A flutter of yellow wings is not a butterfly, but a brimstone moth disturbed from among the leaves; this is what the stick caterpillars will develop into. The brimstone moth belongs to the Geometridae family, so called because the looper caterpillars are geometers or 'ground-measurers'.

Until recently, soot pollution limited the species that would thrive in a town garden, and tolerant plants such as buddleia and the tree of heaven were not only a sensible planting choice, but, in the absence of competition, would often establish themselves. Bumblebees and red admiral butterflies add busy noise and colour to the secluded garden as they feed at the fruity-scented buddleia flowers. Roses did particularly well when soot polluted the air, as the fungus that disfigures the leaves with large black spots is intolerant of pollution. Inner city gardens in the smokiest areas bloomed with cabbage roses and hybrid teas.

Honeysuckle twines up one of the supports of the balcony on the house, and on warm evenings the fragrant, nectar-rich flowers attract silver-Y moths and perhaps a privet hawkmoth. Ivy shrouds the other balcony supports, sheltering the nest of a song thrush in spring, and hibernating small tortoiseshell butterflies in winter. In October it swarms and hums with late-flying bees and large hoverflies collecting nectar from the globular clusters of small flowers.

Orange and bronze wallflowers and purple honesty brighten a sunny corner in spring, and their flowers attract orange tip butterflies. The bare soil around the wallflowers is punctured with neat entrances to the burrows of solitary mining bees, which bask on the warm ground between visits to the flowers.

Later in the summer, scatterings of fine soil particles appear at intervals along the edges of paving slabs. Black ants have been busy extending their underground nests, and preparing the

DRY ROT
This is the fungus most dreaded by householders. It can spread unseen behind wainscoting, under floorboards or in cellars, soon destroying all wood with which it comes into contact. It thrives in moist places which lack circulating fresh air and is particularly likely to attack derelict houses (as here) or little-used weekend cottages. To control it all infected wood must be cut out and damp must be prevented from rising from the foundations.

ORANGE TIP
(right) Perched here on a dead daffodil, this is a female which lacks the orange wing-tips of the male. They are typically butterflies of the countryside, but increasingly use cultivated crucifers, such as white Arabis *and dame's violet, as caterpillar foodplants and so have moved into gardens.*

SEROTINE BAT
(right) This large bat is confined mainly to southern England. Breeding colonies may often be in attics of old houses and they will also hibernate on roof beams. They hunt large moths and beetles over lightly wooded areas such as parks.

EVERGREEN FERNS
(below) Growing here on a shaded wall are wall-rue (top left), black spleenwort (centre left) and maidenhair spleenwort (centre). Found in the wild throughout the British Isles, these ferns may be planted in town gardens.

exits for winged males and females to swarm in July and August.

In the herb patch, sage, marjoram, mint and lemon balm scent the air, which is alive with bees and flies visiting the various shades of mauve and violet flowers. The sorrel, grown as a pungent addition to sauces, has gone to seed, and the tall, pink clusters dip and sway with chattering house sparrows stuffing themselves with the abundant seeds. Nearby, in the flower bed, the papery cups of decorative poppies are crowded with intricately-banded black and yellow hoverflies mopping up the pollen.

The pond, though small, is a focus of attention. A young sparrow and a female blackbird splash in the shallow water, and a feral pigeon ponderously dips its head to drink. Pigeons are the only birds able to swallow, and so do not need to tip their heads to drink. Peer into the water, and there is much to see – water snails browsing the green algae on the pond sides, a small water beetle trundling along, causing the mobile pupae of mosquitoes to loop down from the surface film, and a jigging, dancing swarm of minute water fleas.

BUSTLING BIRDS

The air above is as busy as the water beneath. House martins dart overhead with flickering, twittering flight and swifts swoop screaming between the buildings. The sun glints on the chestnut wings of a kestrel, which pauses to hover motionless above the nearby grassy railway embankment. A carrion crow flaps across with a hoarse squawk, disappears for a minute, and reappears with the limp body of a sparrow that it has struck down from among a feeding flock on the pavement.

Scraps put out on the bird table soon bring down noisy sparrows, squabbling starlings and stately, waddling feral pigeons to fill the small garden with fluttering noise.

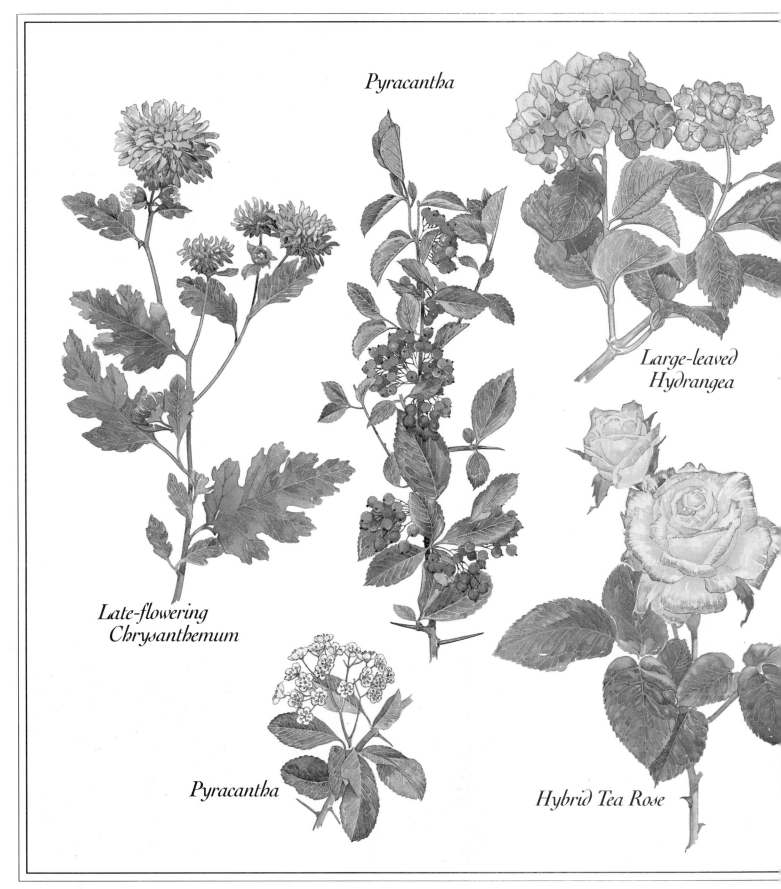

Pyracantha

Late-flowering Chrysanthemum

Large-leaved Hydrangea

Pyracantha

Hybrid Tea Rose

LATE-FLOWERING CHRYSAN-THEMUM (*Chrysanthemum x morifolium*) Native in China and Korea, this popular perennial appears in many golden colours and its heads bear a variety of forms. It produces dark green ovate leaves and sprays of compact daisy-like flowers.

PYRACANTHA (*Pyracantha coccinea*) Also known as Firethorn, this popular evergreen shrub is often grown as a hedge plant, or against a wall. It can reach a height of 15ft (4.5m) and clusters of small white flowers in summer are followed by orange, red or yellow berries.

LARGE-LEAVED HYDRANGEA (*Hydrangea macrophylla*) This perennial shrub will bear red or pink flowers in limy soil and blue flowers if the soil is acid. Its large, shiny and oval leaves have toothed edges. The plant has a rounded shape and will grow from 4-6ft (1.2-2m) in height.

HYBRID TEA ROSE (*Rosa 'Peace'*) Much loved by gardeners for its fragrance, abundant flowering, shiny leaves and its hardiness. It will grow to a bushy shape 5ft (1.5m) high. Unlike many other roses, the spent petals fall suddenly rather than withering on the plant.

Forsythia

Ornamental Quince

Winter Jasmine

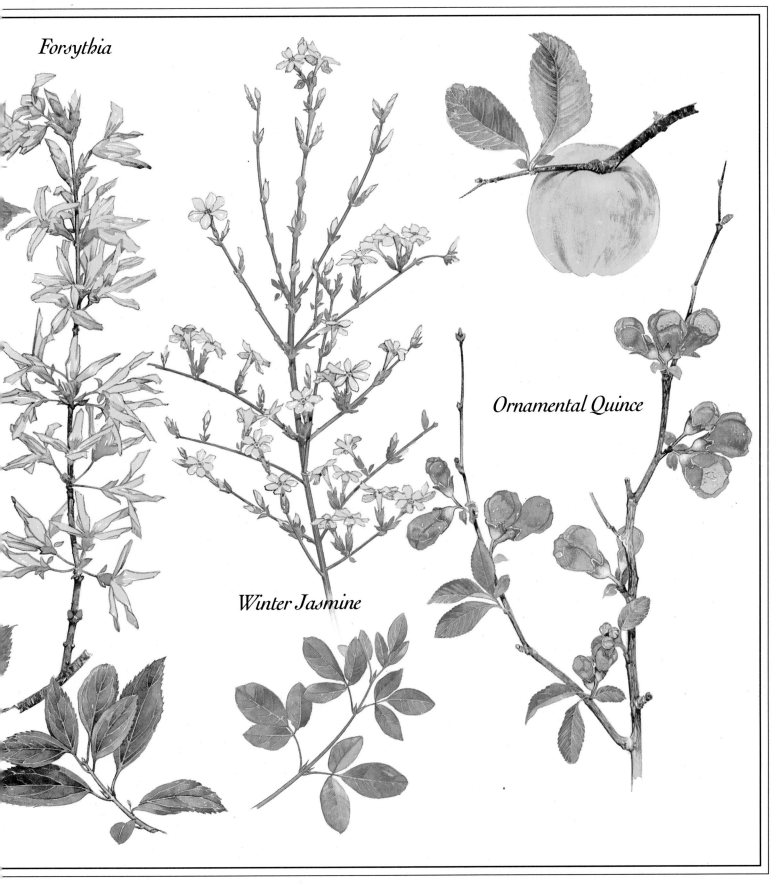

FORSYTHIA *(Forsythia x intermedia)* Introduced from China, this is one of the earliest spring shrubs to flower. It grows into a large bush, reaching 6ft (2m) when mature and its clusters of small yellow flowers are borne on straight, woody stems, before the leaves.

WINTER JASMINE *(Jasminum nudiflorum)* Often grown against a wall, this hardy, scrambling perennial can reach heights of up to 10ft (3m). Bright yellow trumpet-shaped, scentless flowers are borne in clusters on thin, leafless stems from October to March.

ORNAMENTAL QUINCE *(Chaenomeles speciosa)* Also known as Japonica or Japanese quince, this spring-flowering perennial bears large orange to pink blossoms. It will grow to 10ft (3m), and is suitable for growing against walls or in dry, sunny corners.

Plate 2

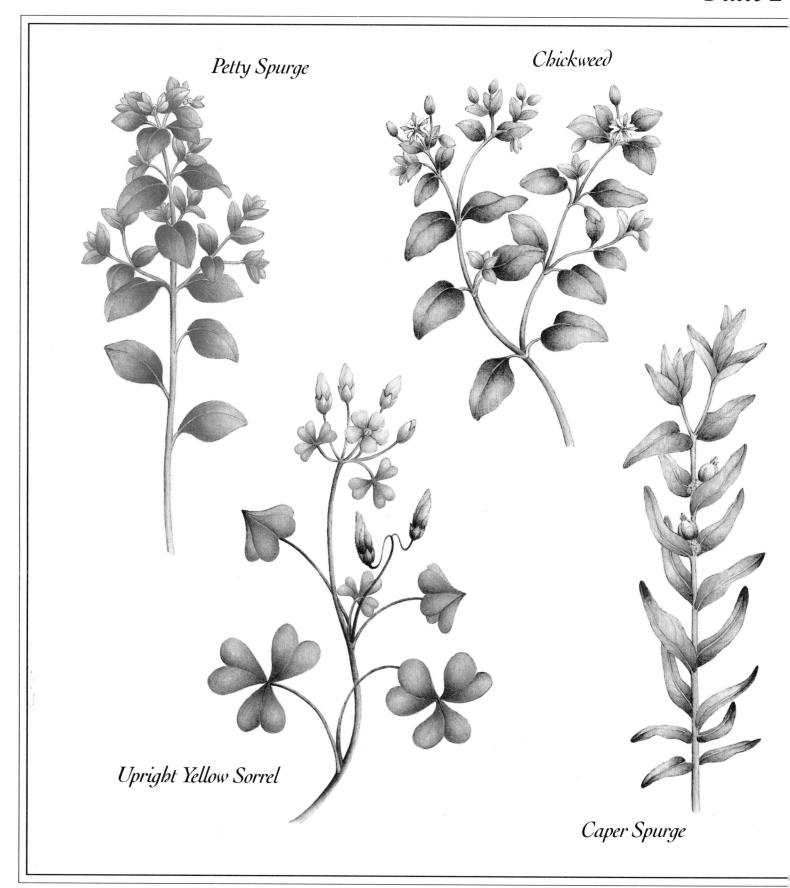

Petty Spurge

Chickweed

Upright Yellow Sorrel

Caper Spurge

UPRIGHT YELLOW SORREL
(Oxalis europaea) This annual
garden weed, commonly found in
south-eastern England, spreads by
means of underground roots. It
bears yellow flowers and purple-
tinged leaves on hairless, erect
stems from June to September.

PETTY SPURGE *(Euphorbia
peplus)* A common garden weed, this
12″ (30cm) annual bears clusters of
tiny naked flowers from March to
November. The flowers have a stalked
ovary and stamens, surrounded by
horned glands. Over 1200 seeds are
produced by each plant.

CHICKWEED *(Stellaria media)*
This common weed of gardens and
wasteland has small, weak stems
but can smother garden plants with
its straggling, spreading habit. It
flowers freely throughout the year,
producing tiny star-like blooms. Its
leaves and shoots are used in salads.

CAPER SPURGE *(Euphorbia
lathyrus)* A 3ft (90cm) biennial once
a much-prized ornamental plant. It
lost favour probably because its
milky juices cause irritation. It
produces poisonous caper-like
fruits and its leaves grow spirally in
pairs, up purplish-red stems.

Daisy

Annual Meadow Grass

Great Plantain

ANNUAL MEADOW GRASS (*Poa annua*) A common dwarf grass with long, broad blunt-ended leaves. Unlike many invasive grasses, it grows in clumps and has no creeping underground root system. It flowers through the year and plumes are borne on 6-12″ (15-30cm) spikelets.

DAISY (*Bellis perennis*) The common name of this familiar weed derives from 'day's eye', as the flower closes at sunset or in dull weather. Easily recognized in lawns by mat-like rosettes of oval leaves and small yellow and white, pink-tinged flowers, from March-October.

GREAT PLANTAIN (*Plantago major*) Also known as Waybread or Rat's Tail, this robust perennial is found on paths, roadsides and in garden beds throughout Britain. It grows up to 6″ (15cm) and bears a long flower spike June-September from which the seeds then develop.

The House Mouse

Often portrayed as harmless and endearing, the house
mouse's preference for sharing our homes and
our food have made it a serious pest.

It is late at night. Only the occasional sound of a passing car ripples across the deep silence of the house. By the skirting board a small nose appears followed by two paws and a pair of beady black eyes. The house mouse has appeared for its nightly forage in the kitchen. It scurries across to the table pausing to take some breadcrumbs at the base of the leg then scampers up on to a cupboard. There it sits, cleaning and preening itself with its paws. Suddenly it stiffens as it hears a click. On the other side of the room the cat, returning from a garden patrol, pushes open the cat flap. Spotting the mouse it tenses and crouches. Tail swishing, it prepares to leap, but before it can do so the mouse has got across the room and back to the skirting board with great speed and agility. The cat turns to washing itself, meanwhile keeping an eye on the mouse-hole.

A LONG PAST

This little drama is played out every evening in homes throughout the country, for the house mouse is one of the most widespread mammals,

being found wherever there is human habitation. Archaeological evidence in fossil remains show it to have existed in Britain since the Iron Age and its wild ancestor probably originated in the steppes of Asia. With such a long past, it is hardly surprising that the house mouse has entered into culture and folklore. Homer, for instance, writes of Apollo Smintheus – a god of mice – and Pliny describes how sooth-sayers valued mice, regarding white ones as a sign of prosperity.

The house mouse varies greatly in its appearance and many different colour forms occur. The British animals are usually a dull greyish-brown colour. Their underparts tend to be only slightly lighter, although they can be a very pale grey. An adult house mouse weighs about an ounce (30g), and is 3¾" (9cm) long excluding the tail, which is as long again. They are usually nocturnal, although not exclusively so.

The peak feeding times are at dusk and just before dawn. House mice tend to live in groups and are rapid and effective colonizers of new habitats. Populations develop a territorial struc-

VERSATILE MAMMALS
*(above) The house mouse
originated in the central
Asian and east European
steppes, where it lived wild
on the seeds of grasses. It has
since become one of the most
widespread mammals in the
world, with about 20
sub-species of varied
appearance. Our mice have
been present here since
before the Iron Age and are
found throughout the British
Isles and Ireland. House mice
thrive particularly well in
man-made environments. In
urban areas they inhabit
houses, shops and factories,
and in the countryside, farm
buildings, mills and, in
warmer weather, hedgerows.*

ture, with the males vigorously defending their own areas from outsiders – whom they will attack – particularly if the population density rises abnormally.

House mice occupy a wide range of urban habitats including houses, mills, factories and warehouses. They are particularly well-suited by their size, habits and ecological preferences to live close to people – especially in their homes as these offer food and shelter. In rural areas they occupy chicken houses, grain stores and all types of farm buildings. Some do, however, leave buildings in the warmth of spring to live in hedgerows, returning to shelter in late autumn.

House mice will eat just about anything. They prefer grain-based foodstuffs, but will take fruit and greens and have even been known to eat glue, plaster and soap. This omnivorous approach is vital in supporting their extremely prolific reproduction.

BREEDING HABITS

In urban habitats, house mice breed continuously, producing 4-8 young 5-10 times a year. The young are born in well-built nests of any available material such as paper, sacking, string, insulation, shredded grass and leaves. Naked at birth the young mice are fully furred at 14 days and mature rapidly. House mice have a short life-span and few live longer than 18 months. Like many animals, they have innate population controls – at increasing densities breeding declines and eventually ceases as the females become infertile.

To man, the house mouse is a considerable and unhygienic pest. It does not just take food, but taints it with its droppings. Unlike other mice, it has a most unsavoury smell and slightly greasy fur. It also carries disease via its fleas –

no longer plague, but bacterial infections such as *leptospirosis*, salmonella food poisoning and intestinal parasites like tapeworms which can be transmitted to man.

Attempts are often made to render houses 'mouse-proof'. Various poisons are also available. But the most effective weapon is probably the old-fashioned mouse trap. In the country there are natural predators of mice like owls, weasels and stoats. In urban areas there is the brown rat and the domestic cat – neither of which are so effective.

It is nearly dawn. The cat returns to the garden, perhaps anticipating better luck with baby birds. The house mouse is once more out again patrolling the kitchen in search of little scraps and leftovers. It seems fairly safe to assume that as long as we are around, the house mouse will continue to be with us.

NIGHT-TIME FORAGERS
(above) The house mouse is most active at night when it leaves its hideaway and sets out in search of food. Kitchen cupboards and larders are its main targets and cereals are its favourite food, although it will eat almost anything, even seemingly inedible substances such as soap, plaster and glue.

TWO BLIND MICE
(left) New-born house mice are hairless, blind and deaf, but within 14 days, they are fully furred and their eyes and ears have opened. Nests are made up from any available soft material, such as sacking, newspaper, string, grass and leaves. Up to 10 young are born at one time, although five to six is the average litter size. The young leave the nest at three weeks old and three weeks later, the female young are ready to breed.

The Collared Dove

**The rapid spread of the delicate, neat, collared dove
throughout much of Britain in less than 20 years
is one of the most dramatic success stories in nature.**

Perched comfortably on a television aerial, the collared dove is such a familiar sight in towns and villages throughout Britain that one would be forgiven for considering it a long-established resident. Surprisingly, however, it is a recent immigrant, having bred in the British Isles only for the last 30 years, and was known only as a rare visitor before then. The story of its relentless colonization reads like a well co-ordinated military campaign.

Recent bird colonizers such as Cetti's warbler have invaded quietly and inconspicuously, but the collared dove was not only anticipated by birdwatchers, but awaited for some 20 years before it finally made its great leap westward. It was originally a Middle Eastern bird, although the Turks, by introduction, had helped it establish a tenuous foothold in south-east Europe in the 17th and 18th centuries. It then began to spread north-west through Europe, by fits and starts. The pattern seemed to be a build-up of the population followed by a wide dispersal.

By 1912 the collared dove had reached the middle Danube region. In 1932, it was perching on Hungarian rooftops and the main spread had begun. By the late 1940s it had reached the Netherlands, Denmark and Sweden. In 1952 it penetrated Belgium and Norway, and the first lone male was heard singing his monotonous song at Manton, Lincolnshire. However, it was not until 1955 that the first nesting record was obtained in Britain, at Cromer, Norfolk. From then onwards, there was no stopping it. The final move was part of a last thrust westward that also carried collared doves to the barren, rocky western islands of Britain and Norway, reaching the limits of their western conquests.

FILLING AN EMPTY NICHE

The secret of the dove's success is that it appears to have found an unfilled niche for a small pigeon of cultivated areas with trees, that was only partly claimed by the long-established turtle dove. Once settled in its new home, the collared dove spread throughout Britain with its customary rapidity, to occupy the whole country except for the upland, treeless areas and the centres of large cities. However, looked

*BATHING BEAUTY
(above) Since its initial
spread in the mid-1950s,
the dapper collared dove has
rapidly become one of the
most familiar – and
conspicuous – garden birds
of villages and suburbs
throughout Britain. It is a
frequent visitor to feeding
stations and bird baths,
where, like other pigeons,
it drinks without raising
its head by sucking up the
water continuously. Its
attractive appearance is,
unfortunately, not matched
by a pleasing voice; indeed,
its doleful, monotonous
cooing, coupled with its
voracious appetite for grain,
has led to it being
regarded as a pest in many
parts of the country.*

HUNGRY SQUABS
At sheltered nest sites, collared doves often begin nesting as early as March and continue to produce young until as late as September. Given ideal conditions, they may rear five broods a year: one of the chief reasons for their efficient colonization of the country. The chicks, or squabs, are fed by both parents on a 'milk' of regurgitated liquid food, growing quickly on this rich diet and fledging within three weeks. The parents defend their young boldly against predators.

IN FLIGHT the collared dove shows a distinctive pattern of grey, pale bluish and unbarred brown feathers and white tail patches. From below, look for the striking black and white tail pattern.

at in detail, its local coverage is less complete than the overall picture suggests.

The unevenness of the collared dove's distribution is linked to two of its basic needs – food and a safe nest-site, hidden from predators. Regarding its diet, the collared dove does not seem to be able to take advantage of growing food sources, unlike the wood pigeon, which can strip bare fields of crops in hours and also take many weed seeds. Instead, it relies largely on farms and other places where grain or animal feedstuffs are available for at least most of the year, and there it has managed to establish small colonies.

The collared dove does not seem to have such obvious success in adapting to life in towns and suburbs, despite the large amounts of food on offer at bird-tables or other feeding sites. This may be because the bigger, bolder domestic pigeons tend to get there first. However, the collared dove manages to fare better where its other need – for a secure nest site – is fulfilled.

As a smallish bird, the collared dove is vulnerable to predators. In winter, when it may be forced to roost in bare trees, it is at risk from tawny owls, and may be threatened by a wide range of predators when nesting. It copes with this threat by hiding itself and its nest in evergreen trees. It favours conifers, particularly the exotic species planted in many parks and gardens, and also dense-leaved trees, such as yews.

Although adept at hiding when necessary, the collared dove can be a noisy bird, especially during the breeding season. It advertises its presence with an incessant, monotonous, mournful three-note call, *coo-coooo-cuk*, with the accent on the second note. When calling its mate to a new nest, it uses only two notes. Also, it often gives a strange, harsh growling call when it flies in to land near one of its own kind, or during the male's rising and falling courtship flight.

YOUNG BIRDS lack the black half collar of the adult and are generally greyer overall. Like the adults, they have slender, blackish bills.

UNTIDY NEST
The collared dove is not the greatest of architects, building a rather untidy, flimsy looking nest of fine twigs, stems and roots. Generally, this is cunningly hidden deep within an evergreen tree, but sometimes, as here, the birds choose to rear their family in a shed or other outbuilding.

EGGS Up to five clutches may be laid in a year, each consisting of two smooth, glossy white eggs.

The Village Pond

Set among the trees of the green, sharing pride of place with the church and the pub, the village pond was once at the very heart of village life across the land. And though seemingly natural features of the landscape, most ponds are as man-made as their surroundings. For it was the pond that held the vital supply of water which the whole village relied upon – for watering livestock, quenching the blacksmith's hot metal, fire-fighting, or even ducking witches. Now, their practical role long since gone, village ponds remain as living reminders of the countryside's ever-changing face.

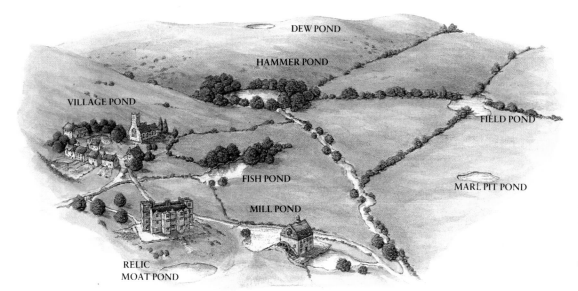

DEW POND

HAMMER POND

VILLAGE POND

FIELD POND

FISH POND

MARL PIT POND

MILL POND

RELIC
MOAT POND

COUNTRY PONDS
The village pond was not the only working pond. Shepherds made dew ponds to water the sheep. The field pond was dug for livestock, at the corner of four enclosed fields. The marl pit pond filled naturally, after marl (a fertilizer) had been dug out. The hammer pond powered tilt hammers for iron smelting. Mill ponds regulated stream water to power the mill wheel. Relic moat ponds are the remains of the manor house moat, and medieval fish ponds held fresh fish for the winter.

Only a few years ago it was impossible to escape hearing the croaking frogs in spring; so numerous were they, and the countryside ponds in which they spawned. Now, sadly, many ponds have disappeared, and with them the sound of the frogs, as piped water supplies have cancelled out their once vital role. Once, though, a pond lay at the centre of almost every village; ponds littered the fields to provide drinking water for cattle, or were the centrepiece of remnant woodland where they had earlier provided power for some ancient industry.

PONDS – MAN'S MARK

Although some ponds have a natural origin, maybe formed when some accident of the landscape damned the flow of a stream, most ponds represent man's mark on the countryside. A clue to this lies in the very origin of the word 'pond.' It comes from an old English source which also gave us the verb 'to pound' meaning to enclose or dam up.

It is easy enough to dam a stream to create a pool of almost still water, and sometimes ponds were made where a spring seeps from the ground. The soil at this wet spot is easy to dig out, making a hollow which soon fills to create a pond – a pond which is, moreover, being continually replenished by the spring to yield a supply of pure, uncontaminated water. Failing a stream or handy spring, a pond can be made by digging at a place where the underground water table nudges close to the surface. A further method, if the soil and bedrock are right, is to dig a hollow which will fill with rain draining from the land around and remain full, because, of course, the first requirement of a pond is that it should be reliable, and rarely dry up.

Dew ponds were also a feature of the open fields, particularly in chalk country, and were

NEATER PONDS
The village pond lives on, but now mainly for its decorative beauty rather than for its practical value. Compared to predecessors, most surviving ponds are now tidier, with concrete edges, goldfish and rafts of water lilies.

made to supply the grazing sheep and cattle with water, though some are to be found in villages. There is a fine round one in the centre of the village of Ashmore, in Dorset, for example.

Dew ponds were the source of many legends and credited with magic qualities, for not only was there a mystery about how they filled, it was thought that they never ran dry. Indeed, it was commonly believed that they were filled by miracle and that dew was a corruption of the old Norman word *Dieu* meaning God.

FOCUS OF THE VILLAGE

The village pond was the focal point of everyday life. In the days when almost every building was capped with thatch, fires must have been very common, and a close-at-hand water supply was essential. The pond was the watering place not only for the village cattle, but also for the slowly

FLOWER POWER
Bankside and pond plants – like these white water lilies and the smaller fringed water lily – build up a peaty soil, filling up the pond and slowly reducing the area of open water.

moving herds and flocks being driven along to market. Where the drovers rested and took their own refreshment while their charges were watered, the village pub put down its roots.

At this popular intersection in the village, local craftsmen would also set up shop. Here would be found the blacksmith. He made horseshoes and metal tools, such as scythes, quenching the red hot metal with water from the pond. In summer, before taking his horses to be shod at the smithy, the carter would often drive his wagon into the village pond, and leave it there for a while. If the weather was very hot and dry, there was a danger that the wooden wheels of the carts would shrink and shed their flat metal tyres.

The village pond was also the setting for some barbarous customs in past centuries. One such was the swimming of witches. A poor unfortunate suspected of witchcraft or sorcery would be tightly bound and thrown into the pool. Staying afloat was taken as a sign of satanic powers and was often enough to condemn the poor wretch to a terrible death at the stake. If the suspected witches did not float, they were not condemned, but could be well near drowned by the time they were pulled out. The last known swimming took place as recently as 1860 in a village pond in Bedfordshire.

Unfortunately, ponds have been disappearing in recent years as they are costly to maintain – for the fact is that any pond is doomed by its own evolution to dry up. Around its edge, reeds and other strongly growing plants are found; when they die their stems and leaves rot down to create a mushy peat, which in time builds up. A pond slowly fills in from its edges in this way. Village ponds which have been saved however, and are maintained for their beauty, have become havens for wildlife and often support more species than their ancient counterparts.

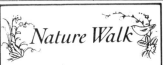

Nature Walk

Some symbols of the past are still found near the village pond. A few are:

DRESSED WELL Flower pictures, made in thanks for the ever-springing waters, decorate some wells.

STOCKS are often found near the village pond, the focal point of everyday life in the past.

OLD PUMP Often beautifully made in cast iron, the communal pump drew water from the well or pond.

POLLARDED WILLOWS close to the pond provided poles to build animal enclosures.

Freshwater Pondlife

In and around the quiet and peaceful village pond is a bustling community of attractive wildlife, from the flowers and birds which adorn its edges to the weird and wonderful underwater creatures.

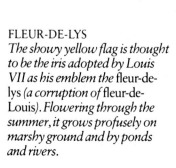

Set like a jewel in the heart of the village green, the pond provides an oasis for a fascinating diversity of wildlife. Even quite small ponds can be excitingly busy places, cram-packed with literally hundreds of different species of plant and animals jostling for space. What makes a pond such an interesting habitat is that it is really a collection of many different 'micro habitats.' From the soft dark mud deep below the water's surface to the fertile marshy border, a pond can provide a home for an enormous number of plants and animals which live in, on and around its clear calm water. But providing a habitat for such a rich variety of life is only possible where the needs of the various species can be finely balanced. Where this balance is upset, the pond may be overrun with weed, choked by reeds or become totally devoid of life.

In a relatively small pond it is the amount of dissolved oxygen in the water which has the greatest effect on the variety and quality of pond life. The most fertile ponds are often fed by bubbling brooks whose waters are rich in oxygen. But most village ponds are stagnant and can only absorb oxygen at their surface and by the action of plants growing in and on the water. But while plants do, indeed, produce oxygen during the hours of daylight, at night they absorb it too, and where the balance is on a knife edge this night-time loss can be disastrous for the larger air breathing creatures such as fish. Even in daylight the picture is complicated, for water which is warmed by the sun holds less oxygen than cold water. So ponds in partial shade may well be lusher than those exposed to the sun.

Yet while plants can clog and choke a pond, when kept in check, either naturally or by man, they not only add to the beauty and variety of pond life but provide food and shelter for the animals which live in and around this watery habitat.

Much of the plant life of the pond is of a very simple kind. In the pond water are myriad microscopic one-celled plants which are the food supply of numerous minute animals. Some of these simple plants are linked in chains which float freely, or form filaments which are seen as slimes on stones and other hard surfaces. Duckweed is a 'free floater' – though much more complex. Its mass of tiny leaves look as though they belong to a single plant, but in fact they are all individual plants each with its own roots trailing beneath the surface. Although extremely successful, free floa-

FLEUR-DE-LYS
The showy yellow flag is thought to be the iris adopted by Louis VII as his emblem the fleur-de-lys *(a corruption of* fleur-de-Louis*). Flowering through the summer, it grows profusely on marshy ground and by ponds and rivers.*

WILDLIFE OF THE VILLAGE POND

The underwater plants and insects provide food for birds and flying insects. Swallows and pied wagtails catch hatching insects, as do dragonflies and damselflies. Mallard filter tiny plants and animals, dabchicks dive for insects or fish and the moorhen feeds on insects, plants and seeds. Pond skaters trap insects that fall onto the water. Under the water, the great diving beetle and water spider hunt for prey.

KEY TO THE SPECIES

1 Horsetail
2 Bulrush
3 Swallow
4 Water plantain
5 Farm duck
6 Dabchick
7 Moorhen
8 White water lily

9 Emperor dragonfly
10 Common duckweed
11 Mallard
12 Amphibious bistort
13 Pond skater
14 Damselfly
15 Whirligig beetles
16 Pied wagtail

17 Frogspawn
18 Water spider
19 Great pond snail
20 Toadspawn
21 Three-spined stickleback
22 Spiked water milfoil
23 Silver water beetle

THE FEROCIOUS GREAT DIVING BEETLE
(above) These large water beetles store air beneath their wing cases as they swim underwater. Bold hunters, they attack everything from insects to small fish.

THE HANDSOME RUDD
This is a fish of stillwaters and is most at home among the water plants. Rudd eat great diving beetles, water snails, insect larvae and plants but fall prey to the voracious pike. Rudd can live for ten years.

FIERCE WATER SHREW
This secretive little grey hunter preys on insects, frogs and even small fish – which it paralyses with its poisonous saliva.

ters can be wiped out if the pond freezes. So to avoid this, duckweeds build up reserves of starch throughout the summer until they become so heavy that they sink to the bottom. There they spend the gloomy, frozen winter months until spring when they are light enough to float to the surface once more.

There are also many plants which are more highly developed. Milfoil is one that roots in the mud of the bottom and remains submerged. It has to cope with a dim light, but has few other plants jostling it for space below the surface. The water lily, on the other hand, is also rooted in the bottom mud, but floats its leaves flat on the surface where they are in direct sunlight. At the edge of the pond grow plants which are little different from those of dry land, but the fact that their roots can survive submerged in the shallow water, where oxygen is scarce, allows them to colonize the fringe of the pond.

Among the pond's animals are numerous water insects, some equipped with gills to take oxygen from the water and others which must come to the surface to breathe. Their differing lifestyles mean they are rarely in direct competition. The great diving beetle, a surface breather, is an active hunter, both as an adult and in its larval form, preying on insects, small fish and tadpoles. Dragonfly nymphs have a similar diet but because they have gills they can wait in ambush, seizing their victims with a hinged 'jaw' that shoots out to snap up prey. The water boatman – a surface breathing

bug – is also an active predator, sucking the body juices from its victims. The slow-moving snails, however, are herbivores. They usually feed by grazing slimes from the leaves of the pond weeds. Surprisingly, snails are not on the menu for adult beetles, even though their jaws are strong enough to deal with the shell, and even though the larva of one beetle – the great silver water beetle – dines on snails almost exclusively.

On the surface, pond skaters and whirligig beetles – both named after the way they move – hunt small flies which fall into the water. The surface which they patrol is, however, not the barrier it may first appear, for both beetles and boatmen do hunt on both sides of it while many flying insects, such as dragonflies and mosquitoes, have larval forms which are aquatic.

The amphibians – frogs, toads and newts – also frequently cross the barrier, spending most of their adult life on land but returning to the pond to lay their eggs. Water shrews, too, are at home both in and out of the water.

The pond's largest underwater predators are the fish – ranging from the small three-spined stickleback to carp, rudd and the voracious pike. Top of the food chain, however, are the birds. Some, such as the dabchick, feed exclusively on the pond, while others, like the moorhen, will be more often seen on the surrounding land. Temporary residents attracted by a seasonal glut of food may range from the stately grey heron, to the flittering swallow and wagtail.

LIFE IN THE BALANCE

Although the pond seems to be a remarkably stable place, with its crowded life in balance, there are several factors which constantly threaten to wreck the ecosystem and end the pond's life.

Pollution poses the major and most serious threat. Farmyard ducks, if there are too many of them, may lead to the serious decline of a pond. Not only are they voracious feeders, soon stripping a small pond bare of life, but they may also pollute it with their droppings. Although pollution can be caused by agricultural chemicals many village ponds are simply polluted by organic waste. Bird droppings, cow pats or the slurry from cattle sheds can all cause havoc.

Such wastes are worked on furiously by bacteria which rapidly use up the oxygen dissolved in the water, thus killing fish and water insects.

Even where such pollution is less severe the results of organic contamination may be equally dire, for the pond may fill with green slimes, flourishing on the nutrients that the bacteria have released. They block the light from the milfoil and other submerged plants which gradually disappear from the polluted pond.

So while the attractive village pond seems such a natural and stable part of the scene, it is, in fact, anything but. Regular cleaning and other active conservation is needed if it is to remain an atractively rich and varied haven for wildlife.

MOTLEY WATERBIRDS
(below) The native moorhen – not a duck – nests on the pond. Tufted ducks may occur naturally but the goldeneye is usually a wing-clipped ornamental. Aylesburys and muscovy ducks are farm birds, bred for eggs and meat.

DELICATE DAMSELFLY
(left) These attractive insects skim low over the water, usually flying into the wind, though they are often blown backwards by it.

NESTING DABCHICK
(below) Also known as the little grebe, the dabchick nests on mounds of plants. It dives frequently for food.

GOLDEN EYE

TUFTED DUCK

MUSCOVY DUCK

AYLESBURY

MOORHEN

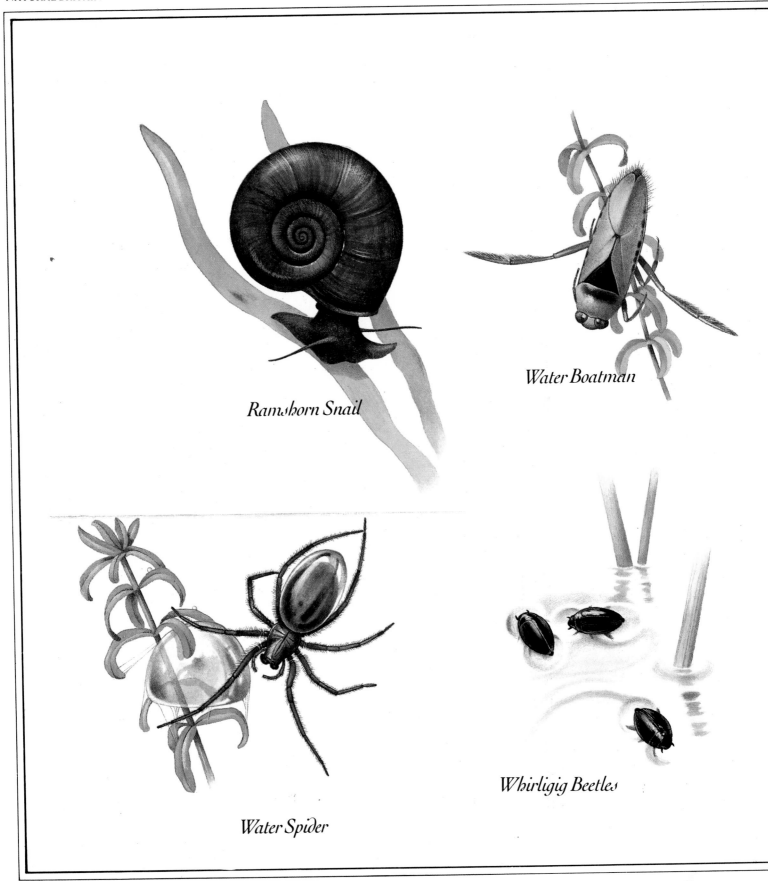

Ramshorn Snail

Water Boatman

Water Spider

Whirligig Beetles

RAMSHORN SNAIL (*Planorbis planorbis*) Recognizable by its flat shell and its slender tentacles, this snail has both male and female sexual parts, and can fertilise its own eggs. It is found in streams, ponds and ditches with plenty of weed. Its red blood is adapted for oxygen.

WATER SPIDER (*Argyroneta aquatica*) The only truly aquatic spider, the water spider can live under water by trapping air in a silk 'bell', attached to plants in still water. It is a plain brown spider, with ferocious fangs, capable of nipping humans, and eating tadpoles.

WATER BOATMAN (*Notonecta glauca*) This is a lively bug which swims on its boat-shaped back, and dives to eat tadpoles, larvae and tiny fish, which it kills by injecting poison from a sharp 'beak'. Eggs are laid in the stems of water-plants in spring, and mature in two months.

WHIRLIGIG BEETLE (*Gyrinus natator*) About 1¼" (6 mm) long, these beetles gyrate in groups over the surface of stagnant water during the summer. Their eyes are divided in two, to enable them to see above and below the water. Feeds on dead insects and fish.

Pond Creatures

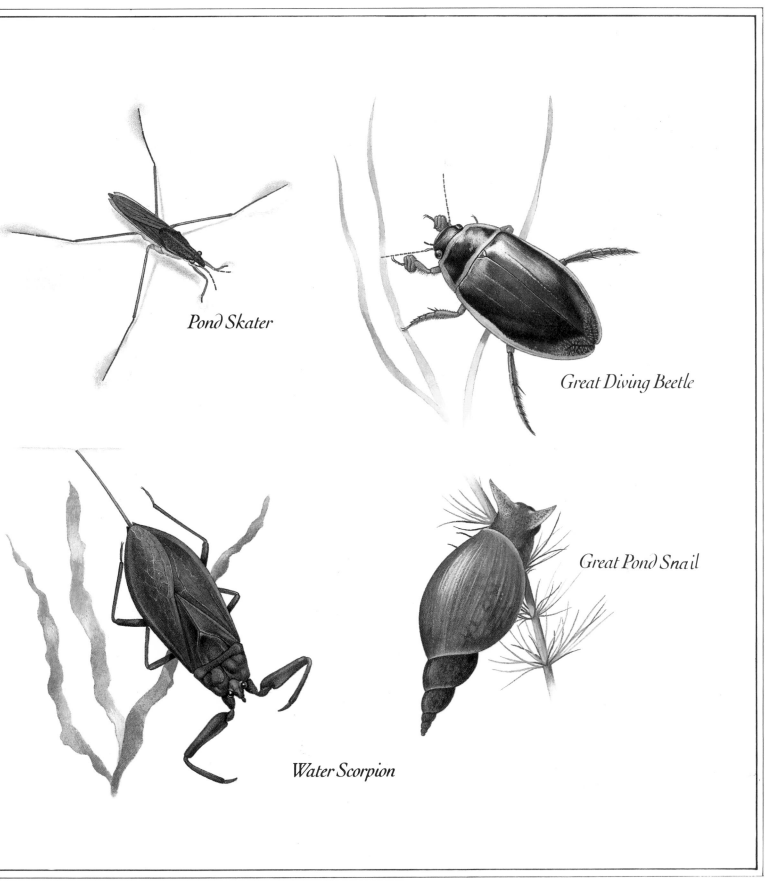

Pond Skater

Great Diving Beetle

Water Scorpion

Great Pond Snail

POND SKATER (*Gerris lacustris*)
This ⅝″ (15 mm) insect uses its four long legs to stand over the pond surface, and its two front legs to hold small insects which it eats with its beak. The eggs are laid in spring and attached to water plants, and hatch as diminutive adults.

WATER SCORPION (*Nepa cinerea*)
An inhabitant of stagnant weedy ponds it has a long tail-spike, through which it breathes oxygen from the surface of the water. The adults are poor swimmers and are usually flightless. It has bright red underwings and a sharp beak.

GREAT DIVING BEETLE (*Dytiscus marginalis*) A greedy carnivore throughout its three years of life, this beetle feeds on insects, small fish and tadpoles, which it paralyses by injection. The adult breathes underwater by trapping oxygen in its wing-cases.

GREAT POND SNAIL (*Lymnaea stagnalis*) A large 2½″ (6 cm) grey-brown shelled snail capable of fertilizing its own eggs. It lives for a year, feeds on algae and the remains of small pond-dwellers, and has to surface in order to breathe. It is prey to fish and water birds.

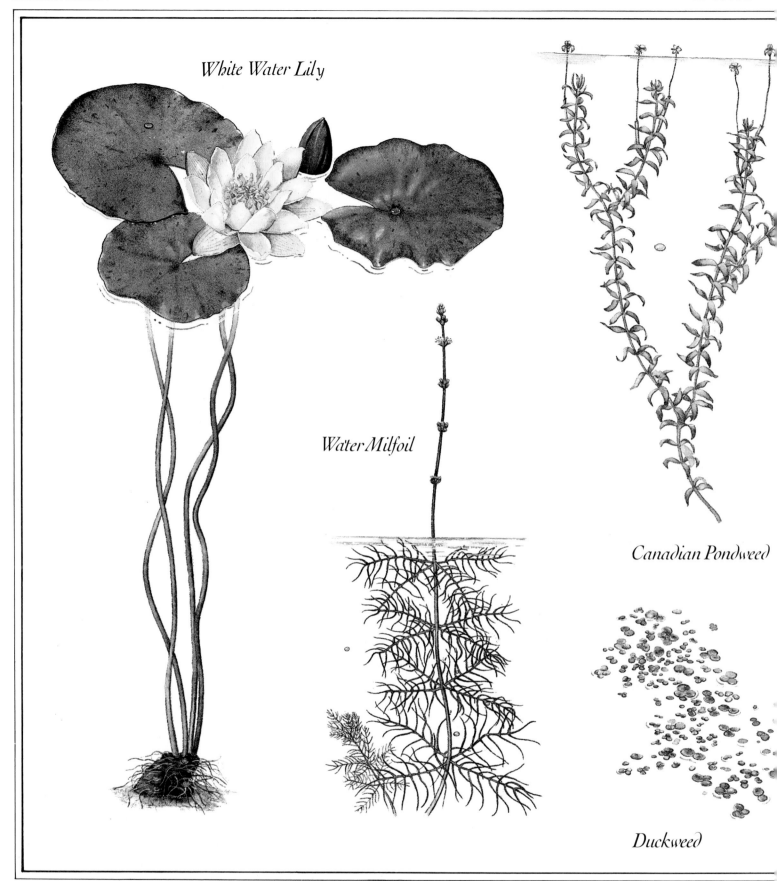

White Water Lily

Water Milfoil

Canadian Pondweed

Duckweed

WHITE WATER LILY (*Nymphaea alba*) White flowers, 4-8" (100-200 mm) across, float among dark round leathery leaves, and open only in full sunshine in late summer; they are widespread in sheltered, fresh water especially in parks and ornamental lakes.

WATER MILFOIL (*Myriophyllum spicatum*) A long feathery waterweed which grows entirely submerged in still or sluggish waters. The deeply cut leaves grow in whorls of four or five, longer than the intervening stem. Spikes of tiny red flowers emerge in June and July.

CANADIAN PONDWEED (*Elodea canadensis*) Introduced in 1842, this plant has spread rapidly. The dark foliage is completely submerged, and the tiny purplish female flowers float on the end of long threadlike stalks. Rarely, male flowers are borne underwater.

DUCKWEED (*Lemna minor*) Tiny free-floating plants which will carpet the surface of any stretch of still water with masses of tiny 1/8" (4 mm) emerald leaves. It will sometimes produce small greenish flowers in June and July. Beneath the leaves, it has thread-like roots.

Aquatic Plants

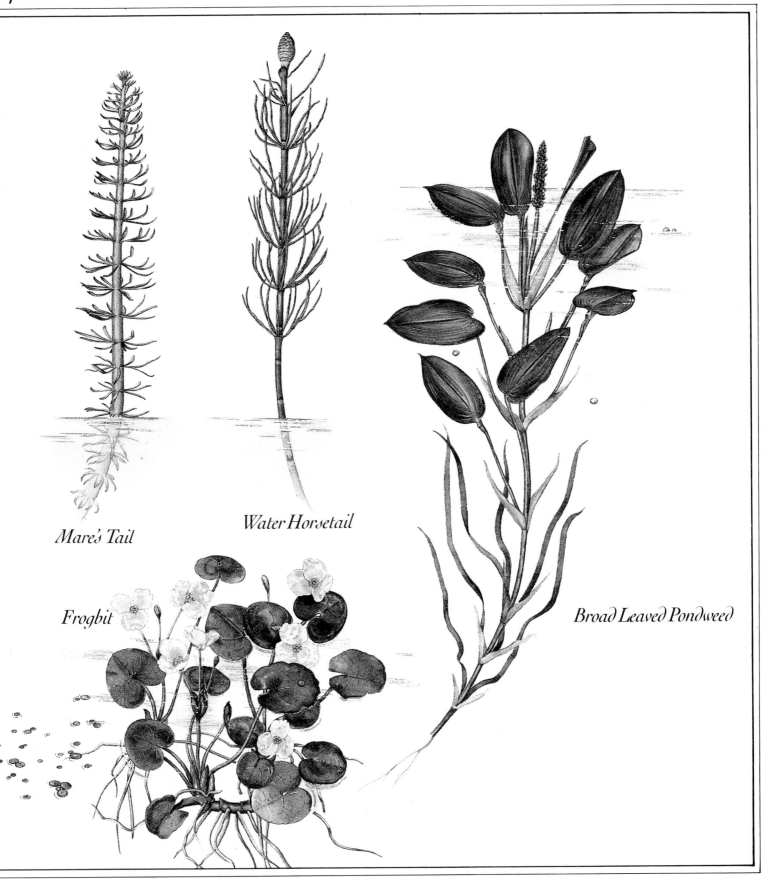

Mare's Tail

Water Horsetail

Frogbit

Broad Leaved Pondweed

MARE'S TAIL *(Hippuris vulgaris)*
Similar, though unrelated to
horsetail, from which it can be
distinguished by its tiny pink flowers
at the base of whorls of soft dark
green leaves. Unlike horsetail it does
not produce terminal cones. Found in
flowing water and lakes.

WATER HORSETAIL *(Equisetum
fluviatile)* This smooth, pale green
plant reaches 5′ (1.6 m), part of
which is generally submerged. It is
widespread in marshes and shallow
lakes, making dense stands of hollow,
furrowed stems tipped with small
black cones in June.

FROGBIT *(Hydrocharis morsus-
ranae)* A free-floating perennial with
1″ (25 mm) dark green, kidney-
shaped leaves, and white flowers
with each of the three petals spotted
yellow at the base produced in July
and August. It is an uncommon
inhabitant of the South of England.

BROAD LEAVED PONDWEED
(Potamogeton natans) The glossy
floating oval leaves of this plant
support spikes of insignificant
greenish flowers which are
pollinated by the wind. It also has
stalk-like leaves which remain
submerged beneath the surface.

The Mallard

At home in town and village, as well as on open country water, the adaptable and well-loved mallard with its 'quack-quack' call is almost everyone's idea of a duckpond duck.

At the sight of children standing by the village pond, bread in hand, the handsome mallard and his mottled brown mate swim urgently towards the titbits. Paddling furiously, necks outstretched, breasts low in the water pushing out bow waves that leave wakes like water darts speeding to a target, mallards from all over the pond quickly home in on the source of food – for the mallard has little fear of man. Indeed, the domestication of this most common of British ducks began many centuries ago and the cross breeding of wild mallards with 'escaped' domesticated birds has made the mallard remarkably tolerant of man.

By tolerating close contact with man mallards are able to use waters that less confiding ducks dare not exploit, whether they be concrete-banked reservoirs, the watercress beds, village pond or even a fountain in a city square. In keeping with this adaptability, mallards will eat almost anything and find rich pickings in man's leftovers as well as more natural food such as waterweed, seeds, insects and molluscs. They may even visit fields to feast on spilt grain or waste potatoes.

The mixture of wild and selectively bred domestic stock has also robed the mallard in a huge variety of plumages: some are pure white, others virtually black, some are pale fawn, others dark brown. But even though the species has such a vast wardrobe of feathers, one detail – in the male birds – shows that it is just one big family wearing different clothes – and this is the characteristic pair of curled-up feathers on the tail.

THE 'CLASSIC' MALLARD

The ancestor of all these mallards, though, can still be seen today, garbed in original colour. This is the 'classic' mallard drake – rich bottle-green head running to a deep chocolate-brown breast with both colours sharply separated by a thin band of white, sitting neatly round its neck like a crisply starched collar. Next to the male, the female is

FEATHER CARE
Preening is an important part of the mallard's daily life, for inadequate feather care can leave the plumage in bad condition and affect the state of the bird's general health. As well as cleaning and tidying up its plumage, the bird also coats its feathers in a waterproofing oil produced by the preen gland, located just above the tail.

During July-September the birds moult and are unable to fly. At this time the male acquires an 'eclipse' plumage similar to that of the female, to better camouflage him from predators.

UP-ENDING
The mallard feeds by dabbling on the surface of the water or up-ending to reach plants and animals found near the bottom of the pond.

quite dowdy and is soberly clothed in mottled shades of brown and buff. But this is for good reason, for it is she who sits on the eggs and her unobtrusive colours help conceal her from her predators.

FINDING A MATE

In spring the winter flocks divide up into pairs and start courting. The boldly coloured males perform a variety of displays, designed to show off their

DOWNIES
Young mallard 'downies' are capable of looking after themselves almost from birth, and often take to the water within a few hours of hatching.

finery to best advantage. All these displays take place in water, and if the pond is small and there are other drake mallards around, passions run high, for the presence of a female mallard ready to mate is like a red rag to a bull.

Attracted by the female a group of anything from three or four up to a dozen or more drakes may gather, and all try to mate with her, squabbling among themselves as they avidly pursue her. Chases develop as she takes to the air in her attempts to escape. Eventually, one or more will successfully mate her in the roughest manner — there have been many cases of females being drowned by the vigorous attentions of too many over-enthusiastic males.

After mating the female finds a nest site and constructs a nest cup, lined with down plucked from her own breast. Although most sites are on the ground, mallards adapt to all kinds of artificial situations and will use nest boxes, and holes in or under buildings. Some females even build in pollarded willows or in the broad branches of waterside trees. The young then have to bounce to the ground to find the nearest water, but this they take in their stride and it does them no harm.

Incubating the eggs and caring for the chicks is left entirely to the female, but if the eggs are lost or the young chicks taken by a predator, she will mate again and produce another clutch. Thus young ducklings can be seen on village ponds throughout the spring and summer months.

Once the chicks are hatched, the female broods them for several hours until their down is dry and they are ready to take to the water. During the first few weeks many of the young will fall prey to pike or rats, or if the weather is cold and wet they may even starve to death. In fact, by the time they learn to fly properly, over half the young will have been lost.

Nevertheless, the mallard population is buoyant, and with up to 150,000 breeding pairs producing up to ten young each year the mallard is likely to remain our most common species of duck.

KEY FACTS

IN FLIGHT the double white wing bars of the drake are clearly visible from a distance and the bright blue speculum of the female helps identification. The neck is held outstretched and the wings are set well back.

ADULT MALES are easily recognised by their striking plumage. But juveniles and males crossed with domestic breeds can still be identified by their two curled up tail feathers.

EGGS are laid usually between March and May and range in colour from white through cream and buff to a pale greenish-blue or olive-brown. Mallards have single broods and lay 11 to 15 eggs.

The Common Frog

The fascinating progress from spawn to tiny froglet – from water to land dweller –
has thrilled countless generations of children. And the lowly frog retains its
miraculous mastery of both elements throughout its five or six years of life.

Welcome harbinger of spring, the frog is more often to be heard than seen when, in February and March, the males croak their amorous song to advertise their presence to females. At other times the frog may be seen sitting stock-still, blinkingly contemplating its next meal with its large golden eyes. When its prey comes in range, out flicks a long, whip-like sticky tongue, which disappears again in the same moment as the frog gulps and blinks. Strangely characteristic, this blinking serves a vital function, for the frog swallows by pulling its eyes down into its head and these push the food down the gullet.

Familiar to almost everyone, the common frog – Britain's only native species – is a surprisingly interesting and complex creature. Often found on land – but seldom far from water – the frog is an amphibian, the name given to vertebrates which start life under water, breathing with gills and later progress to air-breathing. The common frog has achieved a mastery of land and water habitats unequalled by any other animal. As a tadpole it has gills like a fish, but as it grows, it develops lungs, enabling it to escape from its aquatic nursery and breathe air. But the miracle does not end there – frogs have the astounding ability to absorb oxygen through their skins – a fact which allows them to return to the water and spend the winter safe at the bottom of ponds.

Either of these two quite separate ways of obtaining oxygen can be used by itself for long periods of time. On land, frogs mainly use lungs of a kind very similar to our own. The actual mechanism of breathing is rather different though, because frogs have no ribs to expand their chests, and no diaphragm either.

The frog's answer to this problem is a pulsating throat and special valves for opening and closing the nostrils. What happens is that the nostril valves open, the throat is pushed downwards to suck in air, and the valves then close. When the throat contracts back, air cannot get out of the nose and

MASTER OF DISGUISE
Frogs vary enormously in colouration – from grey-green, to yellow, to dark brown – with all sorts of darker marbling and speckling. They can also change colour to suit their environment, and within a matter of minutes can blend with their background. They differ from toads in being, at 4" (10 cm), one third smaller, and having smooth and moist, as opposed to warty and dry, skins. During the mating season, males can be distinguished from females by rough patches which grow on their front feet to help them clasp their mates.

so is forced down into the lungs. In fact, air is usually pumped back and forth between mouth and lungs several times by these throat movements before the nose valves open again, letting out the stale air. One consequence of this way of breathing is that the frog has to keep its mouth closed the whole time, except of course when it is feeding.

The second method, used when underwater, is simply to employ the whole skin surface as a breathing device. This is particularly effective in winter because more oxygen dissolves in cold water than in warm, giving a better supply. Winter hibernation in rivers is therefore made possible, since cold running water contains lots of oxygen and is less likely to freeze over.

Because of their special adaptation, frogs must breed in water, and during the mating weeks the surface of a favoured pool bubbles with multitudes of couples. The male clings, sometimes for days, to the back of a female, and fertilizes her eggs as they are expelled in their thousands. The eggs then sink, until the surrounding jelly has swollen enough to carry them to the pond surface.

In April and May the eggs hatch and a good pond teems with tadpoles in the weed and around the warm, shallow edges. Later, for a week or so around midsummer, the pond again becomes a frog spectacular, with hundreds or thousands of thumbnail-sized babies leaving the water after their metamorphosis from tadpoles.

Many frogs stay in the pond for a month or two after breeding, hiding quietly in the weed until the weather gets warm enough to entice them out on to dry land. During this time in the pond the frogs do not eat anything at all – they cannot feed underwater – and many die of exhaustion or are killed by predators, such as herons, before the spring is out. For the rest of the summer they live mainly in long grass or other vegetation, often in village gardens, where they become the gardener's ally eating all the slugs, snails and insects they can find. At this time of year they will only return to the

COMMUNAL MATING
(above) In spring, a favoured pond will resound with the croaking of hundreds of enamoured males, which attempt to grasp any likely amphibian, or object, in the mating clasp.

TRANSFORMATION
(right) After 10 days, the tadpole digests the spawn jelly and emerges as an algae-eating tadpole. It develops limbs and lungs and leaves the pond at 12 weeks, fully equipped to catch and digest the prey which form its adult diet. At this stage (below) froglets are 1/2" (12 mm) long and vulnerable to a great variety of predators.

pond if the weather becomes very hot and dry; conditions frogs do not like at all.

By the autumn they will be in good shape, with the females already developing next year's eggs, and looking for somewhere to hibernate. Most of the females and some of the males ride out the winter in some suitably protective spot on land, such as the bottom of a compost heap or deep inside a drystone wall. Many males, however, will opt for the pond and sometime in November bury themselves there in the bottom mud. This is a real test of their breathing methods because they may have to spend several months like this with only occasional visits to the surface, during mild spells, for some fresh air.

The dangers of predation, suffocation or starvation are compensated for by the enormous numbers of eggs laid by the female. Possibly only five of the original 1500-3000 eggs will survive to breed, but this still represents progress, and compared to mammals of a similar size, frogs have a generous life-expectancy – up to 12 years.

The Churchyard

Ancient buildings on ancient sacred ground, Britain's country churches and their churchyard plots stand, as many have done since time immemorial, largely untouched and unchanging. Traditionally cordoned off from the surrounding land by a boundary fence, hedge or wall, churchyards enclose small enduring corners of the countryside – fragments of the landscape as it once used to be. And by offering refuge to animals and plants from the ongoing ravages of man on the land around, many churchyard sites present themselves as fascinating living museums of life and times, past and present.

HAWORTH CHURCHYARD
The dank winter scene in the Brontë churchyard near the moors reveals mosses and lichens beneath the trees, with Irish yews in the background. The tightly packed graves leave little room for flowers.

As more and more of our towns and cities bite into the countryside, changing the landscape all around, and as new farming methods continually alter its face, there are increasingly fewer undisturbed rural areas to be found. Yet there is one particular man-made habitat that has remained almost unchanged for centuries – the country churchyard. These sacred places – the spiritual hearts of old rural communities – are remarkably enduring, and generation after generation's respect for them has helped guarantee their preservation.

Many of Britain's rural churches were originally built by the Saxons, from the sixth century onwards, mainly of wood. By the time the Domesday Book was written in 1086 these ancient wooden buildings had largely been replaced by stone-built churches, and there were hundreds, if not a few thousands, in existence across the land. Churches were erected generally close to the centre of the village and enclosed to allow for, and to demarcate, sanctified ground for burials. The enclosure was usually a hefty wall or stockade, sturdy enough to prevent livestock entering the area and despoiling the hallowed ground. Thus the churchyard was simply an area taken from the surrounding meadowland – as almost every village contained extensive hay meadows to provide winter feed for livestock.

A VARIETY OF HABITATS

These meadows were probably already ancient grazing sites themselves, so the corners of churchyards we see today, where no graves or plantings have disturbed the ground, are relic patches of very old meadow – tiny portions of the landscape as our ancestors of over 1,000 years ago saw it. Such patches may contain a scatter of meadow flowers – flowers which were once common to the surrounding fields but which have long since disappeared from them with the constant ploughing and 'laundering' of the fields by modern farming.

The vegetation in parts of the churchyard may also be quite unusual, especially in quieter corners where, perhaps because they have remained untended for many, many years, a natural wild tangle has become firmly established. Protected by the wall from damage by grazing, and from interference by man, such areas may offer an unusual profusion and variety of species. Also standing testament to the churchyard's long

OLD VILLAGE HEART

OLD 'WILD' VEGETATION

RELIC MEADOW

ENCROACHING TOWN SUBURBS

MODERN 'LAUNDERED' FIELDS

WILDLIFE OASIS
(left) Unaltered, perhaps for centuries, the churchyard is often a wildlife oasis in an area that has changed radically all around. Its well-established trees and shrubs will be rich in insects and also offer nest sites for birds. Meadow flowers and their butterflies have gone from the surrounding ploughed fields but flourish in the churchyard's grassy areas. Tarmac and new buildings may have replaced countryside, yet the churchyard remains a haven.

Churchyards are rich in reminders of the past which reveal the antiquity of the site. Here are a few:

CELTIC CROSS Over 1,000 years old, this ancient design of cross, in which the circle symbolizes Eternity, is found mostly in western Britain and Ireland.

LYCHGATE A roofed churchyard gate where bearers waited with the coffin for the priest. Some date from medieval times.

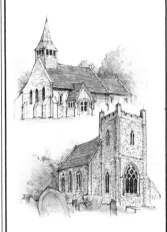

SPIRES AND TOWERS You may come across a timber belfry and spire, or a flint tower with battlements and tracery windows.

undisturbed state are the mighty yews. Gnarled and knotty, some of these Methuselahs among trees have spread their protective arms over the gravestones for over 1000 years.

The churchyard wall itself is usually an interesting mini-habitat, particularly on the churchyard side, and may be colonized by insects and plant life that have learned how to exploit this unchanging place. Indeed, helped by the wet, temperate climate, Britain possesses some of the finest wall vegetation in all Europe.

The lowly compost heap also creates a tiny habitat. Within its rich, warm mulch – perhaps built up over the years in the same place, from decomposed graveyard grass clippings and dead flowers – grass snakes and numerous insects can find a home.

Britain's churchyards, therefore, offer an exciting array of mini habitats all in one. A recently surveyed churchyard in Dyfed, Wales, for instance, revealed an area of grassy heath (a relic of the old countryside), a patch of trees and scrub, a damp

A SAXON CHURCH IN SUSSEX
Perched on the South Downs, the churchyard of St Mary's in Sompting has downland flowers in its short turf and lichens on the church roof.

area with streamside plants and an ancient hedge – all in less than half an acre.

CHANGING CHURCHYARDS

Yet while the churchyard may be beyond the reach of the developer, it may not escape the attentions of a tidy-minded gardener. Not everyone accepts a natural tangle for its own sake – or for the wildlife it encourages. So some churchyards are being ruthlessly tidied up, the mini-habitats cleared away and the grounds weeded of their old meadow 'weeds,' destroying the habitats and the 'real' nature of the churchyard. It is to be hoped that these tiny oases for wildlife, particularly those engulfed among the urban sprawl, live on as they always have, especially in the face of the pace of change in the landscape all around.

A Sanctuary for Wildlife

Bounded by a wall alive with plants and insects, the churchyard is a wildlife wonderland of unusual lichens and flowers and a rich hunting ground for bats and owls.

The modern countryside is, generally, a much tidier place than it was even as little as 50 years ago. The trend nowadays on the part of many farmers and landowners is to clear away old, ruined buildings or to cut down any offending tangle of vegetation. Yet ruined buildings, in their decay, and wild overgrown patches of land which have remained undisturbed for years on end offer rich habitats for wildlife. Today, perhaps the closest we have to these once-common habitats 'run wild' are the many country churchyards of Britain. Though, at first sight, such places may seem surprising candidates, churchyards, in many cases, have remained largely undisturbed for centuries.

The building itself, with its tower or steeple and its high roof, offers roosting sites and nesting ledges and crevices for pigeons, jackdaws, kestrels and owls. While, within the churchyard, a fine balance often exists between all the colonists which has been built up over a long period of time, and a close fitting mosaic of communities can be found. Some may be relic communities – small fragments of countryside long gone. Others are created by the way that the churchyard is managed – for example, the areas of close cut turf and the parts where the grass grows tall may each have a separate spectrum of wild flowers.

Many of the churchyard's inhabitants spend only a part of their time around the churchyard. This is particularly true of the bats. Bats lead remarkably dual lives, behaving quite differently in summer and winter, and often moving to different roosts as the seasons change. In summer, attracted by the insect-rich churchyard, bats congregate in a large breeding colony, often in the church itself. In winter, however, when bats are inactive, many choose quite different roosts and these may be in hollow trees rather than in buildings.

VISITORS AND RESIDENTS

The house martins which nest under the eaves of the church or hunt the churchyard from nests on houses nearby are also attracted by the bountiful insect life. They are said to return to their birth area

WILD DAFFODILS
Churchyards from Wales to East Anglia are havens for our truly wild native daffodil. Sadly, this is no longer common due to overpicking and land drainage. Many garden varieties are, of course, also planted in churchyards.

THE CHURCHYARD'S LIVING HABITATS

The churchyard's micro-habitats – short turf, shrubs, trees, the compost heap and the churchyard wall – are home to countless insects. Bats and house martins catch them in the air and the robin, wren and wolf spider hunt them among the foliage and on the ground. Mice and voles among the undergrowth also feed on insects and are themselves preyed on by owls and the grass snake, which will also eat nestling birds. The holly blue butterfly lays its eggs on holly in the spring and on ivy in the autumn and the caterpillars are eaten by many birds. Lichens encrust the stonework, while ferns, mosses and flowers find niches on the wall.

KEY TO THE SPECIES

1 *Yew tree*	11 *Lichen* Ochrolechia pirella
2 *House martins*	12 *Ants*
3 *Barn owl*	13 *Compost heap*
4 *Pipistrelle bat*	14 *Moss*
5 *Holly blue*	15 *Fern*
6 *Herb Robert*	16 *Rusty-back fern*
7 *Wild daffodil*	17 *Lichen* Xanthoria parietina
8 *Robin*	18 *Wolf spider*
9 *Wren*	19 *Feather moss*
10 *Wall screw moss*	20 *Grass snake*

ANCIENT YEWS
Yews have long been associated with churchyards. The common yew (right) is notoriously difficult to date as the heart wood rots away, leaving a hollow trunk and so making it impossible to count the annual growth rings. However, our oldest trees are likely to be about 1,000 years old. The Irish yew (below), with its typical upswept branches, is a cultivated variety often planted in churchyards.

after their long migration from Africa. If so, these attractive birds may well be among the longest established of village families, having consistently visited and lived in the area over many centuries. Originally, martins nested on river cliffs and rocky crags. But the eruption of stone-built churches after Norman times may well have been followed by a house martin population boom, for they are quick to take advantage of new nest sites. Of the house martin, Shakespeare's Macbeth exclaimed: 'No jutty, frieze, buttress nor coign of vantage, but this bird hath made his pendent bed.' Shakespeare was often an acute observer of the natural world.

Easy hunting also attracts owls to the churchyard where they prey on the mice and grass-eating voles which can be very numerous among the tussocks. The barn owl – traditionally a bird of ruins – may nest in the tower itself. Barn owls, easily identified from afar by their ghostly shriek, are now quite rare, and certainly as likely to be seen near a church as any modern barn.

Lesser birds keep these aristocrats company. Wrens and robins, found in many different habitats, are common churchyard birds, for they like the seclusion and ground cover that the churchyard often gives.

Many churchyards have fine compost heaps and grass snakes take readily to these, using them not only for hibernation but also as nurseries for their eggs – the heat produced by the decaying plants helps their incubation. Grass snakes often spend the summer near water, and here the village pond alongside the churchyard can also be an attraction. The frogs, toads and newts that breed in the pond may also move to the churchyard when they leave the water after mating. These amphibians seek cool, humid surroundings for the summer, so a churchyard containing dense patches of nettles and other plants is an ideal refuge.

The wild flowers of the churchyard vary a great deal, depending on the type of land which was originally enclosed. Flowers typical of meadow, heath, woodland or other habitats may flourish in different churchyards. West Country churchyards, for instance, are often a haven for our truly wild daffodil – known locally as the Lenten lily – which is a traditional woodland and damp pasture flower. The snowdrop's origins are uncertain – it may not be a native species – but spectacular white drifts adorn many churchyards in spring.

The walls surrounding the churchyard form a world of their own, often colonized by rock plants. In this quick-draining micro-habitat, pennywort, wall pepper (which has hot-tasting leaves), wall rocket, wallflower and pellitory-of-the-wall often root in the cracks. Familiar wild and garden plants can also be seen growing on the walls, but are often stunted as a result of the dryness; they also flower and seed earlier than their cousins on the ground.

A number of plants which grew originally on

NODDING SNOWDROPS
One of the first flowers of the year, snowdrops are known as the flower of 'Hope.'

TOMBSTONE LICHEN
Orange Xanthoria parietina *grows on limestone memorials.*

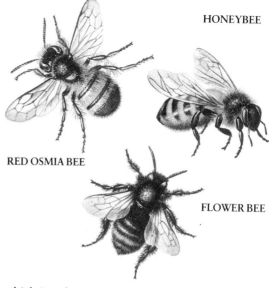

CHURCHYARD BEES
(right) The familiar honeybee compared with two species which burrow into the mortar of the churchyard wall to make their nests.

HONEYBEE

RED OSMIA BEE

FLOWER BEE

GRASS SNAKE
(left) This harmless snake is Britain's largest and commonest snake, and is easily identified by the yellow or white patches on its neck. The warmth of the churchyard's compost heap attracts females from a wide area, each laying up to 40 eggs which hatch in August or September. In winter, grass snakes hibernate for up to six months in the churchyard wall or under tree roots.

which is, of course, lime-based. The churchyard may contain a real library of lichens – up to 180 different species have been recorded in some places. Their ages can be compared from the dates carved into the stones they occupy.

Walls also have a specialized population of insects and spiders. The wall brown butterfly is a grassland species but enjoys basking on the warm stone. Flower bees and the red osmia bee burrow into the loose mortar to make their nests. The hunters include the long-legged harvestman (which may be seen sipping dew) and the funnel web spiders whose webs cover a hole in the wall where they await their prey. Walls make excellent observatories as their small inhabitants can be easily watched as they go about their business.

WREN AT THE NEST
(below) The female wren feeding a nestling with a juicy green caterpillar. She raises two broods, largely on a diet of moth caterpillars. Wrens spend much of their time in thick cover, hunting insects, so the churchyard's tangled vegetation is an ideal habitat.

inland cliff faces are now more likely to be found growing on walls than anywhere else. Ivy-leaved toadflax is one example. It exhibits a fine reproduction strategy adapted to its rocky habitat: once seeded, the stems bend to avoid the sunshine and, as a result, often plant their seeds in cracks in the wall behind them.

Some mosses and ferns are also typical of walls: though one side of the wall may be dry and baking hot, the shaded side will be cool and rather humid, forming a perfect habitat for these plants. The wall and the gravestones are also noted for their lichens. These simple slow-growing plants have no roots: they gain the nourishment they need from mineral traces dissolved in the rain. Some lichens are found on acid stone, others on limestones. Limestone lichens may also be found on acid stone, but they will be growing below the mortar,

RUSTY-BACK FERN
(below) Also known as scaly spleenwort, it grows naturally in cracks in limestone rocks but is more often found on walls, growing from the lime-based mortar.

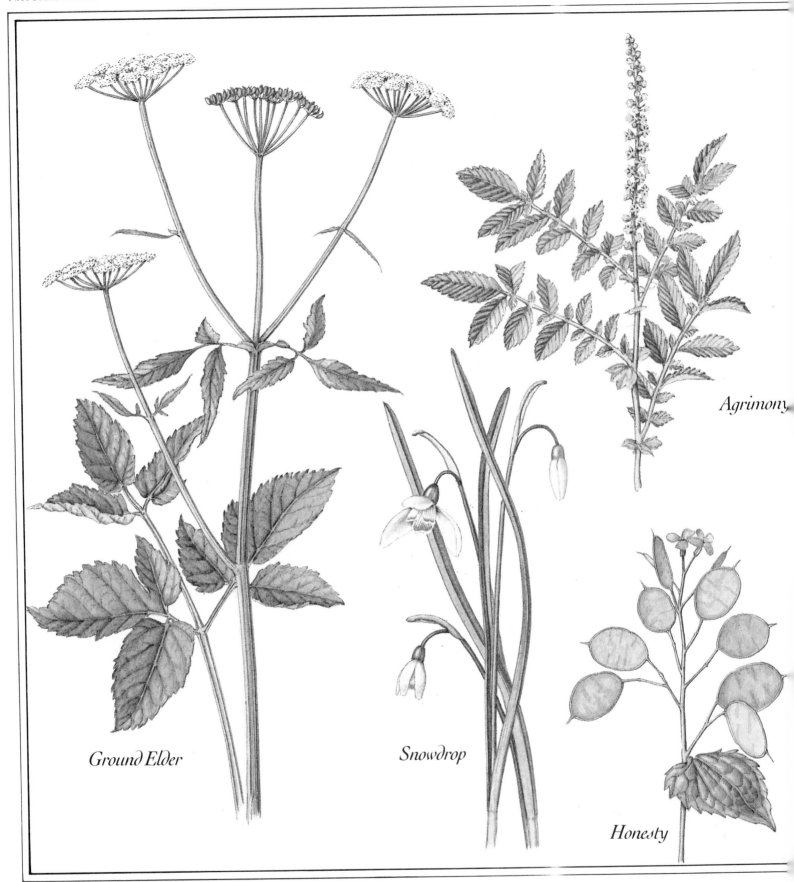

Agrimony

Ground Elder

Snowdrop

Honesty

GROUND ELDER (*Aegopodium podagraria*) An invasive weed of open spaces, this common plant reaches 36″ (90cm), with hollow grooved stems bearing bunches of oval green leaves, and masses of white flowers from June to August. It produces ridged egg-shaped fruit.

SNOWDROP (*Galanthus nivalis*) A welcome sight in January and February, this plant bears solitary white flowers, with inner green-tipped petals. It grows 4-8″ (10-20cm) tall, and can be found in damp and shady places, where its bulbs divide and multiply to flower in thick drifts.

AGRIMONY (*Agrimonia eupatoria*) This is a medicinal plant of grassy places, widespread and common, growing 12″ (30cm) tall, with irregular toothed leaves, and a tapering spike of small yellow flowers from June to August. These become hooked fruits in the autumn.

HONESTY (*Lunaria annua*) An escaped garden plant, which is valued for its transparent papery seed heads, from which the name derives, and which flowers between April and June. It has untidy toothed heart-shaped leaves, and grows to 39″ (1m).

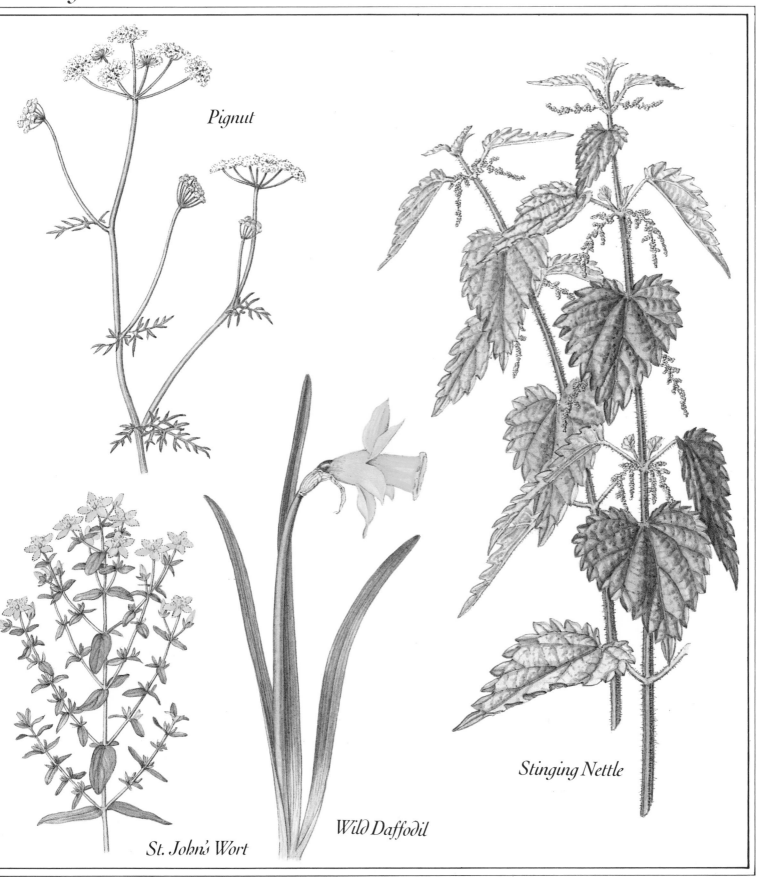

Pignut

Stinging Nettle

Wild Daffodil

St. John's Wort

PERFORATE ST JOHN'S WORT
(*Hypericum perforatum*) This is a
hairless 1-2′ (30-60cm) bushy plant,
whose small oblong leaves are covered
in transparent dots, and whose bright
yellow flowers have black-dotted petal
margins. It flowers from July to
September in woods and hedges.

PIGNUT (*Conopodium majus*) A
slender elegant little 12″ (30cm) plant
which is a feature of woods and
meadows with light dry soils. It has
sparse feathery leaves, and its frothy
white flowers are produced in florets
from May to July. The name derives
from the plant's edible tubers.

WILD DAFFODIL (*Narcissus
pseudonarcissus*) A smaller flower
than most garden varieties, this has
nodding trumpet-like tubes of deep
yellow, cloaked by paler outer
petals. It flowers in March and
April in damp woods and
meadows, mainly in the southwest.

STINGING NETTLE (*Urtica dioica*)
This widespread adaptable weed is
well known for its stinging leaf hairs. It
grows up to 4′ (1.3m) tall, with coarsely
toothed heart-shaped leaves, and
catkins of green flowers between June
and September. The young shoots
can be used in salads and soups.

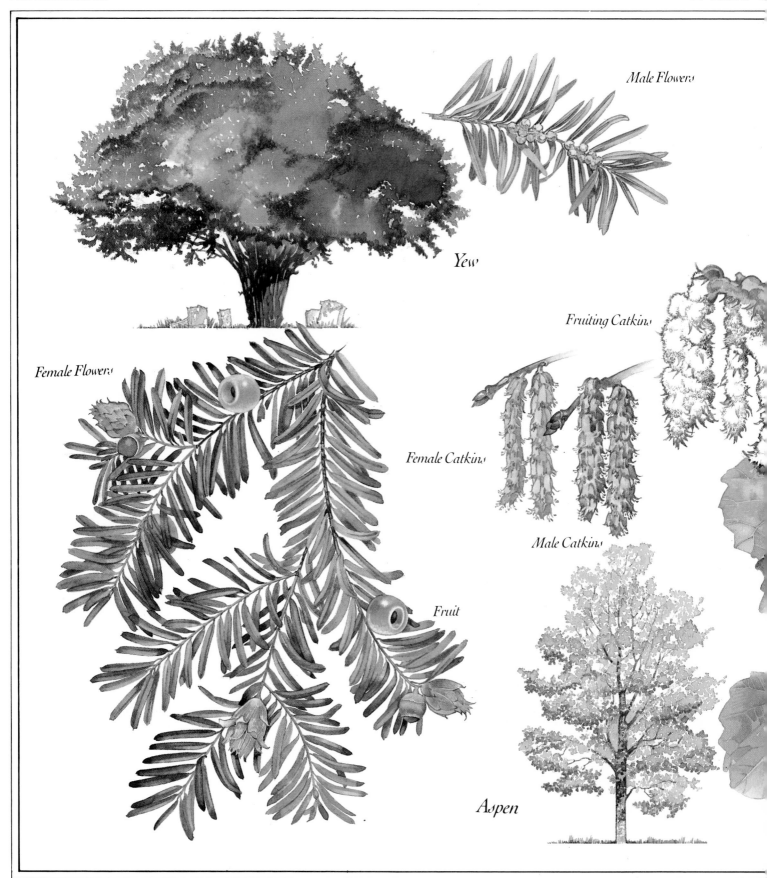

Male Flowers

Yew

Fruiting Catkins

Female Flowers

Female Catkins

Male Catkins

Fruit

Aspen

YEW (*Taxus baccata*) Found locally in woods on dry ground, sometimes forming pure stands on chalk downs, the yew is best known in, and grows to greatest size in, churchyards. A broad evergreen, growing to 60′ (18m) broad, and 45′ (14m) tall in a century, it may live on

for 1000 years. It has dark dense foliage, scaly bark, and produces fleshy pink fruit with poisonous seeds. The needle-like evergreen leaves are particularly toxic to cattle and horses, and churchyard specimens may have been planted to deter domestic stock from grazing there.

ASPEN (*Populus tremula*) The Latin name of this poplar suggests one distinctive characteristic – the leaves are broad and round on very thin flattened stalks, and the slightest breeze sets the whole tree trembling. A tall tree, growing to 65′ (20m) tall and 10-15′ (3-5m) wide, it has grey-brown

bark and produces clumps of thin suckers from its base. The leaves are dark grey-green, paler beneath; the flowers are borne in a catkin which is woolly with white hairs from the seed. Aspen is widespread in damp woods and heaths. Native to North America but common in Europe.

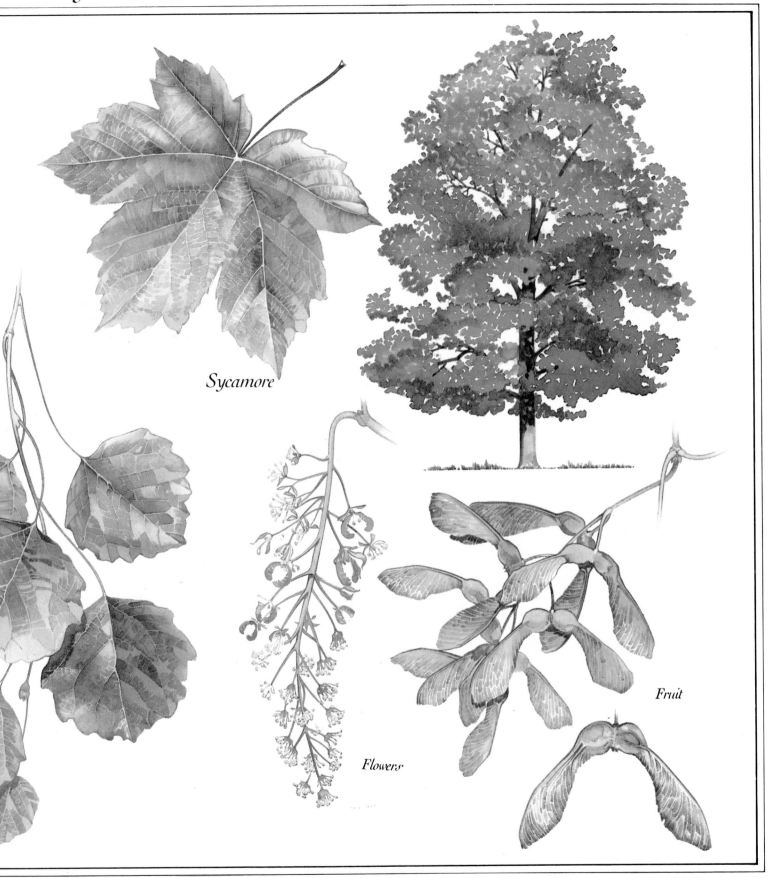

Sycamore

Flowers

Fruit

SYCAMORE (*Acer pseudoplatanus*)
This introduced maple makes a tall 80′
(25m) tree in 60 years, and has broad
ivy-shaped leaves, hairless below, and
frequently sticky in summer, which are
often disfigured by black fungal spots.
The bark is smooth and grey, making
scaly flakes on old trees; the shoots are
smooth, slender and often red,
contrasting with vivid green leaves
or pale green buds. The pale yellow
flowers hang in long clusters and
produce the familiar winged fruits
in pairs which spin away from the
shade of the parent tree in autumn
and seed themselves freely.

The Barn Owl

A silent ghostly hunter of the night, the barn owl's
super-sharp vision and incredibly acute hearing help
it locate prey, even in the dark.

TWILIGHT HUNTER
*This attractive owl, with its
white, heart-shaped face and
piercing eyes, is most commonly
seen in the twilight of dusk or
dawn as it silently quarters the
ground in search of its largely
nocturnal prey. Occasionally,
notably during the breeding
season, the barn owl will hunt by
day to meet the incessant
demands of its hungry young.*

An eerie churchyard at dead of night, the
brooding darkness deepened by the faint,
rhythmic breathing of wind-rustled leaves
and the gentle rubbing of one branch on another.
Suddenly, a spine-chilling drawn-out shriek stabs
through the dark, followed presently by a waver-
ing white shape silently floating among the
tombstones. Surely a ghost? No, simply a barn
owl, calling out as it begins a hunting foray.

Many owls find the short-cropped grass of
churchyards an ideal hunting ground for the
small, nocturnal mammals which form the bulk
of their diet.

But the barn owl is the most frequent visitor

there because it often uses the church tower as a
roosting and nesting site.

Before man changed the landscape, the barn
owl was probably an inhabitant of woodland
glades and fringes where it could both hunt the
grasslands and find suitable nesting holes in old
trees. Then, with the advent of farming, open fields
and hedgerows proved ideal hunting grounds and
farm buildings, wooden barns particularly, provided a range of splendid new nest sites. In the early
days of farming, before the age of motorized
transport, barns were erected in the corners of the
fields where they were needed, but the tractor
changed all that. Today, those old scattered barns

IN FLIGHT this species appears all white when seen from below, but the upperparts are a sandy-orange. The heart-shaped facial disc is distinctive.

have fallen into disrepair and been replaced by modern metal and concrete structures centred at a single site within the farm. The results have been disastrous for the barn owl, which has declined rapidly and become decidedly rare.

Fortunately, the barn owl is not totally dependent on old barns for nesting and roosting sites. Its preferred hideaway is still a large hole in an old tree, although this is just the type of tree that foresters often fell because they consider it dangerous. But it is also happy to nest in old ruins, which have been preserved as ancient monuments; church steeples – many of which are being wired up to keep pigeons from fouling the stonework – and holes in cliffs and caves are other favourite sites.

The barn owl hunts at dusk and again at dawn, then spends the rest of the day hiding up in a convenient hole or building. Its weaving flight is certainly ghost-like as it quarters the fields and hedgerows in the darkening gloom. Like other owls, it has fine, fluffy edges to its trailing wing feathers that serve to quieten the rush of air over them – essential for the silent approach needed to catch sharp-eared prey.

The barn owl is a fine sandy-orange colour on the back and upperwings, with beautiful patterns of spotting which are only apparent close up. The underparts are snowy white. Like man, owls stand upright, and their eyes are set in the front of their flat, heart-shaped face to give them excellent forward vision. The bill, largely hidden by feathers, is sharply hooked for tearing, while the feet are armed with fearsome talons.

The barn owl does not actually construct a nest, but lays its oval white eggs directly on the floor of the barn loft or hole. The eggs are laid at two-day intervals, but are incubated from the first egg. During the 31 days they take to hatch the female seldom leaves them and is dependent on her mate to supply the food she needs. Because they are laid at intervals, the owlets hatch out one at a time. This means that in a brood of five there will be ten days difference in age between the oldest and the youngest, and a considerable difference in size. This difference is important, for the adults always feed the largest and most forceful youngster first, before feeding the smallest. In this way they ensure that, if food is short, at least one survives.

Until quite recently the number of barn owls was closely linked to the abundance or scarcity of their food. If small mammals were abundant the owls bred well, raised as many as nine young in a season, and their numbers increased. Today numbers depend more on the activities of man.

Fortunately, the modern farmer is becoming increasingly aware of the need for conservation. Modern, system-built barns are now being manufactured with special, built-in owl boxes. It will, however, need a lot more thoughtfulness to ensure that our churchyards continue to be haunted by these beautiful birds.

THE TALONS are needle-sharp and are used to catch and kill prey. The outer toe is movable, allowing the bird maximum grip when it attacks.

THE EGGS are whitish in colour and 4-6 are laid at two day intervals during April and May. Incubation lasts about 31 days.

ALL-ROUND VISION
(top) The owl has excellent vision and in dim light can see 100 times better than we can. The eyes, though, are virtually fixed in their sockets, but the owl can swivel its head through almost 180° in both directions for all-round vision.

DIET
The barn owl hunts small mammals up to the size of a rat. Shrews, voles and mice are common prey as their constant squeaking makes them easy to find.

The Bat

Tucked under eaves, squeezed in brick crevices or under roof tiles, bats roost by day
hanging upside down, wings folded carefully around themselves like furled umbrellas.
When the summer's light begins to fade they stream out of hiding and set out on their
nocturnal search for insect prey.

VAMPIRE BATS
Not confined to horror
movies, vampire bats really
exist – but not in Britain –
and drink the blood
of sleeping
animals.

Dark against the dusky sky a small form, swallow-swift, sweeps the aerial avenues between the roof tops and the outstretched fingers of the trees. Flittering fast in pursuit of its airborne prey, the creature's identity remains a mystery until, twisting tightly, its scalloped leathery wings are silhouetted against the silvery light of the long-set sun and show it to be a bat.

Such exciting aerial displays may be seen all over Britain during the warm summer months when, after dusk, colonies of bats stream out of their daytime roosts to begin their night-long swooping, spooling flight, feasting on insects.

There are two families and no less than fifteen different species of bat resident in Britain. Most widespread is the tiny pipistrelle, with a wingspan of eight inches and a body barely larger than a mouse, it weighs less than a quarter of an ounce.

The pipistrelle prefers to roost in confined spaces so is common around buildings where it can squeeze itself under tiles or behind fascia boards. Curiously enough, the pipistrelle actually

One of Britain's most common bats – the long-eared bat (above) – abounds in woodlands, but may be seen in and around the churchyard. It carries its prey, usually too large to eat on the move, to sheltered spots, like the church porch.

prefers modern houses. New ones tend to be better insulated and so have colder roofs which are perfect for the bat's winter hibernation, while the current fashion for hung tiles and shingles proves ideal for bats searching for somewhere safe to spend the daylight hours in summer.

All British bats feed on insects exclusively, so while they commonly roost in buildings the chosen sites are usually on the edge of towns, or near open ground such as parks or graveyards, where insects are plentiful. A lot of food is needed to fuel a bat's fast flittery flight and even the tiny pipistrelle can consume 3000 insects every night.

Bats locate their prey on the wing, using a highly sophisticated form of echo-location. Emitting shrieks over ten times a second – at a pitch so high

A SAFE ROOST
During the day bats roost in the roofs of buildings, in tree holes or, in winter, when they hibernate, in caves and disused mines. In June and July female bats leave the main colony to find a collective nursery roost where they each give birth to a single baby.

NIGHT FLYER
(right) Caught on the wing in graceful flight, the pipistrelle, the tiniest and most common of British bats, begins its daily forage for insects at dusk. It usually catches prey in its mouth and eats while in flight. Larger insects are often caught in the bat's wings and held in the membrane between the tail and leg. The bat takes the food in its mouth from there.

and dirty for bats to colonize. In fact, at different periods of the summer bats need different roost sites, depending on the outside temperatures. For although they are warm-blooded mammals, their body temperature is greatly affected by the surroundings and how recently they have eaten.

In winter when there are few insects about, bats hibernate. Hibernation usually lasts, off and on, through the coldest, greyest months of the winter, and during this period bats require very little energy. The fat, which they have put on during the autumn, provides them with fuel during the winter. For hibernation bats select very cold sites, as warmer temperatures would raise their metabolic rate and quickly burn their energy reserves.

It is during the winter months, however, that bats mate, although the pregnancy does not begin until the spring. Then in June and July the female bats join together to seek out a safe warm roost where they can give birth. So-called nursery colonies typically comprise 50 to 100 females and create a warmer environment for the young. Bats are born hairless and may die if the conditions are too cold. Not all females breed each year, and of those which do only a single offspring is born to a female in any year. This is most likely due to the difficulty a female would have flying if she were encumbered with more than one young. After birth the young bat clings to its mother to suckle and occasionally, if for example a roost is disturbed, it will be carried away to a safer site.

However, if unreliable and wet summer weather means that there are few insects around, bats use internal cooling systems to conserve energy and stay alive for many days without eating. They become torpid – their breathing, heart-beat and other body mechanisms slow down and they cool down to almost the temperature outdoors. Perhaps because of this adaptation to the stress of seasonal food shortages, bats are generally quite long-lived, the longest-living kind being Natterer's bat – this species may live up to 25 years.

we cannot hear them – bats can tell from the echoes they pick up with their ultra-sensitive ears whether any prey is within range.

Once a suitable insect, such as a moth, has been located, the bat alters course and flaps towards it, jaws agape. Much of the rapid, erratic flight so typical of bats could well be due to this highly developed method of prey location combined with needle-sharp reflexes.

Bats are the world's only flying mammals and despite the fact that they appear to lack the highly sophisticated aerodynamics of birds, most bats fly just as well. Averaging between 15 and 20 wing beats per second the pipistrelle is an agile darter, while the related noctule bat with its larger 14″ (36cm) wings is a fast, smooth flier even matching the speed and agility of the swift.

BATS IN THE BELFRY

Despite popular belief bats rarely roost in belfries, since, as they house the bells and clock, they are usually too noisy. Belfries are also too draughty

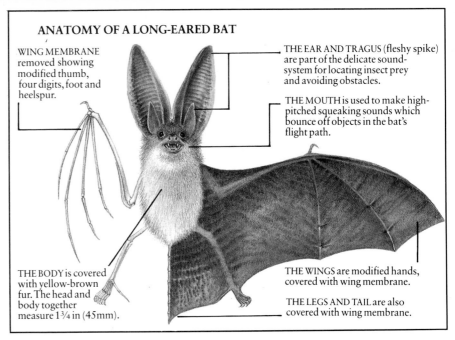

ANATOMY OF A LONG-EARED BAT

WING MEMBRANE removed showing modified thumb, four digits, foot and heelspur.

THE EAR AND TRAGUS (fleshy spike) are part of the delicate sound-system for locating insect prey and avoiding obstacles.

THE MOUTH is used to make high-pitched squeaking sounds which bounce off objects in the bat's flight path.

THE BODY is covered with yellow-brown fur. The head and body together measure 1¾ in (45mm).

THE WINGS are modified hands, covered with wing membrane.

THE LEGS AND TAIL are also covered with wing membrane.

The Cemetery

Cemeteries — large-scale burying grounds unconnected with churches — were an early 19th-century innovation; a response to the ghoulish overcrowding of urban churchyards serving the rapidly expanding cities of the time. Later, the Victorians took up cemetery-building with typically great zeal, cramming them with stone memorials of every sculptural whim and architectural fancy. Now, mellowed by time and the softening effects of nature, many old cemeteries are peaceful overgrown havens which offer valuable sanctuaries for wildlife in the hearts of our cities.

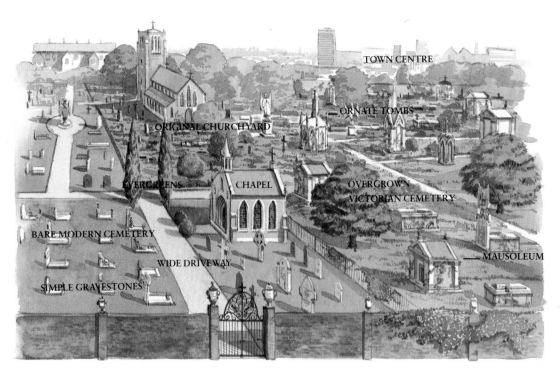

TOWN CENTRE

ORNATE TOMBS

ORIGINAL CHURCHYARD

EVERGREENS   CHAPEL

OVERGROWN
VICTORIAN CEMETERY

BARE MODERN CEMETERY

MAUSOLEUM

WIDE DRIVEWAY

SIMPLE GRAVESTONES

PASSING FASHION
*(left) Cemeteries were
inaugurated at the beginning
of the 19th century for the
interment of increasing
numbers of urban dead
which the urban churchyards
could not take. Cemeteries
were seized on by the
architects and sculptors of
the day as offering
opportunity to create
fantastic statuary and
portentous buildings in a rich
landscaped setting. Modern
cemeteries tend to be much
less ambitious in design,
sacrificing funerary
splendour for considerations
of economy and convenience.*

'Rot and mildew and dead citizens form the uppermost scent.' So wrote Charles Dickens describing early 19th-century London. His words reflect the dire state of affairs concerning the burial of the dead from Britain's rapidly expanding cities. In 1832, for example, a mere 150 churchyards offered the only sites for 'decent and Christian' burial to London's 50,000 annual dead. By contrast, the verdant plots surrounding country churches were picturesque, even romantic, but urban churchyards serving industrialized and overpopulated cities had become overcrowded and were fast decaying into vile and pestilential squalor. Alternative burial grounds had to be found.

As the century progressed, so did public agitation against 'unsanitary' churchyard burial. But while London hosted the advocates of change, provincial cities were the first to act. The very first British cemetery – a burial ground unconnected with a church – was opened in 1819 in Norwich. Then Belfast established two cemeteries – one for protestants and one for catholics, followed by Liverpool, where the St. James Cemetery was opened in 1825 on the site of a disused stone quarry. Greatest of all provincial cemeteries though, was the Glasgow Necropolis (city of the dead), which opened in 1832.

In London the pressure groups multiplied and in July 1832, six months after the first of a series of cholera epidemics hit London, an Act of Parliament allowed the purchase of 54 still wholly rural acres off the Harrow Road at Kensal Green. Here, the capital's first grand cemetery was created. It was an immediate success, attracting both the remains of the famous and the day-trips of the tourists.

By 1840 a further seven cemeteries had formed a ring around London. Despite some opposition from the Church, which regretted the loss of churchyard burial fees, and those like Thomas Carlyle who felt that the new burial grounds typified the worst vulgarities, the cemetery boom continued. In 1850, promoted by another cholera epidemic which again inflated the death rate, the Metropolitan Interments Act put cemeteries into public hands. A system of regulations emerged governing cemeteries, and burial within city limits was virtually abolished.

The Victorians tackled cemetery construction with the same zeal and energy that they applied to other great public works, such as transport, water supply, and the sewers. It was also big business, as the 'black trade' created massive

GREEN IN THE CITY
*(below) Old cemeteries were
often laid out in wooded
areas outside city limits. Left
untended, they soon ran wild
as the fertile soil quickly
sprouts a jungle of brambles,
tree saplings, and thistles,
among which may linger
relics of grander planting
schemes.*

profits from death and its attendant ceremonies.

Architects John Loudon and E. W. Pugin both published treatises on cemetery design in 1843. They envisaged grand gateways, reverential chapels, broad pathways, finely sculptured headstones, all set against a background of trees, flowers and shrubs. The desired effect was to reflect that basic principle of Victorianism which advocated 'The improvement of the moral sentiments and general tastes of all classes, and more especially of the great masses of society'.

In the event, such hopes were not realized in many of the new cemeteries. The monuments of the prosperous middle-classes, still ostentatious even in death, tended towards elaborate, even vulgar, display rather than tasteful restraint. The tomb, wrote Loudon, should denote contemporary taste, but this was frequently interpreted very literally. Every vagary of Victorian architectural fantasy born of a world-wide empire, went on display, often side by side: Egyptian, Classical, Byzantine, Italian baroque, Romanesque, 'Undertakers Gothic', massive subterranean catacombs and imposing family mausolea, all larded with a mixture of sentimental epitaphs.

GLORIES OF THE PAST

These mid-century Victorian creations have a scale and grandeur surpassing everything else that has followed. In more recent times cemetery design has been dictated largely by the demands of the council gang-mower – flat, open lawns with a few scattered evergreen trees, and simple memorial tablets set neatly in the manicured grass. The increasingly popular crematorium, legally sanctioned since 1885, has also further diminished the notion of the cemetery as an attractive landscape feature.

Ironically, it is in those decaying, overgrown, century-old cemeteries which still survive that one can find true mortuary magnificence. Here, within walls now surrounded by urban sprawl remain the valuable enclaves of a bygone age.

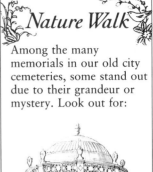

Nature Walk

Among the many memorials in our old city cemeteries, some stand out due to their grandeur or mystery. Look out for:

MAUSOLEUMS, such as this grandly ornate example in the Jewish Cemetery, West Ham. WW1 marked the end of extravagant funerary art.

UNUSUAL HEADSTONES, like these commemorating a pet, and a child, by the clasped hands of the parents.

A COLUMBARIUM, a building where the urns containing funeral ashes found a dignified resting place.

NAVAL CEMETERY *(right) This naval cemetery at Lyness, on the remote Orkney island of Hoy, typifies the bleak simplicity of those cemeteries created to bury the sudden vast numbers of dead caused by two world wars. These casualties of WW1 are laid out in tragic simple anonymity.*

PEACEFUL NEGLECT *(right) An untended corner of Abney Park, North London, where rampant vegetation has overtaken what was once described as 'one of the most complete arboretums in the neighbourhood of London'. This was one of the eight cemeteries ringing London in 1840, and replaced Bunhill Fields as the main burial ground for dissenters. 'General' William Booth, the founder of the Salvation Army is buried here.*

Among Overgrown Plots

The cemetery is a peaceful oasis among the suburban streets providing a hunting ground for owls, nest sites for song birds and meadow-like grass full of flowers and alive with insects.

As the moon pales in the May sky, the last ghostly quavering call of the suburb's resident tawny owl is heard across the cemetery. Then, from within the high brick walls, come the first notes of the dawn chorus. On cue, each song bird joins this natural orchestra. The cock blackbird leads, fluting lengthy cadences and musical twirls. It is soon accompanied by the song thrush, with a terser, more repetitive song.

Now, with a rapidly lightening sky, the liquid notes of the robin can be heard. Then the tiny wren joins in, singing surprisingly loudly for so small a bird.

The rich and varied dawn chorus shows that, behind its walls, at least part of the cemetery must be overgrown enough to offer these songsters secure cover for their nests and plentiful food for their chicks.

Sunshine touches a well tended area of more recent graves, where the grass is regularly mown short. Cypresses and other sombre evergreens march regularly along the paths. Although an occasional native yew stands among them (still relatively small, for the cemetery is no more than 150 years old), the trees are mainly of foreign origin. They have few berries to the liking of the birds, but offer snug winter roosts and nest sites for sparrows and thrushes.

Starlings flight in from their roost. They busily stalk the turf, intent on probing between the grass roots with open bill to pick out worms and soil insects. A blackbird joins them, calling loudly as it lands with tail cocked. While the starlings speculatively probe the soil in a steadily advancing line, the blackbird hunts quite differently. It feeds alone, relying on its eyesight to spot exposed insects.

UNDERGROUND LIFE

The short turf harbours a good many invertebrates. The blackbird will have noticed the casts thrown up by the earthworm *Allolobophora*, and perhaps the tell-tale signs of *Lumbricus*. This earthworm plugs its burrow with a tuft of leaves which may be seen sticking upright in the grass. Smaller heaps of soil are made by lawn bees, which excavate ground nests from which they fly out low over the grass in search of nectar from the cemetery's many flowers.

SEXTON BEETLES
Known also as burying beetles, these are the gravediggers of the insect world. Flying beetles sniff out corpses of small mammals or birds and then bury them as food for their young. If the body is on stony ground it will be dragged to softer soil. The females guard their eggs and then feed the grubs with regurgitated food until they are able to feed on the buried carrion.

WILDLIFE IN THE CEMETERY

In the neat, tended area of the cemetery, the short grass, peppered with daisies and dandelions, is a feeding area for starlings, blackbirds and pigeons. The introduced evergreen trees hold few insects but provide some nest sites. Garden flowers planted on the graves, such as Canterbury bells, may spread to any wild areas. Here, among the older gravestones, trees such as sycamore have seeded themselves. The ground cover is of tall grasses and meadow flowers with ivy and everlasting pea – both climbers – rising above them. Butterflies, moths and other insects are attracted to the plants which offer nectar and other food sources for adults and young, while hedgehogs and many birds hunt the rich invertebrate community.

KEY TO SPECIES

1 Holm oak	14 Nettles	27 Wall moss
2 Blackbird songpost	15 Wren	28 Hover fly
3 Sycamore	16 Hedgehog	29 Wolf spider
4 Blue tit	17 Starlings	30 Black redstart
5 Tawny owl	18 Ivy	31 Garden snail
6 Lawson cypress	19 Bracken	32 Lichen (crottle)
7 Privet hedge	20 Large white	33 Ragwort
8 Lime tree	21 Marbled beauty	34 Silver moth
9 Elder	22 House sparrows	35 Ground elder
10 Peppered moth	23 Canterbury bells	36 Everlasting pea
11 Fox	24 Greenfinch	37 Wasp
12 Pigeon	25 Peacock	38 Ox eye daisy
13 Meadow brown	26 Black knapweed	39 Horsetails

61

They are joined by bumble bees from a hole below the stone foot of a grave. Black ants have also chosen to nest beneath the stone as here they enjoy protection from predators and the warmth which the stone retains long after the sun has set. Later in the year the swarms of mating ants will attract the swifts.

The path marks a frontier, beyond it lies the deserted cemetery. To cut costs, little is done save shaving a strip next to the path for the sake of appearance.

Among the toppling memorials, a young sycamore copse has seeded itself from a garden

BRIGHT GRAVESTONE LICHEN
Patches of orange Xanthoria parietina *stand out from a distance on gravestones and tombs. Less visible are the grey lichens that blend with the weathered limestone memorials.*

SEED-EATING FINCH
Using a fence post to steady itself, this greenfinch is taking advantage of the cottony seeds of rosebay willowherb. This tall plant, growing to 5 ft. (1·5 m), often occurs in cemeteries, particularly on disturbed ground. For the greenfinch the old cemetery not only provides seeds and insect food but also roosting and nest sites in shrubs.

nearby. The trees are already quite tall, elbowing a memorial lime planted half a century ago. In their shade sprawls a jungle of brambles, nettles and elderberry.

It is here that the leaders of the dawn chorus nest. The blackbird chooses the shelter of the overgrown privet hedge, using the nearest sycamore as a songpost. The taller lime is chosen by the song thrush, and its nest may well be among the tree's lower branches. The robin nests in the ivy, which trails like some tropical plant over a broken chest tomb, while the wren nests within the shelter of a deep crack in the stone below.

Rather surprisingly, perhaps, the tawny owls also nest within a broken memorial: they occupy holes in trees by choice, but will even make do with a hole in the ground.

On the edge of the copse, the long grass harbours voles and wood mice. The corpse of one mouse, killed by a feral cat, lies in a pool of deep shadow below the brambles. It is surrounded by a coven of brightly banded sexton beetles, busily scraping away the soil to bury it as a larder for their grubs.

Hedgehogs rest among the undergrowth in the daytime, feeding at night on the worms, slugs and snails which live in the damp shadows.

DRAMATIC CINNABAR MOTH
This striking moth is easily found where ragwort and groundsel – its caterpillars' foodplants – grow. The moth, which is poisonous if eaten, has a weak, fluttering flight.

FOX CUBS PLAYING
Cemeteries are ideal for urban foxes, especially if they have overgrown areas. Here, a breeding den can be hidden and there is cover for the animals to lie up in during the day. In addition, from dusk until dawn cemeteries are usually locked against human intruders.

more commonly seen in the countryside. The meadow brown is one such, as is the skipper which flies moth-like between the grasses in the sunshine.

Day-flying moths also come to the flowers. A typical species is the silver Y, so named from the markings on its forewings. These early silver Y moths belong to the first generation of the year, and are migrants, having recently flown many weary miles from mainland Europe. Later, the home-bred numbers build up and these moths are often quite common in towns in late summer. Neither the moths nor the caterpillars of the silver Y survive the first autumn frosts, however.

The tangled bushes are a daytime hideaway for many other moths. The peppered moth rests on a sycamore, flying at night from early May. But many moths are still in their younger stages at this time, and nearby on the lime are clusters of buff tip caterpillars. Brightly marked with yellow, their colouring is not camouflage but a warning to birds that they are distasteful and best left alone.

SURVIVING LICHENS

In the countryside, the bark of the trees would often carry lichens, but these lowly plants are sensitive to air pollution and the area may be a lichen desert, with only a dusting of the bright green alga *Pleurococcus* on the trunks.

There are few lichens on the gravestones, although vivid orange patches of *Xanthoria parietina* may be seen growing in the sunshine. If the birds choose one of the tombstones as a favourite perch, the lichens benefit, for the droppings which smear the stone below bring welcome nutrients.

In Victorian times gravestone lichens caught the imagination of amateur botanists, for they realized that they can sometimes be dated by the inscription nearby. Lichens were found on old gravestones, but not on more recent ones. The increase in air pollution since they started into life prevented them colonizing new sites. It may well be that the lichens of today's cemeteries hold a tale of their own.

Foxes, too, often have a den in such undisturbed parts of the urban landscape and their cubs gambol in the early morning sunshine before the world is wide awake.

The meadow of long grass between the graves is coloured by flowers and busy with early honey bees visiting from a hive in a back garden half a mile away.

Ox-eye daisies gleam in the sun, indicating that this ground was grassland before the suburb grew up. But common weeds quickly seed themselves into such places, and here dandelion, ground elder and ragwort can be seen.

There are also some garden flowers. Earlier in the year there were nodding clusters of daffodils amid the tangled grass. There is still a late red tulip or two. Once planted on the graves they have since spread. Canterbury bells will flower later. Not far away, a mass of everlasting peas will soon colour the grass pink.

This flowery meadow draws vast numbers of flying insects. Among the butterflies are the strong flying peacocks, tortoiseshells and whites, which are also to be seen in gardens. The cemetery, though, attracts butterflies that are

HOLM OAK
One of the evergreen oaks, this tree comes from the Mediterranean region and is often planted in parks, gardens and cemeteries. Its waxy leaves are an adaptation to prevent water loss in its native dry climate. In winter the tree looks blackish-green but in spring, when new leaves appear, it turns silvery grey. Leaf shape varies markedly, even on the same tree, some being smooth edged, others toothed or holly-like.

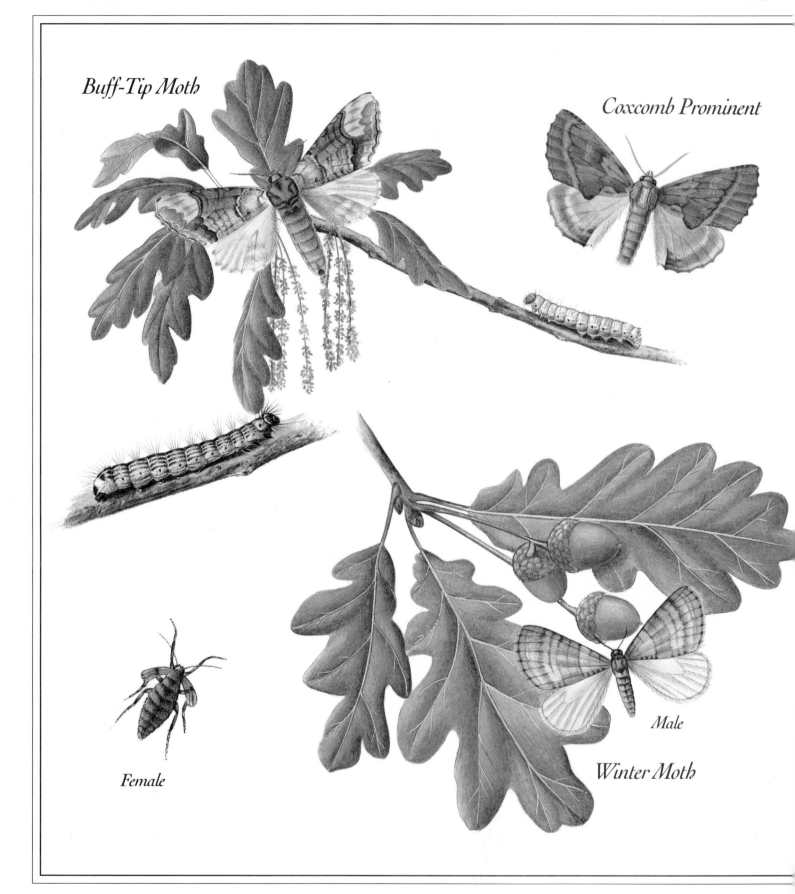

Buff-Tip Moth

Coxcomb Prominent

Female

Male

Winter Moth

BUFF-TIP MOTH *(Phalera bucephala)* This moth with a 2¾″ (68mm) wingspan, flies in summer. At rest it resembles a broken twig, and has also been likened to a cigarette butt. The gregarious caterpillars feed on deciduous trees, especially lime.

WINTER MOTH *(Operophtera brumata)* The larvae of this common moth will feed on almost any deciduous tree or shrub. They pupate in the soil; emerging after the flightless female climbs up the trunk to mate. The 1¼″ (33mm) male is on the wing through late autumn and winter.

COXCOMB PROMINENT *(Ptilodon capucina)* The notched forewing gives this 2″ (50mm) summer-flying moth its name. It is particularly common in suburban areas. The larvae bear a distinctive pair of red points towards the tail and feed on many deciduous trees and shrubs.

Urban Moths

Sycamore Moth

Golden Plusia

Peppered Moth

Marbled Beauty

SYCAMORE MOTH (*Acronicta aceris*) Mainly confined to southern England, where it is common, this moth – wingspan 1¾" (45mm) – flies in June. One of its foodplants is that abundant town tree the sycamore, but the distinctive larvae will also eat the leaves of other deciduous trees.

MARBLED BEAUTY (*Cryphia domestica*) The larvae of this widespread little moth feed on lichen growing on old stone. They pupate in shelters of silk mixed with fragments of lichen. The 1¼" (30mm) adults fly in July and August and are well camouflaged.

PEPPERED MOTH (*Biston betularia*) In industrial areas with soot-blackened tree trunks, the commonest form of this 2½" (62mm) moth is black. In the country it is light and well-disguised on lichen. It flies in summer and the twig-like larva feeds on many deciduous trees.

GOLDEN PLUSIA (*Polychrysia moneta*) Although this 1¾" (44mm) moth was first found here less than a century ago, it is now widely distributed and well-established. The larva feeds on several garden plants including larkspur, and the moth flies in June and July.

65

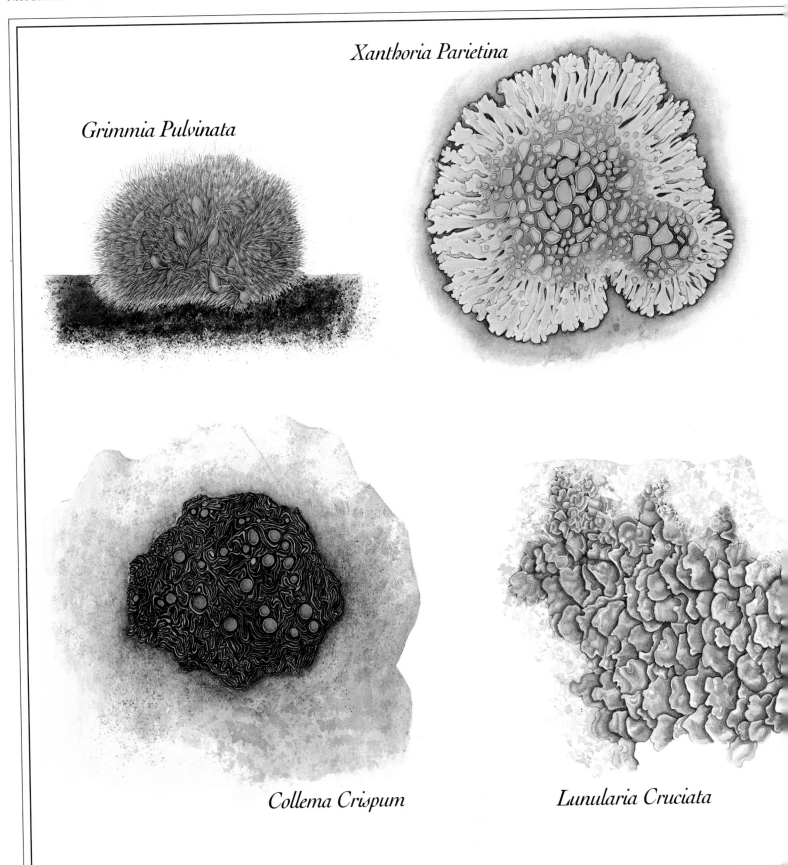

Xanthoria Parietina

Grimmia Pulvinata

Collema Crispum

Lunularia Cruciata

GRIMMIA PULVINATA
Commonly forming domed cushions on rocks and walls, this moss bears very long silvery hair points at the ends of the leaves. The stalks of the spore-bearing capsules are curved and buried in the moss at first, but straighten as the spores ripen.

COLLEMA CRISPUM A jelly-like lichen – an alga and fungus living together symbiotically – found on stone and bark. The dark red discs are spore-producing bodies and the 'plant-body' has small overlapping greenish or blackish-brown lobes, often with small scales at the margins.

XANTHORIA PARIETINA
Common on stone, wood and bark throughout the British Isles, this lichen has deep yellow or orange-yellow lobes. Like many lichens, it produces spores from cup-shaped bodies, which in this case are a deeper orange than the rest of the lichen.

LUNULARIA CRUCIATA
Common on soil, damp rocks and walls, this bright green liverwort is probably Mediterranean in origin. Liverworts are simpler in structure than mosses and, like them, are considered to be amongst the oldest forms of plant life.

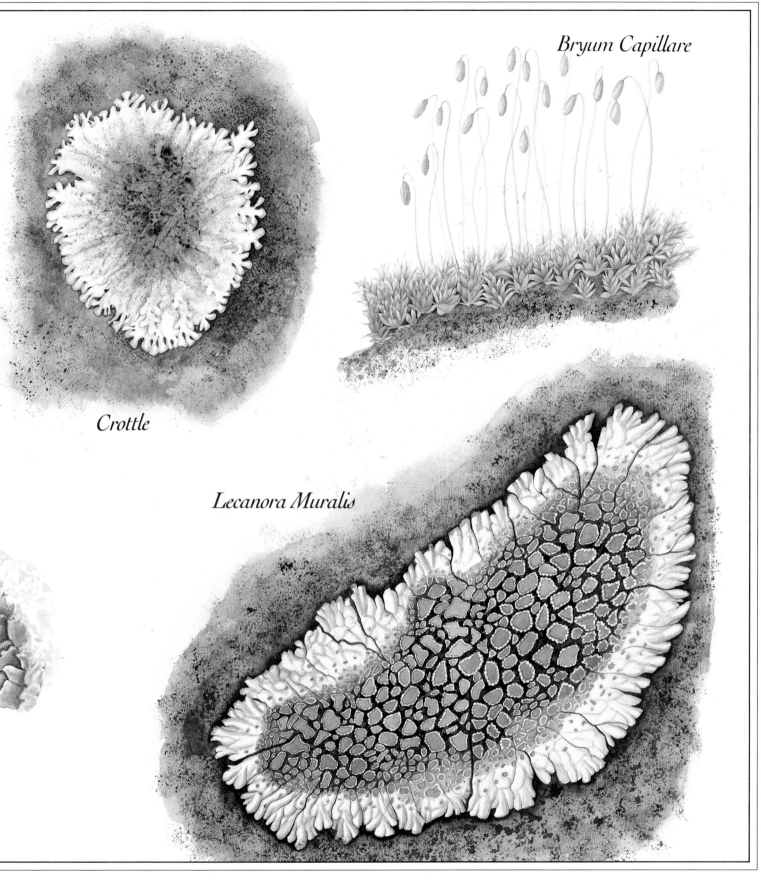

Bryum Capillare

Crottle

Lecanora Muralis

CROTTLE (*Parmelia saxatilis*)
Common throughout the British
Isles, this lichen grows on trees as
well as on walls and stone. The
bluish-grey or grey 'plant-body' is
covered with a network of white
lines and has lobes which are
fan-shaped at the ends.

LECANORA MURALIS This
common lichen forms conspicuous
rosettes on stone, concrete and
walls. It has brown, cup-shaped
spore-producing bodies, which are
crowded together into the centre
of the 'plant-body', which has
numerous small lobes at its margin.

BRYUM CAPILLARE A very
common moss, growing on rocks,
walls and trees. It forms compact
cushions up to 2.5″ (6cm) tall. The
spore capsules are bright green at
first, turning reddish-brown at
maturity and becoming pale after
the spores have been shed.

The Great Tit

Our largest and most common tit, the agile and intelligent great tit is
an opportunist from the woodlands, taking advantage of nesting
holes and abundant insect food in our parks and gardens.

Clearly audible above the other bird calls, a loud metallic *teechah-teechah* rings out from a dumpy little yellow and black bird hanging upside-down on a twig. Suddenly, the singer flits down inquisitively to perch on a gravestone and is revealed as the handsome great tit, easily recognizable by its glossy black cap and bib and striking black stripe running down its yellow belly.

The largest and most common of the tit family, the adaptable great tit lives anywhere, from woodland and farmland to city parks and cemeteries, where there are tree holes to nest in and caterpillars on which to feed its young.

During the autumn and winter, great tits form loose flocks with other tits, goldcrests, treecreepers, wrens, nuthatches and finches, roaming the woodlands in search of food. The bonus of banding together is that there are plenty of sharp eyes to spot predators, and the species avoid competition by feeding at different levels and on different parts of the trees. Great tits spend much more time on the ground than other tits, searching for insects and, particularly

in winter, fruits and seeds, such as beech mast and hazel nuts, which they hold down with one foot while hacking them open with their sharp, stout bills.

They are easily attracted to the garden bird-table in winter, competing aggressively with the other small birds, and performing acrobatics to prise peanuts from their holders. Like blue tits, they also have the unpopular, but clever, knack of opening milk bottle tops to drink the cream. Mentally agile and quick to learn, the trick, first reported in the 1930s, has been passed from one population to another until it is now a widespread habit.

Flocks of tits stay in touch with each other by raucous call notes. The great tit is the noisiest of all and has one of the largest vocabularies of any bird – over 50 distinct calls, ranging from a chaffinch-like *pink-pink* to a penetrating *ti ti si* and the well-known *teechah teechah* of spring, which has earned it the local names of saw sharpener, sharp saw and sawfinch.

As winter turns to spring, the male great tit uses his piercing calls to proclaim his territory.

HANDSOME GREAT TIT
An all-year-round resident, the great tit copes with harsh winters by becoming vegetarian, spending a good deal of its time on the ground searching for seeds and berries. Against the snow its shiny black cap and bib with black band dividing the yellow belly are even more striking.

When the warmer days set in, he chooses a mate and finds a suitable nest-hole in a tree or wall in which the pair can raise their huge brood of up to 15. Being adaptable, they will set up home in drainpipes or even letter boxes and are the most ready of all the tits to use nest boxes.

The female builds the nest, flying into the hole with huge bundles of moss held in the beak. These she deposits in the hole and fashions with movements of her breast to form a bulky cup, which she lines with soft hairs, feathers or wool.

At this stage, she needs every bit of food the male can find to bring her, because she will shortly produce almost her own weight in eggs. She usually lays from 8 to 14, at the rate of one a day, and incubates them for about 14 days. The brown and yellow chicks are very demanding, and both parents are kept busy from dawn until dusk bringing them as many as 700 caterpillars a day. They are fed – and brooded at

night – for 15-18 days, and fly when about three weeks old.

Unlike most other small birds, which rear two or three broods in a season, tits usually have just one large family each year, timed to coincide with the glut of caterpillars in spring. If it pays off, this strategy produces large families, but if

BUSY PARENTS
(above) Parents must fly back and forth non-stop to supply enough caterpillars for their huge brood.

the food supply fails, the population is hard hit.

Chick mortality, as with many other small song birds, is high and nine out of every ten chicks hatched each year will die before they see another spring. Eggs and chicks fall prey to weasels which home in on the noisy young and are adept at climbing into their nest holes. Great spotted woodpeckers will also take advantage of the chicks' natural instinct to beg for food and simply yank the chicks out as soon as their heads appear. Even apparently harmless creatures such as wood mice may help themselves to the eggs if they find the nest hole. Once out of the nest, they face other predators, including jays, owls and, above all, the sparrowhawk. This hawk takes them by surprise as it swoops low over a hedge or around a tree.

However, great tits are highly adaptable and this ensures that they remain one of our most common birds, with over 3 million pairs nesting here each year.

FLITTING FLIGHT
(above) Although an adept acrobat among the branches the great tit is not particularly agile in flight, using its rounded wings to simply flit from tree to tree.

DOMINANT TIT
(right) At 5½" (14cm) long the great tit is the largest of the tits. A bold and aggressive bird, it tends to bully its smaller relatives, the blue-capped blue tit and the more sombre coloured coal tit.

KEY FACTS

IN FLIGHT white wing bars, tail bars and black belly stripe distinguish it from other tits. Wingbeats are fast and flight is undulating.

WHITE PATCHES on the cheeks act as beacons in the dark nest hole. By turning the head to one side they are made more obvious to the mate or young.

THE EGGS are white, speckled with red. A single clutch of 8-14 is laid, usually in a tree hole, in April and May.

The Speckled Wood

Dancing in the dappled light under the shade of trees,
the speckled wood butterfly is in fact defending a
most unlikely territory – a sunbeam.

In the chequered sunlight beneath woodland trees, the delicate speckled wood butterfly may be seen resting with open wings to absorb the sun's warmth, or thronging with other insects, feeding from the nectar-rich blossoms of brambles and honeysuckle. Its subtle shadowy markings provide excellent camouflage when set against the leaf litter and dead vegetation of the enclosed shady places it frequents. But as a further defence against predators, the arresting 'eye-spots' on the top and underside of the wings draw the stabbing beaks of birds safely away from the butterfly's vulnerable body.

Once airborne, however, the speckled wood becomes surprisingly conspicuous, and the males of the species can often be seen fluttering around, 'defending' shafts of sunlight filtering down through the leaf-canopy. A resident male will even chase off intruders, pursuing trespassers high into the trees away from his chosen patch. The reason for this territorial rivalry is that the females congregate in warm corners early in the day to sun themselves, so the males lay claim to these

suntraps in order to vie for their favours.

The male speckled wood also performs the dual function of attracting females and repelling rivals by means of scent glands which release pheromonal messages.

UNIQUE ADAPTATION

The speckled wood butterfly has one characteristic that sets it apart from every other British species – it can overwinter as either caterpillar or pupa, an adaptation which allows it to breed successfully, late in the year.

The combination of an early start in the year, and multiple broods – up to three are produced each year – means that the speckled wood butterfly can be seen on the wing for an unusually long season. It flies from late April through to the autumn, and can be seen as late as October or November in mild years.

After mating the female lays her pale green, ovoid eggs singly on grass stems. After nine or ten days they hatch, and the black-headed, cream coloured caterpillars, or larvae, immediately

SHADES OF BROWN
(above) One of the large family of 'browns', the speckled wood butterfly is discreetly coloured in various shades of brown and dark grey, splashed with cream and dark brown 'eyes' across its 2" (5cm) wingspan. The underwings show a muted and more broken form of the same markings and colours. It is less conspicuous at rest on leaves or on the ground than during its frequent short flights to chase off rivals or to visit flowers. Common in the south and west of the British Isles, it is absent from the north of England and Scotland.

devour the eggshell – a ritual meal of essential nutrients, without which they would die. They then move on in search of food-plants such as cock's foot, couch and other coarse grasses.

The caterpillar feeds both by day and night, and as it matures it changes colour, becoming green to match its surroundings. It feeds constantly for a month (or for up to seven, if it is going to overwinter as a caterpillar), during

which time it moults three times as it grows. Then the caterpillar begins its astonishing transformation from a pedestrian eating machine into a restlessly mobile winged insect whose energies are focused almost entirely on reproduction. This metamorphosis is achieved during pupation.

FROM LARVA TO BUTTERFLY

The pupa emerges from the caterpillar's final moult, head down and attached to a grass stem by a silken thread. The caterpillar skin is cast off, starting at the head, splitting gradually along the body until, with a vigorous flick, the empty husk is shed. It reveals a strange, un-

formed creature with no apparent head or tail. At first this pupa is very soft, but it soon hardens. At this stage in its life, camouflage is all that protects the insect, for the pupa, or chrysalis, is entirely helpless for the weeks or months of its transformation.

Within the pupa, massive changes take place: the digestive system, nerve system and other vital organs change little, but the rest of the creature is broken down into a fluid, from which the sexually mature adult butterfly is formed. Instead of the powerful biting mouthparts of the caterpillar, the butterfly, or imago, has a delicate proboscis or straw-like tongue with which it drinks nectar. The external features of the body bear little relation to the erstwhile caterpillar, and the wings develop miraculously from nothing.

When the emergent butterfly scrambles clear of its case, its wings are still tiny and crumpled. It climbs to an unencumbered twig, and there hangs almost motionless, pumping blood into the veins of its wings for about twenty minutes until they fully expand. It must then wait for over an hour until the wings have dried. Finally its imprisonment is over, and the triumphant speckled wood butterfly can flutter off in search of nectar and a place in the sun.

HUNGRY CATERPILLAR
(above) Having hatched, and eaten the remains of its egg, the larva of the speckled wood butterfly is the size of a match-head, with a hairy, cream coloured body and a large black head. It feeds continuously until it outgrows its skin, which it then splits and sheds. The grass coloured caterpillar that emerges may pupate a few weeks later, or may overwinter in the larval state.

QUIET TRANSFORMATION
(above left) When the caterpillar is ready to pupate, it spins a small silken pad which it attaches to a blade of grass and grips with its rear claspers. It then moults its skin and emerges as a pupa, coloured to blend with its background.

SUBTLY DIFFERENT
The male (far left) and the female (left) of the speckled wood butterfly are subtly different – the male is slightly smaller, with darker markings, and has more pointed wings than the female, with patches of dark scent scales on its forewings. Behavioural differences also help distinguish the sexes. The females cluster in sunny patches in the woodland canopy, attracted to the male's scent, while solo males defend ephemeral pieces of territory against all rivals.

The Waterworks

For thousands of years, people drew water for their domestic routines from local rivers, springs and streams. But as urban settlement grew, demand on local water often outstripped supply. With insufficient water and relatively low standards of personal and civic hygiene, diseases, particularly cholera, were rife among urban populations. It was not until Victorian times, though, that any large-scale attempt was made to solve the problem, and it is to the Victorians that we owe the higher standard of living that came with the building of waterworks across the land.

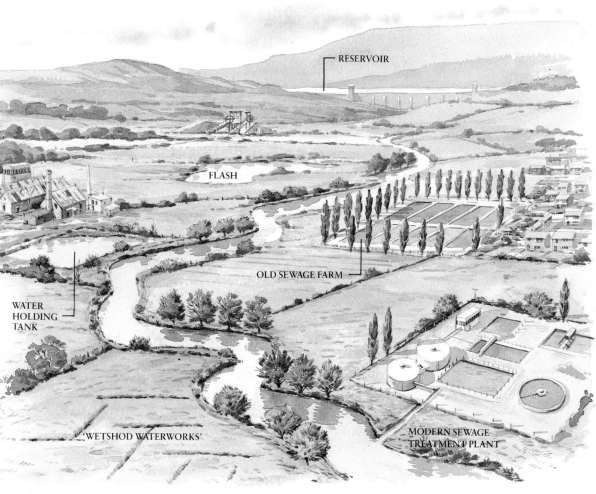

RESERVOIR

FLASH

OLD SEWAGE FARM

WATER
HOLDING
TANK

'WETSHOD WATERWORKS'

MODERN SEWAGE
TREATMENT PLANT

WATERWORKINGS
(left) Man has harnessed
water for domestic,
agricultural and industrial
purposes since early times,
and today the British
landscape is marked with
both abandoned and
working examples of
waterworks. Reservoirs
ensure a constant water
supply, while old-fashioned
sewage farms – a series of
shallow filter pools – and
modern, highly mechanized
sewage treatment plants, deal
with waste. But water has
also provided the power
needed to operate machinery,
and water holding tanks can
be found dotted around the
landscape.

NATURAL WASTE
(below) This small sewage
treatment plant is typical of
those found in rural settings,
which serve a limited local
community. The liquid waste
is sprayed over raised beds of
clinker so that it can be
broken down gradually by
natural processes.

Throughout Britain, towns and villages are linked by a web of modern lifelines. Beneath our roads and patchwork fields stretch hundreds of miles of cables for electricity and telephone, together with pipes carrying North Sea gas. With them lies a complex network of water supply and sewage pipes, servicing almost every domestic, public and industrial building in the British Isles.

In the early days of small settlements, a water supply had to be close to hand, so the first villages and towns were often sited at a spring or waterway guaranteed not to dry out in summer. But a growing population brought an increased demand which the springs and brooks could not meet. More importantly, these natural water sources often became foul, contaminated with sewage and other waste effluent that the towns themselves produced.

London, the Royal capital, reacted early. One of its first waterworks was the Great Conduit in Westcheap, begun in 1285 and filled with water from sources in a then green and rural Paddington. 400 years later, the increase in the number of inhabitants forced the construction of the 'New River', a 36-mile-long waterway bringing clean water from Ware in Hertfordshire, which still forms part of London's supply system.

Another famous landmark in the history of civil engineering is Hobson's Conduit, built in

ABANDONED
(left) Many small local waterworks now lie abandoned, like these old drinking water filter beds in Middlesex, which have been disused since the 1960s. These sites are quickly colonized by a wealth of flora and fauna, and are often worthy of protection as a habitat of special interest.

A whole range of interesting objects connected with water supply still exists. Look for:

1614 to bring fresh spring water to Cambridge. Hobson himself was an entrepreneur (and the origin of the dilemma of Hobson's choice, for he rented out truly appalling horses), and most waterworks supplying London and other growing towns were private companies until well into Victorian times. Some were of dubious merit – only 150 years ago, one was taking water from the Thames at Chelsea 9 feet (3m) from the outlet of a large sewer.

Though sewage was obviously unsavoury, the threat it posed to health was for a long time ignored. In earlier centuries, sewers were rudimentary, and townspeople lived with the stink of dirty water running openly in the streets. In London, the Fleet and other Thames tributaries were little more than noxious open drains. The danger was made clear when cholera and typhus, both waterborne diseases, struck the new Victorian world, with tragic results.

Large reservoirs already existed across the country, built to feed the national canal system. Now vast new ones were constructed to store clean drinking water. One of London's first was at Stoke Newington. Dating from 1834, it was fed by the New River and, like many other drinking water reservoirs, was accompanied by elaborate filter systems of open sanded tanks. These Victorian water supply systems were served by ornate pumping stations, containing beam engines of the kind that had been designed to drain the Cornish tin mines.

STAND TAPS – like this urban iron standard – which supplied water before mains were laid.

BEAM ENGINES – still found in some pumping stations – which pumped water from a local water source to a reservoir.

CLEANING UP

At the same time that the water supply was improved, new sewers were also built. The watery waste was now either discharged directly into a river miles from the town or was led to a sewage farm. Here it was filtered through rows of shallow pools before being allowed to seep back across the fields into the river. In later sewage works, the liquid was sprayed over raised beds of clinker. Both processes relied on the bacteria present in the sewage breaking it down in to harmless products, which happens naturally as long as the bacteria are given enough time and air to work with. Modern treatment plants agitate the waste to achieve the same result in much less space. The purified liquor can then be released into a river with little harm done.

Today, giant waterboards equipped with modern plant and machinery supply homes and workplaces with well over 3000 million gallons of clean water a day (and deal with it when it has been used and dirtied). These, together with older waterworks of many different kinds – often abandoned – furnish a wildlife habitat of great interest.

WATER TOWERS – both new (top) and old (below) – built to store and give a head of water in low-lying areas.

Around the Waterworks

The rich and fascinating microscopic life of freshwater provides the food for larger worms, larvae and insects which attract many birds – especially waders – to both abandoned and functioning waterworks.

The plants and animals of freshwater plankton are microscopic but all other water life depends on them. Scoop up a bottle of water from the muddy bottom of a pool and leave it to settle for a day or two. You may then see some tiny specks of life on the sides of the glass. These will be *Amoebae*, ever-changing 'blobs' which seem the most primitive creatures until they are compared with the really basic bacteria. Then the *Amoeba*, which moves, breathes, feeds and excretes, and also reacts to its surroundings, seems quite well advanced. Beyond that, and keeping a fixed shape, is the *Paramecium*, which has an outer skin covered with tiny hairs, or cilia, which move rapidly and propel the creature along.

A giant leap from these are the water fleas and hydra. Related to jellyfish, hydra are common in freshwater, and can be found in stagnant pools and ditches. They have hollow, tube-like bodies with up to ten tentacles at one end and may be almost 1 inch long. Attaching themselves to duckweed or larger aquatic plants, they usually occur on the underside of leaves.

Water fleas, or *Daphnia*, form the hydra's diet. *Daphnia* jerk and skip their way through ponds and ditches, sometimes in incredible numbers. Their outer shell is transparent and, under a lens, you can examine the pumping heart, the gut and the muscles in dynamic action. They feed on tiny algae and bacteria filtered from the water. As their legs are enclosed within the outer shell, they swim with rhythmic flicks of their antennae.

Where mud has collected at the bottom of abandoned water courses or in stagnant side ditches, there will be worms. *Tubifex*, or sludge worms – similar to earthworms in appearance – may be visible as a reddish patch in the shallows. Colonies live head-down in tubes in the mud, poking out their red tails when not disturbed. *Lumbriculus* is a small brownish worm, very common in still water. Flatworms are very different: they are unsegmented, primitive worms, related to flukes and tapeworms.

LIFE OF MUDDY SHALLOWS

However stagnant the water, some creatures will still thrive in it. In the shallows, where the mud is thick and black with decomposing plant matter, lives the extraordinary rat-tailed maggot. The 'tail' at the end of its maggot-like body is actually a telescopic breathing tube which reaches to the water surface. The rat-tailed maggot is the aquatic larval stage of one of the attractive hoverflies or droneflies that resemble wasps.

At the water's surface, whirligig beetles skim about, water boatmen race in the quieter reaches and pond skaters dimple the surface

GREEN SANDPIPER
Breeding in Scandinavia and eastern Europe, green sandpipers migrate southwards through the British Isles to their winter quarters in the Mediterranean and tropical Africa. They can be seen on their return passage in spring but are commonest from July to October. Small numbers spend the winter in south and east England.

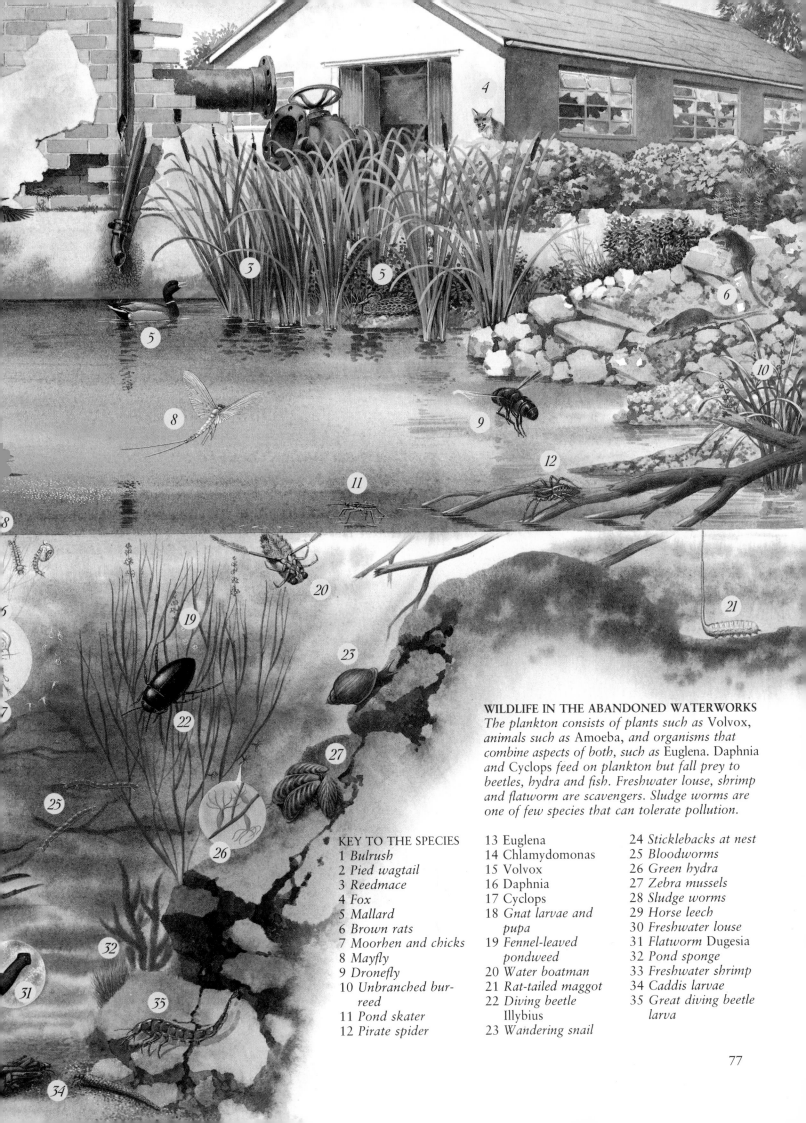

WILDLIFE IN THE ABANDONED WATERWORKS

The plankton consists of plants such as Volvox,
animals such as Amoeba, and organisms that
combine aspects of both, such as Euglena. Daphnia
and Cyclops feed on plankton but fall prey to
beetles, hydra and fish. Freshwater louse, shrimp
and flatworm are scavengers. Sludge worms are
one of few species that can tolerate pollution.

KEY TO THE SPECIES

1 *Bulrush*
2 *Pied wagtail*
3 *Reedmace*
4 *Fox*
5 *Mallard*
6 *Brown rats*
7 *Moorhen and chicks*
8 *Mayfly*
9 *Dronefly*
10 *Unbranched bur-
   reed*
11 *Pond skater*
12 *Pirate spider*

13 *Euglena*
14 *Chlamydomonas*
15 *Volvox*
16 *Daphnia*
17 *Cyclops*
18 *Gnat larvae and
   pupa*
19 *Fennel-leaved
   pondweed*
20 *Water boatman*
21 *Rat-tailed maggot*
22 *Diving beetle
   Illybius*
23 *Wandering snail*

24 *Sticklebacks at nest*
25 *Bloodworms*
26 *Green hydra*
27 *Zebra mussels*
28 *Sludge worms*
29 *Horse leech*
30 *Freshwater louse*
31 *Flatworm Dugesia*
32 *Pond sponge*
33 *Freshwater shrimp*
34 *Caddis larvae*
35 *Great diving beetle
   larva*

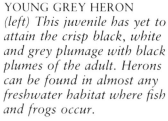

YOUNG GREY HERON
(left) This juvenile has yet to attain the crisp black, white and grey plumage with black plumes of the adult. Herons can be found in almost any freshwater habitat where fish and frogs occur.

INSECT LARVAE
(left) The two rat-tailed maggots are the larvae of droneflies, while the bloodworm is the larvae of a non-biting midge. Both can tolerate water which has been polluted with sewage.

tension as they slide delicately on a layer of air trapped beneath pads of hair. Tiny green blobs of duckweed add a touch of colour. From the shallows grow reedmace, bur-reed and yellow flag.

Old fashioned sewage farms are now things of the past, but are fondly remembered by many experienced birdwatchers. Here, raw sewage was pumped out into shallow beds between steep embankments, with deep sludge covered in a watery film. As they fell into disuse and dried out, so the sludge became overgrown with docks and other plants and the variety of birds to be seen dwindled. The most interesting time was somewhere between the most active period and total degeneration, when the mixture of sludge and wet pools seemed made for migrant wading birds.

FLOCKS OF WADERS

The best sewage farms would attract flocks of redshanks, dunlins, ringed plovers, snipe and lapwings each autumn. Scarce visitors, such as little stints and curlew sandpipers, might drop in, while wood, common and green sandpipers, spotted redshanks, ruffs and greenshanks would all add to the list of exciting birds each year. They each probe and peck for worms and invertebrates in the mud and shallows.

Feeding in a different manner, but also taking the insects of the most watery lagoons, passing common and black terns would swoop down in flight to pick up a morsel. Sand martins and swallows patrolled the air above the water to take emerging flies.

Almost all of these old farms have now been replaced by modern treatment works, often sited near a river or railway, away from human habitation. Comprising circular concrete tanks with constantly revolving sprinkler systems, they would seem at first to be unattractive sites for birds. Yet birds gather in large numbers at these places. Flocks of starlings ride the sprinkler carousels, or stride along the filter beds, jumping up and over the sprinkler arm at each rotation. Pied and yellow wagtails may also be seen feeding here.

More unexpected are the warblers which

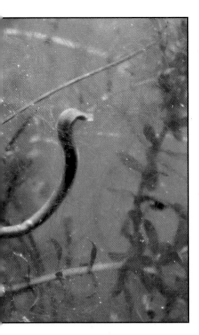

take advantage of the insect life around such treatment works. The chiffchaff is a summer visitor to the British Isles from the Mediterranean, but in recent years increased numbers have stayed through the winter. The blackcap – another summer migrant that spends the winter here in small, but increasing numbers – turns to berries and fruit in winter, but chiffchaffs continue eating insects. In southwest England, large gatherings of chiffchaffs have been watched feeding together at a modern sewage treatment plant where insects are always plentiful.

At abandoned sites, where the water is still and the bankside vegetation more lush, the bird life will be different. There is no short grass or flat ground for the wagtail or pipit to stride across with confidence. The birds here are often bigger ones, able to squeeze through the taller vegetation. The water rail may creep along a well-grown shore. A moorhen will submerge quietly at the approach of danger, keeping its bill just above the surface so that it can breathe without being seen.

FISH-EATING BIRDS

Where there are fish – often they will be sticklebacks if it is a stagnant pond – there will be fish eaters, like the glorious kingfisher. The first sign of a kingfisher is frequently its shrill whistle, as the bird flies off fast and low over the water. For all their strong colours, kingfishers are surprisingly small and are extremely difficult to see when they keep still against a varied background.

An easier bird to spot is the grey heron. Tall and stately, it stands quietly with endless patience, waiting for a fish to come too close. When a fish ventures near, the heron moves with speed. With a lightning lunge and a swift grab with the strong bill, the fish is caught and soon swallowed.

The heron will have more of a struggle if it catches an eel. Although adult eels need access to the sea where they breed, and all young eels travel up from the sea to their freshwater homes, they can be found in old ditches or ponds that have no outlet to a river. This is possible because the eel can leave water for a surprising length of time to wriggle determinedly across wet or moist ground to a nearby ditch. It will live there quite happily – unless it happens to chance upon a heron.

FRESHWATER LEECH
(above) Several species of leech can be found in standing water. Some suck the blood of fish or waterbirds, others feed on snails and worms. A tail end sucker anchors them while awaiting prey.

WATER FLEA SHOAL
(right) Magnified several times, these water fleas are of the Daphnia species which grow to a length of 3mm. They breed rapidly, forming a large part of the diet of some fish.

GREAT REEDMACE
(left) The edges of sludge beds or other abandoned waterworks will quickly become colonized by reedmace. This plant encroaches on the water and soon forms a marshy edge as dead vegetation raises the land level.

POND SKATER
(right) Living on the surface film of ponds or slow-moving water, the pond skater is a predator. It can 'row' itself swiftly over the surface to catch dead and dying insects.

Great Yellow-cress

Fennel Pondweed

Great Water Dock

GREAT YELLOW-CRESS *(Rorippa amphibia)* A perennial with upright grooved stems 16-48″ (40-120cm) tall. Leaves are very variable with only a short stalk. Flowers and oval pods appear June-August. Locally common in wet places, throughout England.

GREAT WATER DOCK *(Rumex hydrolapathum)* Large and robust, this perennial reaches 80″ (200cm), with oval leaves up to 40″ (100cm) long. Common on fertile soils of marsh and waterside, in south and mid England. Branched stems bear whorls of flowers, July-September.

FENNEL PONDWEED *(Potamogeton pectinatus)* Found in fertile, limy waters of lowland Britain and in slightly salty water near the coast, this aquatic plant has thin branched stems to 80″ (200cm). The leaves are translucent, the flowers open all summer.

Marsh Woundwort

Marsh Yellow-cress

Redshank

REDSHANK *(Polygonum persicaria)* A freely-branching annual, which can reach 28″ (70cm), found on cultivated ground, and near water. A dark blotch is usually seen on the lance-shaped leaves. Dense flower spikes appear June-October. Found throughout Britain.

MARSH WOUNDWORT *(Stachys palustris)* A widespread perennial, this 16-40″ (40-100cm) hairy plant is frequently found beside water and in marshes to altitudes of 1500′ (500m). Short-stalked leaves are lance-shaped and toothed. Whorls of flowers open July to September.

MARSH YELLOW-CRESS *(Rorippa palustris)* Common through much of Britain, less so in the West and North, this 3-24″ (8-60cm) annual thrives on muddy banks. Leaves are deeply lobed, with wavy, toothed edges. Small flowers open June-September.

Juvenile

Little Ringed Plover

Kentish Plover

Female

LITTLE RINGED PLOVER (*Charadrius dubius*) Arriving here in March, this plover has been breeding in south-east England since 1944. It is attracted to man-made habitats such as gravel pits, where it nests amongst bare pebbles. After breeding, it gathers near sewage farms and marshes, before flying south for winter. At 6″ (15cm), it is also distinguished from the slightly larger ringed plover, by a white bar over the forehead and yellow eye-rings. 3-4 buff, brown-spotted eggs are laid from April, young are soon active.

KENTISH PLOVER (*Charadrius alexandrinus*) Though once a rare breeding bird of shingly coasts in Kent, this 6″ (15cm) plover is now only an infrequent bird of passage in spring and autumn. Males are told from ringed plovers by their black legs and much smaller areas

Male

Blue-headed Yellow Wagtail

Male

Female

of black on head and chest; females are much paler with brown, not black, markings. They are most often seen at the water's edge, feeding on insects and molluscs – but their colouring makes them hard to spot. Their call is a low, fluffy '*poo-wit-wit*'.

BLUE-HEADED YELLOW WAGTAIL (*Motacilla flava* var. *flava*) This is the central European race of yellow wagtail. It is a regular passage migrant in summer, appearing by water almost anywhere in south-east England – especially in insect-rich

watermeadows. The adult male is distinguished from the yellow wagtail by its slaty-blue head and from the rare vagrant grey-headed and black-headed yellow wagtails by a white eye stripe. All races of yellow wagtail are similar in their behaviour and may interbreed.

The Smew

As white as the floating fragments of ice among which it bobs and dives, the drake smew is the smallest and most elusive of the sawbill ducks, and a scarce winter visitor to our inland reservoirs.

Far out in the small area of ice-free water on the frozen reservoir, among the flock of mallard and coot, the pale winter sun picks out a dazzling white bird. A moment later, it has vanished from sight, as it dives beneath the cold grey water, reappearing some distance away with a fish. Even such a brief glimpse of the drake smew is rewarding, for this scarce winter visitor is one of the most beautiful of all ducks.

Small, neat and supremely elegant, the smew is one of our smallest ducks; the name 'smew' is probably an old version of the word 'small'. From a distance, the drake smew appears completely white, a closer look, however, reveals his delicate markings — a handsome pattern of black patches and lines on head, chest and back contrasting strikingly with his otherwise pure white plumage.

The female, although not so spectacular as her mate, is also an attractive bird. Variously known as a 'redhead' or 'weasel duck', the female smew has a slim head, sporting a russet crown and contrasting white cheeks and throat.

Her body is grey-brown with black and white markings on the wings.

The smew breeds in tree-holes in northern USSR and, in very small numbers, in Scandinavia, migrating south for winter. Its favourite winter haunts are in the Netherlands, but small numbers reach Britain, especially in hard winters. Sadly, though, this dapper little waterbird does not turn up here in anything like its former numbers, with no more than 100 birds being spotted each year.

Smew are remarkably conservative in their choice of winter quarters, returning to the same spot year after year. Despite inhabiting the vast expanses of Russian wilderness, for much of the year, wintering smew will come right into urban areas; favourite haunts include reservoirs in the London area, although large flocks no longer occur at the Brent Reservoir near Neasden, as they used to. Smew also turn up in most years at Virginia Water, Surrey, Abberton Reservoir, Essex, on the coast at Dungeness, Kent and even as far afield as the Chew Valley Reservoir, Somerset.

DISTINCTIVE DRAKE
(above) The handsome drake smew has predominantly white plumage with smart black markings. These comprise a black eye patch which extends to the bill, two black stripes at the back of the head and narrow black lines across the back and flanks, forming a breast band. A small duck, it rarely exceeds 16" (40cm) in length.

STRIKING REDHEADS
(right) Although less distinctivly marked the drake, the female smew also has attractive plumage. A mainly grey-brown body is interspersed with black and white markings, and the white cheeks are topped by a beautiful rusty crown.

RARE WINTER VISITORS
(right) *Although smew are regular winter visitors to Britain, they arrive in very small numbers and only to a handful of favoured locations. Until the 1950s, several hundred smew regularly wintered here – particularly in man-made habitats such as reservoirs and gravel pits, in the London area. This number has now fallen to fewer than 100 a year. Most arrive after Christmas, and leave in mid-March for their breeding grounds in the USSR and parts of Scandinavia.*

KEY FACTS

IN FLIGHT the drake smew is conspicuous with white head and neck, revealing more of his black plumage than when on the ground. The female is less striking, with mottled grey underparts, white neck and red crown.

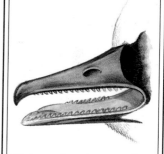

THE BILL has sharp tooth-like serrations along the edge, and is well adapted to catching slippery prey.

THE EGGS are creamy white and laid in a tree hole or nest-box. One clutch of 6-10 is incubated for 30 days.

The first smew are generally spotted during the last week of November, but most do not arrive until after Christmas, with a build-up to maximum number by mid-February. This is followed by a gradual tailing-off, until all except a few stragglers have left us for their northern breeding grounds by mid-March.

Superb underwater swimmers, smew usually dive to a depth of four or five feet, and may stay under for as long as 45 seconds, often surfacing a considerable distance away. A flock often dives in unison, reappearing one by one in various places. Although they take mainly insect food in their breeding grounds, they switch to a diet of fish in winter, when aquatic insects are scarce and hard to find.

Like its much larger relatives the goosander and red-breasted merganser, the smew has a specially adapted 'saw-bill' which is equipped with sharp serrations for catching and holding its slippery prey.

A strong flier once airborne, smew, in common with other driving ducks, take off from the water in a rather laborious fashion, pattering along the surface with their feet and thrashing their wings dramatically to achieve the necessary acceleration; a mallard, by contrast, rises out of the water almost vertically.

Although they do not breed in the British Isles, smew do sometimes begin their communal courtship displays on our waters in spring. These courtship rituals are quite dramatic affairs, with a number of well-defined stages. The drake approaches the female with his head feathers raised to form a crest; he then curves his neck until his head is resting on his back. The display then reaches its climax as the drake rises out of the water, uttering a curious mechanical-sounding creaking call, to which the female, if suitably impressed, responds with a gruff barking and by bobbing in the water.

Although fully protected throughout Britain, the smew still suffers at the hands of egg collectors in Finland, and may be shot on the Continent, its attractive plumage ironically making it popular for mounting and displaying in cases – an ignominious end for such a lively and beautiful bird.

The Farmyard

Basic units of agricultural life, farms have dotted the countryside for countless generations. Embracing pockets of land which traditionally supported a mixed range of crops and livestock, these small self-contained farmsteads helped shape the landscape's familiar rural face. But times have changed and today's farms have become bigger and more specialized and the old-type farm and its farmyard is fast disappearing, the cosy yard with its rich smells and old buildings replaced by clinically clean, almost factory-like structures.

MODEL FARM
(left) The vital components of the farmyard have traditionally been the grain service area centred on the barn, and the cattle quarters in the yard. Each building had its particular function: the cut grain sheaves were stored in the barn, where they were threshed in winter, the chaff blown away by the breeze sweeping through the great doorways: the shelter and cowsheds, stable, pigsty and cart house served the livestock. 200 years ago the open high-roofed Dutch barn was introduced for storing hay and straw.

NEW STOCK
(below right) The interests of efficiency have led to radical changes in cattle-rearing in the last few years: modern milking parlours wash the cows as they approach a shining array of machinery; cattle overwinter in vast sheds. Some cattle even spend the summer indoors – fed on grass cut and delivered by tractor, supplemented by artificial concentrates, their whole diet carefully balanced and monitored. Protection is also given against the infections and parasites which are the main causes of disease. These days cattle are bred to produce either milk or meat, though there are dual-purpose breeds such as the Simmental. Working draught cattle have all but died out in this country, though they are still used elsewhere in Europe.

Farming came to Britain 5000 years ago, brought by New Stone Age man who found a warmer, wetter country than today's, and a landscape entirely covered with wildwood, except for small patches of grassland, moor and marsh. At first, these early farmers simply cleared small pockets of the wildwood to grow corn, and when the thin soil was depleted they moved on. Goats, cattle and sheep helped keep the new clearings open by grazing and trampling down invading saplings. Gradually, over the centuries, more and more land was cleared for agriculture until, today, only nine per cent of this country is now forested, while over 80 per cent is put to some kind of farming use. Consequently, the farm – the focus of agricultural activity – has long been an important feature of the landscape.

PREHISTORIC SMALLHOLDINGS

Very early farmsteads consisted of groups of circular thatched huts surrounded by small fields for crops and livestock. Palisades and ditches protected domestic stock and produce from the ravages of wild animals. Examples have been excavated in Cumbria, Cornwall, Yorkshire and Dartmoor, and a reconstructed Iron Age farm can be seen at Butser Hill in Hampshire.

Bronze Age innovations encouraged a more prosperous and settled agriculture – axes and sickles were commonly available, and greater levels of efficient cultivation could be reached thanks to the beginnings of horse-drawn transport. Settlements aspired to self-sufficiency in tools, food and clothing – an achievement that the Romans exploited and encouraged, introducing various industries, along with the cultivation of the vine, and market gardening.

By Saxon and Norman times strip farming and rudimentary crop rotation were practised, and in villages right across the country, inhabitants worked the surrounding lands together, sharing their draught animals and tools in the service of monastery and lord of the manor. It was not until the Black Death of 1349 had done its grisly work, that villeins were in a position to buy their way out of feudal service, and eventually contemplate the idea of a private self-contained farmstead around its own farmyard.

Later, by the time of Elizabeth I, the enclosure and hedging of open countryside gave rise to farms stationed well outside the village, amid their own fields. Many peasants suffered penury through the loss of grazing rights, but successful owner-farmers had for the first time the power

Nature Walk

Wading through the muck of the farmyard, you may catch sight of curiosities old and new such as:

STADDLE STONES supporting an old wooden barn. These are designed to prevent rodents which would consume or spoil the stored grain, hay or straw, entering the barn.

BROADCASTER

DISC HARROW

MODERN EQUIPMENT such as broadcasters, that spin fertilizer on to the land; and disc harrows that break up newly ploughed soil, to prepare the land for seed.

A GINGANG — a round shed attached to a barn in which a horse or mule walked to drive machinery such as mechanical threshers.

and incentive to improve farming methods. The late 18th and early 19th centuries in particular saw mass enclosure and a revolution in farming techniques, and it is from this era that most farms in the heart of England date — farms elsewhere are frequently much older. Increasingly, prosperous farmers abandoned traditional, functional buildings made from local materials to live in stylish brick-built houses modelled on the great country houses.

In the early 1800s, a succession of poor harvests ruined many small farmers, and their land was absorbed into the estates of the wealthy, worked by tenant farmers. Further changes came with the coming of the railways, opening up new markets for fresh food in the rapidly

HAPPY MIXTURE
Ony five per cent of the farms in the British Isles support the wide range of crops and livestock typical of traditional mixed farming.

expanding industrial cities. Encouraged by competition from imported American grain, which flooded into the country in the late 19th century, farmers in many places began to specialize in dairy and vegetable farming, changing the appearance of the farmyard yet again, as the traditional mixed farm was superseded.

FACTORY FARMING

Today, although many small farms still remain, one third of our most productive land is occupied by a miniscule three per cent of farms. Total food production has doubled in this country over the past 30 years due largely to rigid specialization. While our temperate damp grasslands are ideal for grazing animals — there are more sheep in Britain than in any other European country — intensive livestock rearing and crop growing are becoming more prevalent. Farms specializing in pigs or poultry have replaced chicken runs and pigsties with enclosed 'factory farming' units whose occupants never see the light of day. Cattle are reared without ever setting hoof in a field — known appropriately as zero-grazing. Hedges are obliterated to make way for grainfields of 250 acres or more; and new crops, such as oil-seed rape which has increased over 1500-fold in the last ten years, have altered the face of the country. These changes have also spawned a new breed of tidy concrete farmyards, bordered with vast utilitarian buildings some of which have a definite space-age appearance. Yet despite changes, farmyard wildlife still prospers in those corners untouched by progress.

Around the Farmyard

**Surrounded by open countryside, the farmyard attracts a wealth
of birds and mammals from the fields around, as well as being
home to many creatures of its own.**

Five-thirty on a winter's morning, it is pitch black and a cold wind lashes icy rain against the farmhouse windows. Lights come on in the milking parlour and the milk pump hums. Black and white cows heavy in milk queue patiently.

When milking is over the first glimmers of thin light silhouette the farm buildings against the pale winter sky and bring shape to the dale beyond. A flurry of starlings arrive from the night's roost and sit about the buildings clamouring, before dropping to feed on the spillages in the granary. Mealy deposits on the white walls of the farmhouse reveal their feeding habits. Just as in early autumn purple splodges told the tale of an elderberry feast.

After a hearty breakfast the farmer begins feeding the stock. Small feed potatoes, spent brewer's grains and rolled barley are shovelled off a trailer and into strong wooden troughs in the beef yard. Chaffinches, greenfinches and yellowhammers flit about between the munching mouths of the bullocks. Cocky starlings stand their ground voicing angry objections.

Besides their dairy nuts the milk cows receive much the same feed as the beef animals but fewer stock potatoes and more high quality silage from the clamp. This silage is the result of three cuts of summer grass at its lushest. It is piled into an open pit and covered with black polythene and old tractor tyres. The polythene cuts out the light and the tyres squash out the air. Under these conditions an army of millions goes to work. Invisible to the naked eye, vast colonies of microbes begin to digest the grass, breaking down the hard cellulose fibres of the plant. This makes the sickly sweet smelling silage which weight for weight is more nutritious than the grass itself.

FARMYARD KILLER

By mid-morning the starlings have their crops full and gather in the top of an old ash at the far end of the stack yard. They clamour as on their dawn arrival. Quite suddenly all goes quiet. A chaffinch 'pinks' an alarm and the birds wheel in flight. High above, a sparrowhawk, crosses the valley on its morning patrol, flapping and gliding in characteristic manner. When the sparrowhawk hunts in the farmyard, its arrival goes unnoticed until too late for some unsuspecting bird. It comes crashing in on a low

BROWN RATS
Raiding grain stores, brown rats are vermin to the farmer, and can overrun the farmyard if not controlled. They build nests in underground burrows and excavate several tunnels leading to the nest chamber. Breeding quickly, the female may give birth to five litters, each of ten young, in the course of a year. Brown rats arrived here from Russia in the 18th century.

WILDLIFE IN THE FARMYARD

The barn at the heart of the farmyard may house the increasingly
rare barn owl; Rats also forage and nest in the barn, as may house
sparrows and starlings. The plants of the farmyard, such as Italian
rye grass, provide seeds that will be eaten by sparrows, starlings
and probably the muscovy duck. Homing in to hunt, the
sparrowhawk is after seeds at second hand and, with its long yellow
legs, will pluck an unwary sparrow feeding on spilt grain. The toad
lurks among farmyard rubble and plants. Friesians carry a movable
feast of insects for swooping swallows. The wren, too, lurks and may
build its domed nest among old tyres or farm machinery, but the
smartly attired pied wagtail is a bird of more open spaces, building
its nest in an open-fronted nestbox or atop a wall. Nettles invade
rough ground. The names of chickweed and shepherd's purse reveal
their long association with farms.

KEY TO THE SPECIES

1 *Sparrowhawk*
2 *Rooks*
3 *House martins*
4 *Swallow*
5 *Red valerian*
6 *Barn owl*
7 *Nettles*
8 *Friesians*
9 *Ivy*
10 *Poppies*
11 *Muscovy duck*
12 *House sparrows*
13 *Pied wagtail*
14 *Brown rat*
15 *Common mallow*
16 *Chickweed*
17 *Wren*
18 *Starlings*
19 *Italian rye grass*
20 *House mouse*
21 *Shepherd's purse*
22 *Toad*
23 *Great plantain*
24 *Silverweed*

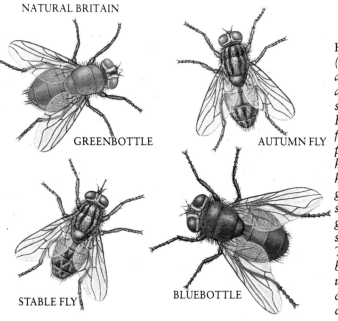

GREENBOTTLE

AUTUMN FLY

STABLE FLY

BLUEBOTTLE

FARM FLIES
(left) The autumn fly actually hibernates in autumn but can be seen flying from February. The stable fly has a longer proboscis (visible here) than the similar housefly. The greenbottle pictured is similar to other greenbottles and is a serious pest to sheep. The bluebottle, which buzzes annoyingly at windows, also has close cousins but is the commonest of its kind.

level attack. Losing altitude a field or so away to avoid detection it accelerates to maximum speed, crossing the beef yard inches from the ground, sending small birds scuttling for cover. Its piercing eyesight locks on to some unfortunate individual. The sparrowhawk has long legs that it lashes out to make good its strike and sharp talons close around the prey in a fatal embrace.

The kill is taken to a favourite post where it is quickly plucked. Feathers float away on the wind like flakes of snow. Momentarily the sparrowhawk stops its work to glare around nervously, feeling insecure in this open position. Disturbed by the farm Jack Russell terrier on its wanderings, the bird takes flight and heads for the cover of a spinney, still gripping the prey in its talons.

The day gives way to better weather. Sunlight encourages a pair of collared doves to climb and

MALE YELLOW DUNG-FLY
(below right) This striking fly has a fascinating life story. Pairs are attracted to cow dung, where they mate. The larvae feed on the dung, pupating in the soil below. Adults, meantime, feed on flower nectar but also prey on other cow pat flies and are even cannibalistic.

SWALLOW QUADS
(below) Safe in a nest on the barn wall, these four young swallows have just sighted a parent flying in and are screaming to be fed. They will fly from the nest 17-24 days after hatching.

glide in a courtship flight and a wren to beat out its punchy song. Mouse-like, wrens search relentlessly for insects and other invertebrates amongst the cracks and crevices in the lichen covered stonework of the farm buildings. In hard winters wrens fare badly when food is short and the nights are long.

The farm's orchard shows evidence of neglect. Branches of the once cared-for apple trees cross as they wind inwards where for years the pruning saw has not been. Rot has worked into the trunks where old boughs have fallen. The holes thus created provide nesting sites for blue and great tits and, eventually, as they become larger, tree sparrows and starlings. The north westward sides of the trunks are green with a soft coating of pleurococcus, an alga that pervades the damper bark surfaces. Squeaky contact calls of small birds break the silence as through the old orchard a mixed party of long-tailed, willow and blue tits, accompanied by diminutive goldcrests, forage. They leave as suddenly as they came. Silently a tree-creeper climbs a trunk examining the intricacies

COLLARED DOVES
(left) A pair of collared doves with brown-capped tree sparrows and greenfinches. Feeding here on spilt grain, collared doves are often seen in large numbers around granaries and farmyards. Their subtly coloured plumage, neatly offsetting a black half-collar, is very attractive, but their monotonous call lacks the soothing charm of the woodpigeon's.

COMMON MALLOW
(right) The wonderful lilac coloured mallow has leaves that resemble pieces of crumpled paper. The petals are lightly candy-striped and the whole plant has a robust sturdiness suited to the farmyard. It flowers strongly from June to September and, dying down over winter, shoots up afresh the following spring.

COCK AND HENS
(below) Descended from jungle birds, this proudly wattled cock supervises his clucking hens. Free range birds are back in favour because of the superior flavour of their flesh and eggs over those of factory chickens. They have, however, always been kept on smallholdings and the older breeds are now much sought after by keen breeders.

of its surface for hidden hibernating insects.

On the ground of the orchard are strewn the dead stems of cow parsley, perennial nettle, hogweed, ground elder and docks. Grey maran hens scratch amongst the debris. Blackbirds, redwings and fieldfares hop about in search of ungathered windfalls. In the spring, regrowth will quickly appear and provide a rich wildlife habitat. A plethora of moths will be generated from it; garden tiger, yellow underwing, magpie, brimstone and small ermine to name but a few. Common shrews, woodmice and bank voles are still in residence, as is the tawny owl that will hunt them. The owl uses its cryptically marked plumage to conceal itself during the daylight hours as it huddles close

to the tree trunk. It will by no means confine its diet to small mammals, but will also hunt roosting birds.

The barn owl uses one of the stone barns as a roosting and nesting site, entering the stronghold through an open ventilation slit in the gable end. Swallows also use the barns as safe nesting sites. The first spring twitterings about the buildings are a welcome sound as they herald the longer days and the turn-out of the dairy cows on to the grass. Often mistaken as a close relative of the swallow, yet in truth not even of the same family, the swifts also turn to the buildings for a place in which to rear their broods. Bands of these long-winged, dark brown, aerial feeding birds scream about the farmyard on the long summer evenings.

The sight and sounds of summer migrant birds seems far away on this cold winter day and by mid afternoon the light is already fading. The starlings gather once more in the ash tree before setting out for their night's roost. The greenfinches, chaffinches and yellowhammers also desert the farmyard.

RODENT ROBBERS

Brown rats and house mice awaken from their daytime slumbers in their hideaways. Five litters of up to ten youngsters in each are born in a year and they can quickly colonize and overrun a farmyard if not controlled. Cats account for large numbers of young rats but an adult rat is a formidable adversary and only the tenacious Jack Russell is fearless enough to take them on. A good ratter is worth its weight in tins of dog meat to the farmer. The grey pelted mouse, like the rat, is an alien to Britain. Grain and dried food form the larger part of its diet and these two creatures cause a real problem in the granary.

As the chill night air grips the land, thick coated farm cats go in search of supper. By 5.30pm it is pitch black again.

Silverweed

Red Goosefoot

Good-King-Henry

RED GOOSEFOOT (*Chenopodium rubrum*) A spràwling annual to 28″ (70cm), the shiny, unevenly toothed leaves, stems and closely-packed clusters of tiny flowers are tinged red. Frequently found on cultivated land in England – rarely elsewhere – it flowers from July to September.

SILVERWEED (*Potentilla anserina*) Long runners to 31″ (80cm) enable this 2-10″ (5-25cm) plant to spread over open wasteland, shingle and grass. Flat, leafy rosettes grow in dry places – upright in wetter areas. Silky leaflets are coarsely toothed, single flowers appear July-August.

GOOD-KING-HENRY (*Chenopodium bonus-henricus*) Growing locally on the rich soil of farms and gardens, this 12-20″ (30-50cm) perennial has ridged, hollow stems and triangular leaves. Heads of tiny, dense green flowers, May-August, ripen to round capsules.

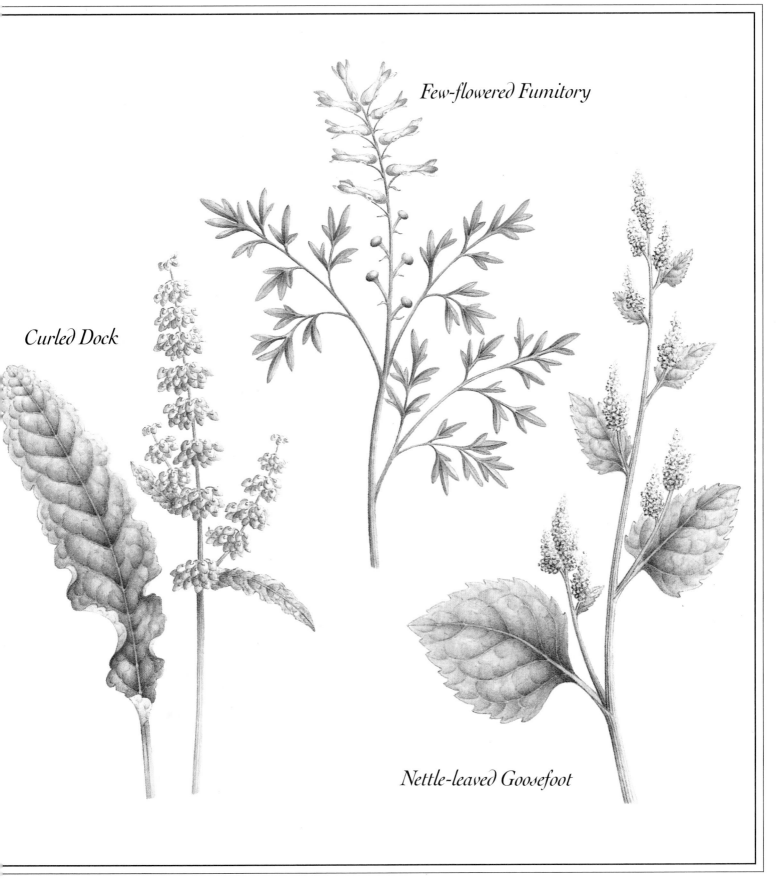

Few-flowered Fumitory

Curled Dock

Nettle-leaved Goosefoot

CURLED DOCK *(Rumex crispus)*
A troublesome arable weed, this
20-40″ (50-100cm), stiffly branched
perennial is very common on verges
and wasteland. Large lance-shaped
leaves have wavy, crimped margins
and whorls of tiny wind-pollinated
flowers are seen June to October.

FEW-FLOWERED FUMITORY
(Fumaria vaillantii) A weakly erect
2-6″ (5-15cm) annual with
branched stems, this is a rare arable
weed of chalky soil. Bluish leaves
have flat, almost linear lobes, and
round fruit follows the loose spire
of small flowers, June to September.

NETTLE-LEAVED GOOSEFOOT
(Chenopodium murale) An annual
weed of arable land in England and
Wales. The hollow ridged stem is
erect and reaches 28″ (70cm),
bearing sharply toothed, mealy
leaves. Short sprays of tiny green
flowers appear July-October.

Cuckoo Bee

Blue Osmia Bee

Cuckoo Bee

BLUE OSMIA BEE *(Osmia caerulescens)* Common in S. England and S. Wales, this is one of the mason bees, making nests in holes in old posts or walls. Up to 12 cells, each with 1 egg, are made from a 'mastic' of chewed leaves. The ½″ (12mm) female is blue, males are dowdy.

CUCKOO BEE *(Psithyrus rupestris)* Scattered in southern England and Ireland, this bee does not collect pollen. ¾″ (18mm) females invade nests of the bumble bee *Bombus lapidarius*, whose shape and colour they mimic, killing the queen. Host workers then raise cuckoo bee eggs.

CUCKOO BEE *(Psithyrus vestalis)* A shiny bee which mimics the bumble bee *Bombus terrestris*. After entering the nest and killing the queen bumble, the ¾″ (18mm) cuckoo female is accepted by host workers who rear her eggs. They occur mainly in the South and East.

Bees and Beetles

Devil's Coach Horse

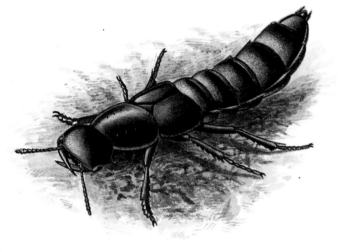

Dung Beetle

Dung Beetle

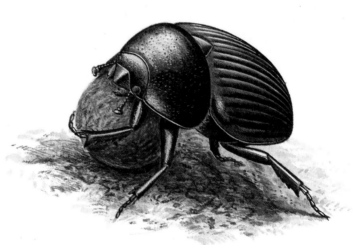

Dor Beetle

DEVIL'S COACH HORSE (*Ocypus olens*) A long, flattish 1″ (25mm) beetle, nocturnal though sometimes seen by day. Both larvae and adult are fiercely predatory, catching small insects and spiders. When threatened, the abdomen curls up to emit foul smelling chemicals.

DUNG BEETLE (*Aphodius rufipes*) Common and widespread in pastures, the brownish dung beetle eats horse sheep or cattle dung. Eggs are laid in the dung and larvae burrow into the ground to pupate. The ½″ (12mm) beetles have ridged wing-cases and fly at night in late summer-autumn.

DUNG BEETLE (*Onthophagus vacca*) Only males of this ⅓″-½″ (8-12mm) beetle have horns. Adults and larvae feed on cow dung – the female buries balls of dung and lays one egg in each. Locally common in south England, it is not found in the North nor Scotland.

DOR BEETLE (*Geotrupes stercorarius*) Common in country areas, both sexes of this 1″ (25mm), glossy beetle cooperate to dig tunnels beneath cow and horse dung. Eggs are laid in dung-balls at the ends of side chambers, guarded by the female until they hatch.

The Pied Wagtail

A familiar sight around human habitation, the slim and dainty
pied wagtail continually bobs its long black tail and darts
about the farmyard in a never-ending search for insects.

Scuttling along the farmyard wall, with black tail bobbing up and down, the pied wagtail suddenly darts into the air, snapping up a passing fly. This elegant little wagtail is usually associated with water – which gives it its country names of water wagtail and polly dish-washer. But old-style farmyards, with less emphasis on cleanliness than modern farms, offer an abundance of insect food throughout the year, as well as ample nesting sites in their ramshackle buildings and sheds.

Widespread in Britain and found in a variety of habitats, pied wagtails show a marked preference for man-made environments and even frequent town centres. They are fairly catholic in their choice of nest sites and settle for virtually any crack or crevice large enough to contain a nest. In rural surroundings the site may be a natural hole in a bank, but in more urban settings, buildings, walls, and other human artifacts, such as abandoned farm machinery, are ideal for nesting.

Prior to nesting in early spring, the male pied wagtail sings to advertise his territory. In contrast to the characteristic call-note – a sharp loud disyllabic *chizzick* – his song is less distinctive, consisting of little more than a series of twitters. However, he makes up for this with a lively courtship display – a dancing flight during which he flutters his wings and fans out his long tail to impress the female.

MULTIPLE BROODS

Once male and female wagtails have paired and settled down in their territory, the female builds a neat nest of moss and dry grass and lays 5 to 6 eggs. She takes most of the share of incubating the clutch for about 14 days but when the eggs hatch the male takes over the responsibility of bringing insect food to the hungry young fledglings. This leaves the female free to replenish her food reserves and gives her the opportunity to construct a new nest so that each pair of pied wagtails can have several broods each year.

With a British population of around 500,000 pairs, the pied wagtail is the commonest of the

BOB-TAIL
The jaunty little pied wagtail, beak characteristically stuffed with insects, stops, head held high and tail pumping up and down, before suddenly dashing off on twinkling legs to add another insect to its meal. With his black cap joined to black bib, black back and white belly, the sparrow-sized male is the more striking bird. In winter however, he becomes greyer-backed like the female. Juveniles are brownish-grey above, dusky below, with a black crescent-shaped breast band.

LODGING WITH MAN

The female pied wagtail is ever ready to build her nest in the safety of an old farm outhouse. The male joins her in flying backwards and forwards with beakfuls of insects for their relatively large brood.

three species of wagtail that breed here. The yellow wagtail, a summer visitor to this country, is rather restricted in its choice of habitat, preferring to nest in old water meadows and pastures. The grey wagtail favours streams and rivers, but unlike the yellow wagtail, is a resident species.

PARTIAL MIGRANT

The pied wagtail is neither a full resident nor a full migrant. Most of the population leaves the summer nesting sites to seek the guaranteed supply of invertebrate food to be found by flowing water. Hence watercress beds and sewage farms support large numbers of pied wagtails during the winter. Individuals vigorously defend a feeding territory from other pied wagtails and even conflict with grey wagtails if their ranges overlap. Some of our pied wagtails, however, particularly the young birds of that year, head for the warmer weather of southern Europe, returning the following spring.

Although territorial in their feeding habits, those that remain in Britain roost communally during the winter – as many as 1000 birds in a single roost. This may bring them safety in numbers but such large flocks inevitably attract the attention of predators, such as sparrowhawks. In recent times pied wagtails have started to use buildings as a substitute for thickets or reedbeds – even greenhouses now provide an ideal and protected roosting site.

The charming pied wagtail has long been a familiar site on farms. With the advent of modern farming practices – the emphasis on cleanliness and the control of insect pests – it might have been expected to suffer. But, on the contrary, this adaptable little bird has coped well with change and is still a widespread companion of man both in the town and on the farm.

IN FLIGHT the pied wagtail, black or grey above with prominent wingbars and white below, repeatedly utters its 'chizzick' call as it undulates through the air.

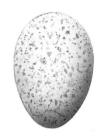

THE WHITE WAGTAIL – a Continental subspecies seen here as a passing migrant – is hard to tell from the pied race. It has a greyer back and rump and its cap and bib do not join.

RESIDENT WATER WAGTAIL

Not quite so recognisable without its normally sleek outline, the wagtail puffs out its feathers against the winter cold. Like most of the others that stay here during the winter the pied or water wagtail heads for streams, reservoirs, and even sewage farms, where it has a guaranteed supply of insects during the harsher months.

THE EGGS are greyish-white speckled with grey or brown. 2-3 broods of 5-6 eggs are laid April-June.

The Pig

All farmyard pigs are the domesticated descendants of the lean, long-snouted, large-tusked wild pig which once freely roamed the forests of Europe and Asia.

A supremely valuable animal to man, the pig is raised in most countries and numbers about 670 million worldwide. It provides around 500 different products from obvious edibles to explosives and leather to lubricating oils, lending weight to the saying that 'every part bar the squeak can be used.' Apart from other primates (apes and monkeys), the pig is the animal most physiologically similar to man, with affinities including its omnivorous diet and comparable digestive system.

EARLY DOMESTICATION

Taming, or domestication, of the wild pig or boar probably started during the late Stone Age about 8000 years ago, though this creature has a history extending back at least six million years.

In Britain, the wild pig was virtually extinct through the impact of hunting and deforestation even in Shakespeare's time – the last one in Windsor royal park was killed by James I in 1617 – and the domesticated pig progressively became a cottager's animal. In Ireland it was known as 'the gentleman who pays the rent' being easily managed and cheaply fed on swill, in a garden pen or on common land.

In time scavenging pigs were elevated to become farm stock worth a little care and capable of being fattened cheaply on dairy by-products and brewers' leftovers. Cross-breeding with varieties brought in from China, Italy and Portugal during the late 1700s wrought improvements as well as dramatic physical changes that led to today's different types.

One of the domestic pig's many surviving links with their wild ancestors is the way a farrowing sow shapes a bed from straw or from plant materials in a dry, sheltered hollow away from other members of the herd.

The sow lies on her side to give birth. Each piglet weighs about 2½lb (1.1kg) and the litter comprises eight to 12 individuals, with up to 20

TAMWORTHS
Among present-day pigs, only the Tamworth (above) vaguely resembles the ancestral wild pig – retaining the physique and hardiness of its wild forbears.
It thrives on poor fare, its coarse pelt protects it from winter chill, and its colour prevents sunburn – a real hazard for outdoor pink-skinned pigs. This resilient and adaptable creature is reared in Britain mainly for lean pork and bacon.

(140-204kg) respectively. Those not marketed at 5½-7 months are kept for breeding purposes in what has become a highly-specialized agricultural industry using genetic 'engineering' and computer-assisted feeding with high proteins and antibiotics.

In a natural setting, the adaptable pig's favourite foods are acorns, beech nuts and vegetable roots which it locates using its keen sense of smell and which it unearths with its sensitive snout.

It is more fastidious than credited, keeping an unsoiled corner of the sty in which to sleep –

or more in exceptional circumstances. At birth each naked piglet immediately and instinctively crawls towards the nipples, sucking its first milk whilst warmed by the mother and massaged with her snout. She is essentially passive, however, and does not intervene to prevent injury when struggles erupt for the nipples containing the most milk, and occasionally injures her young by inadvertently lying on them. A feeding hierarchy is quickly established and birthweight doubles in the first week. A weak or undersized piglet, the 'runt', sometimes dies and first-year mortality is high in some breeds. The litter begins eating other foods within ten days.

Surviving boars (males) and gilts (females under one year) mature fast, growing coarse, bristly hair and achieving average adult weights of 350-500lb (159-230kg) and 300-450lb

MIDDLE WHITE
(above) The increasingly rare middle white pig has a characteristic short fat body and pushed-in snout derived from Chinese pigs which were introduced to this country in 1770.

SADDLEBACK
(right) The British Saddleback is a hardy and prolific animal, reared for both pork and bacon, and perfect as a cottage or smallholding pig. It wallows to keep cool as it has no sweat glands.

another habit acquired in its ancestral days as a forest or woodland 'wanderer', when it used separate areas for feeding, sleeping, excretion and wallowing, all linked by paths worn by frequent trips in its stiff-legged trot.

The rutting season in the wild provoked savage fights between boars who slashed with their teeth in frontal and flank attacks. Domestic boars, however, are kept apart and have no rutting season.

The domestic boar is allowed to fertilize a number of sows, but plays no part in rearing the young. Older boars tend to live in solitude. Sows can be quite fierce after their 111-117 days pregnancy, and they will charge, bite and scream piercingly if alarmed or cornered. However their generally placid demeanor means that life expectancy can be 25 years.

MATERNAL BLISS
(left) Berkshires are small, quickly maturing pigs. Like other breeds, sows may produce two litters per year.

101

The Paddock

Part of the suburban and the country scene, the paddock is a meticulously managed habitat – an enclosed sward of nutritious grasses where horses may feed and exercise all year round. But horses are not the only animals which benefit from the pasture and the shade afforded by overhanging trees. Sited within easy reach of a farm or a private house, the paddock can also provide a refuge for vulnerable lambs or ponies, or donkeys too old for rides. Cattle and sheep may also graze here in summer, while in winter birds flock to probe the turf for seeds and insects.

HARROWING

ROLLING

MIXED GRAZING

The paddock is one of the most evocative of all countryside words, inspiring a whole variety of different images. For some it awakens memories of finely bred horses waiting impatiently to be saddled for the hunt, their coats gleaming and breath steaming in the crisp air of a winter's morning. For others the paddock is the comfortable home of an old pony or donkey – once a child's first ride, now kept as a fond family pet. Still others associate it with springtime, and young lambs gambolling and frolicking under the farmer's caring eye. Indeed, the paddock can be any of these – a vital element of a large, well-organized stable, an enclosed piece of land next to a private house, or part of a busy, working farm, providing shelter and protection for field stock at risk.

One dictionary definition of paddock is a small plot of pasture adjoining the stable.

OUT TO GRASS
Horses and ponies used for riding are most often kept on the 'combined' system – spending some of the time stabled and the remainder in the paddock. Using this system, it may be possible to keep two horses per acre. But where a horse is kept permanently at grass – as are hunters in the summer – then for a paddock to remain both productive and in good condition, the stocking rate should be nearer two acres per horse.

Although a familiar word today, it is of fairly recent origin. Whereas words such as pasture and field are reliably Old English, 'paddock' first appears in written use in the 17th century, although it may derive from an older dialect word *parrock* or 'park'.

Whatever the origins of its name, the paddock came into its own two centuries ago, when widespread changes in farming – especially in the lowlands – resulted in many of the landscape patterns we are familiar with today.

From early times, farmsteads were usually surrounded by a handful of small fenced, hedged or walled fields. Beyond was the ploughland or grazing land which, even in the shires and other parts of the lowlands, were wide and open, largely bare of fences or hedges. These small farmstead enclosures had many uses. They may have provided a scrap of grazing for cattle waiting to be taken to market, or nearby overnight accommodation for a flock of sheep which would otherwise have had to be folded further out; and perhaps weak ewes were brought here to lamb.

RESHAPING THE COUNTRYSIDE

By the 18th century, however, the enclosure movement was well underway. For the sake of better farming, the open ground was being divided into smaller fields; only a few of the commons escaped. A new breed of farmer was emerging – self-assured and definitely his own master. At this time cattle were still the usual draught animals, but horses – for long the symbol of the gentry in the countryside – were adopted by these new farmers, who joined the gentry to make fox hunting a popular sport of all who could be counted masters of the land. And the paddock became a familiar element of the countryside, often sited next to a newly built farmhouse.

Today's farm paddock, tucked behind the farm and often screened from the wind by hedges or a row of planted trees, is as busy as ever. But although its function remains unchanged, today it is carefully managed so that it provides good, nourishing pasture for the horses, cattle or sheep which are kept there.

By their grazing and movements, these

MOWING

SEEDING AND FERTILIZING

NURTURED GRASSLAND
(left) Although the paddock may appear to be a piece of grassland like any other, in order to provide nutritious pasture it needs careful maintenance all year round. Harrowing aerates the soil and tears out matted, dead vegetation, promoting new growth, while rolling flattens the surface. Cattle or sheep may be introduced after several weeks of grazing by horses to prevent the paddock becoming 'horse-sick'. Mixed grazing has the dual advantage of ensuring even grazing and reducing equine parasites, since cattle and sheep consume the long, dung-tainted grass left by the horses. As summer progresses, mowing may be necessary to remove excess grass or tall weeds. Finally, the paddock can be renovated by broadcasting a mixture of seed and fertilizer over the existing grass.

GONE TO SEED
(above) A neglected paddock quickly turns into a wasteland totally unsuitable for grazing horses. Ragwort, which is particularly poisonous to horses, soon takes hold, as do buttercups which are also toxic if eaten in large quantities.

SAFE ENCLOSURE
(right) At lambing time most sheep are folded in a paddock close by the farm where the shepherd can keep a watchful eye on them.

animals create a varied surface within the paddock. In places – along favourite paths or around the water trough – the soil is laid bare. In the summer months this earth may bake hard, making it impossible for new grass to grow, while in winter – unless drainage is good – it may turn into a quagmire. And after just a few weeks a paddock containing horses becomes noticably patchy – some areas are cropped short by heavy grazing, while others sport tall, lush clumps of dung-tainted grass which the horses refuse to eat. Only by mowing or mixed grazing by beef cattle or sheep can the pasture be kept even, but it also needs time to rest (often achieved by rotating the animals between three or four paddocks) and to rejuvenate (helped by harrowing, fertilizing and reseeding).

Although controlled management and intensive grazing means that few wild flowers can be expected, the unploughed soil can be host to fairy rings and other fungi, while the proximity of the farmstead or stables with spilt grain and other rich pickings mean that the paddock also attracts a large number of birds.

Nature Walk

Horses are clipped so that they do not sweat up when worked in winter. Look for:

HUNTER CLIP in which only the saddle patch and leg hair is left on. Ideal for horses in hard work.

BLANKET CLIP where the hair is trimmed from neck and belly. Allows for light work and daily turn-out.

HALF TRACE CLIP along the harness trace line. Useful for horses in light work that are kept at grass.

IRISH CLIP is a light clip which allows the horse to be worked lightly yet offers sufficient protection for it to be kept at grass.

In the Paddock

The paddock's combination of grass and grazing horses is irresistible to some quite exotic insects, while familiar farmland birds search the sward for food and flowers flourish in the dung-enriched soil.

In the centre of the paddock, where the late summer sun has scorched the grass almost yellow, a rose grey-coloured horse is grazing placidly on purple-flowered chickory. As it tugs at the plants, a dapper yellow wagtail is busily snapping up craneflies and other insects disturbed by the movement. After a while, the horse shakes its head vigorously to drive away the flies that buzz around its eyes, and the wary wagtail, easily alarmed, skims away over the grass and up on to a fence post.

At first sight, there seem few other signs of life in the paddock, but a closer look reveals all kinds of birds and insects thriving in the grass, in the ditch and in the hedges and trees around. Over in the shade of an old beech tree, where the horse saunters to drink from the trough, a party of speckled young starlings probe the turf for leatherjackets (larval craneflies). Where the horse plunges its muzzle into the water to drink, mosquito larvae and pupae, suspended from the surface film by their breathing tubes, loop and jerk down in to the water, the pupae like animated commas. Large female mosquitoes with

PADDOCK WILDLIFE
Hedged with beech and shaded by tall chestnuts, the paddock is an inviting habitat. As a thoroughbred horse munches its way through the summer grass, accompanied by a pair of black faced sheep, swallows fly down the insects that fill the air. Overhead, a wood pigeon clatters past while a pair of collared doves bill and coo on the gate. On the ground, crows and magpies probe the turf and colourful yellow wagtail searches for insects. Also adding colour to the scene are the tortoiseshell, orange tip and painted lady butterflies and the crimson cinnabar moth.

KEY TO THE SPECIES

1 Wood pigeon	9 Garden spider web	16 Ragwort	23 Yellow underwing moth
2 Horse chestnut	10 Painted lady butterfly	17 Cinnabar moth	24 Garlic mustard
3 Magpie	11 Orange tip butterfly	18 Small tortoiseshell butterfly	25 Moorhen
4 Creeping thistle	12 Nettles	19 Yellow wagtail	26 Cinnabar moth caterpillars
5 Crow	13 Cranefly	20 Rat's-tail plantain	27 Dung beetle
6 Swallow	14 Horse fly	21 Ringed mosquito	28 Pineapple weed
7 Dock	15 Collared dove	22 Red campion	
8 House sparrows			

conspicuously black- and white-banded legs, rise from the grass beside the horse's hooves, to whine around its twitching ears and sink their mouthparts into its flesh to suck blood.

BITING FLIES

Female mosquitoes are not the only biting flies in the paddock, as the visitor who comes to saddle the horse for a late afternoon hack soon discovers. The painful little bites on the rider's head and neck have no evident origin, hence the American name 'no-see-um' for the tiny biting midges that are the culprits. But there is no mistaking the large, stoutly-built female horse fly, with vast iridescent eyes, which homes in with a deep hum of wing-beats to stab its victim with dagger-like mouthparts. The horse fly lays her eggs in the muddy soil beneath the water trough where the predatory larvae feed ferociously on worms and larval insects.

MORNING FEAST
(above) Field mushrooms gathered early in the morning from the paddock grass make a delicious breakfast, but they must be correctly identified by the delicate ring on the stem and by the gills, starting bright pink but fading to brown.

DOR BEETLE
(right) These shiny beetles feed on horse dung, and carry dung balls deep into underground burrows for their larvae to feed on. They get their name from an old word meaning drone – the sound they make as they fly.

Near the trough is a small pile of hay left for the horse, and here a small party of house sparrows alights with excited twitterings to glean any remaining seeds. In among the sparrows, a plump collared dove moves with matronly tread. Further away, where little piles of horse dung dry out gradually in the sun, black, shiny, rounded dor beetles and scarab beetles scurry to and fro. These beetles not only eat dung, but also excavate tunnels and chambers in the soil

A small tortoiseshell butterfly sails on bright orange and black wings around a patch of nettles, where its yellowish-grey, spiny larvae are feeding. Thistles stand spiky and erect. A large hoverfly, superficially like a honey bee and known as a drone fly, is probing the pale flowers of creeping thistle, and a bright pink and brown painted lady sips nectar from deep within the florets of a darker mauve spear thistle. Some of the early-flowering thistles have already set seed, and linnets and goldfinches tear at the fluffy fruiting heads to feast on the seeds contained within.

Over by the hedge, where the grass is longer, a drab meadow brown flits in and out of the shade, pausing every so often to lay an egg on a grass blade. The caterpillars will overwinter and feed again next spring before pupating. With a jerky flight, an orange small skipper also

ELUSIVE WAGTAIL
(above) Summer visitors to the paddock, yellow wagtails are extremely cautious birds, and their cup-shaped nest of grass in the hedgerow is almost impossible to locate. To avoid revealing the location of the nest, wagtails will fly around or perch on a safe vantage point until an intruder has gone, rather than giving the game away by delivering food to their young.

SHEEP AND MAGPIES
(centre right) A familiar bird of paddocks, often seen singly or in pairs, the magpie has traditionally been a bird of ill-omen, and for small birds and nestlings this reputation may be justified; as magpie numbers have increased in recent years, it is feared that the populations of small birds have been considerably reduced by magpie attacks on their nests.

SELF-HEAL
(near right) This beautiful little flower gets its name from its medicinal properties. In the past, it was applied to wounds inflicted by sickles and billhooks, while the Ancient Greeks are believed to have used it to cure sore throats. Indeed, the latin name, too, Prunella vulgaris derives from the German for a sore throat.

beneath the dung, and into these chambers they laboriously haul small lumps of dung which act as egg-laying sites and food for their developing larvae.

Horses' hooves have flattened much of the vegetation and cut up the turf, but the way horses have torn at the grass as they feed has left a ragged sward with some plants intact. The feathery leaves and pinky-white umbels of yarrow overshadow purple clusters of self-heal and yellow, knob-like heads of aromatic pineapple weed. Here and there are clusters of flower spikes of rat's-tail plantain, above a rosette of broad rounded leaves, and the golden yellow blooms of creeping buttercup – called 'creeping' because it puts out long prostrate stems which root at the ends to form new plants.

moves among the grasses laying eggs. Its caterpillars will hibernate throughout the winter in silken cocoons among the grass stems and not pupate until next summer.

A sudden flash of yellow is a yellow underwing moth disturbed by the moorhen pacing silently on long-toed feet along the ditch, reaching delicately from side to side to snap up insects and spiders. The tiny money spiders, whose gossamer webs shine on the grass on dew-drenched mornings, are not much of a mouthful. But then the moorhen hops up on to the bank and secures a greater prize in the shape of a fat garden spider, hiding beneath a leaf by its orb web in the hedge.

The grass beneath a row of lime trees planted along one side of the paddock has been avoided by the grazing horses and sheep. It is sticky and black with honeydew, excreted by millions of lime aphids. Aphids bite into the sap bearing phloem tissue of plants and to get sufficient amino acids, the building blocks of protein, they have to take in far more sugar than they need, and the surplus is continuously excreted as a sticky honeydew.

ONE FOR SORROW

Further round the paddock, a smart black-and-white magpie flaps over to the hedge on rounded wings, trailing its wedge-shaped tail, to search for late nests of blackbirds or robins. The activities of the magpie disturb a wood-pigeon, which clatters out of the hedge and up into an oak in the nearby copse. The untidy nests of rooks high in the trees are deserted now, and the young birds are following with sedate paces in the wake of a plough in the adjacent field, eating leatherjackets, worms and other tasty morsels turned over with the furrow

of soil. Otherwise, the young birds have a lean time in late summer when the ground is often too hard for them to probe the soil for their invertebrate food.

As the shadows lengthen, a party of twittering swallows lines up on the telephone wire crossing the stable yard. Soon their place in the air, hawking for insects, will be taken by tiny pipistrelle bats, which are already stirring in their roost under the roofing tiles of the stable block. A brown rat peeps cautiously, nose twitching, around the stable door, then retreats hastily as the farmyard cat stretches luxuriously in the last patch of sunlight in the stable yard, then pads off through the gate into the paddock and on into the fields beyond to hunt for voles and incautious young rabbits.

PAINTED LADY
(left) In summer, painted lady butterflies can often be seen seeking nectar from the blooms of thistles in the paddock. But the painted lady cannot survive the British winter in any of its stages, and so migrates to south-west Europe and North Africa, flying on powerful wings that propel it at more than 8 mph.

HORSE FLY
(below) Many species of horse fly can be identified by their iridescent multiple eyes, here spectacularly shown in close-up. Male horse flies feed on juices from plants, but the females are bloodsuckers, and with their strong, piercing mouthparts they can inflict painful bites on humans as well as horses.

HORSE KILLER
(left) Pretty yellow blooms of common ragwort among the grass are a sign that the paddock is neglected, for the ragwort's leaves contain an alkaloid poison that can destroy the liver of any horse that eats them in a matter of months. Horses will avoid areas where ragwort grow, but the leaves may easily get mixed in with hay feed – with fatal consequences. It is from the ragwort, too, that the cinnabar moth derives its poison, stored in its body from the time when it was a caterpillar, which it uses as a defence against birds.

Plate 13

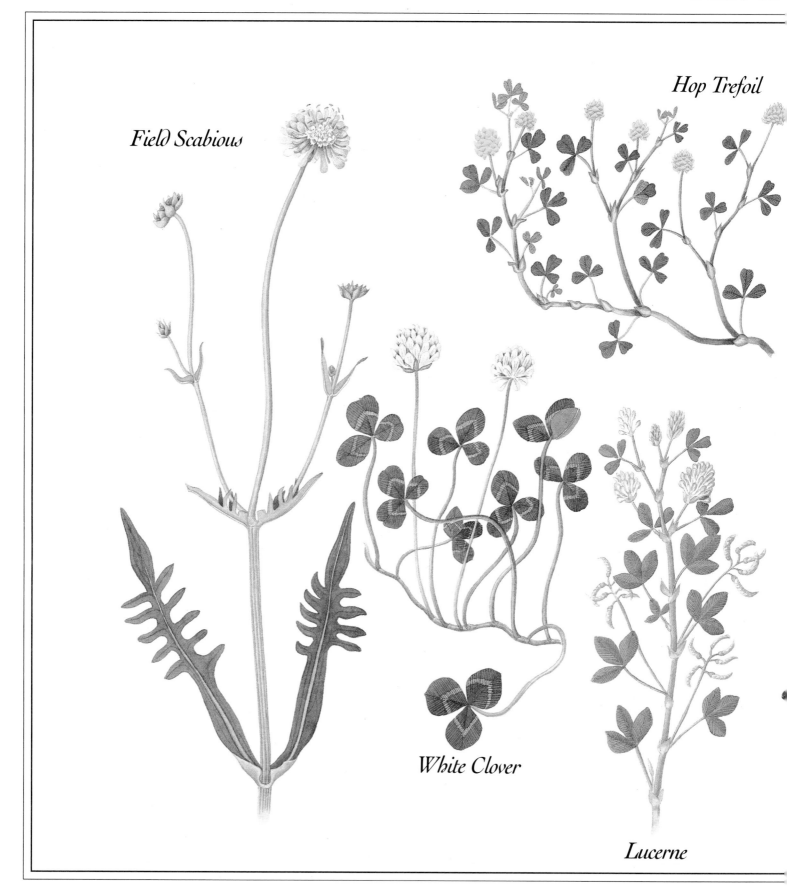

Field Scabious

Hop Trefoil

White Clover

Lucerne

FIELD SCABIOUS *(Knautia arvensis)* A tall perennial reaching 40″ (1m), the scabious grows in the rough grass of pastures and banks, widespread on dry, neutral or chalky soils. Stem leaves are deeply divided and purplish flowerheads are seen from May to September.

WHITE CLOVER *(Trifolium repens)* Very abundant on grassland almost everywhere, creeping stems to 20″ (50cm) root to make large patches on lawn and pasture. The foliage is dark green, with a paler band on each leaflet. Pink or white flowerheads are seen May-October.

HOP TREFOIL *(Trifolium campestre)* Common on wasteland, heaths and short grassland in most areas except north Scotland. This annual has erect stems to 14″ (35cm) and 3 leaflets, of which the middle one has a longer stalk. Flowers appear June-August.

LUCERNE *(Medicago sativa)* Sown extensively to improve pasture and hay, this perennial is now well-established by fields and roads in rural areas. Originally from southern Europe, it makes a bushy plant to 36″ (90cm), flowering April-August. Seedpods are curled.

Paddock Flowers

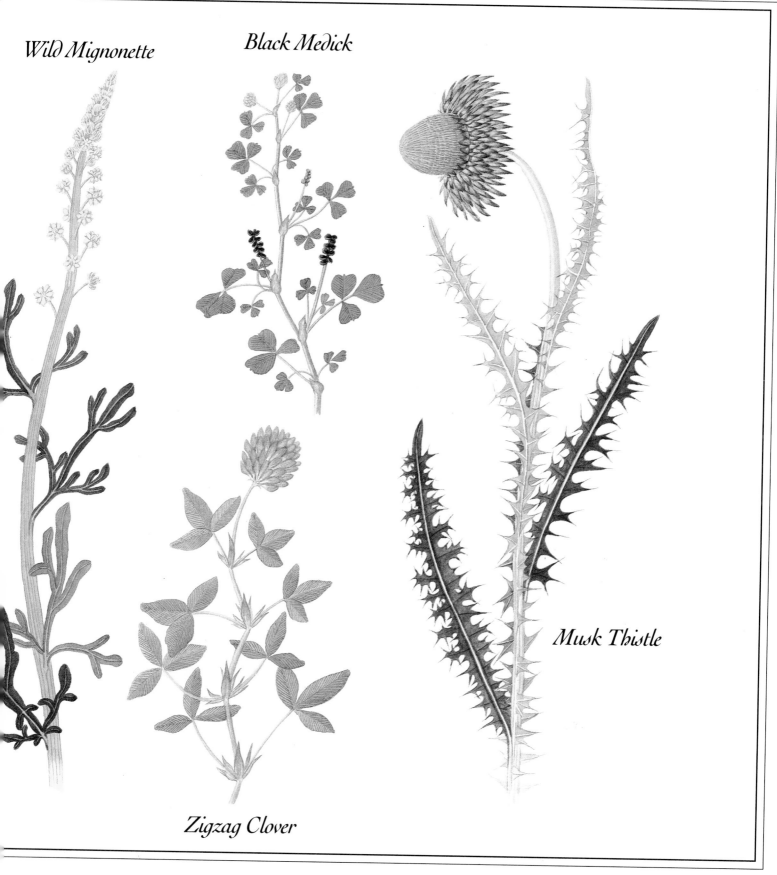

Wild Mignonette

Black Medick

Musk Thistle

Zigzag Clover

WILD MIGNONETTE (*Reseda lutea*) Often found on chalky waste land and disturbed grassland in south and east England, this plant may be biennial or perennial 12-20″ (30-50cm), it is erect and branched, with rough stems. Short spikes of greenish flowers open June-August.

ZIGZAG CLOVER (*Trifolium medium*) Fairly widespread but local, this perennial grows on fertile meadows and waysides. It makes a loose clump, with stems to 20″ (50cm). The lance-shaped leaflets are downy, and a round head of flowers opens June-September.

BLACK MEDICK (*Medicago lupulina*) Very common on grazed or mown grass throughout England and Wales – but not on acid soils, this is a sprawling annual 2-20″ (5-50cm). Small oval heads of flowers are seen May-August; the fruit is a tiny coiled black pod.

MUSK THISTLE (*Carduus nutans*) An 8-40″ (20-100cm) biennial thistle, the stem has partial 'wings'. Both stem and leaves are very spiny, and covered with white cottony hairs. Nodding flowerheads open May-August. Widespread in grassland on dry chalky soils.

Fairy-ring Champignon

Agaricus macrosporus

Dung Roundhead

Parrot Toadstool

FAIRY-RING CHAMPIGNON (*Marasmius oreades*) A common fungus seen May-October, often growing in a ring. The ¾-2½" (2-6cm) wide cap flattens with age, and has pale, wide-spaced gills. Edible – but readily confused with very poisonous species.

DUNG ROUNDHEAD (*Stropharia semiglobata*) Commonly seen from spring to autumn in paddocks and fields, where it sprouts in clumps on horse or cow dung. The sticky, globe-like cap is just ⅓-2" (1-5cm), the gills becoming purplish with age. Stems are slender. Inedible.

AGARICUS MACROSPORUS The thick domed mushroomy cap of this fungus is 3-10" (8-25cm) wide, becoming scaly when mature. Greyish gills darken to brown. It is very good to eat, well worth the time spent hunting for it in pastures during summer and autumn.

PARROT TOADSTOOL (*Hygrocybe psittacina*) A bell-shaped cap ⅓-1¼" (1-3cm) which changes colour from various shades of green to yellow, pink and brown. Cap and yellowish stem are very slimy – making it unpleasant to eat. Found in grassy places in autumn.

St. George's Mushroom

Verdigris Agaric

Giant Puffball

ST. GEORGE'S MUSHROOM (*Tricholoma gambosum*) So-called because it appears in spring around St. George's Day. This thickset fungus, has a domed fleshy cap 2-6″ (5-15cm) wide. Frequent in fields and woodland margins, it has a mealy smell and is good to eat.

GIANT PUFFBALL (*Langermannia gigantea*) Truly a giant, it may reach 32″ (80cm) across. White and leathery when young, at maturity the outer skin splits to release millions of brown spores. Seen in summer, uncommon but plentiful in places. Good to eat when young.

VERDIGRIS AGARIC (*Stropharia aeruginosa*) Clumps of this fungus are commonly found beneath trees and in fields and pastures, spring-autumn. Domed caps ¾-3″ (2-8cm) wide, are covered with blue-green slime, and flatten and dry with age. They are odourless but poisonous.

The Lapwing

One of the most exotic looking of British birds, the lapwing
is a familiar sight running among the furrows of the winter
fields, stabbing at the soil in search of food.

As the sun's weak rays finally admit defeat against the gathering gloom of a winter's afternoon, a large flock of birds rises from a field in ragged formation, the lazy 'lapwing' beats of their broad, rounded wings propelling them slowly through the air. These green-backed plovers, more commonly known as lapwings, are birds of open farmland, which feed in fields, paddocks, meadows, moors, sheep pastures and newly ploughed soil all year round. The farmers welcome them, for with their short black bills the birds peck into the soil for harmful wireworms and leatherjackets. They also take earthworms, snails, spiders, caterpillars, centipedes and beetles, but few seeds and little greenery. Once a flock has landed, the birds spread out to feed, and can be seen making short runs and then standing motionless, tilting their heads forward and then pecking quickly at any movement in the soil.

Lapwings are easily identified – even from a distance. They are large, plump birds about 12 inches (30 cm) in length, with long legs, and a thin upswept head crest. At first they often appear black and white, but close to it is possible to appreciate how beautiful these birds actually are. Their back plumage is not in fact black, but dark metallic green with purple highlights that shine in bright sunlight, while beneath the short tail is a colourful patch of chestnut feathers. The sexes are very similar, the female tending to have more white on her tail and throat and slightly narrower wings.

Towards the end of winter the flocks begin to disperse and the lapwings pair off. As early as February the males begin to establish their territories on grassland, choosing a meadow that has a grey-brown appearance – an indication that the vegetation is of poor quality and will remain short as the season goes on. Small

CAUGHT NAPPING
*A distinctive bird, with its
dapper crest, iridescent
plumage and haunting* peewit
*call, the lapwing is a wader
that is most commonly found
on open farmland. It is
resident in Britain all year,
although in severe winters
huge flocks will gather,
hundreds strong, and fly to
the warmer South-west, and
some may continue on to the
Continent.*

KEY FACTS

IN FLIGHT the lapwing can be identified not only by its striking and distinctive plumage, but also by its broad rounded wings — which are noticeably broader in the male.

JUVENILE lapwings can be easily distinguished from adult birds by their significantly shorter crest and by the pale edges of the green/purple feathers of their wing coverts.

EGGS are a deep brown and covered with large dark blotches. A clutch of four is usually laid March-May and brooded 24-31 days.

A TIGHT SCRAPE
Lapwings lay their clutch of four well camouflaged eggs in a shallow scrape that is made by the male but chosen by the female. Incubation is shared by both birds.

groups nest together — an advantage when it comes to warding off intruders — but the lapwings are much less gregarious now than they are during the rest of the year.

As with many birds, the male lapwing's courtship is a fairly elaborate business. Part of his display is nest building. Finding a patch of bare soil or an area with low-growing plants, usually on a slight rise in the ground and preferably near a tussock of grass for concealment, the male scrapes the ground with his feet then, falling forward on to his breast, turns round in circles to make a smooth hollow. Several of these nests are made, and the female selects the one she likes best.

DARING ACROBATICS

But the male's most spectacular display is the exuberant song flight performance. He rises from the ground with slow 'lapping' wing beats and then when high enough will suddenly twist, roll and spin in what seems an uncontrolled dive to the ground, ending with an upward twist on rapidly beating wings. All the while he makes his distinctive *peewit, peewit* call — the derivation of the lapwing's other common name — peewit.

The time devoted by lapwings to nesting seems fairly brief. The female lays her clutch of four speckled buff eggs between March and May, a time when there are plenty of earthworms, insect larvae and other animals in the soil. The down-covered chicks hatch out in just under a month, and almost immediately run to cover away from the nest. They are fully fledged within four or five weeks. So by mid-summer all nesting and brood rearing activities are complete, and the lapwings re-establish a communal life yet again.

MOTHER AND YOUNG
Soon after they hatch, the mottled, downy young are led away from the often exposed nest scrape, to the cover of nearby vegetation.

The Shire Horse

The noblest of all heavy horses, the Shire is enjoying a revival.
Although on the verge of extinction during the 1960s, today – thanks
to enthusiastic breeders – over 5000 Shires are now in existence.

With a softly-spoken word of command, the pair of massive grey Shires lean into their collars and take the strain. The leather harness creaks and breeching chains rattle as the Shires search for grip, and the steel-banded wheels of the dray inch forward: two tons of horse pulling four tons of beer. Only the stainless steel kegs date a scene little changed in over 200 years. Yet despite now having to share the roads with quite different forms of horse-power, the heavy horse has hauled itself from the very brink of extinction, and is now making a comeback, not only as a decorative addition to shows and ceremonial occasions, but as an alternative source of power, for short haul deliveries in towns and cities.

A typical working Shire stands about 17 hands high (hh) (5' 8") at the withers and weighs nearly a ton, and although it is neither the tallest nor the heaviest of draught horses, it is, without a doubt, the most charismatic. With its strong, well feathered legs, short but massively broad body and large proud head on a long arching neck, it possesses a dignity few heavy horses can match. But despite its popularity today, the Shire has had a surprisingly short and somewhat chequered history.

The exact origins of the Shire have been lost in the mists of time, although it is believed by many to be descended from the Great Horse — the heavy destrier introduced to Britain by William the conqueror in 1066. But for a more certain ancestor we must look, centuries later, to the horse dubbed by Oliver Cromwell in 1644, the Black. Most probably a Friesian, the Black was a sturdy draught horse bred on the farms in the fertile Low Countries. Although not as large as today's heavy horses, combined with the best native descendants of the Great Horse, it probably provided the basis of the modern Shire. The

THE CLASSIC SHIRE
(above) A Shire stallion must be pure black, brown or grey, and stand at least 17hh (5' 8"). The head should be long and lean with a slightly Roman nose and large friendly eyes. The neck should be long in proportion to the body and the back must be short and muscular. The forelegs should be straight with light, silky feathering, and the feet deep and wide. Mares can be black, brown, bay, grey or roan and must stand 16hh or above; geldings can be the same colours as the mares but must stand 16.2hh.

term Shire horse, however, did not appear until 1878 – when the Shire Horse Society was first founded and a Stud Book started.

Named after the intensively farmed shire counties in which it was most widely bred, the Shire became the best known of all the British heavy horse breeds because it proved most adaptable to working in towns. This is due in part to its placid temperament, but also to its conformation. In the words of the old saw: 'it ain't the 'eavy 'aulin' that 'urts the 'orses' 'oofs, it's the 'ammer, 'ammer 'ammer on the 'ard 'ighway.' The Shire, however, has particularly good legs with notably flexible fetlock joints, and so can absorb the impact of steel on stone far better than the other heavy breeds.

Traditionally, Shires were bred on farms in the country, and then broken to harness and sent to work in the towns when aged about four. Much the same applies today except that the majority of Shires stay on the farm, not to

AT WORK
(above right) One of the main functions performed by the Shire horses of today is delivering beer for the breweries. Shires are well adapted for such heavy work for they are bred with weight at the front of their bodies to match their massive quarters. This ensures good balance for hauling when most of the weight is taken by the horse's rear legs. A full-grown gelding weighing almost a ton can comfortably pull double its weight, confirming the old adage that it takes weight to pull weight.

MARE AND FOAL
(right) A Shire foal is born all legs, and to the elbow is almost as tall as its mother. As soon as it can chew, the foal is given a protein and mineral-rich diet to encourage its early development. It is weaned at five or six months, and towards the end of the year will be brought in to winter in a stable block or straw yard where it will be fed on hay and concentrates. Breeding any horse is a risky business, and breeders are grateful for all safe births – and when the Shire breed teetered on the brink of extinction, the cry of 'the foal is alive!' no doubt had a special poignancy.

work but to compete in the show ring, to breed, or simply to provide the highly mechanized modern farmer with a living link to the past, when his fortunes would have been harnessed to his team of heavies and his future prosperity determined by their progeny.

Unlike the thoroughbred which is raised to suit the racing calendar, the Shire is still bred in accordance with the seasons. Mares are put to the stallion in middle or late spring, so that after an 11 month pregnancy the birth of the foal will coincide with the first flush of spring grass which stimulates the mare's milk and so guarantees the foal the best possible start.

Training the horse begins shortly after its birth. A foal a few days old can be comfortably

managed by one man and if it can be trained to accept the restraint of a halter at this stage it will continue to do so even after it has the strength to break free.

Today, Shires are generally handled much more during their early years than was once the case. The horse destined for more serious work will begin schooling sometime after its second birthday. Although still growing, and too young for really heavy work, horses of this age learn faster and the lessons are not forgotten. Once trained, the horse can then be turned away for a year or so before beginning work proper, aged four, after a quick refresher course.

TRADITIONS REVIVED

Guided under the watchful eye of the Shire Horse Society, the Shires being bred today are better than ever and the enthusiasm for them has never been greater. As well as its use for short haul work in towns, there is a growing interest in using the Shire to work the land – even to the extent that new designs of horse-drawn farm machinery are being produced.

But it is the breweries which have most kept faith with this gentle giant of the horse world and who continue to work them in the largest numbers. Breweries, such as Youngs in South London may keep over 20 working geldings all over 17hh and 17cwt in weight. Their horses are worked in pairs pulling a modern, rubber tyred dray and delivering beer to pubs within a three mile radius of the brewery. But on high days and holidays the breweries bring out their massive 19hh show horses. Immaculately groomed and with tails and manes plaited, these magnificent horses are decked out with patent leather harnesses and glittering brasses, and hitched to a colourful show cart – and instead of pulling pints, they pull the crowds, all eager to marvel at the power and majesty of these most noble of horses.

The Orchard

The traditional orchard, with its widely spaced, wizened old trees and green lawns grazed by sheep, pigs and poultry, was once a place for quiet reflection. But today it has been supplanted by regimented rows of dwarf trees capable of high productivity and amenable to mechanical harvesting. No longer peaceful arbours, the modern orchard nonetheless remains a decorative feature, illuminating the landscape in spring when its pink-flushed blossom hangs in fragrant clouds, and again in autumn when clusters of brightly-coloured fruit weigh down the slender boughs.

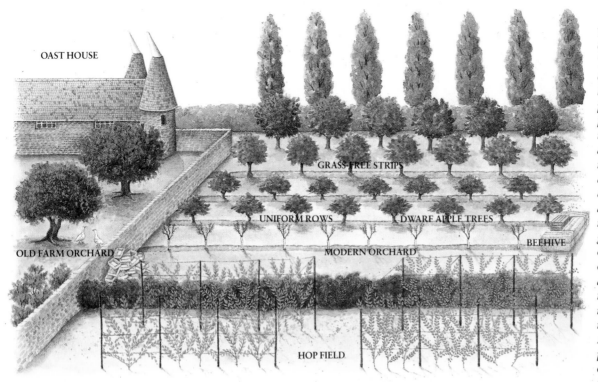

OAST HOUSE

GRASS-FREE STRIPS

UNIFORM ROWS   DWARF APPLE TREES

OLD FARM ORCHARD

MODERN ORCHARD

BEEHIVE

HOP FIELD

NEW AND OLD ORCHARDS
The old farm orchard, usually no larger than a paddock, supported fruit trees as well as grazing animals. In a new orchard dwarf, heavily cropping trees are planted in uniform rows in grass-free strips of soil. These orchards are sprayed against insects and the grass is kept under control by mowing or spraying. Although not as pastoral as the old orchard the yield is higher.

Orchards of fruit trees richly laden with apples, pears, cherries, and plums were once part of the country scene throughout the British Isles. Often no more than a paddock next to the farmhouse, these orchards produced enough fruit for the household with perhaps some extra, in a good year, to sell at the local market.

Such orchards have been with us since the introduction of the cultivated apple, by the Romans, in the first century BC. Before then, the only apple native to our shores was the hard, small and sharp crab apple, which may still be found growing wild in old woods and hedgerows.

The first large orchards, planted to produce fruit for sale, appeared in Norman times and were commonly attached to the great abbeys and monasteries. Indeed, the names of many different strains of apple are first mentioned in monastic documents. One was the pearmain, an eating apple, so called because of its pear shape. Another was the costard, a large cooking apple, popular from the 13th century when it was sold in London by costard-mongers later known as coster mongers – fruit sellers.

As fruit growing became increasingly commercial many smaller orchards disappeared, giving way to larger, better situated plantations mainly in the South. Apples, pears, plums and cherries do best on well drained soils, and they are all sensitive to late frosts which can destroy the newly set fruit. For that reason, gentle slopes above the frost pockets of the lower ground are favoured sites for large scale orchards.

CIDER APPLE BLOSSOM
Even in a modern orchard, with its dwarf trees in neat rows, blossom time is spectacular.

Several southern counties whose warmer climates guaranteed good ripening of the fruit soon became home to large orchards. Kent, the so-called 'Garden of England', once produced around a quarter of Britain's eating apples, as well as fine cherries. Worcestershire also won renown for its apples, plums and pears while the counties of Herefordshire, Gloucestershire, Somerset and Devon grew famous for their sharp and bittersweet cider apples.

As urban populations soared during the Industrial Revolution so too did the demand for fruit – and orchards grew to meet it. Until quite recently however, even new, large orchards remained much the same as their predecessors – monuments to traditional mixed farming. Below the tall thick-trunked trees grew lush grass grazed by geese and flocks of sheep. Pigs were fed on the windfalls – Gloucester Old Spot was a local breed of pig fattened in the orchards of Gloucestershire.

These grazing animals not only kept the grass short around the trees, but they also manured the soil, to the benefit of the fruit. Bees too were kept within the shelter of the orchard, yielding precious honey and wax and ensuring that the fruit would set by pollinating the blossom.

APPLE BLOSSOM TIME

By the mid 19th century commercial orchards were booming as the newly introduced railway system offered cheap transport from orchard to city markets. Public demand had also encouraged the creation of many new strains and there were now well over 2000 different varieties of apple alone. New strains were either cross-bred or originated from 'sports' – natural mutations. These could be easily propagated by grafting and other techniques. Only the finest new varieties received the coveted Gold Medal of the Royal Horticultural Society. Among these was Cox's Orange Pippin, first grown by a retired brewer,

MIXED HUSBANDRY
In a traditional orchard, grazing animals control the grass and fertilize the soil with their droppings.

Richard Cox, sometime before 1836.

Though apple and other fruit trees can be espalier-trained – on stakes or walls – or pruned to grow as a fan of branches along wire supports, most commercial orchards, until recently, grew bushy-topped standard trees, similar to those in the old farm orchards. Today, however, these are being replaced by trees grafted on to dwarf root stock. The result is trees which grow little taller than a man and which, even though they remain productive for 20 years or more, remain slender-trunked. These dwarf trees begin to bear fruit when they are only three or four years old – traditional standards take eight or nine years before they crop heavily. Furthermore, the smaller trees can be grown closer together to treble the yield per acre and are more easily harvested. The latest development in apple root stock is a heavy cropping, hollyhock-like tree with little side wood, derived from a freak mutation found growing in British Columbia.

As animals cannot be allowed to graze beneath these small, accessible trees, the grass which grows there must be mown or sprayed, and herbicides are used regularly to control the weeds which would deprive the trees of nutrients. The trees themselves are regularly sprayed against pests.

Far fewer varieties of fruits are now grown for sale than was formerly the case. Although blemishes do not necessarily impair flavour, consumers tend to favour shiny, regular unblemished products and this has led to just a few modern varieties which exhibit these characteristics dominating the market place.

Sadly, the old pastoral orchards of days gone by have largely disappeared, but where they do still exist, their charm is irresistible.

Nature Walk

A walk in a modern or traditional orchard may reveal some interesting features. Look out for:

TREE-SHAPES New orchards have early-yielding bush or dwarf apple trees rather than large bushy standards.

OAST-HOUSES Hops, used to make beer, were once dried in traditional brick kilns. Now they are dried in oil-fired sheds.

HOP POLES AND WIRES These are supports for hops which are grown over the intricate network.

BEE HIVES In both new and old orchards bees pollinate the spring blossom.

Orchard Wildlife

**Gnarled fruit trees in an old orchard, festooned with
lichens and mistletoe, attract moths, bees and other insects, and
a range of small birds that nest or feed among the trees.**

Tucked away behind the mossy walls which protect the young blossoms from cold spring winds, the old farm orchard can be a hidden sanctuary. Here care is mixed with wild neglect and, as summer days shorten, the atmosphere is warm and apple-scented. Mosses and grey-to-green lichens festoon the branches. Around the cracked bark of the trunks sticky wrappers act like outdoor flypapers, protecting the trees from insect damage by trapping ants, moths and unwary caterpillars. The short, rough grass beneath the trees is well pecked by hens and geese; the year's windfalls are all but gone.

Up the walls grows well established ivy; ferns sprout from mortar cracks; mosses burgeon; and brickwork holes have been occupied by a nesting spotted flycatcher and, not far distant, a tight-sitting blackbird. Wasps stream back and forth to a paper ball nest hidden within the masonry.

At the foot of the wall the vegetation has grown long. Strong grasses thrust above tangled cleavers, ivy, nettles and shaded fungi. A daddy-long-legs flitters up to be adeptly caught by the vigilant flycatcher, sallying out from its feeding perch. Bumble bees, with honey bees from the corner hive, fly busily from red clover to buttercup and ox-eye daisy. House martins swoop low, hawking insects, while a tree sparrow flies to his mate sitting discreetly on a clutch within a tree hole.

The old fruit trees are encrusted with many lichens. Few have common names but there are three main kinds which are easy to recognise: *crusty*, like miniature crazy paving on the bark, *leafy*, like small rosettes flat on the bark, and *shrubby*, like small bunches of ribbons. The rule of thumb is that the further a lichen protrudes from its anchorage, the more sensitive it is to air pollution. (Shrubby lichen is therefore less tolerant of pollution than crusty varieties.) These rather attractive plants, which often form the background for the clever camouflage of moths, are therefore good air pollution indicators. All three kinds will grow where the air is cleanest.

Mistletoe is another plant which grows on old apple trees. A semi-parasite, it takes hold when its seed is wiped on to a branch by a bird eating the berries. The seed sends down rootlets to tap sap tubes beneath the bark. As mistletoe has green, food-producing leaves of its own, it does not really weaken its host to any noticeable degree.

The hoary branches of old apple trees attract a great deal of insect life. Many moths visit them, including some regarded as pests by the growers. One such is the winter moth whose caterpillars feed on the young leaves and may strip them, before falling to the ground in June to pupate. The emerging females lack wings and crawl up the trunks and along the boughs in autumn, to be mated and lay their eggs in the bark and unopened buds. Grease bands are placed around the trunk to trap them. The males, however, have wings and can be seen flying in the winter months.

Shakespeare's 'worm i' the bud' (*Twelfth Night*) was probably a caterpillar of a tortrix moth. It pinions the petals with threads which prevents full flowering and so maintains its

BANDED SNAIL
(left) Common among damp vegetation, this snail may be seen on fungi, like the shaggy ink cap here, in late summer and autumn. The fungus, whose cap changes from white and cylindrical to black and conical, is edible when young. The inky liquid produced with age accounts for the name.

FLOURISHING WILDLIFE OF THE ORCHARD

Many birds are attracted to the orchard by food or nest sites. The goldfinch and hawfinch build delicate nests among the boughs, while tree sparrows and tits seek out holes in the trees or masonry. The bullfinch and hawfinch may feast on fruit buds, and the house martin hunts flying insects. Insects, too, seek food and sites to rear their young. The grey dagger lays its eggs on apple and plum trees; the large yellow underwing lays up to 1000 eggs on a grass blade; and the cranefly injects eggs into the soil where its larvae – leatherjackets – eat plant roots.

KEY TO THE SPECIES

1 House martin
2 Tree sparrow
3 Goldfinch at nest
4 Ivy
5 Bullfinch
6 Blue tit
7 Wood meadow-grass
8 Upright hedge parsley
9 Holly blue
10 Honey bee
11 Hen and chicks
12 Domestic goose
13 Spleenwort
14 Moss
15 Wasps' nest
16 Cranefly
17 Buff-tailed bumble bee
18 Hawfinch
19 Gooseberry
20 *Lichen* Dicranum scoparium
21 Ox-eye daisy
22 Large yellow underwing
23 Red clover
24 Shaggy ink cap fungus
25 Grey dagger moth
26 Garden slug
27 Common wasp

123

FIELDFARE AT
WINDFALL APPLES
*The winter-visiting
fieldfare is fond of fruit,
eating both windfalls and
from the tree. In hard
weather especially, it is
often joined by other
members of the thrush
family, including the
redwing (a fellow winter
visitor), song thrush and
blackbird. Starlings, too,
flock to fallen fruit.*

protective shroud. The maggot of the ripening apple, however, is the caterpillar of the codlin moth which lays its eggs on the skin of the young fruit, leaving the caterpillars to burrow in. Sawflies are also counted a serious pest, for their caterpillars bore into the young blossom and ruin it. A sap-sucking pest on apple and pear trees is the woolly aphid, whose young cluster on a twig in a nest of fluffy, white wax.

The flower-laden boughs are also visited by welcome insects. Best known of these are the bees, both hive honey bees and the wild bumble bees which live in colonies like the honey bee, though these are much smaller. They do a good job pollinating the flowers, and this can be crucial for the crop; hives are often brought into commercial orchards for this reason.

Equally benevolent, but not so regarded, is the common wasp. It acts as an effective pest controller, spending most of its short life collecting caterpillars and other insects to feed to its grubs. In the autumn it is lured by the fermenting juice of the windfalls and may well be a nuisance at picnic-time as it homes in on the jam sandwiches.

Old apple trees often contain holes or crevices and, come spring, many birds head for these handy nest sites. Some familiar birds – the starling, blue tit and great tit, for example – are just as likely to be seen in the garden, but there are others more typical of the old orchard.

No bigger than a house sparrow, the delightful lesser spotted woodpecker drills its own nest hole in a branch or trunk. A shy, quiet bird, it is most easily seen before the leaves appear. In early spring, it drums faintly with its bill on a high, dead branch and the male performs a

marvellous floating display flight to his prospective mate. The weak, high-pitched *pee-pee-pee* call may attract your attention if you are close by.

A woodpecker-like bird with a similar, though stronger, call is the wryneck. A summer visitor from Africa, the wryneck is so called from the way it contorts its neck and head – through 180 degrees – when startled or courting. It bred commonly 150 years ago throughout England, displaying a fondness for holes in old orchard trees. Now it is decidedly rare, though a few pairs may still nest in south-eastern orchards. Interestingly, Scandinavian migrants have recently begun nesting in Scotland where it never previously bred, even when common. Like the green woodpecker it feeds mainly on ants collected from the ground.

The bullfinch is also linked with orchards. It comes especially in those times when its staple food supply, ash seeds, is exhausted. Numbers of these attractive birds are trapped and killed in fruit growing areas, for they take the early

HOLLY BLUE
*(below left) Ivy growing on
the orchard walls attracts
this butterfly in summer.*

BLOOM TIME
*(below) In May, when not
decimated by frosts, birds or
insects, pink or white apple
blossom covers the trees,
holding the promise of a
good autumn crop.*

buds from the twigs, destroying any chance of a good crop. They rarely nest in the fruit trees, though, preferring instead the thicker cover of a hedgerow bush or nearby spinney.

The goldfinch is one of our most colourful wild birds, and is usually seen in 'charms' or flocks roving across open countryside at the end of the summer, dancing from thistle to thistle collecting the seeds. It is, however, also attracted by the scattered, mop-headed trees of the old orchard; it nests out towards the ends of the boughs.

The elusive hawfinch, too, may be seen in orchard country. With its heavy, powerful bill it can crack open cherry stones, but its main foods are beech mast and the fruits of wych elm, hornbeam and maples; it also eats peas from the pod and attacks buds in the spring. It nests in small colonies, often among the branches of apple or pear trees, building a platform of twigs lined with roots and hair, like the bullfinch.

An old orchard can include several 'mini-habitats' within its bounds. The old wall is one: its crevices will harbour countless spiders, and mining bees and other insects may bore into its soft mortar. Plants of many kinds grow up the wall. Ivy attracts the holly blue, one of our most colourful butterflies: though its first generation feeds on holly, the second generation, flying in late summer, lays its eggs on ivy. Flowering in autumn, ivy also provides a welcome nectar for late bees, and winter berries for birds.

The long grass around the trunks and at the foot of the wall may be a habitat in its own right – here are found hammock-web spiders, craneflies and attractive moths, such as the yellow underwing.

One corner of the old orchard may be the traditional dump for the windfalls – the richly rotting fruit can feed toadstools and other fungi.

HUNTING HEDGEHOG *Foraging among the windfalls and through the long grass, the hedgehog finds a rich harvest of slugs, caterpillars and beetles.*

Though rarely seen, mice, voles and shrews thrive within the orchard walls, and tawny owls may come to hunt them, breaking the night-time silence with their long-drawn, quavering hoots.

HONEY BEE

WASP

DELICATE LICHEN *(above) The lichens which grow profusely on the trunks and branches of old fruit trees have no roots. They extract essential minerals and nutrients from the rainwash which flows past them.*

HONEY BEE AND COMMON WASP *(left) These two insects are both commonly seen in the orchard, attracted by different things. Bees visit flowers, sipping nectar and collecting pollen in the sacs on their legs. The nectar and pollen are fed to grubs in the hive or nest. Wasps, however, feed their young on animal food and therefore roam the orchard in search of aphids and caterpillars.*

Blue Tit

Bullfinch Male

Bullfinch Female

Juvenile

BLUE TIT (*Parus caeruleus*) Easily recognised by its distinctive blue cap, yellow belly, and scolding *tsee-tsee-ch-ch-ch-ch* call, this 4½″ (12cm) tit feeds chiefly on insects and nests in tree and wall holes from February. Up to 16 white eggs, spotted red are laid April-May.

BULLFINCH (*Pyrrhula pyrrhula*) This shy 6″ (15cm) finch may only be revealed by its soft, whistled *deu*. It eats seeds, fruit tree buds and insects and builds a platform-style nest in hedges and conifers. 4-5 green-blue eggs, speckled with purple are laid from April-August.

Wryneck

Adult

Tree Sparrow

Goldfinch

WRYNECK (Jynx torquilla)
So named because of its flexible neck, this rare 6½" (16cm) summer visitor is related to woodpeckers. It feeds on insects with its long tongue and lays 7-10 dull white eggs in April and May in an unlined tree or wall crevice.

GOLDFINCH (Carduelis carduelis)
A small, 4½" (12cm) finch, distinguished by its bright yellow wing bars and dancing flight. It feeds on seeds and insects and lays 2-3 clutches of 4-6 bluish-white, brown-speckled eggs in a thistledown-lined nest from April to August.

TREE SPARROW (Passer montanus)
This 5½" (14cm) bird is smaller than the house sparrow, with a chestnut crown and a smaller black throat bib. It eats seeds and insects and nests in holes in trees, walls, thatch or haystacks. 3-5 white, brown-blotched eggs are laid April-July.

Red-belted Clearwing

Lappet

Grey Dagger

**RED-BELTED CLEARWING
(*Aegeria myopaeformis*)** One of a
strange group of moths with almost
completely transparent wings. The
larvae are a pest of apple and pear
trees, feeding on the inner surface
of the bark for 2 years, before
emerging on sunny June mornings.

LAPPET (*Gastropacha quercifolia*)
A large, stout-bodied moth, locally
common in England and Wales,
which at rest is camouflaged by its
resemblance to dead leaves. It can
be an orchard pest, the larvae
feeding on apple leaves. The adult is
on the wing from June to August.

GREY DAGGER (*Acronicta psi*)
A common moth of England and
Wales, the larvae feed on leaves of
fruit and other trees. On the wing in
June, the adults rest by day on tree
trunks and fences where their
mottled colour helps hide them
from avian predators.

Fruit-Tree Moths

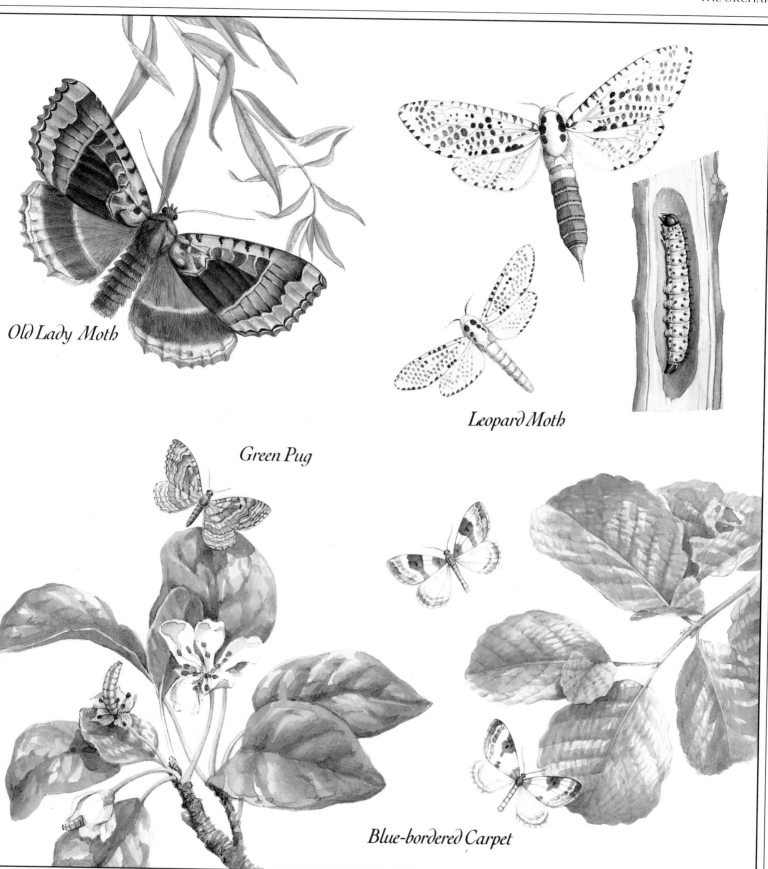

Old Lady Moth

Leopard Moth

Green Pug

Blue-bordered Carpet

OLD LADY (Mormo maura) Flying in July and August and hiding by day in outbuildings and hollow trees, this is one of many fat-bodied moths relished by bats. The larvae feed on low plants in autumn and the new leaves of birch, sallow and fruit trees in spring.

LEOPARD MOTH (Zeuzera pyrina) A scourge of orchard trees, the larvae of this moth feed on the wood of apple and other trees, burrowing beneath the bark for 2-3 years, weakening the branches. Adults fly at night from June-August; females are much larger than males.

GREEN PUG (Chlorocystis rectangulata) Common in orchards and gardens throughout Britain, except in N. Scotland, the larvae feed on the flowers of wild and cultivated apple, pear and hawthorn. On the wing in June and July, the adult has very variable colouring.

BLUE-BORDERED CARPET (Plemyra rubiginata) Locally common throughout Britain, this moth appears before darkness falls in July and August. Often feeding on alder, the larvae are also found in orchards where they eat foliage of plum and apple trees.

The Honey Bee

To make one pound of honey, a colony of bees, under the guidance of its queen, flies a distance equivalent to three times around the world.

FORAGING BEE
The tiny drop of nectar from this flower will be alternately swallowed and regurgitated by a worker bee into a concentrated drop of honey. This is then stored in cells built on to wax combs in the hive. The pollen gathered in the sacs on the bees' thighs is also a food source for the bees and in a single year, a colony may consume 75lb (34kg) of pollen.

Wild bees have been making honey for 20 million years, and for the last 4000 years man has been nurturing bees to tap their sweet harvest. The relationship does not only benefit man. The task of the industrious worker bee, which may have to visit thousands of flowers in single trip to gather its load of pollen and nectar – of up to half its body weight – is made considerably easier by man's planting of orchards. In turn, the bees pollinate the fruit grower's trees and set the crop. For this reason many fruit growers contract commercial honey producers to provide one hive for each acre of orchard.

Bees live in colonies which operate as single social units – in the wild the colony makes its home, or nest, in a hollow tree or cave, but bees take readily to man-made hives. Presiding over the colony, which may be made up of around 50,000 bees, is the most important bee – the queen. By secreting a complex 'scent' of coded messages, 'queen substances', which she passes on to her closest subjects, who pass it to others, she is responsible for directing the running of the colony. But most of the day-to-day activities of the hive centre around the worker bees, female bees, which make up the majority of the population, and it is these bees that are normally seen, buzzing from flower to flower in the summer months. The male bees in the colony are drones – there may be just a few hundred and their sole function is to mate with the queen.

QUEEN BEE

When a queen emerges from pupation, she destroys all cells containing possible rivals, and if two queens emerge at the same time, they search each other out and fight until one of them is stung to death – a sting that does not kill the victor.

For the first few days of adult life, the virgin queen spends most of her time inside the hive feeding on honey, without taking part in any of the hive duties. At first, she is ignored by her future subjects, but this changes after a week or so, when the young queen achieves sexual maturity, and leaves the hive – often the only time in her life that she does so – to go on her nuptial flight. She releases chemical scents, pheromones, which attract a cloud of drones into following her, like the tail of a comet. Of these, five may mate with her – an effort which kills them. The mated queen then returns to the hive to be received by a 'welcoming committee' of courtiers which sets about feeding and grooming her and in turn ingests her 'queen substances'. After this single mating trip, the queen has enough sperm stored inside her body to fertilize all her eggs for the whole of her two to six years life. After a few days she starts to lay, and during her lifetime may produce 200,000 eggs annually.

In high summer, a thriving colony may grow too large for its nest. At this point the queen may release a chemical instruction for the colony to divide. Some of the bees, along with the queen, then leave the nest and swarm as they go out in search of a new home. Before swarming, the queen instructs the workers to construct enlarged queen cells at the edge of the comb, in which the departing queen will deposit fertilized female eggs to produce a successor. If the queen dies unexpectedly without producing a successor, worker bee larvae under three days old can be raised as queens if their diet of royal jelly is extended. Normally, identical worker and queen larvae are differentiated in terms of diet – all larvae start off with three days on royal jelly, a concentrated and highly nutritious protein, but

HIVE OF INDUSTRY

Every honey bee colony centres around the queen. She provides continuity, as generations of her children live and die. Most of these offspring are worker bees, which are responsible for carrying out her instructions for the efficient running of the hive, and which are biologically programmed to perform certain vital tasks at certain stages of their lives. The queen also spawns a small number of drones whose sole function is to mate with the queen. Queen cups – large egg cells – are made on the edge of the comb to allow for the large size of their occupant. All larvae are fed for nine days, after which their cells are closed for varying lengths of time – shortest for a queen and longest for a drone.

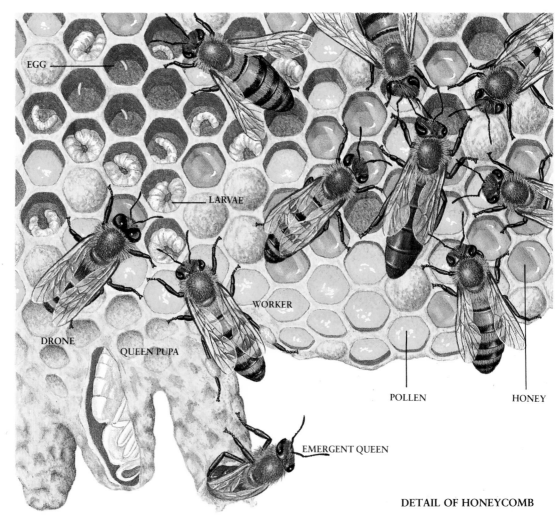

EGG

LARVAE

DRONE

QUEEN PUPA

WORKER

POLLEN

HONEY

EMERGENT QUEEN

DETAIL OF HONEYCOMB

SWARM

Overcrowded colonies may divide and, led by the queen, search for a new nest site. The swarm may settle while scouts seek a permanent site. At this point a beekeeper can induce the swarm to make its home in a hive, otherwise the bees will find a home in a cave or tree.

then workers and drones graduate to honey and pollen. Potential queens, meanwhile, continue their royal jelly feeds.

Unless a swarm leaves the colony, numbers are maintained until the autumn, and the queen lays fewer eggs. As the summer flowers die off and food sources dwindle, drones are refused food, and are eventually evicted from the hive. Over the winter, the queen and a handful of workers survive by feeding on the stored honey and pollen, huddled together in the centre of the hive to keep warm until egg-laying begins again in February. These workers may live as long as six months, having no brood to feed, and no foraging to do.

WORKER'S LIFE

Normally, workers live from four to five weeks, the first three of which are spent in the hive fulfilling various roles as courtier and messenger for the queen, nanny to the larvae and general housekeeper. At first the young worker feeds older larvae on a pollen and honey diet, while developing her own royal jelly producing glands by eating large amounts of pollen. When these are mature, she will graduate to feeding young larvae. Also during this time, she cleans out old cells and makes new ones with wax from special glands, processes honey and stores it, tidies away the pollen dumped by the returning forager bees, clears detritus and bodies from the hive, guards the entrance and feeds the queen. She also begins to take short flights outside. For the final fortnight of her life she becomes a forager, gathering nectar and pollen from flowers. Foraging bees guide themselves by a sophisticated built-in system and the position of the sun, and they communicate the direction of a good food source to other bees by means of a dance performed in the hive.

The Bullfinch

Brightly coloured and attractive, the bullfinch nurtures
a destructive nature, which for centuries has earned it an
evil reputation among farmers and gardeners.

A PRICE ON ITS HEAD
*(above) Since Elizabethan
days the rosy breasted
bullfinch has had a price on
its head. Then, a penny
reward was offered for every
bullfinch killed. For, lovely
though it is, the havoc caused
by its destruction of fruit
and flower buds has meant
that gardeners and fruit
growers over the centuries
have regarded the 'budding
bird' as a troublesome pest.*

A masked robber of fruit trees and bushes,
the outlaw bullfinch carries out its raids
from the sanctuary of its woodland
home. Capable of husking blackcurrant and
gooseberry buds at the rate of 30 a minute and
apple and pear buds at one every ten seconds, a
few pairs of bullfinches can strip an orchard in a
matter of days, discarding the husks like confetti
on the wind, and with them all promise of a
fruitful summer.

BUD PICKER

Perfectly equipped for such villainy, the bullfinch is armed with a sharp-edged, slightly
hooked beak, rather rounder in profile than the
typical wedge-shaped bill of other finches. This
almost parrot-like beak is ideal for biting out
large chunks of plump buds or nipping off the
whole buds and then scooping out the core.

Bullfinches use their beaks in much the same
way as a budgerigar husks seeds: the bud is
rotated in the beak by the bird's short, strong
peg-like tongue, and the outer bud scales are
peeled off by the sharp edges of the bill. But
despite the consummate skill with which the bullfinch can debud an orchard, it is not ideally
suited to a life of 'crime', though some of its
country names – like bud picker and bud bird –
echo its partiality to fruit buds. Its bright scarlet
or rose-pink breast and black cap make it far
too conspicuous a poacher. Furthermore, by
nature the bullfinch is a shy, retiring bird preferring the dense undergrowth bordering woodland margins and clearings to the more exposed
orchard or garden. The woodland habitat also
provides a wealth of seed foods, beginning in
spring with the catkin-like flowers of oak trees,
followed by dandelion and buttercups and pro-
gressing to stitchwort and many other summer
seeds until nettle becomes the favoured food in
early autumn. Once all these have fallen, or
been consumed, the birds turn to dock and

IN FLIGHT the black cap, greyish back, white rump and wing bar are striking. From below the deep rosy breast is evident.

THE BILL, conical in shape and slightly hooked, is used with great efficiency, to pick and husk fruit and flower buds, at a staggering rate.

THE EGGS Usually two clutches of 4-6 grey-blue eggs with purplish markings are laid during the breeding season, April to August.

bramble seeds which often remain available for much of the winter. This diet is supplemented by ash keys in most years, until, in late winter, the buds of blackthorn and hawthorn begin to swell.

It is only when these natural food resources fail that those birds resident close by orchards and gardens turn their attention to the buds of cultivated trees and shrubs. When they do, however, it seems that they find them such a palatable alternative that they can endanger a whole season's fruit crop. For this reason, in some orchard areas, the bullfinch is trapped or shot.

Such controls, however, seem to have little lasting effect on bullfinch numbers, for like many small birds, bullfinches raise 2 clutches of between 4 and 6 eggs each year.

During the breeding season, which extends from April to August, the male bullfinch is rarely far from his mate's side, bobbing up and down, tail cocked and feather plumped up, often singing his whispering wheezy song which sounds like a gently swinging, creaking gate.

Bullfinches generally form pairs for life, after a courting or mating ritual involving bill caressing and gifts of twigs from male to female. Once paired, the female builds a twiggy platform nest supporting a cup of roots lined with hair, concealed deep in the prickly shelter of a hawthorn, blackthorn or gorse thicket.

The pale blue eggs, speckled purplish seem strangely conspicuous, but as soon as they are laid, the well camouflaged female hides them from the view of passing jays and magpies.

Incubation, which lasts 12-14 days, is carried out solely by the female, but the chicks are fed by both parents. Although adult birds are vegetarians they provide their young with a mixed diet of seeds and pre-digested, regurgitated insects and spiders. These are carried back to the nest in capacious, hamster-like cheek pouches. The young spend about 14 days in the nest before fledging. Then the adults establish a new nest and concentrate on raising a second brood.

Once fully fledged, the young bullfinches slowly disperse. They do not stray far, however, and throughout the winter may be seen feeding together in family groups.

MIXED DIET
(right) Although adult bullfinches are vegetarian, they feed their young with a mixture of insect and vegetable material. The adults carry the predigested food to the young in large cheek pouches which are so capacious that the chicks only need to be fed every half-hour.

The Market Garden

For centuries, the costermonger's stall was kept filled with plump, crisp lettuces, luscious strawberries and all kinds of fresh fruit and vegetables grown in market gardens just outside the town – smallholdings tended with the care normally only lavished on a garden. Today, most of our vegetables come from large arable farms, where they are raised alongside wheat and barley – or even from abroad. Yet small and productive market gardens still exist almost everywhere in Britain, growing vegetables and soft fruit in a rich variety unmatched by any of the large arable farms.

LARGE SCALE VEGETABLE GROWING

GRASS LEY FIELDS

CONTROLLED
GREENHOUSE ENVIRONMENT

MODERN MARKET GARDEN
ON GOOD VALLEY SOILS

CROPS UNDER CLOCHES

VEGETABLE PLOTS
(left) The traditional market garden was a small plot on the fringes of the town, growing vegetables and soft fruit to be sold fresh at local markets. Nowadays most of our vegetables are grown on large farms along with cereals in places like the Fenlands. Here, row upon row of vegetables is planted in vast fields and harvested mechanically – fields may have to be left as grass ley every now and then while the soil recovers. The specialist market garden still survives, though, often in modernized form on good valley soils, where crops may be carefully brought on under plastic sheeting called cloches or in vast greenhouses that provide perfectly controlled conditions for optimum growth.

Market gardens growing fresh fruit and vegetables have been an important part of the British countryside for many centuries. In the distant past, villagers grew their own produce in a back plot. But the rapid growth of the towns at the end of the Middle Ages created a new demand, and, in time, every large borough had a belt of market gardens nearby.

Market gardens were a feature noted by many visitors to old London. In Tudor times, market gardens ran from Whitechapel to Islington, and on to St James and Hyde Park. Yet as London grew ever larger, they were pushed further and further out.

By the mid 18th century, there were well over 10,000 acres of market gardens around London covering the gravelly plain from Chelsea to Brentford and beyond, as the notable cartographer John Rocque's map of 1754 clearly reveals. In fact, much of today's London is built on the best market garden soil of the country, quick to warm in spring and easy to dig.

Unlike the plots of earlier days, these 18th century market gardens were being scientifically worked with vegetables grown neatly in well-manured beds. Manuring is something we take for granted today, but it was a practice which only around this time reached Britain from Holland where land was always short. Manuring not only increases the yield but also avoids the need to leave the ground fallow one year in three. So London's horse dung was carted out to its market gardens, and back from the gardens came fresh greens and salads, peas, onions and radishes.

Much the same was later seen in the new conurbations which mushroomed during the Industrial Revolution, and each city and town soon had its own nearby market gardens. Birmingham quickly learnt to rely on the Vale of Evesham for its vegetables. The Ormskirk plain supplied the demands of Liverpool, while the flat ground of the Lancashire-Cheshire border catered for the new mill towns in the hills behind. The Bromham area in Wiltshire supplied Bristol.

Little of this would have been possible but for

UNDER WRAPS
(below) Some of the care traditionally lavished on the small market garden may often be used on a larger scale, such as in the use of cloches to bring on seedlings.

UNDER GLASS
(right) Ever since the Victorian age, glasshouse growing has played an important part in small scale market gardening, for the glasshouse allows the grower to control growing conditions very precisely. The glasshouse shown here, at Loseley Park near Guildford, is growing peppers 'organically' – that is, without the aid of chemical fertilizers and pesticides. The increasing taste for organically grown food and for greater variety in vegetables and herbs may help give the small market garden a new lease of life.

the improved turnpike roads which sped the produce in from outlying market gardens. But it was the coming of the railways which was to have the greatest impact on the pattern of market gardening in Britain. The railways made it possible to bring for sale fresh vegetables grown 100 or more miles away and certain areas favoured by soil or climate could concentrate on large scale vegetable production.

The small market gardens, meanwhile, began to learn the value of greenhouses for flowers or salad vegetables. The Victorian era saw an enormous expansion in the number of greenhouses. At one time there were 4000 acres under glass in Britain, much of it concentrated in London's Lea valley. It was probably the proliferation in greenhouses that first made the tomato – introduced from America – popular. Early lettuces are also grown under glass, though each year around 7000 acres of open land are also devoted to this salad vegetable. Almost as much ground is given over to broad beans, and 3000 acres to runner beans.

Today, 440,000 acres in Britain are devoted to growing vegetables, fruit, flowers and nursery stock in Britain. Much of this is large scale farming, with vast fields growing vegetables and soft fruit, harvested mechanically and sold, as often as not, wholesale for canning, freezing and drying. Yet the traditional small market garden has by no means disappeared. It faces tough competition, not only from the large scale farms, but from abroad as well – cheap air transport and refrigerated lorries mean that today's shoppers can buy fresh beans from Kenya, carrots from Texas and strawberries from Italy. But changes in eating habits may be giving the small market garden a new lease of life. More and more people are coming to appreciate the special taste of fresh vegetables and fruit tended by hand in the traditional way – and to discover the attractions of variety which the large scale farms can simply not match. For the time being, at least, the future of these bountiful plots seems secure.

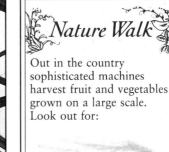

In the Market Garden

The market gardener wages a constant battle against pests but is helped by natural insect, bird and mammal predators that help contain legions of slugs, aphids, cabbage root fly and other damaging invertebrates.

A small grey tractor works feverishly, harrowing the light sandy soil which kicks up and blows on the wind. A black and white Jack Russell terrier sniffs inquisitively along the headland. Beside the remnants of a quickthorn hedge the dog stops and works hard at an old rabbit burrow, throwing out mounds of soil. This light land is ideal for market gardening.

Among the healthy green foliage of a stand of Brussels sprouts, large white butterflies flit on the breeze. In their quest for high energy nectar they are beneficial, acting as pollinators of plants. The females, though, are searching for the sheltered undersides of leaves where they can lay clusters of cylindrical yellow eggs. It is when the caterpillars hatch from the eggs that the problems begin, for they have a voracious appetite for the leaves of brassicas (plants of the cabbage family).

Leaves of brassicas are also sought after by other pests; woodpigeons are the most notorious. During the winter months, when other greens are scarce, the woodpigeon or 'stoggie' takes to sprouts and savoys with a vengeance. However, with the advent of oil seed rape, over the past decade, the market gardener has had an easier time of it from the woodpigeon, for it loves rape. Only when the snow lies deep on the ground, covering the rape plants, do the much taller sprouts become its target.

Rabbits can also completely decimate a crop, eating brassicas right down to the stem, a state from which they cannot recover. Little wonder rabbits are not tolerated in the market garden.

UNDERGROUND PROBLEMS

Not only do the aerial parts of brassicas suffer attack from pests. Both ground and subterranean damage is common. The rasping mouthparts of slugs consume leaves and stems of young plants with astonishing speed. Large black slugs, which leave behind them a silvery trail of mucus on their summer evening wanderings, are not the menace they might appear to be. These slugs feed only on dead and decaying vegetation. The much smaller, reddish-brown netted and garden slugs are the raiders of the seed bed. Field hedge cover is essential if friendly hedgehogs are to be encouraged on their nightly ramblings in pursuit of these troublesome molluscs.

Underneath the soil's surface there is a potential army of pests facing the root systems of the

COMMON CHICKWEED
This common annual weed grows freely on cultivated land and on roadsides, derelict land and in gardens. The stems will sprawl between rows of crops, doing little harm except that they compete for nutrients in the soil. Unusually, the delicate, star-like white flowers may be seen at any time of year but appear most vigorously in spring and autumn.

MARKET GARDEN WILDLIFE

Currants and strawberries, cabbages and carrots, make the market garden a cornucopia for insects and invertebrates. Aphids and flies graze on cabbage leaves, slugs devour young plants and caterpillars feed on leaves. But ground beetles and devil's coach horses prey on other insects and act as natural pest controls. Up above, insect and seed-eating birds flourish.

KEY TO FEATURES AND SPECIES

1 Jackdaw
2 Wood pigeons
3 Pied wagtail
4 Currant bushes
5 Strawberries
6 Mosquitos
7 Tomatoes
8 House sparrows
9 Currant clear wing
10 Field mouse
11 Carrots
12 Rhubarb
13 Nipplewort

14 Garden pebble moth
15 Hoverfly
16 Cabbages
17 Large white
18 Blue tit
19 Common fumitory
20 Red dead nettle
21 Large white caterpillar
22 Cranefly
23 Scarlet pimpernel
24 Black garden ant

25 Garden slug
26 Greenfly
27 Cabbage aphid
28 Cabbage white fly
29 Coltsfoot
30 Shepherd's purse
31 Candle snuff fungus
32 Devil's coach horse
33 Strawberry snail
34 Coral spot fungus
35 Cutworm

36 Blackfly
37 Click beetle
38 Leather jacket
39 Annual meadow grass
40 Netted slug
41 Greenbottle
42 Wireworm
43 Ground beetle
44 Rove beetle

cabbage family, not least of which is the devastating club root fungus. Spores are persistent in infected soil for many years, lying dormant until the introduction of a brassica crop. The fungal colony infests the root system, destroying the root hairs and reducing the tap root to a club-like structure.

Cabbage root fly leaves a similar trail of destruction. This small black fly, rather like a house fly, lays its eggs on the stems of brassicas, close to the ground. The larvae hatch, eat their way into the stem and head downwards, consuming the root as they go. Affected plants wilt in hot weather and eventually die.

Black ground beetles and the devil's coach horse beetle come to the rescue, as they have a healthy appetite for cabbage root fly eggs and larvae. As the pest population increases so do the number of beetle predators, helped by an abundant food supply. Nature strikes a balance when the increasing number of predators achieves control over the pests.

Market garden soils invariably form a good tilth and this seed bed is ideal not only for crop plants but also for annual weeds. Not surprisingly, some of the more difficult crops to keep weed free, such as peas or leeks, share the ground with chickweed, fat hen, pineapple mayweed, wild chamomile, scentless mayweed, speedwell, field bindweed, groundsel, shepherds purse, redshank and nettles. Themselves flowering and seeding within the growing season, they will provide a superb food reserve for flocks of goldfinch, greenfinch and linnet.

Small round holes in the leaves of beans reveal the feeding habits of the tiny, brown pea and bean weevil. Beans also suffer from infestations of a black aphid. Aphids bear many young by virgin birth, which means that many generations may occur as the result of one autumn mating. Little wonder they are so prolific. The flightless generations are helped in their colonization of new plants by red ants. Aphids extract sap from the growing tips of the beans. As a by-product they produce honeydew, a sugary jelly much relished by ants. The ants farm the aphids, introducing them to new plants in order to generate supplies of honeydew.

This aphid husbandry hardly helps the grower, but the green lacewing and ladybirds are silent warriors in the fight against aphid population explosions. Adult and larval forms of both consume vast quantities of the pest. Blue tits and willow warblers will also help to reduce the number of insect pests if they are left a place to nest in the market garden.

On a hump-backed ridge of a potato furrow a red-legged partridge stands erect, grating out a harsh but rhythmical song denoting his territory. At the field boundary, beneath a clump of horse-radish, the female sits close incubating a clutch of a dozen reddish-brown, mottled eggs. Two clutches may be laid, one being incubated by the female and the other simultaneously by the male. This leads to years when 'red-legs' are extremely abundant. The red-legged or French partridge has expanded its range over Britain since its introduction in 1770. It favours light soils in areas of low rainfall.

In a pick-your-own strawberry bed perennial weeds are a problem. Couch grass, docks, and creeping thistle invade the runners and in this entanglement yellow wagtails nest. As the thistles burst into flower elegant peacock butterflies seek them out, resting on the purple heads as they refuel with nectar.

In the warmth of the multispan glass houses a good crop of F_1 hybrid tomatoes is well on its way to setting its fifth truss. Brushing past the leaves puts to flight small white insects that have been feeding on the undersides. These whitefly can become the scourge of the greenhouse. Controllable in the adult form by pesticides, chemicals have little effect upon the eggs which are protected by a scale. A small black calcid wasp is employed to do a sabotage job on the whitefly eggs. Female wasps lay their eggs through ovipositors that pierce the egg scale. When the wasp larva emerges from the egg it

COLORADO BEETLES AND PINKISH LARVAE
These foreign pests must be notified to the police as they can decimate a potato crop.

consumes the contents of the egg scale which turns black as the wasp grub pupates.

Greenhouse waste and spoilt crops are composted at the far end of the market garden. Toads live among the damp debris, feeding on the wealth of invertebrate life. Rosebay willowherb and long-headed poppies grow in some profusion around the edge. On still, warm evenings owl midges cloud the air, to be disrupted by the feeding flights of pied wagtails and a spotted flycatcher.

NATURAL RELATIONSHIPS

Alarming quantities of chemicals are used every year in the market gardener's campaign against pests and diseases but the alternative – natural control by nature's predators – requires that the particular pests become established on the crops first, which inevitably causes some damage. And as long as consumers demand consistent, clean looking produce, the biological control of pests will hardly become popular. Yet some of our most fascinating natural history comes from the continuing evolution of predator-prey relationships.

GREEN LACEWING
(above) These delicate-winged insects are the gardener's friend, as adults and larvae eat large numbers of aphids. Here an adult is devouring blackfly.

MAGPIE MOTH
(below) Attractive though it is, this moth is not popular with gardeners. Caterpillars will strip the leaves of currants and gooseberries.

Small Nettle   *Prickly Sow-thistle*   *Ivy-leaved Speedwell*

SMALL NETTLE *(Urtica urens)* A 4-24″ (10-60cm) annual, the deeply toothed leaves and stiff stems are clothed with unpleasantly stinging hairs. Short spikes of tiny green flowers are seen June-September. It is a weed of light cultivated soil, widespread and locally common.

PRICKLY SOW-THISTLE *(Sonchus asper)* Reaching 60″ (150cm), this robust annual is common on waste and arable land throughout Britain. All leaves have very spiny margins, upper leaves clasp the stem with round lobes. Golden flowerheads open June-August; seeds are cottony.

IVY-LEAVED SPEEDWELL *(Veronica hederifolia)* Weakly straggling over bare ground and field borders, the branched stems of this annual are 4-20″ (10-50cm). Light green leaves are lobed and the short-lived, pale flowers open March-May. Widespread, often common.

Common Poppy

Hoary Cress

Field Penny-cress

COMMON POPPY *(Papaver rhoeas)* Despite its control by herbicides, this 8-24″ (20-60cm) poppy remains common on arable land and rural waysides – but is rarely seen in north Scotland. Large flowers open June-August. Nearly round capsules are hairless, with a circle of pores.

HOARY CRESS *(Cardaria draba)* An introduction from Europe, now common on disturbed and cultivated land in southern and eastern England. 12-35″ (30-90cm) stems branch to make a dense, flat head of small flowers, May-June. Stem leaves are arrow-shaped and clasping.

FIELD PENNY-CRESS *(Thlaspi arvense)* This widespread annual is a pest of arable soils everywhere except the far North. Leafy, upright stems to 24″ (60cm) have a spike of stalked 4-petalled flowers May-July. Round, flat penny-like seedpods are broadly winged.

V-Moth

Garden Pebble

Magpie Moth

GARDEN PEBBLE *(Evergestis forficalis)* This common moth – wingspan 1½″ (38mm) – lays its eggs on brassicas. The destructive caterpillars sometimes bind the leaves together for shelter. There are two broods, the moths flying during May and September.

V-MOTH *(Itame wauaria)* The moth's name refers to the V-shaped mark on its forewings. With a wingspan of 1″ (25mm), it flies during July and lays its eggs on fruit bushes. The larvae are sometimes abundant, destroying the growing shoots of the plants.

MAGPIE MOTH *(Abraxas grossulariata)* This colourful species – wingspan 1½″ (38mm) – can be abundant in the garden. Its similarly-coloured larvae attack currant and gooseberry bushes on which the eggs are laid in July and August. The larvae overwinter, pupating in May.

Currant Clearwing

Currant Pug

Mother of Pearl

Raspberry Moth

CURRANT CLEARWING (*Aegeria tipuliformis*) A wasp-like moth with a ¾″ (19mm) wingspan, often seen resting on currant and gooseberry bushes. The larvae live in the fruit stems causing extensive damage. They pupate within the stems and emerge as adults in June and July.

RASPBERRY MOTH (*Lampronia rubiella*) Flying in June – wingspan ½″ (12mm) – this is a pest of raspberries. The caterpillars feed inside the flowers and hibernate on the ground. The following spring they pupate inside the stems damaging the plant still further.

CURRANT PUG (*Eupithecia assimilata*) This notable pest of the market garden is often found resting on fences or on hops and currants. The two broods are on the wing in June and September. The wings – 1½″ (38mm) across – provide good camouflage.

MOTHER OF PEARL (*Botys ruralis*) Named after the beautiful pearly lustre of its wings – span 1½″ (38mm) – this common moth is seen in market gardens throughout Britain from June to August. The translucent larvae feed on clumps of nearby nettles.

The Carrion Crow

Adaptable, intelligent and bold, the sombre carrion crow has survived years of persecution by the farmer. A scavenger and opportunist, its harsh call is familiar even in the busy city.

Perched high on a telegraph post, a sinister black bird – a carrion crow – is surveying the market garden where the fields are busy with new life. Suddenly, spotting movement on the ground below, the bird launches itself heavily from its perch and swoops. Swiftly snatching a beakful of beetles, it takes to the air again, flapping slowly away to its untidy nest high in the fork of a nearby pear tree where a brood of hungry young awaits.

A BAD REPUTATION

Though much maligned for its scavenging habits – hence its name – the carrion crow is more likely to help the farmer in summer by ridding the fields of pests, than it is to hinder him by plundering crops. Nonetheless, the crow is a great opportunist and will eat a wide range of food, from crabs and frogs to grubs and grain, depending on location and what can be found at different times of year. The summer diet of small mammals and invertebrates is supple-

mented by the eggs and chicks of gamebirds – a reason why some crows end up on gamekeepers' gibbets.

In winter over half the crow's diet is made up of carrion, the rest by grain. Its fondness for cereal seeds is reflected by the naming of the familiar field 'scarecrow'. Indeed, so serious a pest of new-sown fields are they that farm employees of the 19th century used to walk the fields with rattles, similar to those once heard at football matches, to frighten off the thieving birds. Crows even have a notorious reputation for attacking sheep stuck in snow drifts or giving birth to lambs. It has even been claimed that they can kill newborn lambs, though observation surveys show that the lambs are much more likely to be already dead before the crow gets to them.

All in all, the traditional picture of the crow is a highly unpopular one and this is reflected in it being, even now, one of the few birds that can be legally shot as a pest at any time of year. In

THE LONE CROW
(above) Dull black from bill to claw, the sinister carrion crow is a familiar sight everywhere from woodlands to town gardens. It is usually solitary, or with its life-long mate. Sometimes, however, family groups may stay together over winter until the young birds set out on their own in spring.

THE CROW'S NEST
(left) Unlike rooks and jackdaws, which nest in colonies, crows nest alone, in a cup-shaped nest of twigs, high in a tree-fork. Here the young crows feast on a high-protein diet of insects, spiders and other invertebrates. Although the young can fly after a month, the family tends to stay together for up to a year.

HOODED CROW
(below) The handsome and less ominous hooded crow, like the carrion crow, is descended from the European crow.

KEY FACTS

IN FLIGHT wingbeats are slow and elegant and the tail and wings are squarer than those of the less stockily-built rook.

HYBRIDS of the hooded and carrion crow occur where their ranges meet along a band from the Isle of Man to northern Scotland.

THE EGGS are blue-green splashed with darker grey. 4-6 are laid in an untidy cup of twigs in a tall tree, on a cliff or building and sometimes on the ground, March to May.

this, its status is shared by four others – the rook, jackdaw, magpie and jay – of the seven British members of the crow (Corvid) family; the exceptions being the raven and chough.

GREAT SURVIVORS

Despite persecution, the crow has increased in numbers this century, largely due to a reduction in the numbers of gamekeepers, and there are now over one million pairs. Highly adaptable, it is at home on farmland, woodland, moorland, cliffs and open shores. Its harsh croak or 'paarp' car-horn call is even familiar to townsfolk, as the crow has also successfully colonized urban rubbish tips and gardens.

Abundant in England, Wales and southern and eastern Scotland, the all-black carrion crow is absent further north – its place being taken by the hooded crow. The hooded crow probably evolved when an ice barrier during the Ice Age separated the ancestral crow into two groups. Both birds are regarded as belonging to the same species as they can, and do, interbreed, though the hooded crow is quite differently marked, having a grey body. Where the territories overlap, hybrids often occur.

The carrion crow is particularly easy to confuse with the rook as it is about the same size – 18″ (45cm) – and all black. But whereas crows are generally seen alone or with a mate, rooks live in flocks. The country adage 'one rook is a crow; a flock of crows are rooks' does not always apply, however, for rooks sometimes feed on their own and young crows form flocks. Like rooks, a family of crows will remain together for nearly a year after the young are hatched in late April. The young crows depart in early spring, but the adult pair will stay together for life.

BIRDS OF FOLKLORE

The crow is often represented as a white bird that was turned black on some fall from grace. In folklore the crow (and raven) is repeatedly credited as the herald of death and doom. An old countryman seeing a crow perched nearby may still say, only half joking, that it is waiting for his soul. On the other hand, in Czecho-slovakia, the crow was placed in the stork's role of bringing babies. Crows are also supposed to be able to foretell rain, and the sight of a crow stalking into water at dusk is said to be a sure sign of wet weather ahead.

With its sinister appearance and unmelodious voice, the carrion crow is a bird of mystery. Paradoxically it must be familiar to everyone.

The Domestic Goat

Tough and tenacious, and possessing an iron digestion, the
domestic goat thrives on the kind of scrubby, marginal land
on which other livestock can barely survive.

Tough and hardy, the goat has long been one of the most valuable of all domestic animals to man. Goats are animals of marginal lands and can survive and prosper on land too poor and too difficult for sheep and cattle. On scrubby, coarse ground, on which dairy cattle can barely live, goats can yield good quality milk – milk which can give such beautiful cheeses as the French St Maure and Crottin, and is pleasant to drink in its own right.

The goat owes at least some of its hardiness to its remarkable digestive system. It can eat coarse, poor vegetation and extract the maximum possible nourishment because almost one third of its own body by volume is devoted to digestion. Indeed, goats are so good at making the most of poor food that they can actually become sick if let loose on high quality grazing land. To stay healthy goats need to feed on woody, prickly and shrubby foliage as well as good grass.

The goat's ability to eat almost anything and scratch a living in even the most unpromising environment has tarnished its image in the past. Many people seeing pictures of goats demolishing the last wretched tree as the desert advances in Africa or Asia assume that it is the goat which has created the desert. In fact, goats are usually there because they are the only animals that can scrape a living from such overcropped, under-fertilized and abandoned areas.

Similarly, people who have seen a goat chew its way through a carefully grown hedge, or destroy a beautiful garden may decide they are naturally destructive. The truth is that the goat, unlike most other creatures, can include these in its liberal diet.

SCRUBLAND GOATS

In the past, the goat's ability to live on scrubby ground was much appreciated by smallholders. A hundred years ago, one or two goats were

SAANEN GOAT AND KIDS
*(above) The pure white
Saanen goat is the most
popular of all milk-
producing goats. Coming
originally from the Saane and
Simme valleys high in the
Swiss Alps, it was introduced
to Britain in the last century
and often interbred with
native breeds to give a goat
that can, exceptionally, yield
over two tons of milk a year.
The milk of goats like the
Saanen is particularly valued
by mothers whose children
are allergic to cow's milk —
about one in twenty.*

kept on patches of scrub land by thousands of factory and mine workers in the north of England and Wales, and they were once the mainstay of the crofts of the Scottish Highlands before the crofts were 'cleared' in the 18th century. The goat's fortunes declined with the fortunes of the smallholder.

In recent years, however, the goat's unique qualities have begun to be recognized, and the number of goats in Britain has been increasing dramatically. In the mid 1980s, there were around 130,000.

It is the increase in large scale commercial goat keeping – in herds of 200 or more – that has been most marked, but a number of people with large gardens or yards have also begun to appreciate goats as productive pets. Goats make good pets because they are friendly and inquisitive – unlike sheep, for although they look similar, sheep and goats are temper-mentally and biologically distinct. Indeed, sheep and goats have different numbers of chroma-somes (goats have 60 and sheep 54) and cannot interbreed.

SMELLY GOATS

Domestic goats can breed throughout the year. Traditionally, though, they are mated in autumn (September-November). The male goat is well known to need little encouragement to mate, and around this time of year his smell – strong enough at any time – becomes especially pungent, as scent glands near the horns and around the anus exude a powerful musky odour. The 'billy' goat enhances the effect by spraying urine on his front legs, beard and neck.

Nanny goats can conceive when they are as little as three months old, but goat breeders usually will not allow them to mate until they are a year old. The billy can tell a nanny is in mating condition by the smell of her urine.

The kids – normally one to three in a litter –

A NANNY MATE
(right) Goats are becoming increasingly popular as pets with people who have large country gardens. But they need to be kept on a tight leash if they are not to create havoc. Goats will happily eat anything from hedges to prized flowers – and their unusual ability to stand on their hind legs means they can reach tasty morsels the owner may have thought out of reach.

ANGLO-NUBIAN GOATS
(below, left and right) The Anglo-Nubian goat, with its large floppy ears, is among the most distinctive of all goat breeds – but its colouring can vary considerably, from dark chestnut with white ears to mottled black or brown and white.

are born five months after mating (February-April) mimicking the kidding time of their wild forebears. Soon after birth, the kids of breeds of goats that are supposed to be 'hornless' are debudded – that is, the budding horns are removed under anaesthetic. Unfortunately, this rather brutal practice is essential if the goat is to be hornless, for so far it has proved difficult to sustain a breed of truly hornless goats; the horn is associated with fertility, and many matings between truly hornless goats lead to hermaphrodite kids.

In goat farming – unlike dairy cattle farming where the Friesian breed dominates – cross-breeds and hybrids are the rule. Nevertheless, each variety has its own adherents, and rare breeds such as Bagots and Angoras are carefully conserved. Every year, once scorned goat breeds, and goats in general, seem to gain many new admirers.

150

The Fallow Corner

It has long been known that the land cannot keep producing good crops year after year, otherwise it simply becomes exhausted. Thus, for many centuries, arable fields were left unsown to lie fallow – to rest – for one year in every two or three, and the soil's heartiness was restored by enriching it with manure and ploughing vegetation back in. Modern farming techniques, however, mean that this system is no longer necessary, but even today almost every field has its fallow patch – usually in tight corners that are inaccessible to farmers' heavy, tractor-drawn implements.

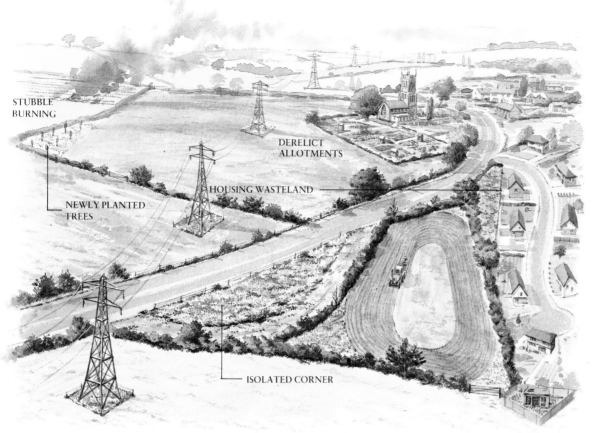

STUBBLE
BURNING

DERELICT
ALLOTMENTS

NEWLY PLANTED
TREES

HOUSING WASTELAND

ISOLATED CORNER

Draped over the land like a blue-green quilt, the young wheat crop grows thick and deep on the rich soil. Every plant is the same – the same height, the same colour. When a gust sweeps across the field, whole swathes move as one, the heavy, grain-laden ears swaying on chemically stiffened stems. Between the rows there is nothing but bare soil, for all competitors of the wheat have been wiped out by selective methods. This is modern monoculture – wheat, and only wheat.

But at the edge of the ploughland, where the rumpled undersheet emerges from beneath the quilt of green, the broken ground is flecked with tiny flowers: creeping scarlet pimpernel, speedwell and pansy. In the field corner, the gaudy poppies nod and flutter above drifts of mayweed. This is fallow land, the realm of weeds.

Farming is a constant struggle against weeds. Sweep them away and more appear almost overnight. This is inevitable, for they thrive on disturbance. They are opportunists, able to sprout, grow and flower within a few weeks, and while more sedate plants are still unfurling their first petals the weeds have scattered their seeds far and wide. A single poppy plant may produce 17,000 seeds, and each seed is capable of lying dormant in the soil for years, until some disturbance of the land makes it sprout. Cultivation does exactly that: the plough turns the soil over, seeds are disturbed, and up come the weeds. If the land is turned a second time to kill the weeds, still more seeds are aroused and germinate in their turn. Only repeated ploughing can cure this, when there are no more seeds to disturb.

This is the basis of the old, traditional farming technique known as bare fallow, which was the principal form of weed control on our farms until fairly recently. The fallow was also necessary to allow the soil to recover between crops. In the original two-field system one field was cultivated while the other was grazed by animals which fertilized the soil with their manure. But by the Middle Ages this primitive system was largely replaced by the more efficient three-field system, where two crops with different demands on the soil were rotated between three fields, allowing two thirds of the land to be put under the plough at one time.

Once a farmer had taken a couple of crops off a field, he would abandon it and let the weeds sprout. The following spring he would plough the weeds back into the soil, adding to its fertility but at the same time causing more to spring up. Repeated ploughings in midsummer and early autumn ensured that most of the weeds were flushed out and destroyed before the field was sown with precious wheat. In practice, another batch of weeds would come up with the crop, but there was little that the farmer could do.

THE MODERN FALLOW

Today the farmer can do something. Selective herbicides sprayed on the growing crops kill broad-leaved weeds without harming the crop itself. But because some of the most pernicious weeds are not broad-leaved there is still value in the fallow technique, with one significant modification: when the weeds come up, they are burnt off with a general weedkiller like paraquat. This way there is no disturbance of the ground so no more weeds germinate. This means that the field no longer has to be left lying fallow for a whole year while weeds are destroyed by repeated cultivation.

Whatever strategy the farmer adopts, the field corners, and sometimes edges, are nearly always left fallow. The reason is simple: modern tractor-mounted ploughs are quite manoeuvrable, and can gain access to all but the tightest corners and this brings on the weeds throughout the field. However, a large crop sprayer (some have a 40 foot span) is a lot less manoeuvrable, and cannot be driven into corners. The seed drill follows the same path and within a few weeks the green shoots of wheat appear in curving rows, while in the corner the weeds flourish.

If, in succeeding years, the plough misses the fallow corner, then many of the weeds will disappear, as they will be displaced by hedge-row plants such as garlic mustard, cow parsley, campion and nettles, which then have time to establish themselves. Eventually, shrubby plants such as bramble and dog rose appear, to be followed by hawthorn, blackthorn and guelder rose. By this stage, the corner will be fallow no longer – overgrown and inpenetrable, it will have turned into a thicket.

FLOWERS AT THE FIELD EDGE
(above) Fallow areas can occur wherever the ground is inaccessible to weed-killing machinery – in tight corners, along the field edge, or on steep, river-side slopes. Here the limit of the crop is defined by a footpath.

Nature Walk

When walking in the country look out for different items of farm machinery used in crop cultivation, such as:

SWING PLOUGH, drawn by oxen and later by horses, and used until the 1950s. There were many local variations in design.

SPRING-TINE HARROW, pulled by a tractor, to slice and crumble the clods of soil after ploughing, in order to prepare an even seed bed.

SEED DRILL, which sows seed in a series of parallel drills and then covers them with soil.

ROLLERS, often used to firm down the seed bed after drilling.

In the Fallow Field

Field corners, where the farmer's seed-drill has not reached, are wildlife havens among the crops – scented with flowers in summer and enlivened by the busy hum of insects and flitting birds.

On a summer's day, yellow and black hoverflies feed on the abundant pollen of poppies, a green-veined white butterfly probes thistle florets with its long proboscis, furry bumble bees are busy at the heads of great knapweed, and orange soldier beetles crawl over the creamy flowers of fool's parsley. A wood mouse scampers up a trailing bramble stem and rabbits scuttle to the safety of their warren, as a fox trots along the field edge.

In the autumn, twittering mixed flocks of dapper tree sparrows, finches and buntings visit the corner to harvest the seeds of teasel, charlock, dock, persicaria and other 'weeds'. The usual farmland birds are augmented by chaffinches from the continent and winter visitors such as bramblings.

Fallow corners and headlands have not always been so hospitable to seed-eating birds. In the last century, when farm labour was plentiful, such rough areas were scythed before the plants had set seed. As a result, goldfinches and other seed-eaters declined. From the 1940s numbers began to pick up, but increasing use of herbicides again decreased the availability of weed seeds. Linnets and others declined steadily in the 1970s and early 1980s.

The marked decline of grey partridges in recent years is linked to the increased use of sprays that reduce both weeds and insects. So now, farmers with shooting interests not only keep sprays away from headlands and field edges, they may also turn off the spray boom on the outer circuit of certain fields. These practices can double the breeding success of partridges, and similar care has helped the populations of linnets and other seed-eaters.

FLOWERS OF THE FIELD EDGE

The varied flora of the fallow corner includes plants that are typically weeds of arable land. Several poppies lift their papery, red flowers to the sun. Golden corn marigolds may mingle with rarer delicate blue cornflowers. The small yellow flowers of charlock attract nectar-feeding orange tip butterflies, whose females lay eggs on the stems and seed pods.

Grasses abound, among them timothy grass, false oat-grass and rat's-tail fescue with its flower heads like tiny brushes. Among the grasses are small nettles, as irritant as the stinging nettle, but these are annuals without the tough, yellow root-stock. Scarlet pimpernel nestles close to the ground, as does dwarf spurge with its tiny, green flowers. On chalky soil, pinkish spikes of red bartsia mingle with

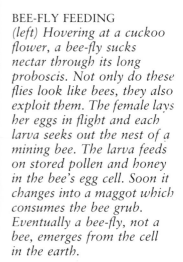

BEE-FLY FEEDING
(left) Hovering at a cuckoo flower, a bee-fly sucks nectar through its long proboscis. Not only do these flies look like bees, they also exploit them. The female lays her eggs in flight and each larva seeks out the nest of a mining bee. The larva feeds on stored pollen and honey in the bee's egg cell. Soon it changes into a maggot which consumes the bee grub. Eventually a bee-fly, not a bee, emerges from the cell in the earth.

WILDLIFE OF THE FIELD CORNER

Untouched by herbicides or insecticides, many plants and their associated fauna flourish here. Poppies, thistles, docks and nettles are all plants of rough ground. Bindweed, or convolvulus, twines the stems of bramble whose flowers attract butterflies. The caterpillars of small skipper butterflies feed on grasses; those of the cream-spot tiger moth feed on dandelion and docks; and those of the large yellow underwing feed on flowers as well as grasses. Adult partridge eat seeds, but their chicks take insects. The linnet and corn bunting are seed-eaters. The mice – the kestrel's prey – also feed on the seeds, while the hedgehog forages for worms and insects, such as plant bugs and various beetles.

KEY TO THE SPECIES

1 Kestrel
2 Painted lady
3 Wheat
4 False oat-grass
5 Cream-spot tiger moth
6 Corn bunting
7 Common poppies
8 Field gromwell
9 Grey partridges
10 Harvest mouse
11 Linnet
12 Teasel
13 Bindweed
14 Couch grass
15 Fool's parsley
16 Long-headed poppy
17 Thistle
18 Small skippers
19 Field forget-me-not
20 Nettle
21 Blackberries
22 Hedgehog
23 Scarlet pimpernel
24 Bee-fly
25 Dock
26 Tortoise beetles
27 Yellow underwing
28 Cleavers
29 Common blue
30 Long-tailed field mouse
31 Mining bee
32 Ants
33 Mining bee's nest
34 Bloody-nosed beetle
35 Heart and dart moth
36 22-spot ladybird
37 Meadow plant bug
38 Bramble

WOOLLY BEAR
(left) Popularly known as the 'woolly bear', this hairy caterpillar is the larva of the garden tiger moth. It feeds on both wild and garden plants. The bright adult moth flies at night and is rarely seen.

TWO HARVEST MICE
(below) Scrambling up the stem of a tall dock, these harvest mice are more likely to be found nesting in the undisturbed field's edge, than among the corn stalks where the combine harvester will destroy their nest of woven vegetation.

the grasses, together with the purple flowers of Venus's looking glass and the spiky fruit sprays of shepherd's needle.

Other flowers are taller, and struggle up through the grasses towards the sunlight. Palest blue field forget-me-nots star the grassy corner, and yellowish-white pansies peep out from among the green stems, together with corn buttercups and pinkish-purple cut-leaved cranesbill flowers. Tansy, with its yellow button-like flowers, and pinky-purple knapweeds force their way through the grassy tangle, and teasel raises its cones of pale lilac flowers on tall, straight stems.

Close by the hedge, which is draped with bindweed and caged in brambles, are stout stands of creeping thistles and clumps of stinging nettles. Growing unobtrusively among the other plants are the sickly-looking spikes of

GREY PARTRIDGES
(left) Our native partridge is a handsome bird with subtly marked plumage. The female lays 9-20 eggs in a scrape among crops or at the foot of a hedge. The insects of the fallow corner are a vital food for the chicks. The tangled plants also provide good nesting cover.

broomrape, with neither green pigment nor leaves. They do not need to manufacture their own food, as they are parasitic on the roots of other plants, including knapweeds and thistles.

The summer flowers attract nectar-feeding butterflies. Orange small skippers fly jerkily from thistle to thistle. Common blues resting, wings closed and camouflaged, on the grass stems, reveal a jewel-like flash of colour as they fly past, and pinky-orange painted ladies dart from flower to flower. So bright and glowing are their colours, they must be freshly emerged butterflies that have passed their caterpillar life feeding on the thistles. In autumn they will migrate southwards or die, and the presence of painted ladies next year will depend on the arrival of new migrants from Mediterranean countries.

A brief flash of vivid yellow is a yellow underwing moth, which in flight reveals its golden-yellow hind wings, but on settling, tucks them beneath its dull brown fore wings. Another moth flutters then settles its fore wings, each with a dark blotch and a dash, flat over its body as it crawls into seclusion; this is a heart and dart moth.

INSECT COMMUNITIES

The thistles are teeming with insect life. A bright green, metallic-looking tortoise beetle crouches on a leaf. Its larvae, which eat 'win-

dows' from the undersides of the leaves, attach their faeces and cast skins to long spines on their back end and hold them as a camouflage umbrella. A tiny blue-black leaf beetle has larvae that tunnel within the thistle leaves. The long-legged soldier beetle on the flower heads preys on visiting insects. Delicate lacebugs feed on the leaves but fall prey to shiny flower bugs.

On the nettles aphids suck the sugary sap, and are hunted by ladybirds, including the 22-spot and the larger 14-spot. Green lacewings flutter over the leaves and lay stalked eggs which develop into larvae that also eat aphids. Caterpillars of many moths chew the leaves, including the leaf-rolling caterpillars of the mother-of-pearl. Froghoppers suck the nettle's watery sap, as does a green capsid bug, and they are eaten by various predatory bugs, including *Heterotoma*, which has curiously thickened front legs.

The insect life provides food for a variety of birds, such as tits and wrens. In the breeding season, yellowhammers, corn buntings, chaf-

finches and other seed-eaters also take insects, which they feed to their nestlings. Staring down into the grass is a kestrel, perched motionless on a dead tree trunk in the hedge as it watches for an unsuspecting vole or wood mouse.

So busy and colourful is the fallow corner, that it has considerable conservation value, in striking contrast to the intensive agriculture that surrounds it. It is ironic that its existence is due to the very size of the modern farmer's efficient machinery.

TORTOISE BEETLE
(top) Seen here on ground ivy, the tortoise beetle is so-called because it can withdraw its legs, head and antennae beneath its toughened carapace.

BRIGHT TANSY
(above) Flowering from July to September, tansy is a herb often found growing at the field's edge.

THREE POPPIES
(right) These poppies are best told apart by the seed pods. The common poppy's is hairless and its length is no more than twice diameter; the rough poppy's is round with bristles; and the long-headed's is long and smooth.

LONG HEADED POPPY

COMMON POPPY

ROUGH POPPY

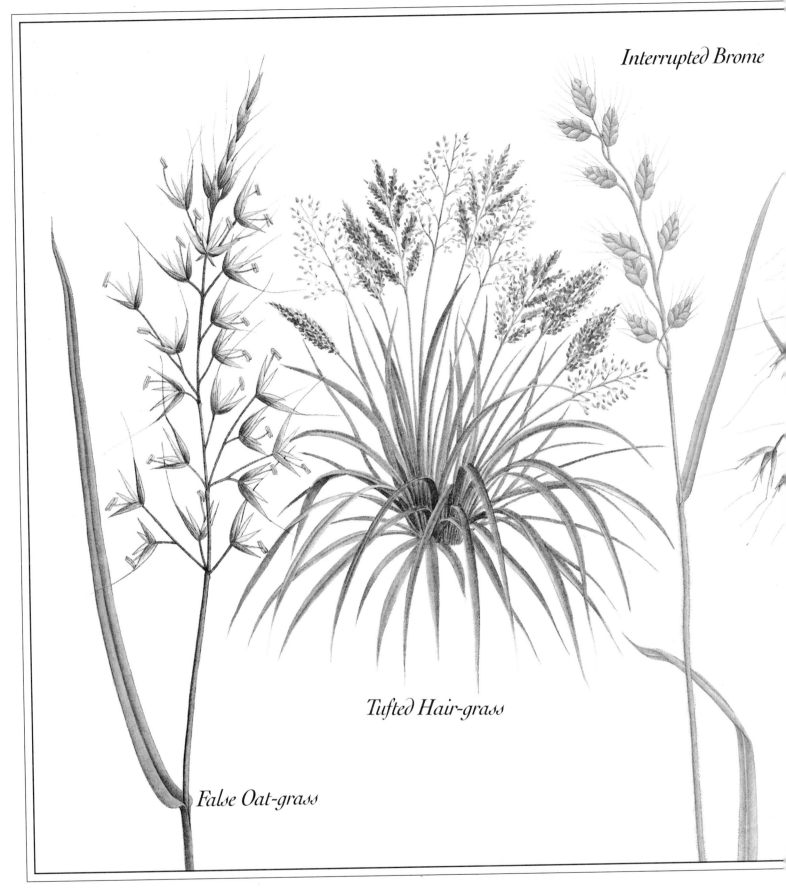

Interrupted Brome

Tufted Hair-grass

False Oat-grass

FALSE OAT-GRASS *(Arrhenatherum elatius)* A coarse perennial that grows in loose tufts, with 20-60″ (50-150cm) stems. Flat leaf blades are rough to touch, and a branched flowerhead opens June to September. Found throughout Britain on wayside and rough grassland.

TUFTED HAIR-GRASS *(Deschampsia cespitosa)* This coarse perennial forms large hummocks with stems to 80″ (200cm). Leaves are flat, the upper surface ribbed and sometimes rounded, and rough. From June to August, silvery flowerheads open. Abundant in wet woods, marshes.

INTERRUPTED BROME *(Bromus interruptus)* An erect hairy annual reaching 40″ (100cm), this was once an arable weed. No longer found in the wild, it was extinct in 1980, but is now grown in botanical gardens. Tight groups of flowers are seen June and July.

Wild Grasses

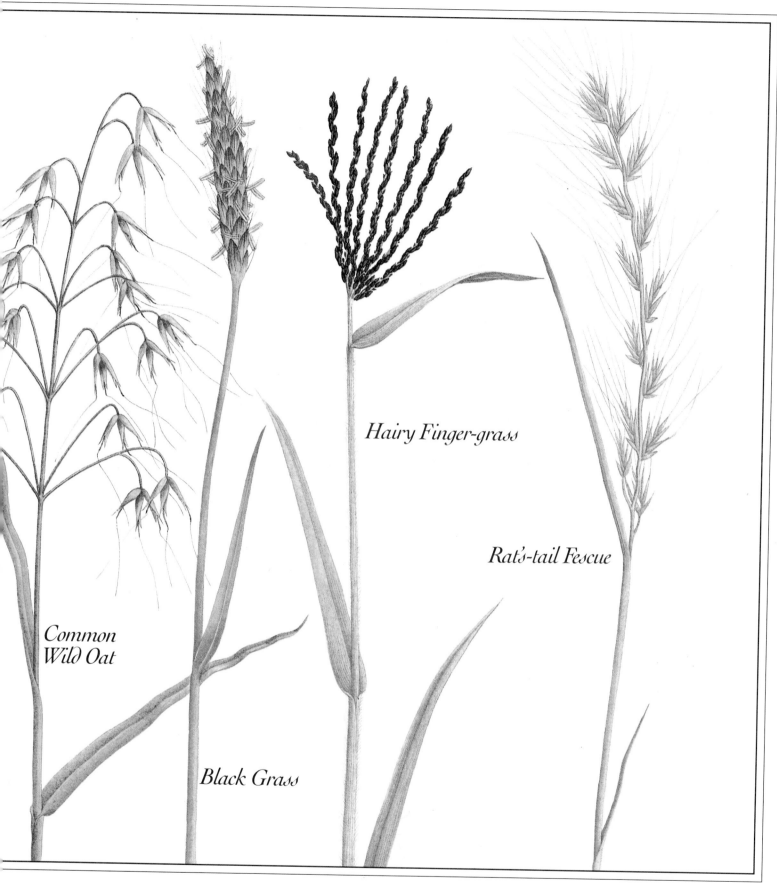

Common Wild Oat

Black Grass

Hairy Finger-grass

Rat's-tail Fescue

COMMON WILD OAT (*Avena fatua*) A common weed of cereal crops in England, this 12-60″ (30-150cm) annual grows in open tufts. The leaf blades are flat and rough. A branched open flowerhead has drooping clusters of 2-3 long-awned flowers, June-August.

BLACK GRASS (*Alopecurus myosuroides*) Common in waste places and arable land in the South East – often a serious weed – this annual has stems 8-32″ (20-80cm), growing in small tufts. Upper surface of leaves is rough, a narrow flowerspike opens May-August.

HAIRY FINGER-GRASS (*Digitaria sanguinalis*) So-called because of the finger-like sprays of 4-10 flowerspikes seen August to September. 4-12″ (10-30cm) high, it is a rare, introduced annual found in arable fields and wasteland near docks, mostly in the South.

RAT'S-TAIL FESCUE (*Vulpia myuros*) Sometimes found in southern Britain and south Ireland on dry sandy soils, waste places or walls. Narrow leaf-blades are rolled, 4-24″ (10-60cm) stems are enclosed by leaf-sheaths to the bristly flower spike, seen June and July. Annual.

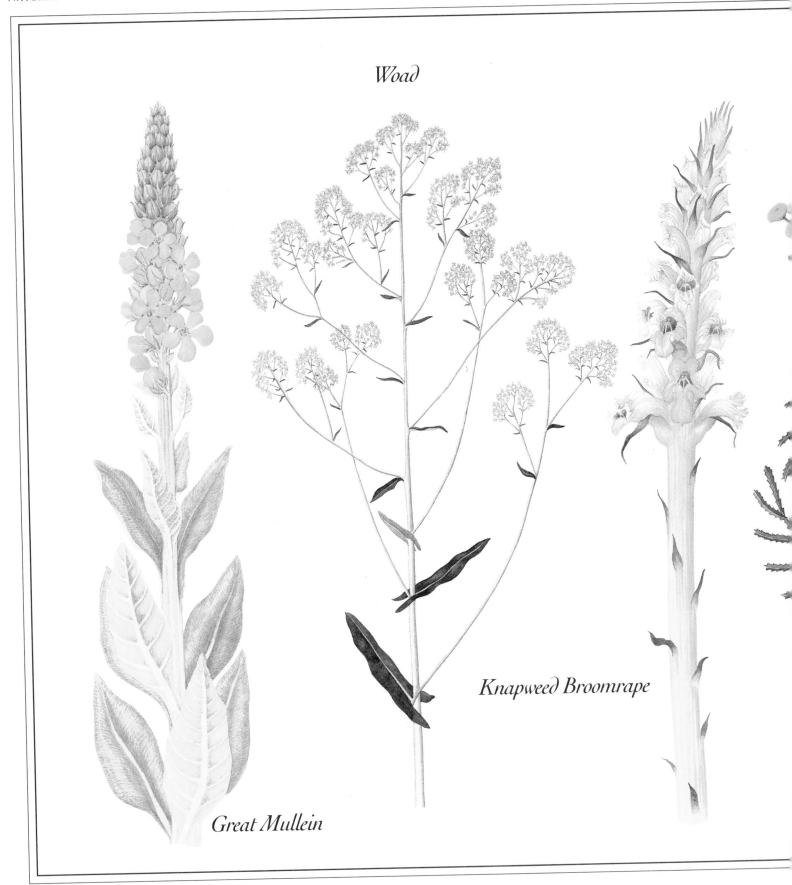

Woad

Knapweed Broomrape

Great Mullein

GREAT MULLEIN (*Verbascum thapsus*) Leaves and stem of this biennial are thick and soft, covered with whitish 'wool'. It reaches 80″ (200cm), with a spire of flowers opening June to August. Frequently seen in hedgerows and waste places on dry soils, rare in the far North.

WOAD (*Isatis tinctoria*) Probably an ancient introduction, this once common biennial now grows only in a few localities in the South. 20-48″ (50-120cm) tall stems bear clasping leaves with basal lobes and heads of flowers, July-August. The shiny winged fruits hang on thin stalks.

KNAPWEED BROOMRAPE (*Orobanche elatior*) Lacking green pigment, this parasitic perennial gets nutrients from greater knapweed. The tubular, hooded flowers open on a thick 6-28″ (15-70cm) stem in July. Local on dry, rough grassland in south and east England.

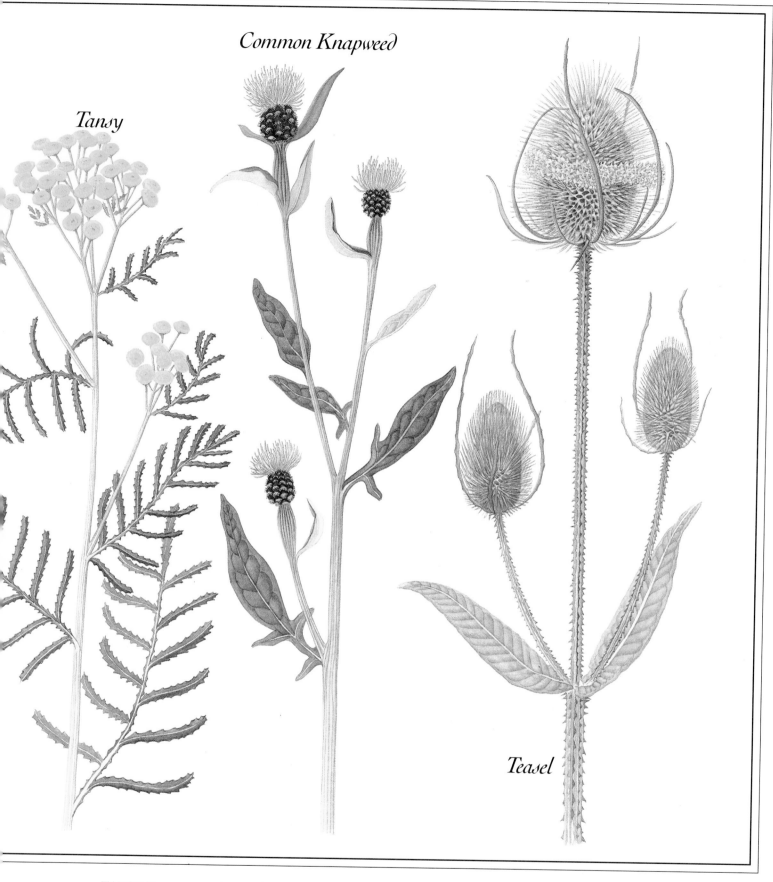

Tansy

Common Knapweed

Teasel

TANSY *(Tanacetum vulgare)* When bruised, the dark fern-like leaves emit a pungent aroma. Arising from creeping roots, erect branched stems to 40″ (100cm) form large clumps in hedges and waste places. Flat sprays of small flowerheads open July to September. Widespread.

COMMON KNAPWEED *(Centaurea nigra)* 6-24″ (15-60cm), a hairy perennial with ridged stems that widen below the flowerheads. These have a hard base with black-fringed scales. Very narrow tubular florets appear July-September. Common and widespread.

TEASEL *(Dipsacus fullonum)* A very stiff, erect biennial, with prickly ridged stems to 80″ (200cm). Large, stalkless leaves make a cup round the stem that holds water. Cylindrical flowerheads open July-August. Common in the South and East.

Web-spinning Spiders

Spiders' webs are extremely varied in their designs,
from the simple to the highly complex, but all
represent ingenious feats of natural engineering.

In the glistening dew of the early hours of morning, a garden spider is busily engaged in an act of silent, but frenzied activity – building itself a new web. Unless it is raining or windy this spider spins a new web every morning, usually just before dawn. Garden spiders may be found almost anywhere but they usually build their webs across a little used part of the garden. Here, the insects on which the spider feeds are all likely to get caught in this web but only if it is fresh and sticky.

Over millions of years spiders have been in contest with insects. The first hunting spiders chased insects over the ground and this may have been one of the reasons why insects developed the power of flight, as a means of escape. However, spiders responded by developing the ability to construct webs which could catch insects in flight. Spiders have shown immense adaptability – they are found everywhere from sand dunes and lakes to coal mines and mountain tops. Their webs are similarly rich in diversity. Some are permanent, some are intended to catch crawling rather than flying insects, some are woolly rather than sticky and a few are most economical on silk.

Spider silk is the strongest natural fibre known. For a given diameter it is as strong as steel, but much lighter and more elastic. Glands in the abdomen of the spider produce silk in liquid form, and this hardens on contact with the air as it passes out through the 'spinnerets' situated at the end of the abdomen. While all spiders manufacture silk, only about half of them use it to build webs. Hunting spiders, for example, use it primarily for purposes such as constructing retreats and egg sacs.

The orb web, a two dimensional structure, is arguably the most impressive of spiders' webs. Other types of webs are built differently and have different strategies. Exposed to the weather, orb webs deteriorate quite rapidly. Before building a fresh web the spider rolls up the old one, small flies and all, and eats it to conserve the protein. The hour-long construction begins with a line of silk being floated out on the breeze; when it attaches to something it is pulled tight. Walking out on this line, the spider lays a second, stronger line (the 'bridge thread') and then returns to the centre of the

THE MASTERFUL ORB WEB
Considered to be the most sophisticated and complex of all spiders' webs, the two-dimensional orb web (above) is built by many species of spider, of which the garden spider is best known. Orb webs are economical to build, requiring less silk than most other webs, but in order to trap insects they must always be fresh and sticky. (Oil on the spider's feet prevent it sticking to its own web.) A typical orb web weaver must therefore build a new web every morning. Before doing so, however, it rolls the old web up into a ball and consumes it, thereby conserving all the nutrients.

MESHED WEB
Spiders which produce meshed webs (left) do so by spinning exceptionally fine strands of silk through microscopic holes in a sieve plate at the end of their abdomens. This produces a tangled network of threads which are not sticky, but are highly effective in ensnaring prey. Meshed webs are most commonly woven around a hole on a tree trunk or old wall. They are extremely durable and, unlike orb webs, do not need to be replaced so often.

first line, attaches a vertical thread and drops down with it. When pulled tight this produces a 'Y' which will form three spokes, or radii, of the orb. Frame threads around the orb are laid next, followed by the rest of the radii. Then the spiral thread is wound round and round from the outside in and given dabs of sticky silk – like beads on a necklace. Finally, lines are tested for tension and the hub, where the spider sits, is completed with a pattern of threads.

The orb web and the cobweb, which is the work of the house spider (family *Agelenidae*), are the two best known kinds of web. The cobweb is a horizontal non-sticky sheet built gradually in the corner of a neglected room where crawling insects such as woodlice, earwigs and beetles may walk on to it. Old webs are simply abandoned when too dusty.

Smaller sheet webs are found abundantly on bushes and in grass during the autumn and are best seen on dewy mornings. The owners (family *Linyphiidae*) hang upside down below the sheet waiting for small jumping insects to land on it or be knocked down by supporting threads.

Spiders of the family *Amaurobiidae* have a sieve plate replacing some of the spinnerets. Strands of extremely fine silk are spun through microscopic holes in the plate, resulting in a bluish, woolly sort of web known as a meshed web, which has great snagging power on insects' legs. These may often be found on tree trunks and old walls, usually issuing from a hole.

Scaffolding webs, built by comb-footed spiders (family *Theridiidae*), can be found in buildings such as garden sheds, or among vegetation. Three-dimensional in structure, a horizontal sheet is supported above and below by sticky lines under tension. In one genus (*Episinus*) the web is reduced to just two vertical threads with one horizontal connecting line, from which the spider hangs, shaped much like a figure 'H'.

SPINNERS AT WORK
(left) Spiders manufacture silk through glands in their abdomens. This is secreted in liquid form through the spinnerets and hardens in contact with the air. Apart from web-spinning, the silk is also used for constructing egg sacs, retreats or for closeting prey or spiderlets.

VEILED WONDERS
(below) These delicate sheet webs are most abundant on bushes and grass on dewy autumn mornings.

The Deserted Railway

Built at vast cost using little more than sheer muscle power, the railways of 19th-century Britain were once one of the engineering wonders of the world. Great networks of lines latticed the countryside, broaching every natural obstacle, all for the transport of people and goods in a newly prosperous industrial age. But after booming for just 60 years or so, decline set in, leaving town and country scarred by miles of deserted track. Fortunately, nature quickly took up where man left off and now many old trackways are flourishing wildlife havens.

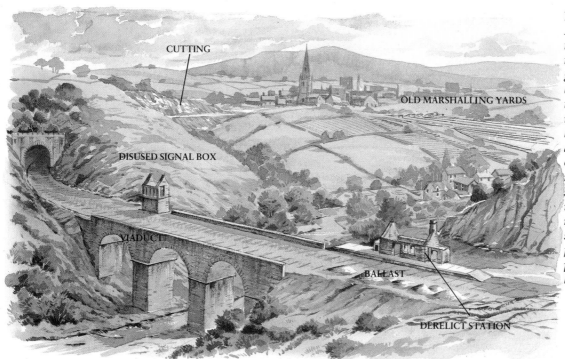

CUTTING

OLD MARSHALLING YARDS

DISUSED SIGNAL BOX

VIADUCT

BALLAST

DERELICT STATION

RELICS OF THE RAILWAYS
All over the country deserted tracks and derelict stations testify to the railways' past glory. Where the rails and ballast have been removed, the trackbed is quickly reabsorbed into the landscape, especially in agricultural areas, where it is often reploughed. But the new towns which originally sprang up to service the railways remain, along with monumental viaducts and spectacular cuttings carved from bare rock, leaving a permanent mark on the landscape.

High in the bleak moorlands of north Wales, not far from the great slate quarries of Blaenau Ffestiniog, the Bala and Ffestiniog railway soars across the valley of the Afon Prysor on nine high Romanesque arches, before sweeping westwards along a narrow ledge chiselled into the hard black rock of the mountain. It is an awesome feat of civil engineering, carved out of the landscape by manual labour in the 1880s to carry Welsh slate and granite to the industrial Midlands. Today, in the 1980s, it is deserted. The trackbed which once shook under the steam-hauled slate trains hammering up from Trawsfynydd is now a footpath. The rails have gone; in their place nothing save grass.

RADICAL SURGERY

Last used in 1961, this 16-mile stretch of railway is only a fraction of the 8000 or so miles of line closed in England and Wales since the railways were nationalized in 1948. Two thirds of these closures took place after 1963, when the Railways Board under Dr Richard Beeching recommended radical surgery on the network to cut out all the unprofitable cross-country routes. This policy sliced great holes in the capillary system which had served every corner of Britain in a pre-motor age, leaving only the main arteries intact.

Many of these routes enjoyed less than a century of useful life. Most of the early railways, built in the 1830s and 1840s, were planned to link major cities and industrial areas in the reasonable expectation of heavy demand and big profits. The result was the inter-city network which still forms the backbone of British Rail. It was only in the 1850s and 1860s that the railway companies began to expand into the sparsely populated rural areas. In an

age when road transport still moved at the pace of a horse, these cross-country routes attracted good trade and provided the railway shareholders with a steady, if unspectacular, dividend.

But after 1918 the cross-country network faced growing competition from road transport and was increasingly subsidized by the more profitable lines. A loss of £87 million in 1962 finally proved too much: the Beeching report – and mile upon mile of redundant trackbed, cuttings, embankments, tunnels and bridges – was the result.

Much of the engineering work which makes deserted railways so spectacular would be unnecessary on a railway built today. But in the 19th century limited locomotive power meant that the railways had to be built, as far as possible, on the flat. In hilly country this

ON THE RIGHT TRACK
(below) A flat, agricultural landscape is broken by the green ribbon of a disused cutting. Too expensive to fill in and replough, it is left undisturbed, as a nature reserve.

ECHOES OF THE PAST
(below) Unsuitable for any other use, a Victorian railway station stands deserted, overlooking an abandoned country line. Although the rails have been removed, the ballast remains on the trackbed, the loose limestone chippings inhibiting the growth of encroaching vegetation.

initially meant that contour-hugging lines went miles out of their way to skirt hills and valleys, involving tight, slow curves that made fast working impossible. But as train speeds and fare-paying passenger traffic increased this became intolerable, and by the 1840s the continuous 'direct' route was adopted – a far more expensive option, which involved colossal engineering works in the form of viaducts, embankments, cuttings and tunnels. A celebrated example of this approach is the 73-mile Settle to Carlisle railway – scheduled for closure – which was carved out of the fells of eastern Cumbria in the 1870s at a cost of £47,500 per mile; at relative cost, the most expensive stretch of railway ever built in Britain.

CHANGING THE LANDSCAPE

We take these engineering feats for granted on a working railway, but on a disused line they can be seen for what they really are – a complete redefining of the local landscape, introducing cliffs, ravines, and great linear earthworks which have become havens for wild plants and animals in retreat from intensive agriculture and relentless urbanization. In industrial areas old railway cuttings often act as unofficial nature reserves, their steep sides pockmarked with rabbit burrows and the occasional fox's earth; a tangle of brambles and wild rose.

Many of the old railways remain in this state because it is simply too much trouble to do anything else with them. Although the British Rail Property Board has sold most of the land, few of the new landowners will go to the expense of filling in cuttings or flattening embankments. They often buy because the railway crosses their property – not because they need the land. Sometimes the overgrown trackbed is valued for shooting; more often it is used as a dump for rubbish or a convenient site for a few caravans; only rarely does it become an official long-distance footpath or cycle track.

Nature Walk

As you walk along a deserted line, look out for relics which give a clue to its past life, such as:

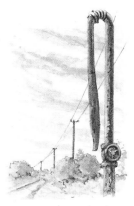

WATER CRANE'S leather hose used to fill locomotives in the days of steam.

STONE RAMP built to herd cattle, or to unload quarried stone into waggons.

BOUNDARY MARKING showing which company owned the line.

MARKER POSTS showing distances in chains, made before selling off the land.

Along Lost Lines

Deserted railway lines, like linear nature reserves, provide an increasingly valuable refuge for a range of wildlife as varied as the countryside through which they pass.

Scrambling down the embankment of a deserted railway line you enter a strangely linear world, often only yards wide but miles long. These wild green lanes, which track through some of Britain's most beautiful backwaters, unify a diversity of habitats which reflect the countryside through which they pass.

In summer the banks are bright with colour and the air is heavy with scent as cow parsley waves its frothy flowers above a grassy sward dotted with purple vetches scrambling up amongst the moon-faced ox-eye daisies and golden buttercups. It is worth pausing briefly to try and determine which of the ten or so buttercups found in the British isles, these are, as the different types are good indicators of the degree of moisture in the soil. Bulbous buttercup, for example, so called because of its bulb-like swollen basal stem, is found on dry soils and prefers lime, whereas creeping buttercup loves damp soils and differs from the meadow buttercup in favouring bare ground.

The flora will generally be typical of the local area. However the economy of 'cut and fill' engineering can transport materials some distance, and with Britain's varied geology, it is possible to find some surprises. Strapwort has only one truly native habitat, in Slapton Ley, Devon, but has been found on inland railways.

The structures built to carry the railway across difficult terrain have also become a habitat for certain plants, notably ferns. Brittle bladder fern is native to the rugged areas of the north and west but the railway has spread it to the south and east lowland areas.

Another, more familiar, railway line traveller is Oxford ragwort. Introduced to the Oxford botanical gardens from southern Italy where it is a native of volcanic soils, it was first recorded growing wild in Oxford in 1794 and by 1879 had spread as far as Reading along the Great Western Railway. It is now a common sight throughout Britain.

Other 'escapes' from cultivation to be found along the railway, either from adjacent gardens or from when wartime allotments were common on railway land, are everlasting pea and Michaelmas daisy, golden rod and red hot poker.

Relatively free from the effects of farmers' spraying as well as the traditional burning,

TRACKSIDE TUNNELS
Keeping the grass down long after the line has been deserted, rabbits thrive on the overgrown embankments. Tunnelling easily into the soft banks, they rapidly establish sprawling warrens from which they spread along the line and into surrounding pasture land.

LIFE ON THE LINE

Not long after the passing of the last train, nature begins to reclaim the deserted line. Ash and birch, planted to stabilize the banks, grow tall beside a laburnum – a garden escape – and attract woodland birds to nest and feed. Unmanaged, the trackside grasses are lit up with flowers among which nectar feeding bees compete with butterflies. Reedmace and marsh orchid grow beside pools which attract moorhen. A lizard basks in the sun while a grass snake slithers from the pool. Tunnelling into the embankment, rabbits, badgers and sand martins make their home, but for the horseshoe bat the man-made tunnel provides the perfect roost.

KEY TO SPECIES

1 Holly blue	14 Rusty back fern	27 Large skipper
2 Gatekeeper butterfly	15 Badger	28 Large red damselfly
3 Sand martins	16 Lords and ladies	29 Plume moth
4 Ash	17 Horsetail	30 Mining bees
5 Silver birch	18 Grass snake	31 Yellow rattle
6 Willow warbler	19 Moorhen	32 Small copper
7 Speckled bush cricket	20 Song thrush	33 Hunting spider
8 Dog rose	21 Rabbits	34 Cock pheasant
9 Honey bee	22 Pyramidal orchid	35 Amber snail
10 Whitethroat	23 Marsh orchids	36 Common lizard
11 Laburnum	24 Frog	37 Cowslip
12 Horseshoe bat	25 Common centaury	38 Bloody-nosed beetle
13 Reedmace	26 Oat grass	39 Crab spider

169

STATION PLANTS
(left) As old station buildings slowly decay, the crumbling stonework is colonized by specialist plants such as stonecrop (centre) – more commonly found in dry rocky habitats – while climbers such as ivy and damp, shade-loving ferns each find a niche along the platform's edge.

BRANCH LINE CHAFFINCH
(below) A bird of Britain's rapidly diminishing natural woodland, the seed-eating chaffinch has been quick to exploit the overgrown railway line both for food and as a safe corridor along which it can travel from one isolated woodland to another. And as trees and shrubs slowly succeed the grass and scrub, the line can also become a valuable nesting site for forest fringe and hedgerow birds.

slashing or spraying regimes of management, the cuttings and embankments are once again ablaze with typical grassland plants. Abandoned railways are much richer reservoirs of plants than other corridor habitats such as motorways due to their greater age and history. Seed sources were much more plentiful in the nineteenth century when railways were first built, and many species established themselves on the newly formed embankments. Today the use of herbicides on farmed land has decimated our native wild flowers and hence the stock available for colonizing newly formed earthworks is substantially reduced.

MIXED WOODLAND

Wooded areas on embankments are of relatively recent origin and so do not usually display the richness of our native woodlands. Trees and shrubs were encouraged on embankments to stabilize the soil. The bladder senna shrub is one which was widely planted. In more urban areas sycamore dominates, an introduced tree much maligned by naturalists because it supports less than 20 species of insects compared to our native oak's generous support of nearly 300. Rivalling the common sycamore, comes ash; both trees have winged seeds which are dispersed on the wind.

Where ash predominates the ground flora is much less impoverished than under sycamore, as ash casts a much lighter shade, and comes into leaf later. The spring flowers of our native woodland edges – primrose, ramsons, bluebells and wood avens – can often be found.

The butterflies benefit from the warmth and shelter of the cutting. It is possible to find at least ten different types along an old railway in summer. The most easily recognized are prob-

ably the red admiral, painted lady, the large white and small white butterflies. Others worth looking out for are the common blue, meadow brown, gatekeeper and small tortoiseshell. The dense banks of ivy which smother old railway buildings, particularly in more urban areas, are a vital source of nectar for late flying insects as the flowers bloom in autumn. Bramble is also valuable as a food source and cover for small mammals and birds as well as insects.

Amongst the myriad insects inhabiting the railway, are hover flies. The adult hover fly feeds upon nectar but its larvae prey upon aphids – each one consuming up to 1000. Aphids are an important food source for another attractive insect, the ladybird. The ladybird belongs to the biggest group of insects, the beetles. Different types of beetle feed on both living and decaying matter and are a vital part of the food chain. The wasp beetle, so called because of its yellow and black colouring, belongs to the longhorn group of beetles, identified by the long antennae. It is a wood borer and is important in its grub stage as a food source for woodpeckers.

Birds which make use of the railway line do so because it is a readily available source of nourishment, with insects and the seeds and fruits of plants, and for the larger birds of prey, small mammals such as voles and mice. Others will find a roost there or suitable nest sites. The birds add another dimension to the pleasure of walking abandoned railway lines, comple-

WORRIED WOOD MOUSE
Easily recognizable by its large ears and pale underside, the wood, or long-tailed field-, mouse is a common resident of the woodland fringe, leaving its burrow at night to feed on insects and plant shoots, buds and berries. Extremely fastidious at all times, the wood mouse will also groom its fur and three-inch long tail when frightened.

GLOW WORM
This insect is not a worm but a female wingless beetle which advertises its presence to its winged mate with a greenish glow generated by a chemical reaction.

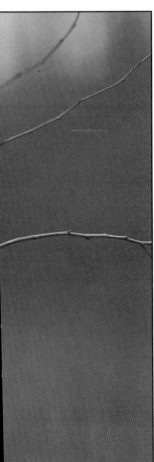

TRACKSIDE FLOWERS
(below right) For the first few years after desertion the grassy trackside often resembles a flower meadow as the open sward of grass allows (clockwise from bottom) primrose, false oxlip and cowslip to brighten the embankments with their subtly different shades of yellow. But left unmanaged, more aggressive grasses, such as fescues, and scrub, dominated by bramble and blackthorn, soon prevail, reducing the diversity of the flora.

menting the visual display of plants with their song. The warblers are notable songsters, and as summer visitors to Britain make their nests in dense vegetation near the ground. Charms of bright goldfinches can be seen in autumn feeding on the seed heads of teasels or thistle. Where woodland has developed one may see, or more likely hear, the elegant long-tailed tit, greater spotted woodpecker or chirpy bullfinch. The tawny owl may occasionally be seen at dusk hunting for small rodents along the line of the railway. Bats, too, often swoop through the darkening skies hunting for insects caught up in warm drifts of air. When sufficiently dry and draught free, tunnels provide ideal roosts for these protected creatures.

INTER-CITY SCAVENGER

The fox has also used the railway to good effect. Coming into the fringes of cities, it has benefited from the rich pickings of our wasteful consumer society. The fox is omnivorous and the railway provides it with a good hunting ground for berries, small mammals such as voles and mice, the eggs of ground nesting birds as well as beetles and earthworms, although a significant proportion of the urban fox's diet is made up of fat-bodied moths.

Badgers will make the railway their home if it is sufficiently secluded and has banks in which they can excavate their extensive network of underground passages. Their favoured habitat is woodland near to pasture and occasionally the combination may be provided by the incidence of the abandoned railway. Like foxes they are nocturnal and omnivorous, feeding mainly on earthworms.

With the loss of hundreds of miles of hedgerow and acres of woodland, disused railway lines have become increasingly important as linear nature reserves – thin green lines along which species of the woodland fringe can gain some measure of security.

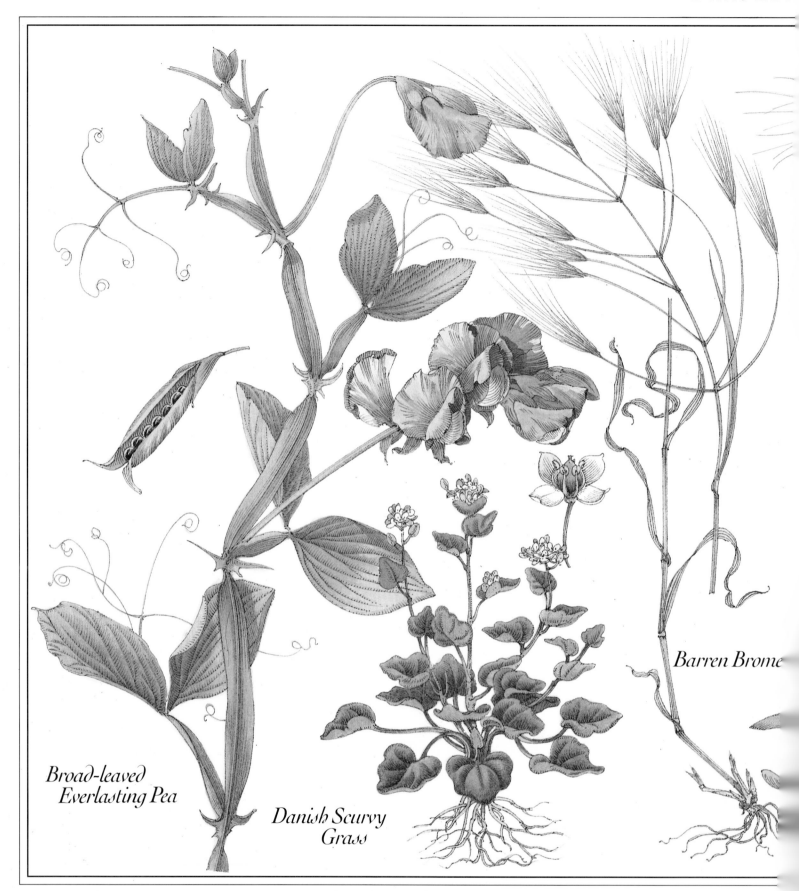

Broad-leaved
Everlasting Pea

Danish Scurvy
Grass

Barren Brome

**BROAD-LEAVED
EVERLASTING PEA** (*Lathyrus
latifolius*) A tall, 80″ (200cm)
perennial which climbs using
tendrils. Stems are winged and the
leaves divided into oval leaflets. A
garden escape now seen on wastes
in South. It flowers June to August.

DANISH SCURVY GRASS
(*Cochlearia danica*) Chiefly found
on coastal cliffs and shores, this 4-
8″ (10-20cm) annual also occurs
inland, growing on the shingle on
railway tracks. Leaves are stalked
and fleshy, the lowest heart-shaped.
Flowers open February to June.

BARREN BROME (*Bromus
sterilis*) Growing as single stems or
in open tufts to 40″ (100cm), this
annual or biennial grass is
widespread and common in
lowland Britain. Purple tinged
leaves have short hairs, and loose
drooping, flowers seen May – July.

Great Horsetail

Garden Lupin

Narrow-leaved Meadow-Grass

GARDEN LUPIN (*Lupinus polyphyllus*) Increasingly common beside railways and roads, this 24-48″ (61-120cm) garden escape originally came from North America. Perennial, with tall flower-spikes June-July on upright stems, its palmate leaves have 9-16 leaflets.

GREAT HORSETAIL (*Equisetum telmateia*) Widespread but local, rare in Scotland, this perennial grows in damp chalky shaded places. 40-80″ (1-2m) pale, sterile stems with many branches appear in spring, shorter unbranched fertile stems are brownish. Spores shed in April.

NARROW-LEAVED MEADOW-GRASS (*Poa angustifolia*) Most common in southern England on dry gravel banks, chalky or sandy hills, this perennial grass grows in small tufts 8-24″ (20-60cm). Leaves are slender and stiff, the purplish and spreading flowerheads open April-June.

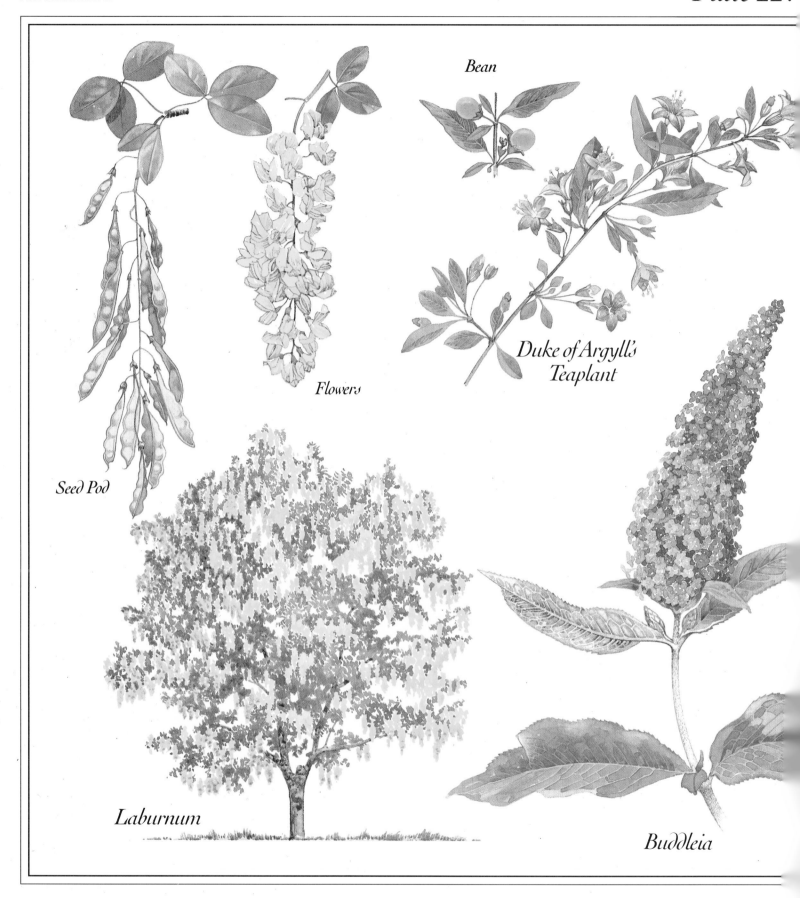

Bean

Duke of Argyll's
Teaplant

Flowers

Seed Pod

Laburnum

Buddleia

LABURNUM *(Laburnum anagyroides)* Popular in gardens, where drooping sprays of blooms are most attractive May and June, this small tree up to 23′ (7m) is self-sown on banks and waysides. All parts are poisonous, particularly the seeds borne in long pods.

DUKE OF ARGYLL'S TEAPLANT *(Lycium barbarum)* Naturalized in hedgebanks throughout England, the arching stems of this 3-10′ (1-3m) shrub have scattered spines. Narrow leaves are bluish-green and small flowers, June-September, are followed by oval red berries.

BUDDLEIA *(Buddleia davidii)* Growing on derelict sites and by railways even in the heart of cities, this 3- 16′ (1-5m) garden escape has toothed leaves, cottony below. Long narrow heads of numerous tiny flowers appear June-October, and attract butterflies.

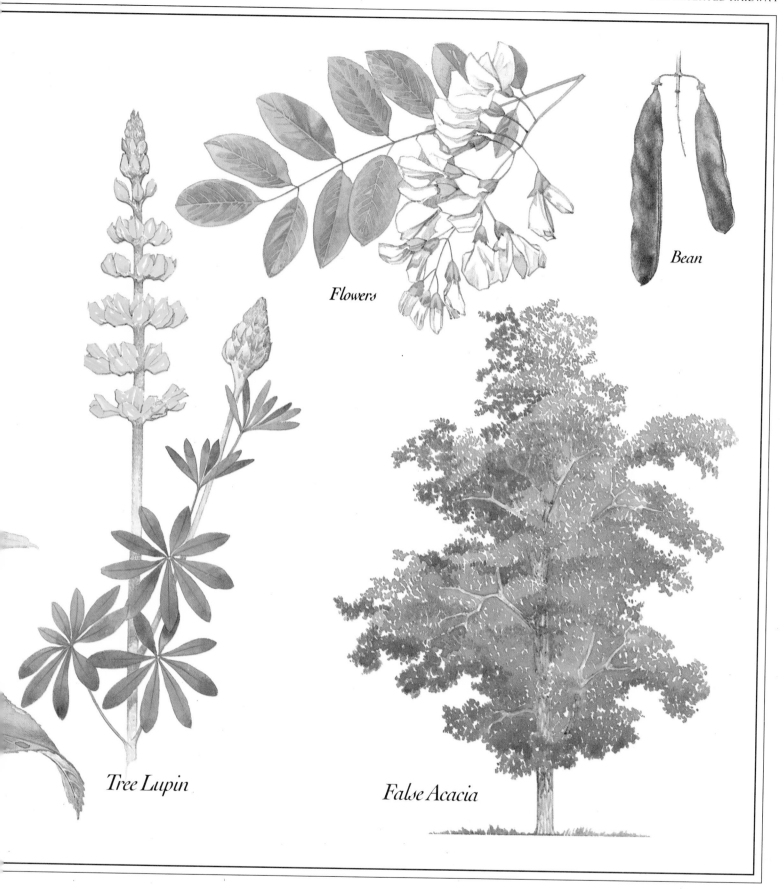

Flowers

Bean

Tree Lupin

False Acacia

TREE LUPIN (*Lupinus arboreus*) A garden escape now established on sandy or stony wasteland and banks, mostly in the South and East, this woody shrub reaches 10′ (3m). Its erect branches bear tall spikes of flowers June-September, and leaves with 7-11 leaflets, silky below.

FALSE ACACIA (*Robinia pseudacacia*) An open-crowned tree to 80′ (25m), often planted, it can spread freely by means of suckers. It is most common on sandy soils of the South and Midlands. Drooping sprays of fragrant blossoms open in June. Twigs bear short spines.

The Field Vole

A timid inhabitant of lush grassland, the field vole spends
its brief life within the confines of a small territory,
ever mindful of the predators who pose a constant threat.

Amongst the thick lush grass at the edge of an overgrown railway track, a small solitary creature emerges from a hidden nest and stops, nose twitching to sniff the air, before scampering on to feed on the succulent stems of the tall grass. It is a field vole (also known as the short-tailed vole), one of the most abundant of Britain's small rodents.

Greyish-brown on the upper parts, dull white or grey below, the field vole has small eyes and ears and a blunt snout. The head and body measure 3½-4 inches (90-115mm) when fully grown, and the tail 1-1¼ inches (30-45mm). These small creatures weigh little more than half an ounce (17g) in winter, but increase their weight in spring in readiness for the breeding season, the male fattening up to 1½oz (42g) and the female to 1oz (28g).

FANTASTIC FECUNDITY

The field vole is noted for its high reproductive rate – in theory, a pair of voles could generate 700 or more descendants in a single breeding season. Consequently, the species is widespread in England, Scotland and Wales, though it is absent from Ireland and many of our outlying islands.

In spring, the female builds a nest of shredded grass leaves at ground level, and her first litter – of four to six naked and helpless young –

TERRITORIAL VOLE
The field vole makes its home in areas of long rough grass in the proximity of a large number of its kind, but defends its own small territory with aggressive determination. Field voles are the staff of life for a whole host of predators, including foxes and owls, but these make little impression on their population, which is constantly buoyed up by a prolific reproductive rate.

A TINY HERBIVORE *(right) One of the most specialized and highly evolved species of rodent, the little field vole is a strict herbivore, specifically adapted to feed on the green leaves and grasses which form its staple diet. Grass is both tough to chew and difficult to digest, and unlike other rodents that live on diets of meat, seed or fruit, the field vole has molar teeth which grow from the bottom as quickly as they wear away at the top.*

piles of greenish droppings in the runways to signal its presence to other voles.

Field voles have eventful social lives; big mature males have home ranges which might include the home ranges of several females. If one of these dominant animals meets another male they are quite likely to fight. With quick, darting movements, they approach each other, tails high, bodies held high off the ground and the fur on the backs bristling. They gnash their teeth, and a fight might ensue, with boxing, wrestling and biting. A young vole may quickly submit by throwing himself on to his back in front of the dominant vole, who respects this signal of submission and withdraws. Females are only aggressive in the last stages of pregnancy and when they are nursing a litter.

VOLE PLAGUES

Unlike all other British rodents, field voles show very wide fluctuations in numbers; in many areas there is a population explosion once every three to five years. On the European mainland, this can lead to 'vole plagues', noticeable when countless thousands of these creatures cause massive damage to crops. In Britain such plagues are not generally a problem – the last one occurred in the Scottish borders during the 1890s, when the field voles did so much damage to pastures that sheep had to be moved elsewhere to graze; the tiny herbivore totally out-ate the bigger one.

No one knows why or how vole population explosions happen – it is one of the unsolved problems of mammal ecology. And although high concentrations attract large numbers of predators – foxes, weasels, stoats, kestrels, buzzards, harriers and owls – these are not the main cause of reducing the plague population. It may be that this ill-understood phenomenon is a means of satiating the appetites of the predators, so that at least some of the voles can extend their range and breed in new areas.

appears in April. The youngs' eyes open in a fortnight and they are weaned about a week later. By then, the females of the litter can be sexually mature and may easily become pregnant within a few days of leaving the nest. The mother mates again as soon as she has given birth, and within three weeks gives birth again. With an average life expectancy of just 7½ months only those voles born in late summer are likely to survive to breed the next spring.

From the nest, a system of runways spreads in all directions, tunnelling under the surface of the ground and winding through the vegetation. This is the vole's home range, which it patrols and defends for 24 hours of the day, leaving

MOTHER AND BABES *(below) The female builds a nest of shredded grass at the base of grass tussocks or under logs lying in the long grass. She produces four or five litters of four to six young between April and September: those born early in the season usually breed the same year and rarely survive until winter.*

A NEAR RELATION
(below) Occasionally found amongst the long grass favoured by the field vole, the bank vole is distinguishable by its reddish coat, its smaller, more pointed head and shorter tail.

The Slow-worm

The harmless slow-worm is a common inhabitant of deserted
railway embankments. Always alert for predators, it seeks shelter,
in thick cover and is only rarely seen in the open.

Something moves in the long grass on the slopes of a deserted railway embankment. The stems undulate gently as if a snake is weaving its way through them. Eventually, where the grass gives way to a bare patch of earth, a slow-worm emerges, slowly slithering from cover to bask where the summer sun's rays warm the ground.

Despite their name and their appearance, slow-worms are neither slow nor are they worms – nor indeed are they snakes: they are legless lizards. Slow-worms have several features which indicate their relation to lizards; they have broad, flat tongues – unlike the long, thin or forked tongues of snakes; they can also close their eyes and have the ability to break off their tails (a process called 'autotomy') – neither of which snakes can do. The slow-worm's relation to lizards can be further seen in their skeletons, which show vestiges of the bones to which the front legs would have been attached.

Like the common lizard, the slow-worm is common throughout England, Scotland and Wales, but is not found in Ireland. Its favoured habitats are those with a good cover of vegetation such as hedgerows, roadside verges, overgrown gardens and especially railway embankments. This last type of habitat is particularly to their liking because of the dry, well-drained slopes. The slow-worm's liking for railway embankments has even enabled it to colonize parts of central London.

In common with its relatives, the slow-worm's slender body is covered with overlapping shiny scales, giving its skin a smooth, polished gloss which is sometimes mistaken for sliminess. Generally coppery-brown in colour, the males have a more uniform appearance with some dark mottling on their under-surface. The slightly larger females have dark stripes along their back and sides, and dark brown flanks. Some of the older males develop ornamental blue spots, the reason for which is unknown.

SNAKE IN THE GRASS?
(above) Once thought to be a snake, the slow-worm is actually a member of the lizard family. However, unlike other lizards, its ear holes are not external, legs are absent and its smooth, polished scales give it a shinier coat than that of its reptilian relatives. The slow-worm is to be found in habitats with abundant vegetation, such as hedge banks, roadside verges and railway embankments.

NEW-BORN

(above) Slow-worms are born encased in their egg-membrane but hatch out in a few seconds. The young, average about 3in. long, and emerge a brighter colour than their parents.

Slow-worms can grow up to 16″ (40cm) long, the largest recorded being 19½″ (49cm).

The slow-worm's ability to shed its tail is an effective means of escaping predators. The tail wriggles for some time after it has been shed, attracting the attention of the predator while the animal makes off quietly into the undergrowth. The truncated stump eventually grows a new tip, albeit somewhat reduced in size.

WINTER HIBERNATION

Being cold-blooded creatures, slow-worms are forced to escape the rigours of winter by hibernating from October to March in an underground chamber. The first mild weather of spring causes them to wake and return to the surface, and it is at this time that they are most often seen basking in the sunshine. Slow-worms bask out of necessity for without external heat their bodies cannot reach the required temperature to enable their vital systems to function.

Mating takes place in April and May and is quite a vigorous affair. Initially, the male grasps the female with his mouth and in response, she

DEAD SKIN

Like snakes and lizards, slow-worms periodically slough (shed) their surface layer of skin (below). As their skin does not stretch, they have to slough it in order to grow.

MATING DANCE

(above) Slow-worms mate in the spring, after the winter period spent in hibernation. The male clasps the female with his mouth and the two lie coiled together for several hours.

coils around him. The pair remain locked in this embrace for several hours. The young slow-worms develop inside the female's body and are not born until late summer. The length of time involved depends largely upon the temperature – the greater the heat, the quicker the eggs develop.

Birth often takes place in a warm safe retreat, such as a compost heap, and for the first few moments of life the young remain encased in egg-membranes. These membranes quickly rupture and the 10-15 young emerge, dispersing almost immediately to go in search of food. Young slow-worms are born a more golden colour than the coppery-brown adults, and have a black dorsal stripe.

The food of both adults and young consists largely of invertebrates such as slugs, snails, spiders and insects. Due to their poor eyesight, movement is the key factor which enables slow-worms to spot their prey. Slow-worms themselves fall prey to many animals; and even domestic cats are all more than ready to make a meal of an unsuspecting slow-worm. In captivity, slow-worms have been known to live for up to 50 years, but in the wild the perils they face reduce life expectancy to just a few years.

The Golf Course

Long, open fairways spotted with sandy bunkers, smooth, close-cropped greens and surrounding rough – long grass, heather or gorse – are all familiar features of the golf course, and now account for some 250,000 acres of the British countryside. These diverse elements of the modern golf course originated from the natural links of the Scottish coast, where golf was first played. But as the game grew increasingly popular they were recreated artificially inland, redefining the local landscape and providing new habitats for wildlife in town and country.

THE GOLFING LANDSCAPE
Today, golf courses are found in every type of landscape – on commons and heaths, at the heart of conurbations, on sites in the open countryside and on the coast, where the game first developed. Although the appearance of courses differs according to the nature of the surrounding countryside, they all exhibit similar characteristics which are created artificially, though usually in sympathy with the local landscape.

Golf courses are widespread throughout Britain and occur almost anywhere where there is a centre of population within easy reach. Smaller towns almost certainly have a golf course on their outskirts, and larger cities may have several. A glance at the map of Greater London reveals 85 courses. There are well over 1200 courses in England, 380 in Scotland, 120 in Wales, 78 in Ulster and 160 in the Republic of Ireland.

Although no two golf courses are identical, they all share the same basic features: large open expanses of grass, often landscaped into gentle rolling hills, occasional sand bunkers and smaller areas of flat, short-cropped grass known as greens. On larger courses small copses, streams, lakes, bushes and shrubs often appear so well established that it is difficult to believe that the course is not a natural landscape, but one constructed artificially purely for the sport of golf.

THE ORIGINAL LINKS

The reason that most modern courses share such remarkably similar characteristics is because their features all derive from the 400 year old 'Old Course' at St Andrews in Scotland, where the first recorded game of golf was played in 1552. The site of this course is an area of land known as the links – wild, rough, sheep-grazing land on the coast, which was created when the sea receded after the last Ice Age. This undulating wilderness was gradually colonized by gorse and heather; fine grasses grew on the better drained raised ground and sandy depressions occured where sheep sheltered from the wind.

As the possibilities for playing golf on the links became known, other Scottish clubs (like Leith and Edinburgh) were founded on similar terrain, and golf spread rapidly throughout Scotland. The game was slower to develop in England: although an early society was formed at Blackheath, near London, in 1608, it was not until the 19th century that the sport became popular. Courses in England did not imitate the Scottish ones at first – early players simply dug holes from day to day. When courses were deliberately designed, usually by ex-professional golfers turned course architects, they tended towards a formal garden design, with square tees, oblong bunkers and smartly shaped greens.

But towards the end of the 19th century there was a reaction against this formal approach, and courses began to take on a more natural

LINKS WITH THE PAST
(below) The features of modern-day courses all originate from the natural landscape of the seaside links, which provided ideal conditions for the development of the game. Short, springy turf grew on the well-drained raised areas of sandy ground, while the undulating terrain, sandy bunkers and rough, gorse or heather-covered ground, provided exciting natural hazards. There are many links courses to this day.

Many an historical landmark lies tucked away on golf courses around Britain. Look for:

BRUCE'S CASTLE once a base for Robert the Bruce, now in ruins at the ninth hole at Turnberry, signposted by a lighthouse.

CAESAR'S CAMP the remains of an Iron Age fort which stood near the 7th, 10th and 11th holes at Wimbledon.

INSPECTION POINTS at Coombe Hill, Kingston, built for Cardinal Wolsey's water supply line around 1520.

GRIM'S DYKE at Pinner, the only important earthwork in Middlesex – a frontier between hostile tribes around 400AD.

appearance. Inland courses, based on the natural links, began to appear, with varying degrees of success. At first many town courses were built on unsuitable loamy soil, and the ground became boggy during the winter months and rock hard during the summer. Other courses were built on rougher, but better drained, stretches of heathland. Britain's first successful inland course was the Royal Wimbledon, built on the common in 1865. Sunningdale in Berkshire was another notable heathland course, built in 1900.

Today, golf courses are found in every type of landscape – by the sea, in built-up urban areas, in the open countryside. Many started out very remote from the original links type course, and because hazards such as water courses, lakes and sand bunkers did not occur naturally they had to be introduced. Courses are generally created in sympathy with the surrounding countryside and existing features such as woodland are retained where they can be incorporated into the overall design. The resulting diversity of habitats provides an important refuge for many birds and animals, especially in the otherwise spartan environment of our sprawling conurbations.

RICH DIVERSITY *(above) The diverse elements of the golf course ensure a variety of habitats for wildlife species. This is especially true of town and inland courses, where hazards like sandy bunkers and water obstacles are created artificially and may be unique in the area. Grass left deliberately uncut at the edge of the fairway is also a valuable refuge for many small mammals.*

Around the Links

The golf course's mix of natural and man-made habitats bustles with wildlife and – in the suburban setting – provides a welcome stretch of open countryside among the surrounding houses.

A spinney of tall, closely planted oak and ash shelters a monotonously crooning stock dove and rings with the laugh of a green woodpecker. The waving grasses of meadowland are alive with orange, brown and blue butterflies, while high above, a skylark churns out its musical-box song. A blackcap warbles from a hawthorn hedge and, sheltered deep within a derelict barn, a dozing owl opens one round eye and shifts position. Swallows dip and swoop over a pond, catching insects, and blue and brown dragonflies hawk up and down the meandering stream.

These varied natural habitats can all be found around a golf course, maintained as a setting for the greens and fairways of the course proper, and providing a challenge for the golfer who hits the ball off line.

ON THE SHORT TURF

The informal and natural appearance of the rough contrasts markedly with the mown grass of the fairways and the velvety sward of the greens. But these too attract wildlife, being valuable feeding grounds for birds. Food is more accessible to ground-feeding birds in short grass, and they prefer to forage in the open, where they can see approaching predators.

Noisy flocks of starlings strut about and probe the turf with their sharp beaks. Dapper black-headed gulls, which roost on a nearby reservoir, come here to feed, especially in winter. And if the greens are watered, they attract young rooks in summer when feeding is difficult on the dry, hard soil of arable land.

All these birds are picking from the turf the root-feeding insects which cause headaches for groundsmen by interfering with grass quality. There are the rather greasy-looking, fat caterpillars of yellow underwing moths, shiny wireworms, which develop into click beetles, and leatherjackets, the elongated larvae of crane-flies. Sometimes in autumn the adult crane-flies, or daddy-long-legs, are particularly abundant, clinging to long grass stems and, when disturbed, taking ungainly flight, trailing their long legs.

Fairy ring champignons emerge in the grass from spring until autumn. The ring widens year by year as the underground, thread-like hyphae move out into rich, unexploited soil beyond the circle already exhausted of nutrients. Much of the plant is below ground, forming a branch-like network. The visible fungi are temporary

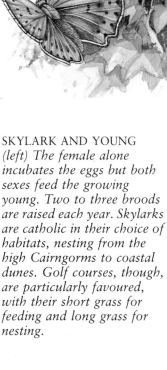

SKYLARK AND YOUNG
(left) The female alone incubates the eggs but both sexes feed the growing young. Two to three broods are raised each year. Skylarks are catholic in their choice of habitats, nesting from the high Cairngorms to coastal dunes. Golf courses, though, are particularly favoured, with their short grass for feeding and long grass for nesting.

WILDLIFE AROUND THE GOLF COURSE

The pond provides a safe breeding site for frogs, newts and sticklebacks, as well as territorial dragonflies and damselflies. The reed bunting and moorhen – which may be seen feeding on the fairways – nest in waterside vegetation. Of the butterflies, the small copper, holly blue and green hairstreak all hold territories and will chase away other species. In the dry, sandy bank mining bees and rabbits make their burrows, and elder – unpalatable to rabbits – and gorse grow here. The dunnock feeds on the ground near cover but mistle thrushes and flocks of rooks, gulls and starlings seek insects on the fairways and greens. Voles fall prey to the kestrel and to the tawny owl, which will also take roosting finches.

KEY TO FEATURES AND SPECIES

1 Holly
2 Rookery
3 Kestrel
4 Tawny owl
5 Relic hedge
6 Greenfinch
7 Silver birch
8 Mistle thrush
9 Black-headed gulls
10 Starlings
11 Ancient pollard
12 Holly blue
13 Meadow brown

14 Brown hare
15 Gorse
16 Green hairstreak
17 Elder
18 Ivy
19 Moorhen
20 Cock reed bunting
21 Green-veined white
22 Skylark's nest
23 Brown aeshna
24 Small copper
25 Yellow water-lily
26 Brooklime

27 Cuckoo flower
28 Mining bee
29 Rabbit burrow
30 Blue-tailed damselfly
31 Common frog
32 Sweet flag
33 Dunnock
34 Harebells
35 Three-spined stickleback
36 Water horsetail
37 Common newt
38 Field vole

and are pushed up to distribute the reproductive spores.

Elsewhere, puffballs have erupted from the
ground, to release dust-like clouds of fine
spores when prodded. And there may be clusters
of delicate, slender-stalked liberty caps, the
halucenogenic 'magic mushrooms'.

If undisturbed, the sandy soil at the edge of
bunkers is excavated by furry, rufous-coloured
mining bees. They are solitary bees, although
there may be several burrows close together.

IN THE ROUGH

Away from the rigours of the mowing machine,
plants grow unhindered. Drifts of ox-eye daisies
star the long grass among which harebells nestle.
The sturdy flower spikes of pyramidal orchids
gleam rosy-purple amid the grass stems, and
spikes of yellow rattle, like little yellow snap-
dragons, sway in the breeze. Yellow rattle is a
semi-parasite, absorbing some of its nutrients
from grass roots.

The grassy expanses are being invaded by
birch scrub, which if unchecked will shade and
alter the habitat. Now it is sunny, open meadowland, buzzing with bumble bees and hoverflies feeding at pignut, hogweed and other
umbellifers. All around are bursts of rasping
song produced by small, brown grasshoppers
rubbing their hind legs against strengthened
areas on their wings.

Tents of silk on the grasses, supported within
scaffolding-like webs, house the eggs or tiny
spiderlings of *Pisaura mirabilis*. The mother is a
slender, greyish spider with a black-edged pale
stripe along her body. She rests near her nursery
in a characteristic pose, with her two front pairs
of legs close together and held out at an angle of
30°. On autumn mornings, the sun sparkles on
dew trapped in thousands of small horizontal
webs constructed by money spiders.

Rabbits, which feed at dusk and dawn on the
deserted fairways, have excavated a maze of

NATTERJACK TOAD
*(above) Distinguished from
the common toad by the
yellow stripe down its back,
the rare natterjack toad is a
protected species. Most at
home in the warmth of Spain
or France, natterjacks are
found only in the warmer
parts of Britain where
they favour the warm
sandy soils of heaths and
sand dunes. They spend most
of the day in a sandy burrow,
the males emerging at night
to croak noisily to attract
females.*

YELLOW RATTLE
*(right) So-called because its
seeds rattle in their capsule,
this plant is common in
grassland, flowering from
May to August.*

GREEN WOODPECKER
*(below right) The largest of
Britain's woodpeckers (none
breed in Ireland), the green
woodpecker is very much at
home on the golf course.
Unlike the two spotted
woodpeckers it spends a
good deal of time feeding on
the ground, eating
caterpillars and spiders but
searching especially for ants.
The short turf of the fairway,
where the ground is warmed
by the sun, holds large and
varied populations of ants,
especially in heathy areas.*

burrows in a sandy slope. Yellow ragwort,
downy, maroon-flowered hound's-tongue, and
stately foxgloves flourish here, as rabbits find
their leaves distasteful. For the same reason,
elder with its creamy heads of fruity-smelling
flowers, thrives in the ancient boundary hedge
atop the slope. White bryony, with its cucumber-
like leaves, climbs and twines up the hawthorn
and blackthorn.

The thick hedge shelters nesting robins,
dunnocks and blackbirds; a pugnacious blue tit
carols from a topmost branch; and a diminutive
wren gives its breathless, musical jingle. Tent-
like webs of silk on hawthorns and brambles
house hundreds of colourful, hairy caterpillars,
which eventually defoliate the bushes. They will
develop into brown-tail moths. These whitish
moths have tufts of hairs on the tip of the
abdomen, which the female sheds to cover and
protect her eggs.

On the stream banks is a froth of fragrant

meadowsweet, and here and there the oblong, reddish flowerheads of great burnet or the purple, shaving-brush flowers of marsh thistles. Near the pond, where the ground is marshy, is a clump of sunshine-yellow marsh marigolds, drifts of palest pink cuckoo flowers and ranks of stiff horsetails.

A male orange tip butterfly alights to feed at a cuckoo flower, and seems to disappear from view as he closes his wings to reveal the camouflaged underside. Meadow browns flit, wraith-like, in and out of the clumps of grass, the females pausing every so often to lay an egg. Angular, orange small skippers zigzag from flower to flower. Their caterpillars, like those of meadow browns, feed on grasses.

WATER HAZARDS

In the shallows of the stream stands a heron intent on rudd in a nearby pool. It ignores the too small sticklebacks that swim around its legs. A smart, black-headed male reed bunting gives a metallic alarm call from the reeds, as a sinuous weasel trots quickly across an open patch of ground. Forewarned, a water vole plops into the water, and foraging field voles crouch motionless in their runways beneath the matted grass stems and roots.

MINING BEE
(above) Poised here at the entrance to her egg burrow, the female has arrived laden with pollen. She can carry half her own weight in pollen. Half a dozen trips are needed to stock an earthen cell with a ball of nectar and pollen on which she will lay an egg before closing the cell. Three to six cells may be made along the tunnel dug by the female. She dies after egg laying and the offspring emerge the following year.

THICK ROUGH
(above right) The dark mauve flowers of scabious brighten the long grass where many a ball has been lost. Brambles add a further hazard for the wayward golfer.

GIANT PUFFBALL
(right) This giant among fungi can grow to over 2 feet in diameter but is more commonly football-sized. Found throughout the country, often in banks and ditches bordering grassland and woods. Edible while young, white and firm, the fruiting body turns brown and powdery as it ages, sometimes exploding to release a cloud of spores into the air.

The semi-natural habitats of suburban golf courses have considerable significance for conservation, particularly of meadow plants and their associated animals. Field ponds are preserved, and with them frogs and newts, including the great crested newt.

Sandy courses on dunes, particularly in eastern and south-eastern counties, provide relatively undisturbed habitats for uncommon and endangered plants and animals. Brownish, white-spotted sand lizards bask in the sun, scuttling out of sight as you approach. Rare dune flowers, such as the curious and exotic-looking lizard orchid, bloom on at least one golf course, where a spectator stand was carefully sited so as to protect the flowers from trampling.

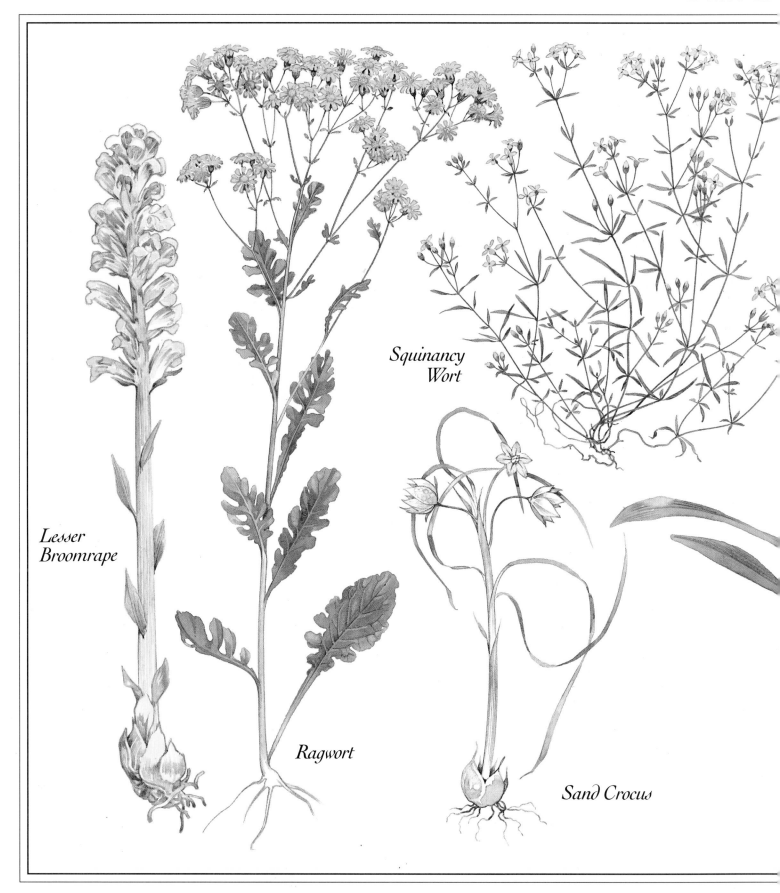

Lesser Broomrape

Squinancy Wort

Ragwort

Sand Crocus

LESSER BROOMRAPE (*Orobanche minor*) This 4-20″ (10-50cm) annual or perennial has no photosynthetic material and lives as a parasite upon members of the clover and dandelion families. It haunts grassy places, flowering from June to September.

RAGWORT (*Senecio jacobaea*) One of the most familiar flowers of rough grassland, this 6-30″ (15-75cm) perennial occurs almost everywhere. It is in flower throughout the summer and autumn. Poisonous to livestock and difficult to eradicate.

SAND CROCUS (*Romulea columnae*) On sandy soils near the sea in Devon and the Channel Isles, this little perennial bejewels short turf, including that of golf course roughs. It has slender, wiry leaves, and the solitary flowers appear in spring on 1-3″ (2-7cm) stalks.

SQUINANCY WORT (*Asperula cynanchica*) Once used as a gargle for sore throats, this tufted perennial grows in dry, grassy places, often on chalk and mainly in the South. 4-9″ (10-23cm) stems arise from a woody stock, bearing flowers from July-September.

Grassland Flowers

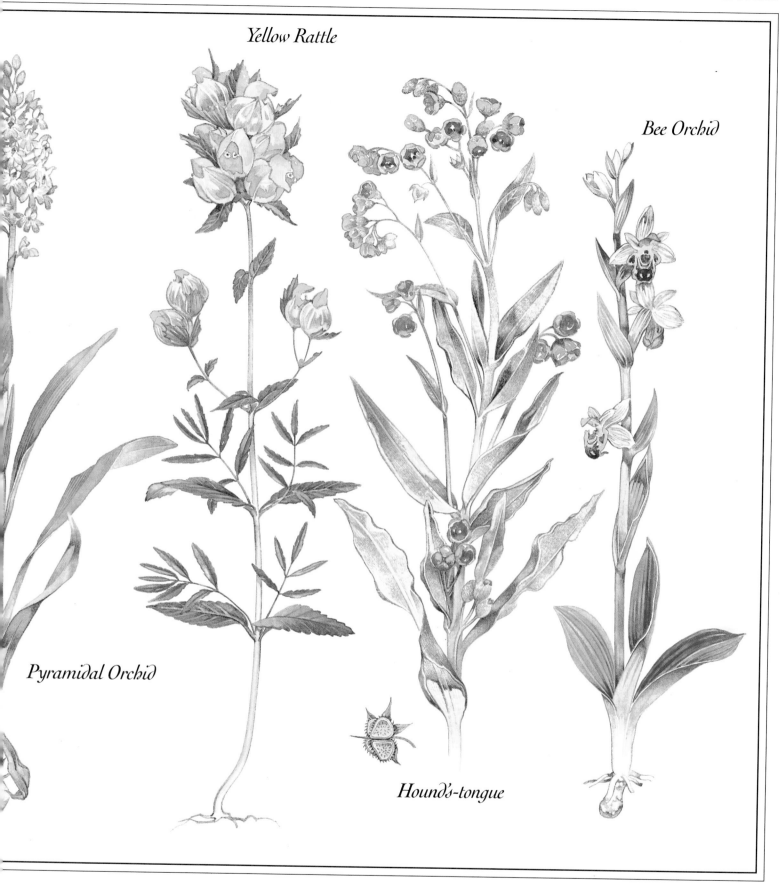

Yellow Rattle

Bee Orchid

Pyramidal Orchid

Hound's-tongue

PYRAMIDAL ORCHID
(*Anacamptis pyramidalis*) One of our more common orchids, the many-flowered heads of this widespread 8-20″ (20-50cm) perennial appear in summer in grassland – usually on chalk or limestone – and on dunes.

YELLOW RATTLE (*Rhinanthus minor*) Widespread and frequent in unimproved grassland, this 3-18″ (8-45cm) annual is a semi-parasite of grasses. The stem is often black spotted and flowers appear May – September. The name comes from the sound of the seeds in the pods.

HOUND'S-TONGUE
(*Cynoglossum officinale*) The fruits of this 1-3′ (30-90cm) biennial give it its name; they are flattened and covered in short, hooked bristles. It flowers during the summer and is found in dry rough grassland, but is uncommon in the North and West.

BEE ORCHID (*Ophrys apifera*) One of our less fussy orchids, this widespread but rather local perennial grows in a variety of grassy habitats. The 2-6 flowers, which are visited by male bumble bees, appear in June and July on a 6-18″ (15-45cm) stalk.

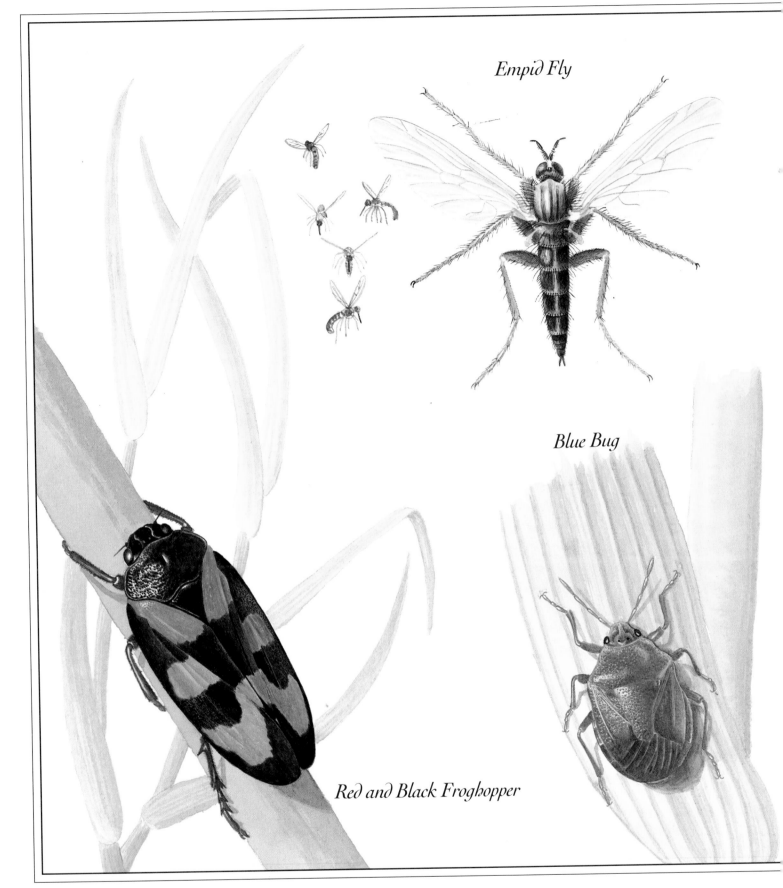

Empid Fly

Blue Bug

Red and Black Froghopper

RED & BLACK FROGHOPPER
(*Cercopis vulnerata*) The familiar
warning colours of distasteful
insects belong in this case to the
largest of our froghoppers. It is a
common species in the South and is
found upon bushes and trees. The
larvae feed on the sap of roots.

EMPID FLY (*Empis tesselata*)
Widespread and common, this fly –
the largest of our several species of
empid – appears in large numbers
throughout the summer, often
around hawthorn flowers. It feeds
partly on nectar but will also
eat other insects.

BLUE BUG (*Zicrona caerulea*) This
bug is found from mid to late
summer and is fairly common
except in the North. Eggs are laid
on a variety of plants in early
summer. The young spend their
early days in groups, but their full
life history is a mystery.

Invertebrates

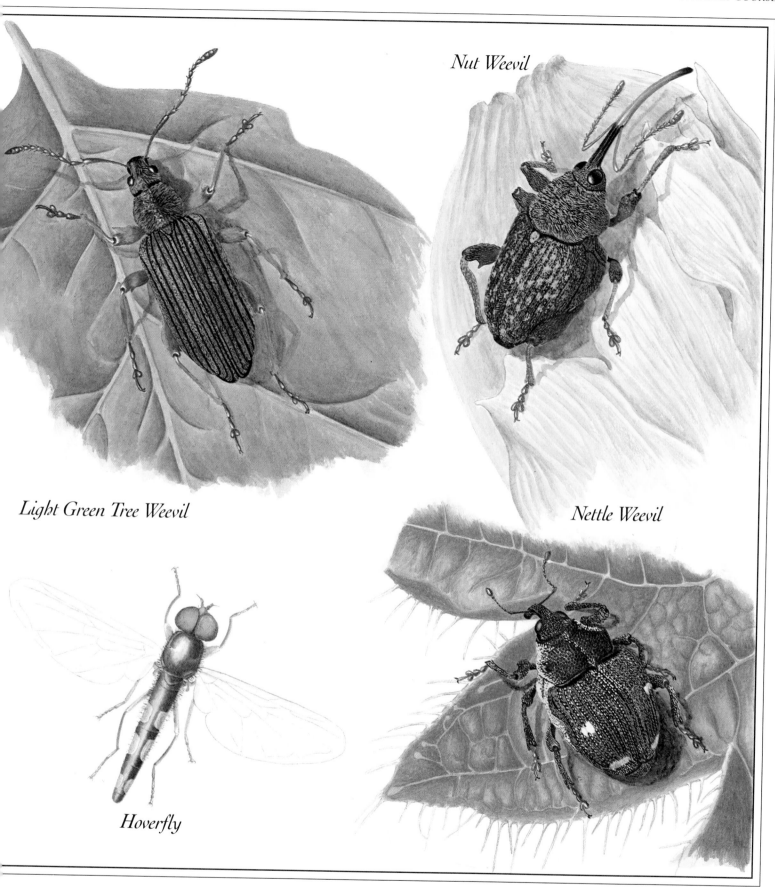

Nut Weevil

Light Green Tree Weevil

Nettle Weevil

Hoverfly

LIGHT GREEN TREE WEEVIL (*Phyllobius calcaratus*) The larvae of this weevil live in the soil, feeding upon roots. The adults may be found in early summer, eating into the new leaves of young trees. Their appearance becomes patchy with age as their scales wear away.

NUT WEEVIL (*Curculio nucum*) In summer, when the young green nuts form on hazel bushes, the female nut weevil bores into them to lay her eggs, one in each nut. The larva feeds inside the nut, exiting to pupate when it falls in autumn, and an adult emerges the next spring.

HOVERFLY (*Melanostoma scalare*) One of our most familiar and common hoverflies, this species occurs almost everywhere. The adults feed on pollen, particularly that of grasses. The eggs are laid on the underneath of leaves and the larvae prey upon aphids.

NETTLE WEEVIL (*Cidnorhinus 4-maculatus*) In rough grassland where stinging nettles grow, this little weevil may often be found; the larvae feed inside the rootstock. When alarmed, the adult, like many weevils, curls its legs under its body and feigns death.

The Great Crested Newt

The vibrantly coloured great crested newt is a rare and elusive
animal, usually only sighted in spring when it leaves dry land for the
still ponds and streams which it inhabits during the breeding season.

Seldom seen, it is only the occasional disturbance of the tranquil surface of slow-flowing waters, lakes and ponds which betrays the presence of a great crested newt. Woodland pools and lakes and ponds on golf courses are particularly good places to find this miniature 'dinosaur' – largest of our native species of newt.

The great crested newt earns its name from the crest which, in the breeding male, runs along the back from the eyes to the tail. The female is slightly larger than the male – about 6½ inches (16.5cm) overall – and has no crest, but sports skin flaps above and below the tail. Both sexes generally appear brown from above, with variable black spots on their backs and flanks. Their skin is covered with minute fleshy white lumps which have given this amphibian its other name – the warty newt. In contrast with their dull brown backs, both male and female newts have a vivid orange belly, strikingly marked with black blotches. The appearance of the male is further enhanced by a silver stripe along the side of the tail.

Like our two other native species – the palmate and the common newt – the great crested newt emerges from its winter hibernation as the warmer weather arrives in early spring and makes its way to nearby water to breed. Here,

KING OF THE NEWTS
(left) The largest of our native species of newt, the great crested newt is now rare in Britain, but is instantly recognizable by its size and striking colouring. Each newt has its own individual belly patterning.

on the bed of the pond during April, the male performs an elaborate courtship display; after pursuing a female round the pond, he darts in front of her, arching his back to display his crest and markings to best effect, and vibrates his tail in a series of wave and whip movements to waft his scent to his prospective mate. If the female is receptive the male deposits a spermatophor (a small bag of sperm). The female moves over it and takes it into her body to fertilize her eggs. With courtship over, male and female go their separate ways.

The female now begins her laborious task of egg-laying. Up to 300 eggs are laid, and great care is taken to wrap each one individually in the leaf of a water plant to protect it from predators. Tadpoles hatch about a week after the egg is laid, and because of the time it takes the female to lay her eggs, they can be found at various stages of development from May to August, when metamorphosis is usually complete. Tadpoles which hatch late in the season, sometimes well into July, overwinter in the pond in tadpole form and metamorphose the following year.

Both tadpoles and adults are entirely carnivorous, their diet consisting mainly of fresh-

A CAUTIOUS EFT
(above) Apart from their frilly external gills, which remain until metamorphosis is complete in August or September, the translucent efts, or tadpoles, look like miniature versions of the adult newts. They mature in the pond during the summer, taking refuge amongst the pondweed which hides them from predators.

WINTER SLEEP
(above left) With the onset of cold weather in autumn, the great crested newt becomes increasingly inactive. From November to February it hibernates under logs or stones, often in the company of other newts, until the warmer spring temperatures disturb its torpor.

A CHANGE OF CLOTHES
(left) Like other newts, the great crested newt sheds its skin at the beginning of the breeding season when it migrates from dry land to water. The tough 'land' skin, which stops it drying out, is exchanged for a more permeable one suitable for aquatic life.

water invertebrates. Almost anything of a suitable size which moves will be taken – waterfleas, freshwater shrimps and insects. In their turn, great crested newts fall prey to a variety of predators. Young tadpoles are particularly vulnerable to predation from all kinds of fish, and although adults are protected to some degree by their size and the poison produced by their warty skin, they are still attacked and eaten by owls, crows, weasels, stoats, rats, hedgehogs, foxes and even domestic cats.

BACK ON DRY LAND

The adult newts leave the pond in midsummer and take up residence on land, hiding in long grass or under stones and logs by day and emerging at night to hunt for worms and slugs. The young follow them in August or September and remain on land until they have reached breeding age. Because of its larger size, the great crested newt takes longer to reach maturity than other species of newt, and it is not until they are at least two years old that newts are able to return to their pond of origin and reproduce. In some cases, newly matured newts go further afield and colonize new ponds.

Great crested newts have always been a popular quarry for children on pond-dipping expeditions, and have suffered in the past from over-collecting. Now, although scattered throughout England, Scotland and Wales, they are still relatively uncommon, and are afforded special protection by the law. This not only helps to protect these beautiful creatures from collectors, but also from two much more wide-ranging and potentially devastating threats – pollution and habitat destruction.

The Stately Home

Created solely for the pleasure of their wealthy owners, the stately homes of Britain have made a lasting impact on the landscape. In the past, many acres of farmland – even villages – were obliterated to make way for vast parks that rolled right up beneath the elegant windows of these great houses. Once emparked, the landscape was moulded and manicured to recreate an ideal vision of nature – rolling grassland, calm lakes and pretty coppices of trees. Many stately homes and their parks have survived, softened and matured over the centuries, to provide some of the country's most tranquil and pleasant scenery.

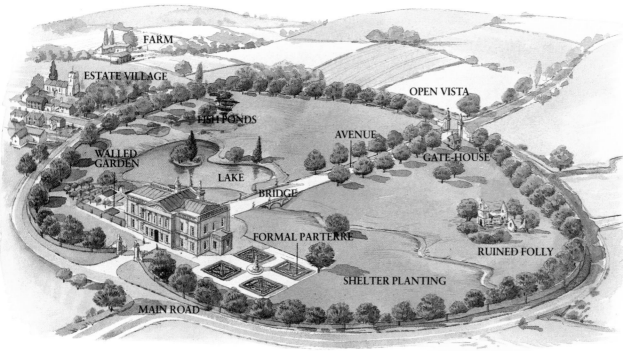

PLEASURE GROUNDS *(left) Apparently natural, but carefully contrived – to the extent of transplanting entire villages – the boundary walls of the stately home contained a miniature world of diverse elements, both decorative and utilitarian, ranging from the walled vegetable and fruit garden, to the artificially created lake. Tenant farmers supplied what the park could not.*

The stately homes of England stand within gardens and parkland which embody the passing passions and interests of succeeding generations of owners. These ranged from the intricate sophistication of the earliest forays into purely decorative gardening in the 16th and 17th centuries, through the endless emulations of Arcadian countryside which daubed country estates with a uniform green in the 18th century to the grand schemes of the last great era of the garden – the 19th century. In this last period there was still money enough for designs incorporating elements from the past combined with a love of colour satisfied by the introduction of plants from all over the world.

FEUDAL FORTRESSES

Stately homes grace every county of Britain, though most embellish the wealthy southern lowlands. Many have their origins in medieval manor houses, around which village life revolved, and whose lords ruled with despotic power over villein and bondsman. Not surprisingly, early manors combined beauty with fortification, and existing examples abound in moats, crenellated battlements, towers and defensive walls.

The gardens of such homes answered a practical need for fresh food; herb and kitchen gardens, orchards and allotments, all contributed to the seasonal and limited diet. Fish came from the pond and meat from the park in which deer, wild cattle and boar roamed, providing sport and sustenance throughout the year. Of these parkland homes, among the earliest remaining are Woodstock near Oxford, and Chillingham in Northumberland, which date from the 12th and 13th centuries. At their peak there were more than 2000 deer parks in Britain, the rank of the feudal baron being reckoned by the number of deer parks licensed to him by the monarch.

By Tudor times the wealthy and powerful were at last safe to forsake their castles and indulge a passion for elaborate decorative buildings, with large glazed windows from which the view was uninterrupted by defensive walls. This led naturally to the origination of what was to become a peculiarly English passion and genius – the decorative garden.

Springing from severely regimented and utilitarian kitchen gardens, the first pleasure gardens – pleasaunces – followed this established style: they were in effect extremely formal outdoor rooms, walled spaces celebrating nature tamed, while the surrounding parkland resounded with the calls of animals both wild and dangerous. A reverence for order was reflected in the elements within the garden walls – diminutive clipped evergreen hedges depicted mottoes, heraldic emblems, or intricate patterns; water was contained in rectangles or long canals; straight avenues of trees were planted, often clipped or pleached to form solid rectangles of foliage; single specimens underwent the contortions of topiary. Elizabethan gardens stripped nature of all that was natural.

ELYSIAN FIELDS

In the 18th century a new fashion for naturalism swept through the country; considerable money was spent, and earth shifted, with the objective of perfecting nature. The fashion began· at Chiswick House, where Lord Burlington sought to reproduce the effect of the classic landscapes of ancient Rome, as an authentic setting for his neo-Palladian villa. Tired of keeping nature in a straight-jacket, the *nouveau riche* followed suit and landscaped with a vengeance, creating 'natural' valleys, hillocks, lakes and groves where none had existed. Rejecting the sheltered sites of Tudor manors, they built on the hill-tops, proclaiming their power for all the world to see.

The unrelieved greenness of this landscape was shattered by the colourful excesses of the 19th century – exotic new plants were brought into the gardener's repertoire from all over the

world. A passion for the picturesque spawned pagodas and temples, towers and ruins. Nostalgia turned the wheel full circle, and 'Elizabethan' gardens proliferated once again.

World War 1 brought about social changes which depleted the battalions of gardeners necessary to preserve this demanding splendour and the last 50 years have hastened the process of decay – food shortages during World War 2 put many parks under the plough, and subsequently motorways and housing estates have eaten away at the remainder.

But the irreplaceable grandeur of these historic stately homes is now recognized and preserved wherever possible. Opening the house and grounds to the public – which may be a disagreeable economic imperative for the owner – is an unprecedented stroke of luck for visitors, enabling them to explore a richly unique part of the countryside, complete with its unusual wildlife, once inaccessible to all but the privileged few.

WOODED VALLEY (above) Stonor Park, near High Wycombe, is a fine example of a country house set in a wooded deer park. The foundations were laid in this sheltered Chiltern valley towards the end of the 12th century, and the ancestors of the present owners have occupied and added to the house for 800 years.

APPARENT ANTIQUITY (left) The great parterre of Drummond Castle harks back in style to Jacobean times. In fact the 13 acres of intricate bedding, laid out to form a St Andrew's cross, was begun in 1820. The multi-coloured filigree of the gardens makes a dramatic contrast with the grim grey castle. Beyond the confines of the formal garden, with its nostalgic panoply of topiary, terraces, urns and statues, lies the natural landscape of woods and streams.

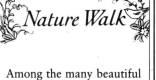

Nature Walk

Among the many beautiful and intriguing decorative features to be seen on a stroll in the grounds are:

BRIDGES in many different styles, spanning natural and artificial waterways, and providing vantage points.

TEMPLES and follies, designed to catch the eye and excite the imagination, completing or presenting a commanding view.

MAZES created from clipped evergreens, much loved by Elizabethan gardeners.

TOWERS either incorporated in a newer building or added to give an air of hoary antiquity.

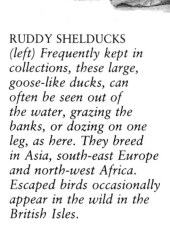

In Open Parkland

A mix of native and exotic species, the open park is graced by herds of deer and majestic trees, leading to the ornamental lake where introduced wildfowl swim alongside familiar moorhens.

An early summer heat haze shimmers over the parkland. The fallow deer fawns, little over a fortnight old, are long-legged and sprightly. Chasing each other with abandon, they play follow-my-leader over the grass tussocks. At the sight of a human intruder, however, they end their gambolling and rush to the does.

The does, too, are wary but are quickly reassured and soon resume grazing peacefully, heads down, only their long tails flicking regularly to brush away the irritating flies. Centuries of peaceful domestication have accustomed them to the sight of man in the confines of the park, though instinct still dictates that they shun a close approach.

Fallow deer appear in a range of colour variations – an unusual feature among deer. Chestnut brown spotted with white is a typical summer colouring, but 'menils' are pale brown with spots, and there are also black, white and intermediate varieties. The full range is more likely in a wild herd rather than among park animals.

Far across the park, separate from the does, the handsomely antlered bucks sit peaceably together, ruminating. In autumn, however, there will be conflict as rivals fight for possession of the harems.

Fallow deer have lived in Britain and Ireland for hundreds of years, both in parks and running wild in our forests. Sika deer, though, are relative newcomers. They were introduced, just over a century ago, as an ornament in a number of parks. These deer prefer to keep to the cover of the wooded knolls in the long summer days, only venturing into the open to graze the grass at dawn and dusk. Many estates now also run a herd of longhorned cattle, kept primarily for their stately good looks.

The close sward created by the deer and cattle has no peer. Untouched by the plough or by fertilizers, the long established grassland may be speckled with low growing flowers. Here and there the short turf is pockmarked with anthills, while long patches of grass grow under the trees and waves of bracken carpet the slopes.

RUDDY SHELDUCKS (left) *Frequently kept in collections, these large, goose-like ducks, can often be seen out of the water, grazing the banks, or dozing on one leg, as here. They breed in Asia, south-east Europe and north-west Africa. Escaped birds occasionally appear in the wild in the British Isles.*

WILDLIFE IN THE STATELY PARK

Over the parkland grazed by deer and cattle, a hobby pursues an agile swift. Tree holes attract nesting jackdaws and little owls, and provide roost sites for bats. The resident waterfowl – mallards, moorhens and grebes – are joined by flamingoes, pelicans and exotic ducks. The large white is a visitor from the Continent, while the painted lady has flown here from North Africa. The dragonfly, which breeds in the lake, hunts other insects but may itself fall prey to the hobby. Breeding in rotten wood, the rose chafer flies off to feed in the rose garden.

KEY TO FEATURES AND SPECIES

 1 Hobby
 2 Swifts
 3 Great crested grebe
 4 Jackdaws
 5 Oak
 6 Browse line
 7 Peacocks
 8 Redwoods
 9 Atlas cedar
10 Little owl
11 Beech
12 Longhorn cattle
13 Fallow deer
14 Molehills
15 Long-eared bat
16 Emperor dragonfly
17 Flamingoes
18 Great reedmace
19 Pelicans
20 Painted lady
21 Rose chafer
22 Moorhen
23 Yellow flag
24 Pheasants
25 Bracken
26 Mallard pair
27 Large white
28 White water lily
29 Ferruginous duck
30 Cuckoo flower
31 Beefsteak fungus

The grazing animals also take the foliage of the trees, creating a browse line over six feet from the ground. The fallow deer reach highest, standing on their hind legs to eat the tasty leaves.

Throughout the long day, a succession of busy life surrounds the deer in the park. Jackdaws have nested in holes in the massive old pollard oak, dispossessing even the owl, and they are now busy feeding their large young.

Overhead swoops a rare, fast flying falcon, the hobby. A breathtaking flier, the male's aerobatics are most dramatic during courtship. In late May and early June, the male sweeps in

PÈRE DAVID'S DEER
(above) In the 19th century, Père Armand David, a French missionary, discovered the only known herd of this species in Peking's Imperial Hunting Park. Several were exported to Europe, including a pair to Woburn in Bedfordshire. The 11th Duke of Bedford acquired others from Europe and began to successfully breed them. The Chinese herd was later wiped out, and all those that today roam stately parks are descendants of the Woburn herd.

GOLDEN ORFE
(above right) Swirling shoals of golden orfe are often kept as ornamental fish. They swim and feed near the surface and tend to muddy the water far less than goldfish or carp. The golden variety, bred for their decorative qualities, are descended from greyer cousins that occur naturally in the rivers and lakes of Eastern Europe and Scandinavia.

BLACK SWAN
(left) These graceful birds are native to Australia. Once scarce, even in wildfowl collections, they now breed in captivity and are becoming a familiar sight on ornamental lakes.

arcs and figures-of-eight over the perched female, culminating in high velocity swoops and loops around her, followed by a ceremonial presentation of a freshly killed bird.

Now, however, he dips down over the lake and deftly captures a flying dragonfly in his talons. Banking upwards, he nibbles it as he flies. Later in the season, when feeding the chicks, he will fly down house martins and even swifts in thrilling high speed chases.

A cock pheasant appears on the grass but stays close to the security of the covert which was specifically planted for its ancestors in Victorian days. Its gaudy hues challenge the colours of the peacock which haunts the proximity of the house. This is a truly splendid ornamental bird. When breeding, though, its charisma lessens, for it is apt to begin its loud, disturbing raucous calls at first light.

The exotic colours of the peacock can be equalled by the plumage of ornamental water-

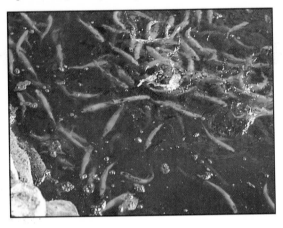

fowl on the lake, the mandarin, Carolina and ferruginous duck among them. They sometimes escape to the countryside round about and they have now established small breeding populations in the wild.

Also on the lake are moorhens, so light that they can daintily pace the water lily leaves. From early April they will be fussily chiding their oddly blue-pated chicks. Familiar mallards may be swimming among exotic pelicans and even flamingoes.

ON THE WING

Other visitors from abroad are the long ranging butterflies, such as the painted lady and the large white. They weave across the park, shining in the sun. Later in the year new generations will be on the wing.

Activity continues as dusk falls, long after the rooks have noisily returned to the tall trees near the Great House. Now the bats emerge from crevices and cracks in the ancient trees. Seen only briefly against the fading light, their flight may give them away — noctules, for instance, fly high, even among the swifts in the last of the sunset. The long-eared bat threads its way between tree branches and can take the cockchafer, the big 'maybug', before it has had time to stir from its daytime roost among the oak leaves. This familiar beetle is lured by the lights of the house, and will enter rooms through open windows.

Its cousin, the shiny green rose chafer, is also seen in parkland. It breeds in rotten stumps and leaf mould. Sadly, this beautiful insect is much more local than it once was.

Decaying wood is an important habitat for many beetles. The grubs of stag beetles, weevils and chafers all live in it and are commonly found in parkland where rotten wood is plentiful. Giant limbs are often left to lie where they fall, and the old trees have innumerable cracks and rents of age. Stag-headed oaks – with dead branches atop a new lower green crown – are also a common feature.

This abundance of old trees (now hard to find in the manicured countryside) is the result of the park's long history. Deer grazing means that young saplings have no chance of survival – any planted trees have to be protected by wooden or metal cradles. In grazed parkland the oak and others are allowed to grow tall and old. The trees are valued for their picturesqueness, and even their diseased and dead limbs, which would cause a forester to fell them, are tolerated.

But parks also abound with interesting, as well as old, trees. Landscape designers have long favoured planting trees from the wider world. The spreading cedar of Lebanon is as much an emblem of the stately home as are its herds of deer.

By early Victorian times, scientific curiosity had added a sharp edge to fashion, and many

now superb specimens of conifers were planted as ornaments in the park. Two trees have added interest. These are the maidenhair tree, with its odd but immediately recognizable cloven leaves, and the dawn redwood. They are living fossils, thought extinct until found growing in remote areas of China.

With its grand views, its exotic flora and fauna, and a rich bank of native species that are now less common in the surrounding farmed countryside, the stately house and its park provide a wealth of wildlife interest.

LEISLER'S BAT YAWNING
A woodland species, Leisler's bat generally roosts in tree holes, emerging shortly after sunset to hunt around the tree tops. Wooded parkland suits it well. Although it is widespread and fairly abundant in Ireland, in England it is confined predominantly to the Midlands and the South.

ROSE CHAFER
(above) Strikingly armoured in metallic green, rose chafers can be seen throughout the summer, often perched on flower heads. They feed on the leaves and flowers of numerous plants, including roses. In flight their wing-cases make them highly conspicuous.

ORNAMENTAL PLANTING
(left) The centrepiece of this colourful lakeside display is a tall, bronzed swamp cypress. Brought over from Florida and adjacent American states, it grows well in or near water, producing distinctive 'knobby knee' roots above the ground. Although it is a conifer it is not an evergreen: the leaves turn bronze in autumn and fall in winter.

Plate 2

Coast Redwood

Dawn Redwood

Cedar of Lebanon

COAST REDWOOD *(Sequoia sempervirens)* The world's tallest tree, up to 375′ (114m) in its native USA, but too sensitive to cold and pollution to reach more than 130′ (40m) in Britain. Green shoots bear tiny male flowers. Round conelets ripen into brown woody cones.

DAWN REDWOOD *(Metasequoia glyptostroboides)* Thought long extinct until discovered in China in 1941, it is now often planted in parks. It is deciduous with flat needles and cones about 1″ (2.5cm) long that ripen in 1 year. The crown is narrow and spire-shaped.

CEDAR OF LEBANON *(Cedrus libani)* An impressive, stately tree up to 130′ (40m) – the flat spreading crown very prone to snow damage. Whorls of stiff, dark ¾″ (2cm) needles are borne on short shoots. Winged seeds fall from the ripe 5″ (13cm) long cones and are wind-dispersed.

Wellingtonia

Atlas Cedar

Deodar

WELLINGTONIA (*Sequoiadendron giganteum*) Very tall with massive girth in its native California – it has so far reached 160′ (50m) tall in Britain. It has thick, soft bark and scale-like leaves. Tiny male flowers ripen in spring, pollinating 3″ (7.5cm) long cones that take 2 years to mature.

DEODAR (*Cedrus deodara*) A tall narrow-topped cedar reaching 120′ (36m), with drooping branch tips. Sharply pointed 2″ (5cm) needles are in whorls – and female flowers develop into oval cones 4″ (10cm) long. It is native to the Himalayan Mountains.

ATLAS CEDAR (*Cedrus atlantica*) The variety *glauca* is often planted for its attractive blue needles. Mature trees reach 120′ (36m), with broadly conical crowns, ascending branches and erect leading shoots. Cones take two years to mature. Brought to Britain from North Africa in 1845.

Plate 20

Wood Blewit

Earth Star

Common W
Helvei

Pholiota

WOOD BLEWIT *(Lepista nuda)*
Often growing in rings on disturbed
humus-rich soil, this common fungus
fruits September-December. The 2-5″
(5-12cm) flattish cap has a rounded
edge and thin crowded gills
shedding pale pink spores. The lilac
colour fades to buff with age. Edible.

PHOLIOTA *(Pholiota adiposa)*
Appearing in autumn, forming
dense tufts at the base of beech
trees, this uncommon fungus has a
sticky 1-7″ (3-17cm) cap with rings
of scales. The curved stem is also
scaly. Yellow gills turn rust-brown
as the ripe spores fall. Not edible.

EARTH STAR *(Geastrum triplex)*
Occasionally found among leaf
litter in beechwoods August-October.
Bulb-like at first, the outer layer
splits to form a 4-8 pointed star
2-4″ (5-10cm) across leaving a round
spore-sac sitting in a 'saucer'. The
spores are dark brown. Not edible.

COMMON WHITE HELVELLA
(Helvella crispa) Very distinctive
with its fluted, hollow stem and
saddle-shaped 1-2″ (3-5cm) wide
cap – it does not have gills. Spores
are white. Usually appearing
August to November in clearings in
woods, a common fungus. Edible.

Verdigris Agaric

Grisette

Porcelain Fungus

Black Bulgar

VERDIGRIS AGARIC *(Stropharia aeruginosa)* A poisonous fungus with a bell-shaped 1-3" (2-8cm) cap that becomes flat with age, losing the greeny slime and white scales. White gills turn purple-brown as the spores ripen. Common June to November on heaths and forest floors.

PORCELAIN FUNGUS *(Oudemansiella mucida)* The convex 1-3" (2-8cm) caps are thin, delicate and very slimy, with widely spaced white gills, borne on curved stems, scaly at the base. Seen on trunks of beech trees in autumn, often in large groups. White spores, edible.

GRISETTE *(Amanita vaginata)* The 2-4" (5-9cm) fragile cap has a finely grooved margin and variable colour. Crowded gills and spores are white. Arising out of a cup-like 'volva', the hollow stem tapers. Found on heaths and in woods. Edible but very similar to deadly species.

BLACK BULGAR *(Bulgaria inquinans)* Growing in close-packed groups on the bark of dead oak and beech trees, inedible ½-2" (1-5cm) fruit bodies are round and rubbery when young, opening to smooth flat discs. Half the spores are brown, half colourless. Common in autumn.

The Peacock

Moving with almost ceremonious dignity and grace across the well
kept lawns and terraces of stately homes, the peacock provides a
superlative expression of wealth, pride and grandeur.

As if showing off to the visiting public, the peacock elegantly lifts his magnificent train, fanning the feathers into a halo of metallic green, purple, blue and bronze. To the peacock courting his harem of peahens the display is an exercise of prowess and dominance – hence the expression 'proud as a peacock'. Poised in front of the chosen female he gently vibrates the quills so that they rustle and shimmer, then pivots his hologram of feathers so they catch the light at a different angle and flash with iridescent brilliance.

The striking plumage and courtship display of this the world's largest member of the pheasant family, complement the grandeur of the stately home perfectly and it is small wonder that peafowl (the collective name for the male peacock and female peahen) have been kept as ornamental birds for thousands of years. Exactly when they were introduced to Britain from their native

THE PEACOCK 'TAIL'
*The peacock's spectacular
4 foot train is not its true tail.
The 150 or so quills are
elongated feathers called
coverts which overlie the
supportive grey-brown tail
feathers. Lacking these coverts
the peahen at 38" (96.5cm)
long is half the male's size.*

India and Ceylon is not known. The Phoenicians were responsible for introducing them to the Pharaohs of Egypt, and Alexander the Great is attributed with bringing them to Europe where they quickly became a symbol of opulence.

By late medieval times peafowl had become a culinary delicacy as well as a feast for the eye and no formal banquet was considered complete without a lordly dish of peacock. It was only after the more tender turkey was introduced into this country from Mexico in the 17th century that the peacock lost its appeal as a table bird.

Long revered and protected in some parts of India, native peafowl have gradually begun to trust man, foraging close to towns and villages and becoming very tame. Although naturally shy in the wild, they are, however, easy to manage in captivity, providing they have sufficient space. Reluctant to fly, they can lift off into a strong, lumbering and surprisingly fast flight when necessary, though pinioning (wing amputation) or a fence about 9 feet high is usually enough to keep ornamental birds within bounds.

Omnivorous in their native jungle habitat, captive birds thrive on the same cereal pellets given to farmed turkeys. Although extremely hardy birds they appreciate the provision of a lean-to building in which to roost at night. In the wild they roost in trees, which they ascend in stages during late afternoon.

HAREMS OF HENS

Peafowl breed readily throughout most of the year, the male taking a harem of between two and five peahens. Apart from displaying and uttering his raucous, screaming breeding call, the cock takes no part in family duties after mating. The nest, made by the peahen, is usually a hollow scraped in the ground filled with leaves, small sticks, grass and other debris. In the wild the hen may lay in an old vulture's nest or in the hollows of the branches of large trees.

Kept within limited confines, the peahen cannot readily escape the male's advances and may produce up to 30 chicks in a season. For commercial breeding purposes, this natural fecundity is further encouraged by removing the eggs soon after they are laid. In common with other pheasants, the peahen is not a good mother, a problem sometimes overcome with captive birds by using a bantam hen as a nanny.

The brown peafowl chicks hatch after some 30 days – males being distinguished by their heavier brownish-black markings. Both males and females try to display from as little as one week old – the peahens generally lose this inclination but the still-drab young males carry on, sometimes in quite a comical fashion.

Hens develop a dark chestnut-brown crest, dark metallic green and dull brown upperparts, and a pale-buff abdomen. At two years males have a very short train but the colourful 'eye' markings are yet to appear. After 4 more years the fully-grown peacock is able to parade his rainbow-coloured plumage in its full glory.

SAFE ROOST
With surprising grace for such bulky birds, hens and cocks begin to roost in trees during the late afternoon.

PERFORMING PEACOCK
The male's courtship display is heralded by a shattering high-pitched call and brassy scream like the miaow of a giant cat. Displaying his semi-circular train, then shaking his lowered orange-brown wing feathers he turns to reveal the tail feathers that support it. He spins to show his colourful 'face' once more, and if she crouches, he runs to her and mates.

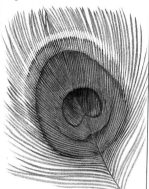

207

The Old Wall

Built of anything from jagged sandstone chunks tumbled together to neat rows of brick secured with mortar, walls have long been a familiar part of the landscape, constructed over the centuries for a wide variety of purposes. Some were built to pen animals and divide fields; some to provide shelter from the elements; some to act as stout defence against enemies. But whatever their original function, durable old walls soften and mellow with time, as wind and rain assaults the exposed faces, and nature soon gains a foothold on them.

RUINED NORMAN
STONE BLOCK WALL

DRY-STONE WALL

FLINT WALL

LOCAL BRICK WALL

A WALLED LANDSCAPE
*(left) Old walls are visible
almost everywhere in the
landscape, but their age and
construction may vary
enormously, from roughly
laid dry-stone walls, some
dating back to the Bronze
Age, to the massive cut block
walls of Norman castles and
abbeys, and the neat
mortared bricks of Victorian
terraced houses.*

THE OLD BRICK WALL
*(below left) Pristine, neat and
barren when first built, brick
walls mellow over the years,
as the weather softens their
colour and plants and wild
creatures find a niche on
the masonry.*

W alls have criss-crossed the British landscape almost since the day people first settled down permanently to farm, perhaps 5000 years ago. And through the centuries all kinds of materials have been exploited to make these solid boundaries – stone, brick, slate, flint, concrete.

The age and condition of these walls varies enormously. Some stone walls are still sound after hundreds of years, while others lie ruined, their masonry strewn on the ground, after little more than a few decades. But they were all built to last, and if properly maintained and protected may stand for thousands of years. Fences, hedges and dwellings made of wood rarely survive long, but walls of stone and brick often become permanent features of the landscape. Even ruined walls may leave a lasting trace, as the prehistoric hut circles jumbled among the bracken on Dartmoor and in the Pennines bear witness.

Some of the oldest walls in Britain are found in the extremities of the country, intact after thousands of years. At Skara Brae in the Orkneys, coastal dunes shifted in a tempest in 1850 to reveal a prehistoric village, with massive walls built solidly of dry-stone masonry as long ago as 2500 BC. At Carn Brea, in Cornwall, the dry-stone wall that once enclosed a Neolithic village has survived equally long.

Over the rest of the country, however, wood was plentiful, and there was little need for prehistoric Britons to build of stone. Their timber dwellings disappeared long ago, leaving few traces but undulations in the ground and signs of post-holes beneath the earth.

It was the Romans who bequeathed the country's most impressive ancient wall – Hadrian's wall, built of well-finished squared blocks of stone and running for more than 70 miles across the bleak northern Pennines. Hadrian's wall is ample testimony to the engineering skill of the Romans, and their ability to make the most of slave labour. But

DRY-STONE WALL
(right) In upland Britain, many field walls are built from great boulders carefully piled together to form a dry-stone wall. Where massive boulders like this are used, wide gaps are left in the wall which all kinds of mosses and plants can colonize swiftly, soon covering the wall with a cloak of vegetation.

LOCAL STONE
(below) Dry-stone walls are invariably built of stone found nearby, and, once flowers and lichens begin to grow over the blocks, the wall blends naturally into the landscape.

there are many other Roman walls in Britain – at Horncastle near Lincoln, for instance, and in London near the Tower. And in the upland areas of Britain, some of the dry-stone walls that mark out the fields may be Roman in origin, repaired and rebuilt many times over the centuries.

WALLS FOR DEFENCE

In the Dark Ages, however, people preferred to build in wood, and it was not until the Normans arrived that stone walls became important once more. Countless castles, halls, cathedrals and churches contain Norman work, and from Norman times and the Middle Ages, we have inherited an enormous number of stone walls – some massive, such as those of the mighty castles, others barely noticeable. For many centuries, though, solid walls tended to remain an exclusive feature of public buildings and the great houses of the aristocracy – the majority of people built their homes of stick and mud.

Brick walls did not begin to appear until much later. It was only in the 18th century that brick began to be used in any quantity. Then, richer lowland villages each had their own brickfields, yielding distinctively coloured bricks. Roving gangs of brickies not only dug the clay but fired it and then built the squire's new house or the wall to enclose his garden.

In the 19th century, when massive urban expansion demanded millions of new, permanent homes, and thousands of factories were erected, brick became a major industry. Railways allowed brickworks to supply vast areas – often with distinctive coloured bricks, such as the bright red of Lancashire, or pale fawn weathering to grey of East Anglia. It is from this time that date so many of the old brick walls we see today, whether in the sprawling factories and rows of terraced houses that characterize the great industrial cities or in the mellow walls of old cottage gardens and ivy-covered rectories.

Nature Walk

Walls differ greatly in construction and appearance, and often incorporate specific features. Look for:

BRICKS laid in different patterns or bonds. The most common are the English (top), stretcher and Flemish bonds (bottom).

CRINKLE CRANKLE WALLS, common in Suffolk. The sinuous shape is self-strengthening.

BOLES, or niches, set into old formal garden walls, built to house bee-hives.

NESTING HOLES, sometimes exposed in ruined dovecots, which may date from medieval times.

Around the Old Wall

**Mottled with lichens and moss, the old wall harbours a
thriving community of flowers and insects in its cracks
and crevices, and ferns and snails shelter in its lee.**

The late afternoon sun rakes across the
crumbling ochre masonry of the old wall,
sharply defining in patterns of light and
shade all the minute cracks and indentations
that roughen its surface. After a day bathed in
sunshine, the stones are warm and dry, and the
faintly musty scent of the damp morning is all
but gone.

The old wall has mellowed with time, softened
by long exposure to wind and rain, and it is no
longer the vertical man-made desert it was
when first erected. Over the years, nature has
slowly established a foothold, aided by the
gradual crumbling of the brick and stone, and
now a surprisingly rich community of small plants
and creatures cling to its once barren surface.

Here and there, the even tone of the brickwork is mottled by myriad coloured patches of
different kinds of lichen, looking like flaking
splashes of faded paint. On the acidic granite
walls of the north-west of England, bright green
patches of the lichen *Rhizocarpon geographicum*
are often seen, while on sandstone walls in the

WALL CLIMBER
*The ivy-leaved toadflax – here the rarer white
variety – secures itself to the old wall with
numerous rootlets pushed into cracks.*

South, crab's eye lichen (once an important
source of red wool dye), with its flesh pink
'eyes', forms a white crust on many old walls.

Slow-growing and long lived, lichen survives
entirely on nourishment carried in the rainwater
that sluices down the wall and so needs no soil.
But its dependence on rainwater makes it doubly
sensitive to air pollution, and, in towns and
industrial areas, even the oldest wall is often
bare of lichen. Only a few lichens, such as
Lecanora dispersa, with its dark grey crust
and white-rimmed discs, and grey-green
Lecanora conizaeoides grow successfully on the
urban wall.

Where the wall has become cracked and
fissured, wind-blow soil can lodge. Here all
kinds of plants and wild flowers take root, and
summer may see the entire wall covered in a
colourful patchwork of blooms. Golden carpets
of biting stonecrop spill out over the top of the
wall from deep crevices. Delicate pink shining
cranesbill finds a niche near the ground, while
broad-leaved willowherb, and aptly named
pellitory-of-the-wall, sprout from deep crevices.

Here and there, ivy-leafed toadflax scrambles
across the masonry, its tiny snapdragon-like
flowers lilac in the afternoon sun, and its glossy
ivy-like foliage hanging in festoons. The toadflax
is especially well adapted to life on the wall, for,
once the flowers of toadflax have been fertilized,
the seed stalks curl slowly back to push the
capsules into cracks in the wall. Then ridges on
the seed wedge it firmly in place as the new root
becomes established.

All summer, bees and butterflies hover round
the flowers, revelling in the reflected warmth of
the sun-soaked wall. The wall brown butterfly
basks against old brickwork, while red admirals
and small tortoiseshells flutter in to sip the
nectar of red valerian. Late in summer, the
year's second generation of holly blue butterfly
lay their eggs on the leaves of the ivy that seems
to scramble over so many old walls.

Many bees are drawn to the wall not only by
the flowers but in search of nests. The flower
bee and the mining bee tunnel into old mortar,
or even crumbling stone if it is soft enough,
while the red Osmia bee nests in any small hole
available. Wall mason wasps, too, dig out nests

LIFE ON THE OLD WALL
*On the warm, dry, sunny side
of the old wall, ivy-leaved
toadflax and other flowers
scramble over the lichen-
mottled stone, and root in
the cracks where the
Amaurobius spider lurks and
wall mason wasps excavate
nests. On the damper, shady
face, polypody fern and
spleenwort find a sheltered
niche, and slugs and snails
a cool resting place. Up
above, flutter holly
blue butterflies,
and a wren
bobs and
darts.*

16

2

27

KEY TO THE SPECIES
1 *Red valerian*
2 *Wren*
3 *Ruby-tailed wasp*
4 *Cluster flies*
5 *Ivy*
6 *Holly blue*
7 *Red velvet mites*
8 *Polypody fern*
9 *Trained apple tree*
10 *Red admiral*
11 *Herb robert*
12 *House sparrows*
13 *Pellitory-of-the-wall*
14 *Black garden ants*
15 *Wall brown*
16 *Biting stonecrop*
17 *Grey cushion moss*
18 *Zebra spider*
19 *Ivy-leaved toadflax*
20 Amaurobius *spider*
21 *Wall mason wasp*
22 *Lichen* Lecanora muralis
23 *Crane-fly*
24 *Two-toothed door snail*
25 *Wall rue*
26 *Garden snail*
27 *Maidenhair spleenwort*
28 *Silvery thread moss*
29 *Grey dagger moth*
30 *Flower bee*
31 *Yellow slug*
32 *Lichen* Ochrolechia
33 *Garden spider*
34 *Lichen* Xanthoria aureola
35 *Garden flowers*
36 *Common liverwort*
37 Bryum argenteum
38 *Pill millipede*
39 *Silky wall feather moss*

NIGHT MOVES
(left) The cracks and crevices of the damper north face of the old wall provide a sheltered haven for the garden snail during the day, but at night it wanders far in search of food before returning to its daytime resting place just as dawn breaks.

WALLFLOWER
(right) Cultivated as a garden flower for centuries, the wallflower often grows wild, and, in spring, brilliant yellow blooms of the 'wild' wallflower brighten many an old wall.

in the wall, making cosy brood cells in the soft mortar and stocking a larder with caterpillars and other creatures. The wall mason owes its name to its habit of sealing off this nursery with mortar of its own.

Sometimes, beautiful ruby-tailed wasps can be seen scooting over the brickwork, tapping with their antennae as they go. They are not searching for a nest site of their own, but for the hollow galleries of other bees and wasps — where they will lay their eggs and plunder the larders of their unwitting hosts.

From their nest below the wall's foot, ants scurry up their exactly marked trail, while cluster flies, bluebottles, and countless hover-flies rest on the sun-baked brick.

All these insects, of course, provide a rich feast for predatory spiders, and a fine web spanning a deep hole in the masonry betrays the sinister presence of the *Amaurobius* spider. Lurking quietly in its lair are often one or two much smaller, pinkish spiders. These, like sorcerer's apprentices, steal titbits from the *Amaurobius's* table.

But just as they hunt, so the spiders too are hunted by the birds that often frequent the wall in summer. Wrens and robins from the fields and woods around swoop in to take advantage of the rich pickings.

TWO SIDES OF A WALL

Many walls have two very distinct sides, and on the north side, the range of wildlife is often very different from the sun-soaked south side. Here, in the shade, protected from the dessi-cating rays of the sun, grows fine, powdery *Pleurococcus* algae, dusting the wall green over large areas. So little does *Pleurococcus* like the drying effect of the sun that walkers once used it like a compass, for it often only grows on the north sides of tree trunks.

The shady side of the wall harbours other damp-loving plants, too. Along the bottom of the wall, cluster flat green 'leaves' of liverwort

MAIDENHAIR SPLEENWORT
(above) Like all ferns, the small maidenhair spleenwort appreciates shade, and is often to be found in the shadow of old walls, especially in western Britain.

LIME-LOVER
(right) The lichen Caloplaca heppiana *is happy only on relatively lime-rich surfaces, and on old brick walls, the pattern of the pointing may be traced out by bright orange rosettes of this lichen as it colonizes the mortar but shuns the acidic bricks.*

WALL BROWN
*(below) Bricks retain warmth
well, and wall brown
butterflies can sometimes be
seen basking on the old wall
long after the sun has
passed.*

SUMMER VISITOR
*(below right) A summer
visitor, the whinchat
usually nests in thick
upland undergrowth, where
its nest can be well
hidden. But it may
sometimes conceal the
nest in the matted grass
at the foot of an old
dry-stone wall, safe from
prying eyes.*

which must remain moist at all times. Within
crevices, and all over the masonry – wherever
there is a pocket of soil for spores to lodge –
many kinds of moss may grow: feathery catkin-
like fronds of silvery thread moss, and vivid
green velvety cushion mosses.

Many ferns, too, thrive in the moist shade of
the north-facing wall, especially in limestone
country. Deep in the shade of the limestone wall
grows Hart's tongue fern, with its large solid
green, pointed fronds, and sprouting from a
crevice are the shiny rows of green discs along
the fronds of maidenhair spleenwort. From
other cracks in the damp wall emerge parsley
fern and wall rue. And where the masonry is
mossiest, common polypody may sprout.

Many small creatures, too, love the moist
shade of the north side of a wall. A yellow slug
winds slowly between moss fronds while garden
snails sit motionless through the day. Only after

dark does the garden snail wander off to look
for grazing, often travelling some distance before
returning to exactly the same spot at the first
hint of dawn, leaving a glistening trail to mark
its nocturnal journey. Skittle shaped door snails
rest in the moss by day, too, while nearby lurks
a harvestman. The harvestman is a distant
relative of the spider, and is equally carnivorous,
but it needs damper conditions to prevent its
thin skin drying out, and it is often seen drinking
drops of dew.

As the years pass, the old wall is increasingly
cloaked by lichens and flowers, mosses and
ferns, and insects and small creatures continue
to excavate the mortar. Gradually, the wall
crumbles and weakens, and in wet or windy
weather, parts of it collapse. Soil collects between the tumbled masonry, and grass begins to
grow over the ruined wall. Slowly but steadily,
the old wall begins to vanish.

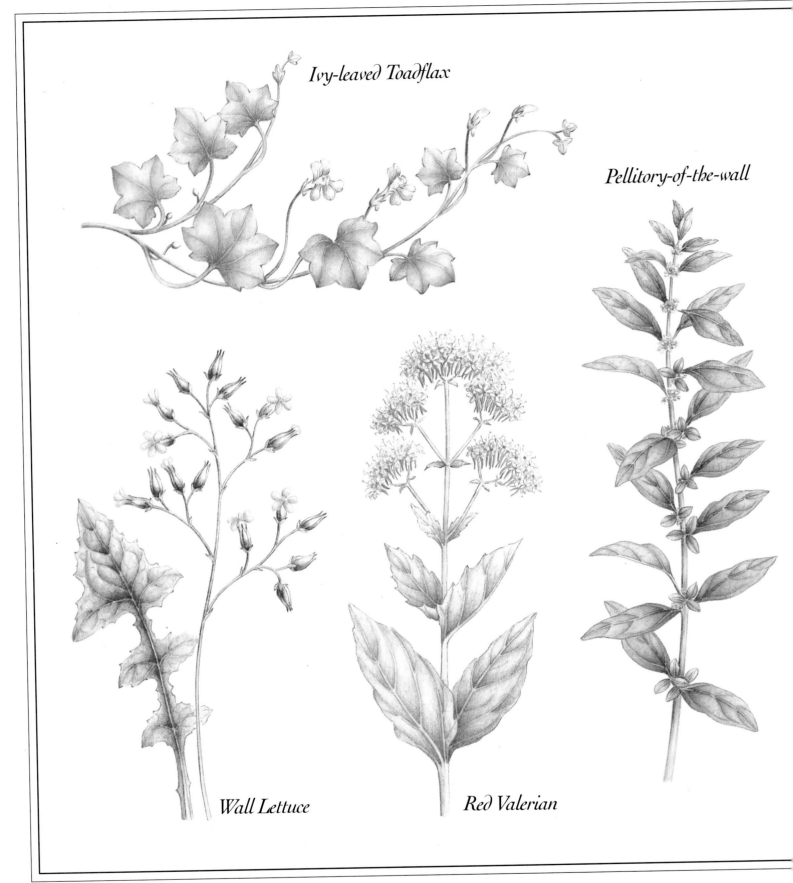

Ivy-leaved Toadflax

Pellitory-of-the-wall

Wall Lettuce

Red Valerian

WALL LETTUCE *(Mycelis muralis)* A tall plant, with a slender, hairless stem growing to 24″ (60cm) or more. The green leaves can be eaten in salads. Yellow flowers, each with five petals, bloom in a spreading cluster from July to September.

IVY-LEAVED TOADFLAX *(Cymbalaria muralis)* A creeping plant found on walls over much of Britain, its leaves are broadly-toothed on long stalks, often purplish. Long stems support tiny lilac snapdragon-like flowers with a yellow spot on the lower lip and a short spur.

RED VALERIAN *(Centranthus ruber)* A common plant of dry, limy banks and walls in the South. From clusters of oval leaves and greyish stems up to 32″ (80cm) tall grow small reddish-pink (sometimes white) flowers which bloom from May to July.

PELLITORY-OF-THE-WALL *(Parietaria diffusa)* A member of the nettle family, growing up to 14″ (35cm) tall, this leafy plant grows along walls and steep banks throughout most of Britain except the North. Its tiny greenish flowers bloom on red stems June to October.

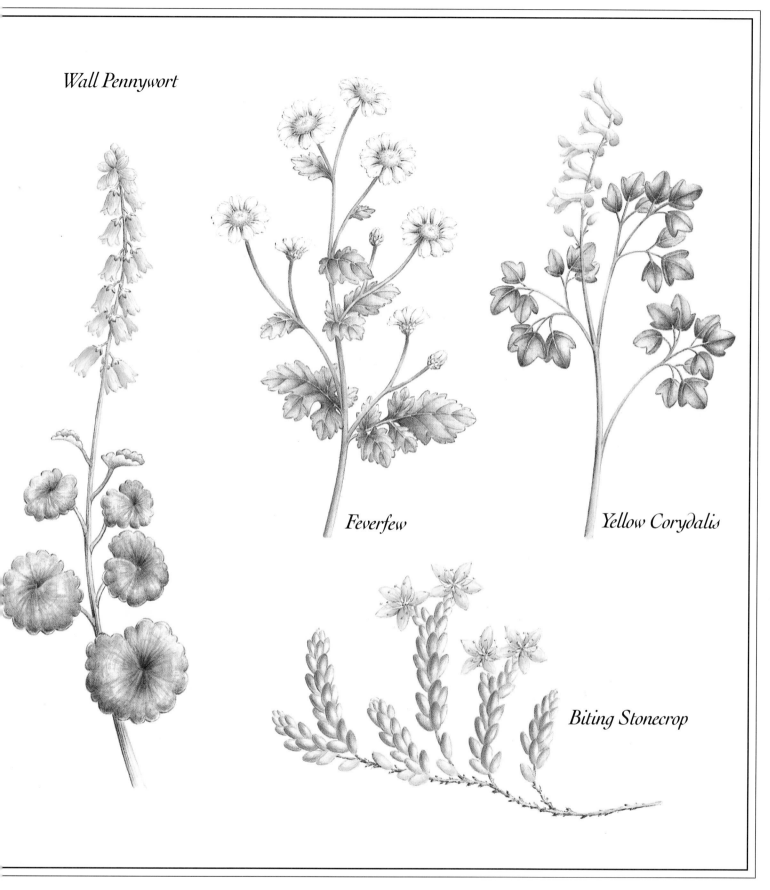

Wall Pennywort

Feverfew

Yellow Corydalis

Biting Stonecrop

WALL PENNYWORT *(Umbilicus rupestris)* A 4-16″ (10-40cm) perennial on walls and rock crevices, which prefers the damp climate of west Britain, and southern Ireland. From clusters of shiny, dimpled leaves grow spikes of yellowish tubular flowers. Blooms May to August.

FEVERFEW *(Tanacetum parthenium)* Common in and near gardens and along grassy walls, the bright aromatic leaves of this 20″ (45cm) perennial are believed to cure fever and migraine. Daisy-like yellow and white flowers appear from July to August.

BITING STONECROP *(Sedum acre)* Also known as wallpepper, this small plant, growing up to 4″ (10cm) tall, is common on walls, sand dunes and bare ground. The spreading cluster of thick yellowish leaves taste peppery. Yellow flowers appear June to July.

YELLOW CORYDALIS *(Corydalis lutea)* Also known as yellow fumitory, this 6″ (15cm) tall, bushy plant has neatly divided greyish leaves and slender, hairless stems that sprout from crevices in walls near gardens. Vivid yellow clusters of flowers appear May to August.

Wall Screw Moss

Silvery Thread Moss

Silky Wall Feather Moss

SILKY WALL FEATHER MOSS
(*Camptothecium lutescens*) Found
mainly on chalky or limestone
downs, this is a loose, tufted moss,
with rather yellowish tips to its
leaves, on slender, branched stems.
The bases of tussocks are red-
brown. Each leaf is serrated.

WALL SCREW MOSS (*Tortula
muralis*) Very common on walls,
forming neat, small, furry cushions
with silvery 'hairs' at the tip of the
leaves. The upright stalks bear
yellow capsules which turn
purplish, then release spores once
the pointed hood has dropped off.

SILVERY THREAD MOSS
(*Camptothecium sericeum*) A
distinctive moss of walls, boulders
and trees, this grows in branching,
triangular stems flattened into
broad silky mats. It is glossy, but
curls up at the sides when dry to
make a feathery, fern-like cluster.

Southern Polypody

Bryum capillare

Grey Cushion Moss

SOUTHERN POLYPODY
(*Polypodium australe*) Growing on limestone rocks and old mortared walls in the warmer South and West, this fern has narrow, triangular fronds up to 12″ (30cm) long with the second pair of lobes widest, and the edges of each lobe slightly toothed.

BRYUM CAPILLARE This deep green moss grows in cushions up to 2½″ (6cm) throughout Britain on rocks, walls and trees. Its leaves are concave and spreading while large pendulous, reddish-brown spore capsules are borne on 1″ (2.5cm) stalks.

GREY CUSHION MOSS
(*Grimmia pulvinata*) Tight, domed cushions of this pale grey moss often cover limestone walls and roofs. The leaves have very long, silky, silvery hairs, and the spores are borne on short, curved stalks which gradually straighten out with age.

The Wren

**Our commonest bird, the jaunty little wren is found
throughout Britain, and its noisy trill is a familiar
sound in both town and country.**

From deep within the dark ivy that sprawls across the old brick wall, a bird sings: a sweet, fast warbling, interspersed with a raucous trill. The trill is loud and intense, and suggests the leaves hide a large bird. But it is just the tiny wren, bobbing in and out of the foliage more like mouse than a bird, before whirring away to a nearby bush on short stubby wings.

The little brown wren is not only one of Britain's smallest birds, just 3¾ inches (9.5cm) long, but also the commonest, with as many as 10 million pairs breeding in Britain each year. It is fortunate that it is so numerous, for many wrens die in severe winters – in the harsh winter of 1962-3, for instance, some 75 per cent of British wrens may have perished. But the wren's remarkable reproductive rate brought the population back up to normal within four years.

It is partly the wren's small size that makes it so susceptible to cold, for it loses heat quickly. But the wren is also one of the few birds to remain in Britain all year round that eats nothing but insects. When the snow lays deep, or the vegetation is frozen, insects may be impossible to find.

Wrens often survive the bitter winter nights by crowding together into roosting sites in large numbers, so that the combined body heat of all the birds keeps them warm. Favourite roosting sites are unlined nests, built by the males for roosting, not egg-laying, and nest-boxes. Even though they are so small, it is astonishing how many wrens are able to cram into a single site; the record is 61 birds in one nest-box.

Although they spend much of their time

creeping about the undergrowth, wrens are easily seen as they pause briefly to deliver their loud songs from the top of a wall. They seem to show little fear of humans and allow them to approach closely – although the folklore associated with wrens gives them every reason to be wary.

In the past, the wren was widely regarded as God's bird, a magic bird, or King of the Birds, and was given special protection for most of the year. But during the period between Christmas and Epiphany (6 January) – especially in Celtic regions – the wren was hunted, and often killed, after elaborate rituals. The custom persists in diluted form in parts of Ireland, where,

SINGLE MOTHER
*(left) Cock wrens may mate with many partners,
and the hen may be left to rear her brood
alone, in the nest he builds and she lines.*

VERSATILE NESTER
(below) The adaptable little wren will build its ball-shaped nest anywhere from old walls to garden sheds, lining it with dried grass and moss.

INSECTIVORE
(above) The wren relies entirely on insects for food, and risks starvation in very severe winters when insects become very hard to find.

KEY FACTS

IN FLIGHT Fast and direct, the wren has a distinctive, whirring flight on short, rounded wings. Plumage is reddish-brown on mainland Britain.

BOBBED TAIL
The stubby, cocked tail of the adult wren when perched is unmistakable.

THE EGGS Two clutches of five to eight speckled black or reddish-brown eggs are laid each year, in April and August.

although the birds are not actually caught, small boys go from door to door reciting verses about the wren and collecting money 'for the King'.

THE WIDE-RANGING WREN

The wealth of local names given to the wren, from 'stumpy' (referring to its cheekily cocked tail) to Titty Todger (from its small size) are a testament to its familiarity all over the country. Indeed, the wren probably occupies a greater range of habitats than any other British bird, being equally at home in dense woodland, city centres and on bare mountain slopes.

Its forceful song and equally loud, explosive 'ticc-ticc-ticc' sequence, often run together into a churring trill, can even be heard resounding over the lonely sea-cliffs of our most remote islands. Such isolated populations of wrens have evolved into four distinct subspecies: the slightly greyer Fair Isle and Hebrides wrens, the larger, greyer, paler St Kilda wren, and the similarly sized but darker Shetland race.

Not surprisingly, for a bird that occupies so many different habitats, wrens nest in a great variety of sites, from hedges and clumps of ivy to holes in walls, in trees and among rocks, or even among tools, shoes or old teapots in a garden shed.

In April, the male wren builds a number of unlined 'cock's nests', using whatever materials are available, such as moss, feathers, dead leaves and grass, to fashion a neat, domed structure with an entrance on one side near the top. Soon a female selects one of these nests, and lines it with feathers. On this soft bed, she lays her delicately spotted eggs – usually from five to eight, but sometimes as many as 16 – and incubates them for 14 or 15 days. Both parents are kept busy bringing caterpillars to their rapidly growing young, which fledge about 17 days after hatching.

Wrens usually rear a second brood, laying their second clutches as late as mid August. Many males are polygamous, installing a series of females in different nests and helping each mate rear her brood. It is strategies like these that ensure a population large enough to survive predation and the rigours of winter.

The Country Lane

A gentle amble along a country lane, just wide enough for a cart to pass, is the beginning of a journey following the footsteps of travellers long past whose wanderings carved out the many miles of country lane now found across Britain's landscape. Once the only means of communication between farms, villages and towns, these quietly meandering byways have largely been superseded by throbbing modern road systems. Nevertheless, many lanes still remain, some in daily use, and are often direct routes straight into the peaceful, leafy world at the very heart of our countryside.

WINDING COURSE

SUNKEN LANE

OLD FIELDS

MODERN ROAD AND BRIDGE

OLD FARMSTEAD

FORD

WIDE VERGES

NEW LANE

THE LANE'S PROGRESS
Many old winding lanes, made when fields were carved out of woodlands, are still in use. Sunken, with no verges, these steep-banked tree-lined lanes usually run between old farmsteads. Often a lane is crossed by an arm of the network of the modern road system. If a country lane is straight with wide grassy verges it is likely that it would have been established during the eighteenth century when many open fields were 'enclosed', providing for more direct routes between centres.

As the din of the traffic-jammed highway slowly fades behind, to be replaced by birdsong and the hum of insects, the traveller of the leafy lane is transported back to a bygone age when progress was at horse's pace and distances were measured in days, not miles. From behind the wheel of a car, leaving the orderly network of modern roads and navigating the spidery web of rural byways can be a bewildering experience, as they weave their way in confusing duplication as if undecided on their destination. Much of this confusion has been brought about by the razing of farms and hamlets which the now quiet roads once served. But explored on foot, map in hand, much can be learned of these old rural highways and the people who once travelled them.

THE SUNKEN LANE

Wending their way through the green heart of the British countryside, shrouded by the out-stretched limbs of hedgerow trees and shielded by high banks, many country lanes appear sunken as if worn down by countless feet over countless generations.

Few lanes are extremely ancient, however, as the first clearly defined tracks between settlements, which followed a more or less straight path across higher ground, have, more often than not, become the main roads of today. Other old tracks have long since been ploughed up, although some still show up as crop marks – lines of greener growth showing where the original roadside ditches were filled in.

AN ANCIENT BYWAY
(above) Winding between steep, primrose-strewn banks a sunken lane follows an ancient route.

GREEN LANE
(below) Surviving trackways, ridgeways or drover's routes, if not adopted into the road system, may still be used for farm transport.

It was during the Dark Ages, following the end of Roman rule, that many of today's villages, and the lanes which served them came into being. Roads joined the new settlements and ran from clusters of villages to nearby towns. Later other tracks came into being, marking the course of pathways around the boundaries of the newly established parishes and great estates as they were established by the church and the nobility. Yet more paths were trodden out by the villagers trudging daily to labour in the nearby fields and woods. Many of these old routes, now lined by hedges, have become the gently winding country lanes we still enjoy today.

Not all lanes originated in this way, however, some, such as those found in deepest Devon and Dorset, the Welsh Marshes, Sussex and parts of Essex, were formed in medieval times by farmers clearing irregularly shaped fields from the woods. The new farmsteads they established were far from the established villages. The fields they created were often separated from each other with earth banks. Earth banks also lined the tracks. Now set with hedges and trees, these banks make the deep worn lane whose twisting, turning course follows the erratic boundaries of the fields seem even deeper.

For centuries all these byways were unsurfaced, rutted, muddy paths, but the highways linking the towns were not much better. Some followed the old Roman roads, but without upkeep the surfaces eventually broke up, and their ditches filled. Badly damaged or flooded sections were bypassed in wide arcs, so changing the long straight tracks into winding highways.

TOLL ROADS AND TURNPIKES

With the golden age of the stage coach, however, came some improvements. A system of improved turnpike roads was created by private companies who charged tolls for their use. At this time much of the open countryside of the shires was being enclosed in neat square fields, and many old lanes were straightened and drainage ditches dug at this time.

The long, inter-county 'drove roads' on which cattle walked their way to the main markets remained green, but in time the main roads of all kinds became 'macadamised' – surfaced with graded rock. Later on, when tar became cheap, roads and lanes were both topped with tarmac – tar mixed with graded slag or other stone – ready for the age of the car. These improvements instantly elevated many rural roadways to the status of major thoroughfares. But many more were simply cut off. Bypassed by new, wider, straighter highways, the endless tangle of country lanes was left to slowly slide into disrepair. Now carrying little traffic, and receiving even less maintenance, these rural byways have regained something of their old character; a safe thoroughfare for wildlife as well as man. With verges decked with flowers, the country lane has once again become a place to explore for its own sake and not merely a route to somewhere else.

225

Along the Leafy Lane

**Off the beaten track, the banks and hedges of country
lanes offer fine opportunities for the quiet enjoyment of scented flowers,
ever-active birds, insects and well-hidden mammals.**

A stroll along a country lane, winding between banks topped by hedges and old standard trees, conveys the rich feeling of being deep in the countryside. Here, as the sunken lane dips down, the trees meet overhead, casting a deep, cool shade on the steep earth banks where an old burrow – rabbit, or fox perhaps – disappears beneath tree roots. Breasting the rise, the breeze carries a heady waft of bluebells and cow parsley; bright rays of sunshine illuminate a dry, sloping hedgebank alive with flowers, the humming of bees and the unseen rustles and squeaks of a shrew. A basking lizard scuttles for cover. The flittering shadow of a butterfly crosses the tarmac en route to the bramble flowers, the rattling song of a wren bursts from the hedgefoot and dappled sunshine plays over wild strawberries in flower. A hedgehog snuffles along the bank top, squeezing under the five-barred gate, and from far off, across the fields, the soft coo of woodpigeons carries faintly.

Country lanes are part of the old farming countryside. They encompass many mini-habitats as they pass from light to shade and cut through different soils on their criss-cross journeys over the country. Each lane can thus offer the walker a glimpse into the rich world of wildlife little changed for centuries.

ANCIENT WOODLAND MEDLEY

Hedgerows along the twisting lanes dating from medieval times have a wide medley of fine trees, echoing the variety once found in the ancient woodland which grew there. In addition to oak and ash, beech may grow, or a statuesque wild cherry, while dark green hollies reach untrimmed tree status. And in the autumn, the vivid yellow leaves of a field maple stand out: though usually seen as a shrub in the hedgerow, it can become a dainty tree with finely fissured bark.

The woody shrubs in the hedge are equally varied. Delicate spindle, sallows, hawthorn, nutty hazel, heavily scented elder, brightly berried guelder rose and wayfaring tree and, ubiquitously, the tough blackthorn – alive with white blossom in early spring and laden with sloes in autumn – are typical species.

Many of the old trees are peppered with cracks and holes which attract nesting birds. The little owl is one: it is not a native species but was introduced from Europe in the last century. A cross looking bird, it can be seen during the day, often attracting attention with its plaintive *kiu* call. The mistle thrush is drawn to the hedgerow trees, building its large nest where the branches fork. Its country name of

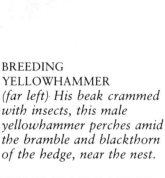

**BREEDING
YELLOWHAMMER**
*(far left)· His beak crammed
with insects, this male
yellowhammer perches amid
the bramble and blackthorn
of the hedge, near the nest.*

VIOLET GROUND BEETLE
*(left) About 1" long and
generally active at night, this
beetle can be seen in the hedgebank on mild wet evenings,
hunting earthworms, slugs,
snails and insects. Its sharp,
notched jaws can hold the
slipperiest of prey.*

COUNTRY LANE WILDLIFE

The rich plant life of the lane's hedges and banks attracts many insects. Flowers are visited by numerous bees and by the hedge brown butterfly whose caterpillars feed on grasses. The leaf-cutter bee snips dog rose leaves for her nest. Spiders and beetles hunt the varied insect life, and slugs and snails steadily eat leaves and fruit. Lizards, shrews and nesting birds are avid hunters of insects and other invertebrates, while rabbits crop the vegetation: all are at risk from the carnivorous stoat and from another hunter, the little owl, which may nest in a tree hole. Bumble bees and mining bees favour the driest of the banks for their nest sites.

KEY TO SPECIES

1 Mistle thrush
2 Field maple
3 Robin
4 Little owl
5 Wild cherry
6 Holly
7 Dog rose
8 Bramble
9 Hedge brown butterfly
10 Leaf-cutter bee
11 Bumble bee nest
12 Rabbit
13 Wren
14 Goose grass
15 Common lizard
16 Mining bee holes
17 Stoat
18 Bluebell
19 Red campion
20 Crab spider
21 Greater stitchwort
22 Wild strawberry
23 Bush vetch
24 Wolf spider
25 Grove snail
26 Pygmy shrew
27 Ground beetle
28 Garden snail

'storm cock' derives from its loud ringing song which it delivers from the topmost branches in the face of an approaching storm – a time when most birdsong is stilled.

The dense cover of the hedge attracts not only nesting birds familiar from the garden – blackbird, song thrush, wren and chaffinch – but also farmland species such as the yellow-hammer and the corn bunting, whose song resembles a jangling bunch of keys. Mingling with the melodic songs of robin and dunnock are the summery sounds of visiting warblers: the willow warbler's descending trill, the white-throat's high-pitched chatter and perhaps the rich melody of a blackcap as it sits seemingly lost in its own exquisite waterfall of notes.

FLOWERING MAY
(above) The common haw-thorn or May is at its most conspicuous in the month of May when smothered with white blossoms. Growing singly or in small clumps, this thorny tree can be a striking feature of hedgerows which grow alongside the winding medieval lane. In later times, hedges of hawthorn were often planted around the enclosure fields.

ORANGE TIP
(top right) Seen here perched on a dandelion, the orange tip is commonly found along country lanes. Its caterpillars feed on hedge mustard and cuckoo flower which grow on the banks.

ROMAN SNAILS MATING
(left) Eaten since Roman times, Britain's largest snail – the shell is about 1¾" across – is found in hedgebanks on chalk or limestone soils in south-east England. Active from spring to autumn, it hibernates in winter.

Up the banks of the sunken lane grows a textured weave of plants which, in spring, can be as colourful as a rug. In western counties, bluebells, deep-blushing red campions and the pure white flowers of stitchwort make a mosaic along the lanes. These flowers are perennials, repeating their show year after year.

After the leaves of the bluebell have died down the thin scatter of grass grows tall, and vetches sprawl across the bank or, using tendrils, climb up the hedge. The quickly growing cleavers also scrambles up vegetation. Often called goosegrass, its bristled seeds, which stick to clothing, are a familiar country nuisance. Ivy is also common: it likes a well drained soil and the hedgebank of the deep lane suits it.

ACTIVE INSECTS

The warm, dry banks of the lane also attract many different kinds of bees. Honey bees can be seen sipping nectar from the flowers – flying, perhaps, not from a hive but from a wild colony in one of the hollow trees nearby, for many swarms live free. The larger-bodied bumble bees are among the first insects seen on the wing in spring. These early fliers are queens, which alone survive the winter.

The bumble bee queens feed on the nectar and pollen of the spring flowers, while searching for a nest site – red-tailed and buff-tailed bumbles often choose an empty mouse burrow. Here the queen builds a set of cells, stocks them with honey and nectar and lays eggs in them. When the new young bumbles eventually fly, the old queen allows them to take over the food gathering and concentrates her energies on laying more eggs.

Several species of solitary bee may also nest in the hedgebank. One such is the mining bee. The queen excavates a tunnel and stocks it with egg cells filled with honey and pollen, but dies before the grubs hatch. The queen leaf-cutter bee, another solitary species, breeds in a similar way. She scissors the leaves of the wild roses in the hedge, taking the pieces back to her nest in a tree hole, where she rolls them into cells which she stocks with food for the grubs before laying her eggs into them. She, too, dies before her brood hatches.

HEDGEROW THRUSHES

These closely related thrushes are not always easy to tell apart. The largest is the mistle thrush (10½"), followed by the blackbird (10") and then the song thrush (9"). The female blackbird has dark legs and is chocolate brown above with variable mottling on the brown chest and belly (juveniles are even lighter below with clearer mottling). The mistle thrush, when seen side-on, is decidedly pot-bellied. Bigger and deeper-chested than the song thrush, it is paler and greyer and has bolder, more distinct spots on its underparts. When feeding on the ground, the mistle thrush hops boldly; the song thrush hops or runs and often pauses with its head on one side (as here).

MISTLE THRUSH

BLACKBIRD

SONG THRUSH

The bankside is also an excellent place to observe spiders. Their webs differ markedly, not only in shape and pattern but also in such things as the angle at which they are spun. Sticky webs trap the spider's struggling prey but on webs without sticky threads the resident spider is only warned by the movement of the web, and must catch its prey either by stealth or speed.

Some spiders do not spin webs. The bank is often the hunting ground of the wolf spiders –

FEMALE LITTLE OWL
(below left) Quite at home in the daylight, this small owl – the same length as a starling but a good deal chubbier – is often to be seen perched on a bough or gate post. When curious or alarmed it quaintly bobs its head before flying off in a bounding, woodpecker-like fashion. It is found mainly in England and Wales.

HAWTHORN SHIELD BUG
(below) Perched here on bracken, these attractive insects are particularly associated with the hawthorn from which they suck nutritious juices from the leaves and fruit.

they run down their prey. Crab spiders have another strategy: they are not web spinners but wait motionless on a leaf or among the petals of a flower. Their colouring makes them almost invisible (some are green, others yellowish to suit their background) and they take any hapless insect that lands nearby.

Preying on the spiders, insects and invertebrates are mice and shrews, which are common in hedgerows of all kinds. They – along with the plant-eating voles – are likely to be heard rather than seen: the shrews, particularly, have noisy confrontations at the borders of their fiercely held territories. Weasels and stoats may also be seen coursing the hedgebank in search of rodents and they will take large prey such as rabbits.

In the warm tranquility of the country lane much is going on, often unseen by the passing motorist, each animal occupying its own niche, breeding or feeding as best it can among predators and prey alike.

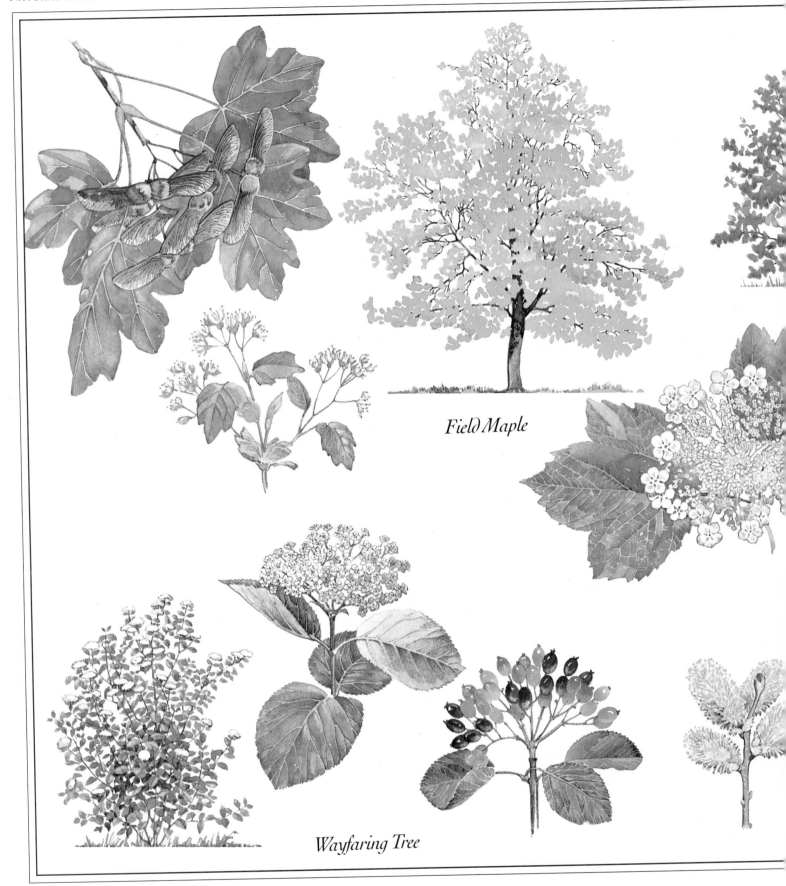

Field Maple

Wayfaring Tree

WAYFARING TREE *(Viburnum lantana)* The fragrant flowers of this small tree or bush open between April and June, and are followed by fruits which are black when ripe. The soft leaves have pale flocked undersides. It is common on limy soils in the South.

FIELD MAPLE *(Acer campestre)* This small deciduous tree is often grown as a hedgerow bush. It has grey furrowed bark, and more rounded leaves than the similar sycamore, which turn bright red and yellow in autumn. The winged fruits are carried by the wind.

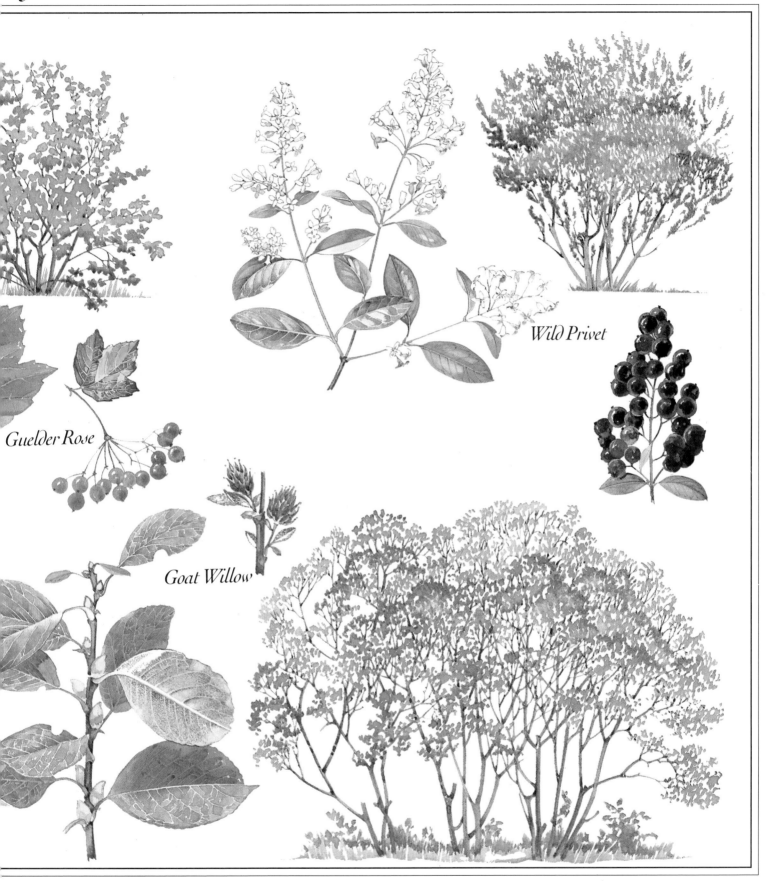

Wild Privet

Guelder Rose

Goat Willow

GUELDER ROSE *(Viburnum opulus)* This deciduous 13′ (4m) tree or shrub carries flat flower heads from May to July, which consist of a mass of tiny fertile flowers surrounded by larger sterile ones. The leaves and bunches of berries turn scarlet in autumn.

GOAT WILLOW *(Salix caprea)* With its silky catkins, this 30′ (10m) tree – also known as sallow – is a striking feature of the early spring. Common in many parts of Britain, it favours damp soil, and grows in hedges, and around the shores of lakes.

WILD PRIVET *(Ligustrum vulgare)* This poisonous evergreen shrub has much narrower leaves than its cultivated counterpart. It has short spikes of strongly scented flowers in May and June, which become sprays of black berries. It is common in the South on chalk.

Plate 3

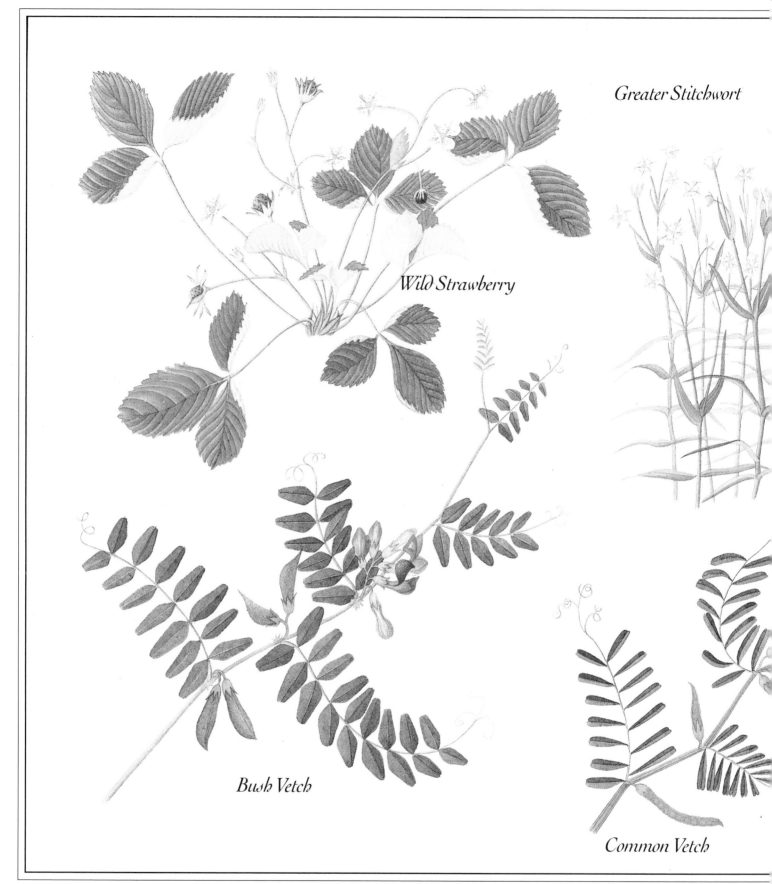

Greater Stitchwort

Wild Strawberry

Bush Vetch

Common Vetch

WILD STRAWBERRY *(Fragaria vesca)* This pretty perennial flowers from April to July, and produces delicious small edible berries. New plants grow at the ends of long runners and quickly form thick mats. It is a common plant throughout the British Isles.

BUSH VETCH *(Vicia sepium)* This common downy perennial sprawls through hedges and banks throughout Britain. It produces mauve, or sometimes yellow flowers from May to September, in clusters of 2 to 6, which develop pods of black seeds, hence the other name – crow-peas.

GREATER STITCHWORT *(Stellaria holostea)* has straggly stems up to 24″ (60cm) long, with starry flowers which burst open in the spring and summer. It is common in hedge-banks, and was reputed to cure the 'stitch' when taken in wine. It is also called adder's meat.

COMMON VETCH *(Vicia sativa* This annual climber bears bright pink flowers singly or in pairs from May to September. There is often black spot at the base of the down leaves. It grows in hedge banks and grassy places in the south-east of England.

Wayside Flowers

Bugle

Tufted Vetch

Goosegrass

TUFTED VETCH (Vicia cracca)
This summer flowering perennial of roadsides and hedges throughout the British Isles climbs up to 6′ (2m) by means of spring-like tendrils at the ends of the leaf-fronds. The one-sided spike of flowers is held on a long stem.

BUGLE (Ajuga reptans) This creeping perennial whose 12″ (30cm) stems are hairy on opposite sides, is common throughout Britain. It produces purple or white flowers from May to July. The bronze leaves are killed by cold, but the stems root where they touch damp earth.

GOOSEGRASS (Galium aparine)
This annual straggles among other hedge plants supporting itself by hooked bristles on the leaf-edges, and the corners of its square stems. Also called cleavers, it produces minute flowers from May to August which become bristled burrs.

The Common Shrew

Working round the clock to fill a tiny but demanding belly, the shrew's short life is a frantic race with starvation, as it energetically patrols its patch, battling with its brethren.

TUNNEL VISION
A relative of the mole and hedgehog, the shrew shares their poor eyesight and hearing and, like the mole, lives much of its life in underground tunnels. Known in the 16th century as the blind mouse, and accredited – wrongly – with a poisonous bite.

The shrews of the British Isles lead lives which are nasty, brutish and short. Day and night, with very short rest periods, they are condemned to spend their 18 month lives in an unrelenting and hazardous search for food. They suffer from the law of diminishing returns as applied to mammals – the smaller the creature, the more it has to eat in proportion to its size just to keep pace with its energy expenditure. A pregnant shrew for example, has to eat one and a half times her own weight daily, and if a shrew has to fast for as little as three hours, it will die of starvation. Added to this, the low nutritional value of the shrew's favoured diet – maggots and mealworms, which are 70 per cent water; and in hard times, baby mice and earthworms, which are 85 per cent water – hardly eases the pressure.

While hunting, the common shrew bustles among the low vegetation, and delves into the leaf-litter twittering softly to itself, with an almost inaudible bird-like sound. The main tool used in its foraging expeditions is its sensitive snout with its panoply of whiskers. Equipped with these, the shrew bustles under cover along the tunnels it builds, or those made by other small mammals, tracking down a variety of creatures which supplement its basic diet – from woodlice and moths, to spiders and snails.

The shrew spends most of its life hidden from view, though in emergencies it will both climb and swim. It has many enemies, and its only defence is a foul odour exuded by glands on its flanks. Unfortunately for the shrew, this is ineffective against cats and owls, its two main predators, since owls have a poor sense of smell, and cats kill shrews for sport, not for eating. Stoats, weasels and other mammals thin their numbers too, but the greatest toll is taken by winter and starvation.

WOOD MOUSE

BANK VOLE

COMMON SHREW

These three small mammals share a similar habitat and can be difficult to tell apart at a glance. However, side by side, they all show quite different features. The common shrew, at 3" (75mm) is the smallest of this trio, the bank vole is 3½" (90mm) head and body, and the wood mouse is the largest, at 3¾" (95mm). The wood mouse enjoys the same diet as the shrew with the addition of seeds, buds and shoots, and is the only nocturnal member of the three. The bank vole is entirely vegetarian.

The shrew does not hibernate, and must continue its quest for insects throughout the impoverished months of winter. Young shrews grow a thicker and darker coat as autumn approaches, but adults which have already survived one winter never grow a second winter coat, and usually die with the onset of cold weather. The new generation which has not yet bred is left to continue the species.

Within a few weeks of birth the young stake out their territory, which at roughly the size of a tennis court is surprisingly vast for such a tiny creature. This they do by leaving scent markers, warning any would-be-intruders to steer clear. The common shrew is extremely aggressive by nature, and chooses to live a solitary life. If a shrew accidentally bumbles into the home range of another a fierce battle is bound to ensue. A pair of shrews locked in combat is oblivious to danger, but the battle is often very ritualized, and shrews rarely injure each other; verbal abuse is as important as physical conflict and their shrill chatter can be heard several yards away.

THE MATING OF THE SHREW

The only time two shrews can meet without fighting is at intervals from April onwards, when the female is receptive to mating. At this time the male will tolerate her on his turf, but only for the time it takes to complete the peremptory and brusque mating-act. Back in her own territory the female constructs a nest of grasses and dried leaves, usually under cover of a tree stump or fallen branch. As her appetite increases with the progress of her pregnancy, she becomes frantically active, eating furiously for half an hour, then stopping in her tracks for an impromptu nap, after which she may spare a moment or two to groom before dashing on in search of another meal.

The pregnancy lasts 18-21 days, and the

female mates again as soon as the litter is born, so that she is continuously pregnant and suckling throughout the summer. Within a day of the first litter being weaned, the second is born.

As its name suggests, the common shrew is the most widespread of the three native species, which also include the water shrew and our smallest mammal, the pygmy shrew. It can be found throughout the mainland and on some islands around the coast, though it is not found in Ireland. The country lane, bordered with banks of rich plant and insect life, provides a perfect habitat for this fiery little bundle of energy.

FAST GROWERS
Shrews are born blind and naked, weighing less than a pea, but after a fortnight their eyes open, and a week later they are weaned and ready to fend for themselves. The litter size varies from 3 to 10, but it is usually around half a dozen. Females have 3 or 4 litters each year.

235

The Blackbird

From spring to late summer, the blackbird's exhilarating
dawn song proclaims the day's beginning, while at dusk its voice
offers a haunting valediction to close the day.

Plaintive and melancholy, yet rich and mellow, the song of the blackbird is one of the first to ring out across the woods, fields and country lanes in the rosy dawns of spring and summer. It is the easy cadences and liquid sounds of the blackbird which open the day, and although it is by no means silent during the day, its velvety tones are once again prominent when, at the end of the day, it leads the evening birdsong. Heard continuously from late February to early July, the blackbird's song, a musical succession of freely composed phrases of great variety, is comparable to that of the nightingale for sheer beauty.

Originally a shy woodland bird, the blackbird has successfully spread into many man-made habitats and is as much at home in an urban setting, among town gardens and city parks, as it is in farmland among hedgerows and country lanes.

Through song the male blackbird establishes the territory in which he intends to live and breed. Young blackbirds spend much time listening to the songs of older birds and experimenting with their own compositions — as a result they generally gain territories and mates later in the breeding season than mature birds.

SOLICITING THE MALE

Early in the year resident blackbirds set up territories and form pairs — older birds that have survived the winter usually reclaim last year's territory and often pair up with former mates. By the time the blackbird population is in full song in early March, some pairs of older

FEEDING THE BROOD
Once the eggs have hatched, the male blackbird (above) his yellow-ringed eye and beak contrasting strikingly with his sleek black plumage, shares in the feeding of his young chicks. Prior to their hatching he takes no part in the incubation, except to perch nearby the nest and sing for long periods of time.

SUNBATHER
(Right) A young blackbird, with speckled breast, spreads its wings and tail feathers, basking in the warm sun. This is thought to be part of the bird's preening process. The heat makes feather parasites move around, enabling the bird to get rid of them more easily when it cleans its feathers.

THE MALE blackbird with jet-black plumage, gold beak and yellow eye-ring is easily identifiable. The female, with dusky plumage and speckled throat and neck, is often mistaken for a song thrush. Juveniles are heavily speckled and appear leggy and dumpy.

LISTENING POST When foraging for worms blackbirds stand with their heads cocked as if listening for underground sounds.

THE EGGS Several clutches of 3-5 light blue-green eggs with brown blotches are laid during the breeding season.

birds will be feeding their first brood.

The female, once paired, starts building nests with the male in close attendance. Using grass and leaves strengthened with mud she makes a sturdy bowl-shaped nest in a bush, tree, hedge or bramble thicket. When the nest is built she takes an active part in the mating display, seeming to solicit the male's attentions. She points her bill and tail straight up in the air, and running ahead of him, gives a high-pitched call. The males takes the hint and follows with bursts of song and much fanning of feathers.

Soon after, a day at a time, the female lays three to five eggs, which she incubates for about two weeks. Apart from short breaks for feeding

WHEN IS A BLACKBIRD WHITE?
Answer: The blackbird species is prone to albinism and white blackbirds are not uncommon. Sometimes partial and progressive albinism occurs where at first only a few white feather patches are visible.

and preening she covers the eggs herself day and night. The male, meanwhile, perches nearby singing for long periods of time, advertising his lordship of the territory. Once the eggs hatch he takes a more active interest in proceedings, helping to feed the hungry brood. The chicks, born blind with just a few patches of down, grow rapidly and are ready to leave the nest in just under two weeks.

CHICKS AT RISK

For the first few days after fledging the chicks are incapable of sustained flight but they run or bounce along the ground with great alacrity. At this time they are extremely vulnerable, and the strident 'pink-pink-pink-pink' alarm call is often heard as the parents try noisily to fend off predators, usually cats, jays, magpies and crows.

Blackbirds usually raise two or three broods in a season. All of the chicks from the earliest brood are likely to survive since they are born well before most of the usual predators are about. Adult birds are also vulnerable to attack from cats and other birds including sparrowhawks. To escape the attentions of the sparrowhawk blackbirds dip and fly low out of cover especially across roads and lanes. Sadly this low flying defence often results in blackbirds being hit by passing cars. If attacked by birds such as magpies or crows blackbirds defend themselves by having a 'fright' moult in the jaws of the attacker, leaving it with a mouthful of feathers.

As the summer progresses the melodic song of the blackbird is heard less frequently until, by the end of August, it dies away completely. Young birds disperse widely, some going to Ireland and others to France. The resident population is joined by over-wintering Continental visitors from Scandinavia. Many young and inexperienced birds perish during the cold, hard winters, but those which survive go on to become the harbingers of the new year's spring.

238

The Harvest Hedge

Always much more than simple boundary markers, hedgerows yield a harvest that can be as rich and varied as the fields and woods between. Myriad creatures flock to the hedge to take advantage of the abundant food, and the year-round hedgerow harvest was once a vital part of the rural economy. In the past, many hedges were cultivated to provide regular supplies of timber and smallwood, while gathering the wild berries and nuts that ripen in the hedges in late summer gave a welcome taste of luxury to the plain country diet.

OAK

OLD HEDGE LINE

WILD HEDGE

TRIMMED HEDGE

BEECH

ELM STUMPS

COPPICED HEDGE

LAID HEDGE
(right) Traditionally, winter was the time when the hedgerow harvest of wood was reaped – when the sap is down. It was also the time when 'laid' hedges were woven into dense stock-proof barriers. Armed with billhook and axe, a skilled hedge-layer could lay up to 30 yards of hedge in a day.

THE MANAGED HEDGE
(above) In recent years, many hedgerows have been grubbed up to increase farming efficiency, but many of those that remain bear witness to the ways in which hedgerows were once managed to maximize the valuable harvest of timber they yielded. Many were planted with oak, beech and elm, often pollarded (cut-off at the bole) to provide a ready supply of straight spars, and elm trees in particular became a familiar part of the English hedgerow – until they were felled by Dutch elm disease in the 1970s. Smaller hedgerow trees, such as hazel, might be coppiced (cut back to the stump) every 10 years or so while around fields where livestock was kept, hedges had to be laid – woven into impenetrable barriers. But for birds and bees and butterflies – and many country people – it is the wild, unmanaged hedgerows, where nuts and berries burgeon, which provide the richest harvest of all.

Hedges line lanes and fields all over Britain, from Cornwall to Cape Wrath. Some are short, tangled mats of hazel scrub; some are huge, bushy hedges studded with mature beech and oak trees; and in the warmth of the Channel Islands, beautiful hedges of fuchsia bloom. But whatever their character, country hedges were once working hedges, with a particular job to do.

Nowadays, besides acting as boundary markers, hedges are kept primarily for the shelter they give. Horticultural districts such as the Wirral and South Hampshire have high shelter hedges, while parts of East Anglia have recently gained willow hedges designed to prevent the wind or 'fen blow' eroding the soil. But in the past, hedges had many uses which are all but forgotten today.

In many parts of the country, hedges were a vital source of fuel for poor country people, although the poor could only exploit this where the commons right of 'hedgebote' existed. This right also allowed them to collect dead branches to feed their animals in winter – the bark was especially valuable.

Hedges were also an important source of timber, especially in areas which had been extensively cleared and many hedges were planted with elm, ash, oak and beech trees – though often only the landowner could take wood from hedges.

For those who could cut trees, the quick growing field elm was immensely useful. Its timber made good planks for cladding barns or making chair seats; its trunk could be hollowed to make water pipes; and even its fresh foliage could be fed to cattle. Often large elms, oaks and beeches would be pollarded – cut-off at the bole high enough to prevent stock grazing the new shoots. In the South-east, smaller hedge-row trees such as hazel were coppiced in exactly the same way as woodlands. Every 10 to 15 years, the trees were cut right down to their stumps, yielding excellent wood for hurdles and thatching spars. Because thick hedges were needed to keep livestock in, fields between newly coppiced hedges were usually ploughed up for corn or roots. Only when the saplings springing from the stumps had grown tall and thick again were the fields returned to pasture.

For the poor, though, it was as a source of wild food that the hedge was especially cherished.

Besides the rich harvest of berries every autumn, there were 'nuts in May' to be gathered – these nuts were actually the tubers of pignut, dug and boiled like potatoes. In autumn, there were hazel or 'cob' nuts to be gathered, and through much of the summer, mushrooms and all kinds of fungi.

Many other hedgerow plants that count for little today had real value in the past. The tuberous roots of cuckoo pint, for example, were boiled to yield a starch used to stiffen ruffs in the reign of Elizabeth I, while woundwort was good for staunching blood from wounds.

From early times the foxgloves that often grew beneath the hedge were held in awe, for eating even a couple of its leaves could prove fatal. Yet for centuries, the plant was a valued treatment for dropsy and, more recently, digitalis made from foxglove leaves became an effective weapon in the fight against heart failure.

In World War 2, the siege of Britain reminded people of the real value of the harvest hedge. Tons of herbs were gathered for drugs and country schoolchildren regularly spent some of their classtime collecting rose hips from the hedgerows to make a syrup rich in vitamin C. And nettles were brought back into use for dyeing camouflage clothing.

From the very earliest times, country people have made the most of the creatures drawn to the hedgerow by the abundant supply of food. Thrushes and other birds were killed for the pot or 'limed' and sent to London. Later, rabbits, too – netted as they emerged from their burrows at the hedge foot – were valuable supplements to the poor country people's meagre diet. These days, however, the bountiful hedgerow harvest is left almost unreaped. But if we have forgotten the value of the hedge, wild creatures have not and, all year round, the hedgerow is alive with myriad birds and small mammals.

HEDGEROW ELMS (left) Elm trees were the most popular of all the large trees planted in hedgerows, and, in the South, great rows of elm trees along field boundaries were once a common sight. The elm not only grew quickly but provided tough, durable wood for anything from field drains to cart wheel hubs.

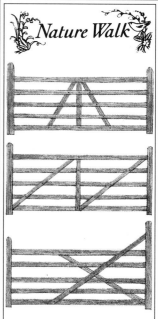

TRADITIONAL GATES. From the top – Inverness, East Riding, and the iron-braced Gloucester gates.

BLACKBIRD NESTS. Found in the fork of a tree or shrub, usually 3ft or more off the ground, lined with mud.

WHITETHROAT NESTS. Usually 1ft off the ground – loosely built lined with roots and hair, and wedged in twigs.

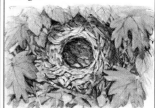

WREN NESTS. Solid domed nests, built into tree hollows, from ground level upwards.

Nature Walk

241

Along the Hedgerow

The flowers and fruits of the harvest hedge draw hordes of hungry birds, mammals and insects, many of which earn their meal by fertilizing and dispersing the seed of the hedgerow plants and shrubs.

The harvest hedge is a bright scene of plenty, glowing with berries and busy with feasting. The juicy black fruits of the bramble attract wasps that become drowsily replete. An elegant red admiral butterfly alights on an over-ripe berry and uncoils its long tongue to suck the juices.

A family party of mistle thrushes strips the hawthorn of its pendulous red fruits, and blackbirds peck at the scarlet berries of white and black bryony. The two sorts of bryony are unrelated, white bryony being a member of the cucumber family and black of the yam family; they are named for the colour of their roots.

Orange-red hips, sometimes collected for rose hip syrup, adorn the thorny dog rose. Velvety-purple sloes cluster on the blackthorn. Gathered for sloe gin or wine and jam-making, these fruits are equally attractive to the birds. Noisy starlings and blackbirds also strip the elder of its tiny black berries, another fruit sought by wine-makers.

Deep within the hedge lurk the sinister berries of deadly nightshade, like glossy, black, miniature cherries. Pheasants are said to eat them, but they are poisonous to humans and many animals, being rich in alkaloids that affect the nervous system.

SEED DISPERSAL

Many plants have evolved sweet fruit pulp around their seeds as a mechanism for dispersal. The bright, tasty fruit, often an inviting red colour, entices animals to eat the flesh and its enclosed seeds. A mistle thrush that eats a haw whole, or a blackbird that gulps down a blackberry, is helping the plant to reproduce. They digest the nutritious fruit tissue and excrete the seeds, usually some distance from the parent plant. Thus the plant's evolutionary strategy has worked. But the wasp or butterfly that sucks at fruit juices, and the caterpillar that munches away at the crab-apple, are fruit thieves. They are opportunistic feeders and are of no benefit to the plant.

By late summer most of the hedgerow flowers have withered and fruits and seeds have developed in their place, but there is still some nectar available for flower-feeding insects. A tortoiseshell butterfly investigates the sweet-scented honeysuckle draping the hedge, then flutters down to probe the yellow flowers of

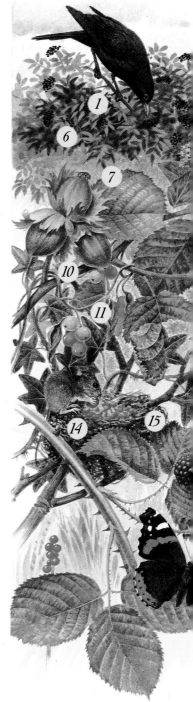

MONEY SPIDER WEBS
Early in the morning, when there is a touch of autumn in the air and the night has been cold, the sun glints on the dew. Myriad tiny, horizontal spider webs glisten, rising up the hedge like steps. These are the webs of small money spiders. They use their sheet webs as traps, lurking beneath to bite and pull through any tiny creature wallowing on the insubstantial surface.

AUTUMN

SPRING

KEY TO AUTUMN SPECIES

1 *Blackbird*
2 *Long-tailed tits*
3 *Blue tits*
4 *Sloes*
5 *Fieldfare*
6 *Elderberries*
7 *Nut weevil*
8 *Ivy flowers*
9 *Haws*
10 *Hazelnuts*
11 *Black bryony berries*
12 *Hibernating brimstone*
13 *Dog rose hips*
14 *Wood mouse*
15 *Chewed hips in bird's nest*
16 *Female holly blue: late summer brood*
17 *Comma*
18 *Bramble*
19 *Common wasp*
20 *Arum berries*
21 *Red campion*
22 *Red admiral*
23 *Flesh fly*
24 *Mushrooms*

HEDGEROW WILDLIFE

In autumn, berries attract insects, birds and mammals. Insects seek nectar from the late flowers of ivy and red campion. Tits search the foliage for invertebrates.

In spring, leaves and flowers burst out afresh. Caterpillars and newly hatched insects provide food for breeding birds. The hunting stoat may feed on partridge eggs, a vole or an unwary rabbit.

KEY TO SPRING SPECIES

1 *Male bullfinch*
2 *Ash*
3 *Cuckoo*
4 *Oak eggar caterpillar*
5 *Oak*
6 *Hawthorn*
7 *Blackthorn*
8 *Brimstone*
9 *Bramble*
10 *Hedge brown*
11 *Grey partridge*
12 *Red campion*
13 *Green-veined white*
14 *Arum*
15 *Stoat*
16 *Pignut*
17 *Morel*
18 *Common cat's ear*
19 *Small skipper*
20 *Frog hopper*
21 *Rabbit*
22 *Female holly blue: spring brood*
23 *Bank vole*

243

HIBERNATING LADYBIRDS
(left) Clustered here on the dead head of a teasel, these seven-spot ladybirds have chosen a prickly site on which to overwinter. Many do not survive until the spring as they are prone to fungal attack. They have no need to hide away – their bright colours warn birds that they are poisonous.

WOODY NIGHTSHADE
(right) The bright berries, which turn from green to yellow and then to red when ripe, often decorate the hedgerow long into winter after the plant's leaves have withered and fallen. The plant climbs among hedgerow shrubs, and from June to September its beautiful purple and yellow flowers enliven the scene.

FIELDFARE ON HAWS
(right) Large numbers of wintering fieldfares and redwings join their resident cousins – the mistle thrush, song thrush and blackbird – to feast on the hedgerow harvest. In a good autumn the hedgerow is laden with fruit – hips, haws, sloes, elderberries, blackberries and rowan berries.

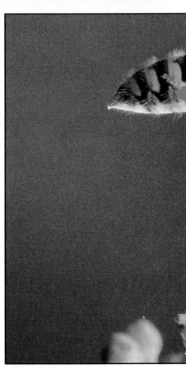

hedge mustard. The last ring of lilac-coloured flowers at the base of the cone-like flowerheads of a tall teasel is a fuelling stop for a painted lady butterfly. As summer turns into autumn and the temperature drops, painted ladies migrate southwards or die; neither adult, egg, caterpillar nor pupa can survive the cold British winter.

A few white trumpets remain on the hedge bindweed, and these are visited early in the day by bees and hoverflies hungry for their pollen. The focus of activity for the flower-feeders is the ivy cloaking a dead stump of elm. The small, greenish-yellow flowers, arranged in globular clusters, produce copious nectar which is avidly lapped up by bees and hoverflies.

Many of the larger hoverflies on the ivy look superficially like honey bees. They are drone flies, named after male honey bees, since, like them, they have no sting. These robust flies are able to hibernate as adults and so are often seen on warm autumn or spring days. Their maggot-like larvae feed on decaying organic material and are often found in water, breathing by means of a tube up to 15cm long. Sometimes they are found in wet carrion, and are thought to be the source of Samson's riddle about a swarm of bees and honey in a lion carcass.

Hedgerows in southern England and Wales are often covered with old man's beard or traveller's joy. As autumn unfolds the flowers of this clematis give way to feathery clusters of plumed seeds. Wind disperses the clematis seeds, but the little seeds of another common climber, goosegrass or cleavers, are covered with hooked spines that lodge in the fur of passing mammals and are dispersed in this way.

Teasels produce seeds in the spiky 'cones' at the top of their tall stems. The plants sway and dip as goldfinches, bright and dapper as guardsmen, perch to lever out the tiny seeds. A patch of thistles hosts a twittering party of linnets and more goldfinches after the seeds. At the end of the nineteenth century, when farm labour was cheap, and field edges were regularly scythed, goldfinches became quite rare. Recently their numbers have increased and a twittering charm of goldfinches is again a familiar sound in the countryside.

Far less visible are the tiny money spiders that float through the air on gossamer strands, appearing as though from nowhere and hanging in mid-air without apparent support. Young money spiders disperse by climbing to the top of plants, raising their abdomens in the air and paying out silken strands from their spinerets. Once the breeze catches the gossamer thread, they let go and float away.

Compared with early summer, the hedge seems quiet. Most of the birds have fallen silent now that their courtship and nesting are finished.

A LITTER OF YOUNG STOATS
(left) Although stoats mate in the summer, the young – from 5 to 12 in a litter – are not born until the following spring. Blind at first, they are suckled for several weeks before being introduced to solid food. Once they leave the den they learn to hunt alongside their mother.

Only the companionable robin still sings, as it moults its feathers. A stately pheasant struts with measured tread in the shade of the hedge, while above, a solitary blackcap inquisitively searches the hawthorn leaves for bugs and flies. The flash of their white rumps betrays two young bullfinches, dowdy brown compared with their black and pink father. A magpie swoops in over the field, lands on an ash tree emerging from the hedge, and disturbs a family of long-tailed tits. They erupt out of the tree and flit along the hedge, looking like flying acrobats supporting their long tails on their shorter, stumpy bodies.

ANIMALS OF THE EVENING

As each day draws to a close and the shadows lengthen, a little muntjac deer picks its way delicately and silently along the base of the hedge. Rabbits furtively creep out of their warren in a sandy bank, ready to scuttle back to the safety of the burrows at the least sign of danger. They have yet to notice the family party of stoats snaking their way sinuously along the far side of the hedge. But the red-brown bank vole gnawing at seeds among the ash roots has sensed the advance of the marauders, and it retreats quietly into its tunnel beneath the grass roots. So, too, has the bright-eyed wood mouse, which pauses just long enough to collect a sloe, before taking the fruit into a secluded crevice in the thorny blackthorn tangle.

When plump, brown hazelnuts ripen in September or October, both voles and mice will gnaw them open to reach the nutritious kernels. Their technique, however, is different, so their teeth marks can be identified on empty shells. Having made a hole, bank voles insert the snout and gnaw inwards on the nearest side; wood mice insert the lower incisors and gnaw outwards on the far side of the nut.

A young fox, already old enough to have left its family, trots towards the rabbit warren, but is too slow and inexperienced to do more than give the rabbits a scare. It follows a well-worn track compacted by the feet of badgers.

As the golden globe of the harvest moon rises above the hedge, a female badger lumbers into view along the track, her three growing cubs following behind, making whickering noises as they gallop up to where she has excavated a bumble bee nest in an abandoned mouse run. They, too, have their share of the hedge's harvest, as they feast on the juicy bumble bee grubs and stored honey.

GOLDFINCH ON TEASEL
(left) Roaming family parties of goldfinches are much in evidence in late summer and autumn. Thistle and teasel seeds are favourite foods.

MIDSUMMER HEDGE
(below) White dog rose and climbing honeysuckle dominate this hedge, flowering together in June and July.

COMMON WASP ON IVY
(left) Flowering in autumn, ivy provides a late source of nectar which attracts many pollinating insects.

White Bryony

Wild Hop

Wild Madder

WHITE BRYONY *(Bryonia dioica)*
This perennial herb has long, branched stems 13′ (4m) or more, which climb by means of tendrils. The flowers are borne on separate male and female plants from May until August. Locally common in hedges and scrub.

WILD HOP *(Humulus lupulus)* A widespread native 10-20′ (3-6m) perennial, the hop clambered in our hedges long before it was cultivated. The stems climb by twisting in a clockwise direction. Only the female flowers, which appear in late summer are used in making beer.

WILD MADDER *(Rubia peregrina)* Restricted to south and south-west England, this 1-4′ (30-120cm) perennial scrambles in hedges, scrub and thickets. The four-angled stem has rough prickly edges, as do the leaves, which grow in whorls of 4 to 6. Flowers from June to August.

Hedge Bedstraw

Woody Nightshade

Hedge Bindweed

HEDGE BEDSTRAW *(Galium mollugo)* This perennial herb is found throughout the British Isles. Its four-angled 1-4′ (30-120cm) stems trail in hedges, on banks and in open woodland. The little flowers appear in July and are followed by smooth rounded fruit.

WOODY NIGHTSHADE *(Solanum dulcamara)* This scrambling 1-7′ (30-210cm) woody perennial is a member of the potato family. Flowering from June to September the red fruits are poisonous. It is widespread in hedges and woods and on waste ground and shingle beaches.

HEDGE BINDWEED *(Calystegia sepium)* The 3-10′ (90-300cm) stems of this perennial climb by twisting in an anticlockwise direction. It blooms from July to September; the flowers are followed by capsules containing brown seeds. Common in much of England and throughout Ireland.

Bullace

Medlar

Lesser Sweetbriar

BULLACE (*Prunus domestica insititia*) Once widely grown for its fruit, the bullace has been replaced by larger varieties of plum. Usually reaching about 20′ (6m), it may occasionally be found in hedges in many parts of the British Isles. It flowers in April and May.

LESSER SWEETBRIAR (*Rosa micrantha*) The arching stems of this 4-7′ (1-2m) shrub are a frequent sight in hedges, woods and scrub in England and Wales, particularly on calcareous soil. The prickles are hooked and the flowers are borne in June and July.

MEDLAR (*Mespilus germanica*) This thorny shrub of 7-10′ (2-3m) bears solitary flowers in May and June. It is naturalized in hedges through much of England. The small, apple-shaped fruit remains hard until softened by the first frosts of autumn; then it is ready to eat.

Plymouth Pear

Sour Cherry

Cherry Plum

PLYMOUTH PEAR (*Pyrus cordata*) A thorny little shrub only found in hedges around Plymouth, in the counties of both Devon and Cornwall. It reaches 10-14′ (3-4m), flowers in April and May and the fruit is small – less than 1″ (25mm) long – and rounded.

CHERRY PLUM (*Prunus cerasifera*) A small, introduced hedgerow tree which reaches 25′ (7.5m). The flowers, which are often solitary, appear in March and April among the opening leaves. Usually the first of the wild cherries to flower, it is found in many parts of England.

SOUR CHERRY (*Prunus cerasus*) This introduced hedgerow shrub grows up to 25′ (7.5m) tall, often with drooping branches, it flowers in April and May and is the wild ancestor of the morello cherry. Uncommon in northern England and Scotland, but widespread elsewhere.

Female

Brown Hairstreak

Male

Wall Brown

Dingy Skipper

BROWN HAIRSTREAK (*Thecla betulae*) On the wing in August and September, this butterfly occurs mainly in southern England and the Midlands. The adult – wingspan 1⅛″ (35mm) – prefers to stay among the tree-tops. Eggs are laid on sloe and overwinter before hatching.

DINGY SKIPPER (*Erynnis tages*) This 1″ (25mm) skipper is on the wing in May and June, sometimes earlier, in much of Britain. On dull days it folds its wings over its back like a moth. The larvae feed on bird's-foot trefoil, hibernating and pupating in a tent of leaves.

WALL BROWN (*Lasiommata megera*) This 2″ (50mm) sun-loving butterfly is often found basking along low hedgerows and on banks and walls. It is common as far north as southern Scotland, flying in May and again in July and August. The larvae feed on a range of coarse grasses.

Butterflies

Grizzled Skipper

Small Copper

Marbled White

GRIZZLED SKIPPER (*Pyrgus malvae*) Confined to southern and central England, this 1⅛″ (28mm) skipper lives in small colonies. The eggs are laid singly on such herbs as wild strawberry and cinqfoil. It appears in May, and has a rapid flight with blurred wings.

SMALL COPPER (*Lycaena phlaeas*) There are usually three broods of this 1⅛″ (28mm) butterfly a year, so it may be seen on the wing from May until the frosts of autumn. It is territorial, darting towards any intruding butterfly. The larvae feed on sorrel and docks.

MARBLED WHITE (*Melanargia galathea*) One of the most distinctive of the brown butterflies, with a 2⅛″ (54mm) wingspan, it is found in the Midlands and the West in late summer. Eggs are dropped in vege-tation; larvae hibernate over winter and feed up on grasses in the spring.

The Yellowhammer

The cheerful, jingling song of the bright golden yellowhammer
is one of the most familiar country sounds, ringing out
from the hedgerows on long, hot summer days.

Its brilliant plumage glowing gold in the morning sun, the yellowhammer perches boldly in the topmost branch of a hedgerow hawthorn and bursts into song. All day long, its familiar, repetitive song, popularly rendered as 'little-bit-of-bread-and-no-cheese', echoes across the cornfield.

Often, the song of the yellowhammer is the only sound to be heard in the hot, dry harvest landscape, and it is known to country people all over Britain. For the yellowhammer, the rich harvest of seeds to be gleaned from the hedgerow is irresistible, and it is one of the commonest of all hedgerow birds.

The familiarity of this cheerful little bird to country people is reflected in its many common names. In Northumberland, it is called the 'yellow yowlie'; in parts of Scotland the 'yellow yoit'; and in the Norfolk Breckland, the 'guler', perhaps after the Dutch gold coin the guilder.

Such familiarity has not always been in the yellowhammer's favour. In northern Scotland,

it had the unfortunate reputation of drinking a drop of the devil's blood every morning in May, and was once mercilessly persecuted for this reason. In many parts of England, it was believed the dark markings on the yellowhammer's eggs were bloodstains, left as punishment after the birds became stained with blood as they fluttered around the Cross at the Crucifixion. Many country boys were taught it was their duty to destroy the eggs.

Fortunately, the yellowhammer has survived such persecution and the song of the male yellowhammer is a common hedgerow sound on fine days as early in the year as March, or even February. This spring song is a declamatory song, designed to announce the male's territory to rivals, but it is also a mating song attracting female birds.

The courtship of the yellowhammer is a boisterous affair, with the male vigorously seeing off rivals or chasing helter skelter after females, only for both to tumble into the hedge

HEDGE FEEDER
(above) *Like all buntings,
the yellowhammer feeds
mainly on seeds – though in
the breeding season it
will often eat insects and
larvae – and the abundant
supply of seeds and berries
makes the harvest hedge a
popular haunt for this
little bird.*

IN FLIGHT the bright lemon yellow head of the male yellowhammer is prominent, set off against a chestnut body. From underneath, the rich brown breast band and streaks are visible.

HUNGRY NESTLINGS
(above) Keeping the young chicks fed on a high-protein diet of insects and caterpillars is a never-ending task for the adult yellowhammer.

SONG POST
(below) To sing its characteristic 'little-bit-of-bread-and-no-cheese', the yellowhammer likes to find a prominent perch amid the hedgerow.

SHORT BILL Like all buntings, yellowhammers have a short, stout bill perfectly adapted to picking up seeds from the ground.

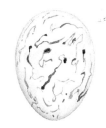

EGGS Two or three clutches of three to five eggs are laid, pale blue with dark 'scribbled' markings.

in a flurry of feathers. Sometimes, the male struts around in front of the female with crest raised, tail fanned, head up and bill wide open; at other times, male and female confront each other face to face, with outspread, fluttering wings.

Once mated, usually in April, the female begins to build a cup-shaped nest of grass, plant stems and moss, lined with hair and fine grass. Her favourite sites are among rough grass on the ground, at the foot of the hedgerow, or in an overgrown bank or ditch, though occasionally she may build in a bush a few feet above the ground.

During the summer, the female yellowhammer may lay two or three broods, each with three or four pale eggs covered in distinctive scribble markings. The female incubates the eggs, but once they are hatched, both parents care for the hungry nestlings, feeding them on a high-protein diet of insects rather than seeds although the adults themselves will sometimes eat insects in the summer. The chicks are ready to leave the nest within a fortnight.

As the hot summer days shorten into autumn, the yellowhammers set about eating in earnest to build up their vital reserves of fat to help them through the bleak winter days. They roam farmland in search of spilled grain, weed seeds and other foods, moving from field to field in a light, bounding flight, singing as they go. As they search the ground diligently, they keep themselves warm by puffing up their feathers.

Gregarious birds, yellowhammers search for seeds in large flocks, but so well camouflaged are they against the golden stubble of the autumn cornfield that they can be difficult to see. Often chaffinches, greenfinches, bramblings and linnets, and occasionally skylarks and sparrows, will join the yellowhammers, and these large flocks may stay together right through the winter.

Throughout the cold weather of autumn and winter, yellowhammers roost together in large groups in reedbeds, or in dense hedgerows, which shelter the birds from the biting winds and helps them save precious energy.

The Fallen Tree

In a clearing deep in the wood lie the shattered limbs of a fallen tree, its weakened trunk severed violently from its roots leaving only a jagged stump rising forlornly from the forest floor as a temporary reminder of past glory. Once a common sight in Britain's woodland, today fallen trees are often sawn up for timber as soon as they topple – apart from the south of England, where so many trees were destroyed by a storm in the autumn of 1987 that many are still lying where they fell. Where they are left, the dead wood is quickly covered with a carpet of velvety green moss and claimed by the myriad insects and fungi which speed its decay and return its nutrients to the soil, guaranteeing future life in the wood.

OPEN GLADE

STAG-HEADED OAKS

PARKLAND

NATURE RESERVE

SAPLINGS

CUT TIMBER

RELIC
WET WOODLAND

DIVERSE FATES

Throughout the countryside there are countless numbers of trees in woods and parkland, coppices and hedgerows, but fallen trees are relatively few. This is because of the value of timber – many trees are sawn up soon after they fall, and it is generally only in parkland and unproductive or commercially useless woodland, like the alder and sallow woods found in marshy areas, that fallen trees are allowed to remain. In areas of heavy grazing by sheep or deer, the glade created by the fallen tree remains open. Only occasionally – in a protected environment – is the fallen tree replaced by natural succession, and the glade replenished with new trees.

Since the end of the last Ice Age, when the first birch and Scots pine trees colonized Britain, woodland has been an important feature of the British landscape, and the death of trees part of the eternal cycle of the forest.

In these ancient natural wildwoods, untouched by man, disease and animal damage took an annual toll of the trees, and at any one time vast numbers of toppled trunks and broken branches would litter the forest floor, providing a habitat for thousands of species of animals and fungi which in turn hastened the process of their decay. The fall of each ancient tree punctuated the forest cycle, creating a glade in the forest and enabling the sun to break through the canopy and encourage the growth of bright spring flowers. In time the clearing would be replaced by a thicket, beloved by song birds, and then by young saplings, taking root in the enriched soil and spreading wide to close the gap in the canopy.

This natural cycle is rarely witnessed today, even though we still have vast areas of trees – some 1,200,000 acres of broadleaved woodland, three times that acreage of conifer plantations, and an estimated 88 million trees growing singly along hedges or in belts or clumps in the patchwork countryside. The scarcity of dead and decaying wood is mainly due to the modern value of timber – many woodlands are now maintained as timber reserves and most woodland trees are felled in their prime, free of disease, long before they would naturally fall.

Nowadays old and fallen trees are more likely where trees are valued not for their timber, but for their appearance. It is in open parkland and in hedgerows that many of our oldest trees are found. Some of these have had their timber value destroyed by pollarding which has opened the trunk to decay.

AN INDEFINITE LIFESPAN

Decay does not necessarily spell the end of a tree. Trees do not age and die in the same way as animals with their predetermined lifespans – they take many years to reach maturity, and then survive for as long as the income from their leaves and roots matches the demands of trunk and branches. Some species reach three, four or five times the human span as a matter of course: gnarled, dead limbs stretch unclothed amongst the foliage of living branches, but still the tree stands, its blasted, hollow trunk living on surrounded by myth and folklore.

Throughout its life, a tree is attacked by animals of many kinds. Squirrels tear the bark from upper branches, while deer strip the exposed roots. Beetle grubs and some caterpillars burrow to eat their way through the timber and insects devour the leaves. A tree can survive most of these attentions, although sometimes, especially when heavy insect infestation is followed by drought, some of the higher boughs may die. The tree can grow a new vigorous canopy of green leaves below, but the dead limbs may remain to give it a 'stag head'.

Fungal infection is much more dangerous, and permeates living – as well as dead – timber, weakening it so that in time it falls. Fungi may also kill a tree by blocking sap tubes – the effect of Dutch elm disease which decimated our hedgerow elms. Fungal spores spread quickly, carried by wind and also by insects, and it is because of this that fallen timber is quickly cut up and cleared from productive woodland – the forester considers it too risky to leave.

Where a fallen tree is allowed to remain in the cool, moist shade of the forest floor, it retains its bark and becomes host to a multitude of animals and plants. For this reason, in woods which are being managed as nature reserves, branches and even trunks are allowed to lie and rot. Indeed, such is the wealth of animal life associated with a fallen tree that it can be counted a nature reserve in its own right.

AN ENRICHED WOODLAND HABITAT
(above) In some woodlands, dead trees are left as part of a conservation policy, and provide a habitat for a wide variety of flora and fauna.

THE ANCIENT OAK
(left) Of all our native trees, the mighty oak has the longest lifespan, and may live for as long as 800 years. Some of the oldest standing trees are found in our parklands and woodlands; their hollow, blasted trunks and dry, twisted boughs tell of their age and the extent of their decay. Limbs may fall, but still the tree stands, an ancient giant, surrounded with legend.

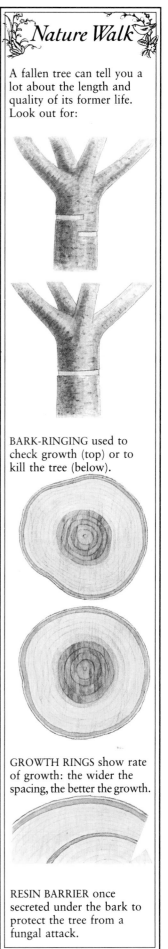

Nature Walk

A fallen tree can tell you a lot about the length and quality of its former life. Look out for:

BARK-RINGING used to check growth (top) or to kill the tree (below).

GROWTH RINGS show rate of growth: the wider the spacing, the better the growth.

RESIN BARRIER once secreted under the bark to protect the tree from a fungal attack.

Life After Death

Trees are constantly under attack from fungi, insects and even birds but this decay accelerates apace when the tree crashes to the woodland floor.

After growing tall and strong for more than two centuries, the great gnarled tree in the midst of the forest is old now, and fragile. Its crumbling, rotten bark is deeply fissured, and many branches are withered and twisted. Boughs once limber and supple are weak and frail, creaking ominously in even the slightest breeze. Many dead branches already lie scattered beneath the tree, and each strong gust of wind snaps off another. With every spring, the tree sends forth fewer and fewer young green shoots, and the ancient bole of the tree is now partially hollow. It will not be long before some fierce winter gale brings the tree itself crashing to the ground.

But in the death of the tree there is life, for the dying tree is the habitat of a fascinating variety of wildlife. For many creatures and organisms, the dying tree provides not just a home but sustenance too. Often, it is their very presence that causes – or hastens – the decay.

While the tree is yet living, many kinds of insects and fungi will find food there. In spring,

SHAGGY PHOLIOTA ON AN OAK STUMP
This vigorously growing fungus adds a splash of cinnamon colour to the autumnal scene. It grows in clusters, mainly on deciduous trees.

hordes of caterpillars and other small invertebrates devour the succulent green foliage. Rolled up in the leaves of an old oak, for instance, are the caterpillars of the green oak tortrix (or 'oak roller') moth, their droppings pattering on the woodland floor like drops of rain. Safe from marauding tits in their leafy tunnels, the caterpillars devour the young leaves voraciously, so that by the middle of June the tree looks as bare as in winter. A healthy tree can send out fresh leaves late in the summer, but for an already decaying tree, the effects of defoliation by these and other caterpillars can be devastating.

Meanwhile, hidden from sight under the bark, equally destructive mouths may be at work. For up to four years, the foul smelling caterpillar of the goat moth burrows tunnels, the thickness of a finger, deep into ash, lime, oak and elm trunks, while down near the base of these trees – often penetrating the roots – white hornet moth caterpillars dig away in the dark, emerging years later to spin their cocoons in a hole in the bark.

BURROWING BARK BEETLES

Burrowing away within the tree, too, are the grubs of bark and ambrosia beetles, each species eating away its own unique pattern of tunnels; when the tree, or branch, falls to the ground and the bark peels away, these gallery patterns are clearly revealed. Bark beetle larvae feed on the wood itself, while ambrosia beetle larvae eat the ambrosia fungus that coats their tunnels. But both can wreak havoc in a tree already weakened by frost or drought. Even healthy trees may eventually succumb – especially if the beetles lay them open to attack by other insects or to fungal infections. The great spruce bark beetle – an invader from Europe – is especially feared by foresters, while the devastating effect on elms of infestation by elm bark beetles, which carry the deadly fungal infection Dutch elm disease, is all too well known.

The Dutch Elm disease is microscopic, and can penetrate to the heart of the tree. But many

AROUND THE FALLEN TREE

Plants soon colonize the clearing made by the fallen tree. Bramble flowers attract the high brown fritillary. Grasshopper warblers and nightingales nest in the undergrowth. Redstarts and woodpeckers occupy holes in decaying trees, as may the hornet. The larvae of many beetles burrow in standing and fallen timber, encouraging fungal infection. The invisible feeding threads of many fungi break down the wood, putting forth colourful fruiting bodies.

KEY TO FEATURES AND SPECIES

 1 *Pipistrelle bat*
 2 *Usnea lichens*
 3 *Oak*
 4 *Nightingale*
 5 *Male redstart*
 6 *Great spotted woodpecker*
 7 *Birch trees*
 8 *Hornet*
 9 *Male sparrowhawk*
10 *Foxglove*
11 *Sycamore seedlings*
12 *Bracken*
13 *Old tree stump*
14 *Grasshopper warbler*
15 *Tinder fungus*
16 *Deer-stripped bark*
17 *Coral spot fungus*
18 *Parmelia lichen*
19 *Stag beetles*
20 *Beetle galleries*
21 *Primroses*
22 *Coral-root orchid*
23 *Bugle*
24 *Bramble*
25 *Bracken*
26 *St John's wort*
27 *Honey fungus*
28 *Moss*
29 *Ant beetle*
30 *Woodlice*
31 *Crumble cap fungus*
32 *Ground beetle*
33 *Common cow wheat*
34 *Beefsteak fungus*
35 *High brown fritillary*
36 *Molehill*
37 *Wasp beetle*
38 *Hawthorn*

SPARROWHAWK WITH PREY
Hunting along woodland rides or swerving between tree trunks, the sparrowhawk takes its prey by surprise. It may also hunt along hedgerows, darting over the top to catch feeding birds unawares. It usually strikes down its quarry in flight, before flying off with the luckless bird to a plucking post. Here a female sparrowhawk – the larger of the sexes – is plucking a great tit on a dead branch. A fallen tree in a clearing makes a convenient plucking block which may be used many times.

DISAPPEARING FROM VIEW
(below) The fallen tree is soon hidden by grasses, brambles and flowers. The rotting wood is covered by carpets of moss and clumps of fungi which break down the timber.

NEST SITES

It is not all decay, though, for the weakening of the tree opens up potential nesting sites for myriad woodland birds. In summer, little willow tits are ever flitting in and out of the nestholes they have excavated themselves in rotting alder, willow and birch trunks, while the distinctive *pchew* of the marsh tit may often be heard in the branches of the old tree where it has found a suitable crack to make its nest. Woodpeckers, meanwhile, delve into the wood with their hammering beaks, looking for food.

But as time wears on and the tree becomes more and more rotten and cracked, new insects and fungi will colonize, sometimes driving out the original inhabitants, sometimes living side by side. Many of these species accelerate the decay. The sandy yellow root fomes fungus can devastate conifers, weakening the roots so much that the tree is easily blown down. Infestation continues, branches and boughs die and drop off, and eventually the whole tree is brought crashing to the ground.

At first, the scene around the great fallen trunk is one of terrible destruction, as shattered branches and boughs lie strewn across the ground, and broken limbs dangle from trees caught in the fall. But the fall has cleared a sunny glade in which many woodland flowers will soon flourish, and many of the tree's own internal community have survived the fall. Soon the original inhabitants will be joined by myriads more. In time, they will reduce the

other kinds of fungi may grow in the living wood, speeding the process of decay, as their fine feeding threads permeate the tree, softening and weakening the wood.

Fungi of all shapes and sizes may live off the ageing tree, from elaborately sculpted 'bracket' fungi that cling to the trunk like wall brackets, to the toadstools that cluster around the base – even the powdery looking spots and patches that cover old trees are usually tiny fungi, such as the deathly white patches of *Hyphodontia sambuci*. Largest of all the bracket fungi is the giant dryad's saddle which grows rapidly after summer rain up to 2 ft (60 cm) across. For sustaining this vast fungus, the host tree is repaid with an attack of white rot, as it is by the hoof-shaped oyster fungus. A brown discus of birch fungus on a birch tree signals the onset of heart rot in the tree, which turns the heartwood rust-coloured and breaks it into crumbling blocks.

Another danger signal is a cluster of 20 or more honey fungi, like a pile of cornflakes around the base of the tree. This is the tree's death warrant, for the feeding threads of honey fungus cause a flaky white rot in the wood. Timber killed this way is luminous, shining slightly in the dark.

Trees can often survive insect and fungal attack for many years – even decades – while individual branches die and fall, and even the trunk hollows out. But as the tree cracks open it lets in more and more infestations. The black, gelatinous witches' butter fungus, for instance, colonizes dead branches on the tree, while the descriptively named Jew's ear fungus lodges in frost cracks on the trunk.

FOXGLOVE
(left) This woodland flower often springs up in clearings made by fallen trees. A year or two later it may be found growing from a crack in the decaying trunk. It flowers from June to September.

EYED LONGHORN
(above right) This beetle gets its name from its long antennae and the eye-like markings on its wing cases. Its grubs excavate galleries under the bark of decaying deciduous trees.

FEEDING WOODPECKER
(below left) Hammering here at a fallen branch, this great spotted woodpecker is searching for grubs. Woodpeckers hasten the fall of living trees as their drillings encourage damaging fungi.

HORNET'S NEST
(below right) As well as being the largest British wasp, the hornet is one of the rarest. It generally breeds in holes in tree trunks or stumps, chewing the soft wood to make the cells of its nest (visible here).

tree's colossal bulk to nought.

Among the many fungi that feed upon the shattered remains of the tree are poisonous yellow sulphur tufts, crinkly hairy stereums that cluster like little roof tiles on the log, and withered, black dead man's fingers which favour beech tree stumps. In rotting oak stumps, the grubs of stag beetles – one of our largest insects – live hidden for several years, eating the soft wood around them. The adults, too, often hide in cavities, emerging only in the evening for mating forays. The timberman beetle, easily recognized by its exceptionally long head feelers, prefers rotting pine wood.

Once the wood begins to dry out, insects notorious in many homes, such as the death watch beetle and woodworm (the furniture beetle), begin to bore their intricate maze of holes. The death watch gets its name for the way it taps its head on the walls of its gallery to attract a mate, the effect sounding like an ominously ticking watch.

A fallen tree may also become home to many snails, worms, woodlice and other creatures of the woodland floor. These tiny creatures range surprising distances after dark, returning at dawn to safe refuges beneath the bark or in the honeycombed timber. By feeding on the decaying wood, they too hasten the breakdown of the timber into fine soil.

All the while, of course, the prone tree is frequently visited by woodland birds. The brightly-coloured redstart flickers down to feed on the abundant insect and invertebrate life, while the sparrowhawk tarries a while to pluck newly captured prey on the stump.

Soon the vegetation thriving in the sunny glade created by the fall of the tree is lapping up around its diminishing bulk. Ivy and other climbers scramble over it. Purple foxgloves, coral root orchid and many other plants spring up in crevices. Slowly and surely, the old tree vanishes into the woodland background, leaving only the rich community of plants and wild creatures that it fostered.

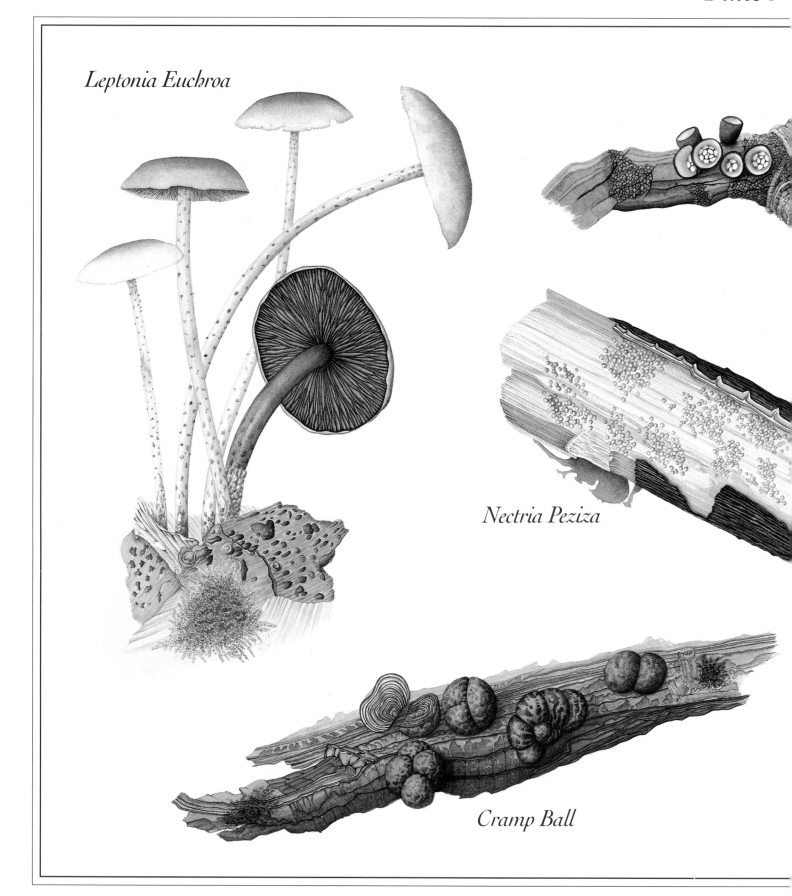

Leptonia Euchroa

Nectria Peziza

Cramp Ball

LEPTONIA EUCHROA This uncommon fungus has a silky, domed cap ½-2″ (1-5cm) across, violet to deep purple, on a slender stem. The gills are also a dark violet and shed pink spores. Tufts grow mostly on fallen hazel and alder, July to November. Edible.

CRAMP BALL (Daldinia concentrica) Growing mostly on dead ash wood, this fungus produces very woody, rounded fruit bodies up to 4″ (10cm) across, throughout the year. Black and shiny when mature, they shed millions of spores each night. Clearly banded inside. Not edible.

NECTRIA PEZIZA Fairly common throughout the year, this fungus grows on decaying bracket fungi and rotting wood. Very numerous, microscopic globular fruiting bodies have spores that are dispersed by drops of rain. Cup-shaped when dry. Not edible.

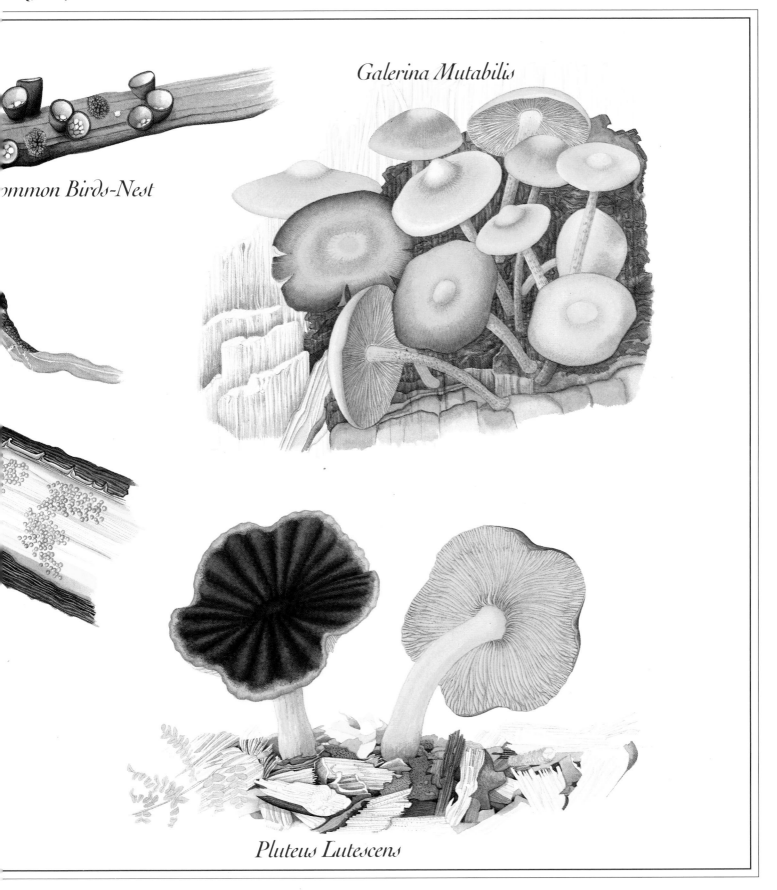

Galerina Mutabilis

Common Birds-Nest

Pluteus Lutescens

COMMON BIRDS-NEST
(*Crucibulum laeve*) Found growing
in clusters on fallen twigs and other
plant remains, autumn-spring. The
fruiting bodies are at first globular,
ripening to a 'nest' about ¼" (6mm)
across. Egg-like capsules contain
white spores. Inedible.

PLUTEUS LUTESCENS Living on
rotten wood, mostly beech, groups
of this uncommon fungus appear
May-October. The dark, pale-edged
cap is ½-2" (1-5cm) wide with
whitish gills turning pink as spores
are shed. The stem is bright yellow.
Supposedly edible, not recommended.

GALERINA MUTABILIS A
common fungus growing in crowded
tufts on tree stumps, seen late spring
to autumn. Caps are 1½-3" (3-6cm)
wide, flattening and drying with
age. The pale gills turn cinnamon as
dark-coloured spores fall. Scaly stem
has a ring below the cap. Edible.

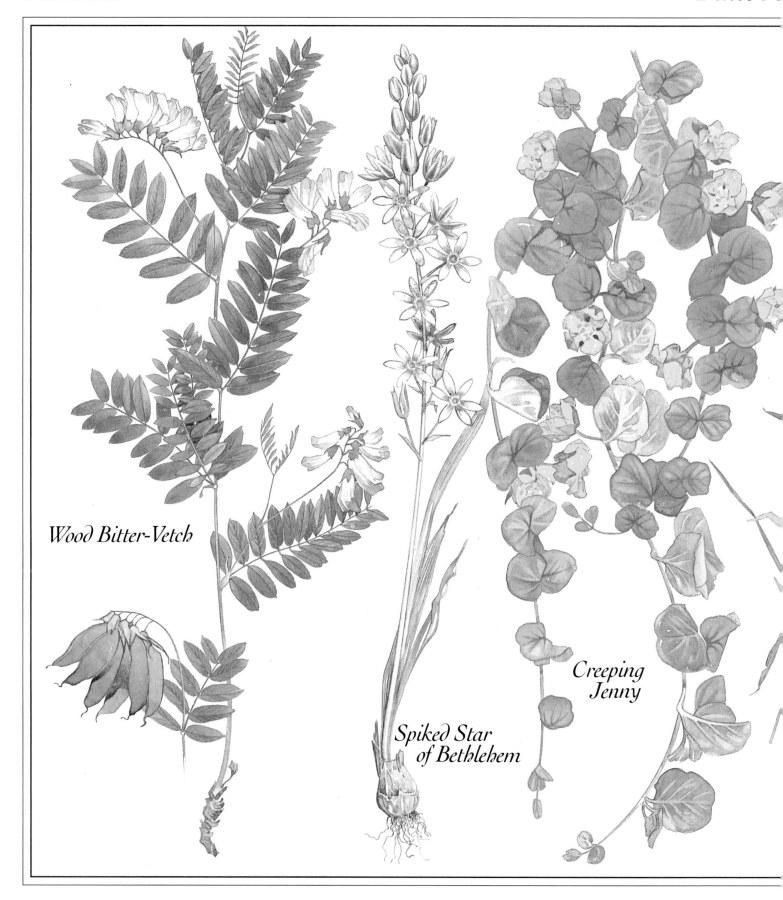

Wood Bitter-Vetch

Spiked Star
of Bethlehem

Creeping
Jenny

WOOD BITTER-VETCH *(Vicia orobus)* An increasingly rare plant of rocky woods in western Britain, this robust perennial has branched stems 12-24″ (30-60cm). Its leaves divide into 6-9 pairs of hairy leaflets – tendrils are absent. Spikes of 6-20 flowers appear June to September.

SPIKED STAR OF BETHLEHEM *(Ornithogalum pyrenaicum)* Very local and chiefly confined to woodlands on Cotswold limestone, this plant has linear, bluish leaves which fade in spring. The tall 20-40″ (50-100cm) flower stem bears over 20 blooms, June-July.

CREEPING JENNY *(Lysimachia nummularia)* A widespread trailing perennial of shady, damp banks and clearings, it forms a low carpet of stems up to 24″ (60cm) long. Rounded leaves are dotted with tiny glands, yellow flowers are borne singly June-August.

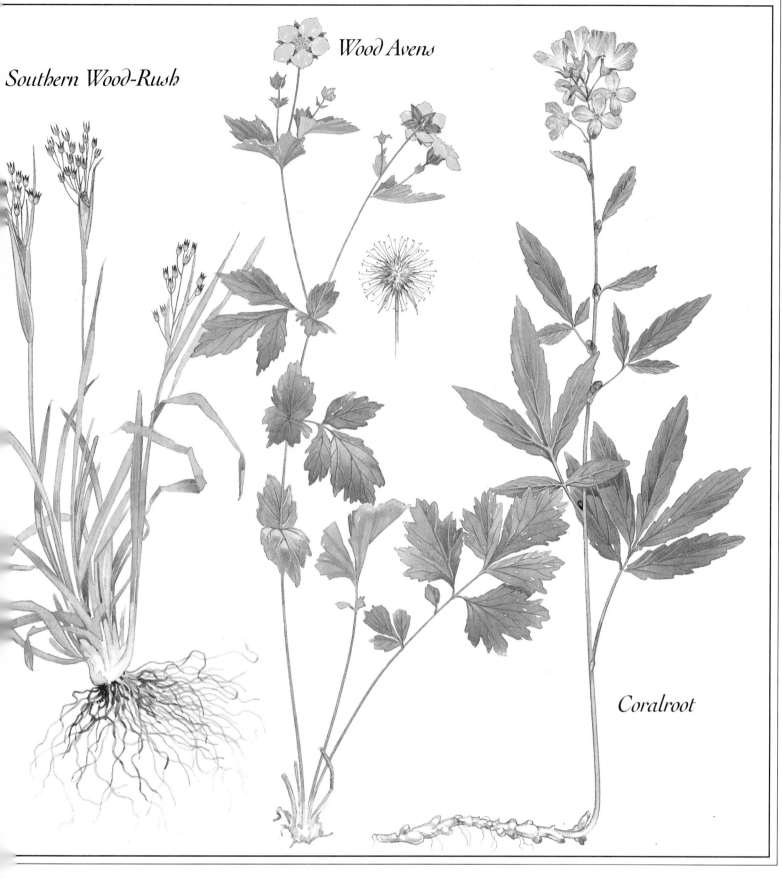

Southern Wood-Rush

Wood Avens

Coralroot

SOUTHERN WOOD-RUSH (*Luzula forsteri*) Often plentiful in woods of south Britain, narrow leaves of this 4-10″ (10-25cm) tufty perennial are easily told from grass by the fine cottony hairs around the edge. An open head of flowers that droops to one side can be seen April-June.

WOOD AVENS (*Geum urbanum*) A downy perennial growing in open clumps, stems to 24″ (60cm), with stalked flowers and hooked seeds, June-August. Leaves are unequally divided into toothed leaflets. It is widespread and common in shady woods, banks and waysides.

CORALROOT (*Cardamine bulbifera*) An erect, 12-28″ (30-70cm) perennial with thick, scaly roots, local to woods of Chilterns and the Weald. Top leaves are simple, lower divided into 3-7 leaflets. Flowering April-May, it reproduces by small buds in the leaf axils – its seeds rarely set.

Ghost Orchid

Common Cow-Wheat

GHOST ORCHID *(Epipogium aphyllum)* A very rare, protected orchid found in a few spots in deep shady beechwoods on the Chilterns. Weak, 2-10″ (5-25cm) stems and scale-like leaves lack green pigment and obtain all nutrients from rotting leaves. Flowers weakly June-August.

COMMON COW-WHEAT *(Melampyrum pratense)* Very variable, this 3-24″ (8-60cm) sprawling annual has long tubular flowers yellow when growing in woodland glades, white with pink marks when on open moors. It flowers May to October.

Purple Toothwort

Toothwort

TOOTHWORT *(Lathraea squamaria)* Widespread but local, seen mostly in damp chalky places, this parasite on roots of hazel and elm, is completely lacking in green pigment. Short-stalked, dull flowers borne along one side of a curved stem reaching 12″ (30cm), March-May.

PURPLE TOOTHWORT *(Lathraea clandestina)* A rare garden escape, found by streams and ponds in south and east England, this perennial parasitizes willow and poplar roots. Branched stems are hidden below the ground, only the bunches of long-stalked flowers emerging, April-May.

The Wood Ant

From their spectacular nests deep in the forest, armies of wood ants march out along radiating paths to comb the trees for prey. Highly organized, they are virtual rulers of their patch of woodland.

To come across a wood ant nest while walking through the forest can be an alarming experience. At first sight it seems innocent enough: a mound of leaves, twigs and pine needles, usually about 3 feet (1 metre) high, looking as if someone has dumped all the sweepings of the forest in a heap.

A closer look, however, will reveal that the heap is alive, its whole surface crawling with ants. A single nest may contain over 300,000 wood ants, and on one of those warm, dull humid days typical of the British summer most of them will be out and about, foraging for food. These foragers are the worker ants – non-breeding females whose function is to collect food, build, clean and repair the nest, and defend it against predators and rival ants.

DETERMINED HUNTERS

Wood ants feed on other insects, particularly the caterpillars of moths and sawflies which they hunt in trees near the nest. When a wood ant finds its prey, it attracts other workers with excited movements, and like a pack of dogs they surround the quarry and drag it down. The ant's principal weapon is chemical – having got a grip with its jaws an ant will curve its tail forward between its legs to spray a jet of corrosive formic acid which penetrates the skin of the prey, paralyzing it and destroying its tissues.

Co-operation does not stop at the kill – the ants also work together to drag their victim back to the nest. Unfortunately, the orchestration is often far from perfect – the ants will pull in different directions at the same time, and it may be some minutes before they sort themselves into an effective team. An average-sized colony may collect over 100,000 insects a day, as well as an equivalent weight of sugary honeydew milked from aphids and scale insects.

HUNGRY DEPENDANTS

Back at the nest much of this food is fed to the queens and larvae. The queens lay eggs all summer, so there are larvae at all stages of growth in the nest. These legless grubs rely on the adults to feed and groom them. As they grow big and fat on the food they are brought, they begin to develop adult features, and eventually each spins a cocoon to protect it while it changes into an adult proper.

Exactly what kind of adult finally emerges depends partly on the egg, and partly on the way the developing larva is treated. Most of the fertile eggs develop into workers, but if some of

the larvae are particularly well fed under the right temperature conditions they may grow into fully-fledged queens. Each year a few unfertilized eggs are also produced, and these develop into males. Their function is simply to mate, after which they die: there is no such thing as a male worker ant.

When they emerge as adults, both males and queens have wings, and some time in June when the weather is just right – windless and humid – they take off for their nuptial flight. Those that escape the notice of aerial predators such as

A DEFENSIVE WORKER
Common in oak and conifer woodlands throughout England, the wood ant is Britain's largest ant. Worker ants are about ¼" (6mm) long, and queens and males ³/₈" (9.5mm). With abdomen raised, this worker is ready to defend itself from attack by spraying formic acid from its anal glands.

swifts and martins will mate in the air or fall back to earth to mate on the ground where the males soon die.

Once mated, the queen is fertilized for life. She no longer needs her wings, so they fall off, and she crawls away to find a nesting site. This is a dangerous time for the queens: many are killed, not only by predators such as birds, toads and spiders, but also by other ants which resent the intrusion into their territory.

Some queens play safe and re-enter the old nest, but many start entirely new colonies. Selecting a suitable site, usually under an old tree stump, the queen digs a small hole and lays some eggs. The first larvae to hatch eat the remaining eggs and in due course emerge as workers who collect food for the next batch of

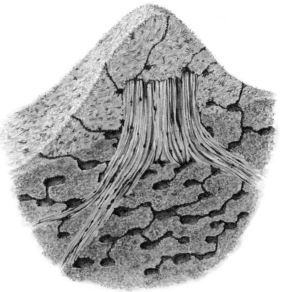

INSIDE THE NEST
(left) Under the characteristic mound of twigs and pine needles which shelter the nest lies a system of underground tunnels and chambers where the queen and young are tended by the workers. Inside, the conditions are humid, and eggs are transported from one chamber to another to ensure their proper development. Workers guard the entrances vigilantly and defend the nest against unwelcome intruders.

WORKING TOGETHER
(right) Workers join forces to carry a brimstone butterfly back to their nest. Each colony has its own territory in the forest and a series of permanent trackways links the nest with the hunting grounds. Wood ants can detect strangers from another colony by smell and defend their territory to the death. Battles between neighbouring colonies have been known to last for days, even weeks, especially when food is scarce and each colony is trying to increase its foraging range.

A VIRGIN QUEEN
(below) Only very few of the larvae develop into queens – perhaps as few as one in every thousand worker ants. When a queen emerges from her cocoon, she is winged, like the male, and retains her wings until her nuptial flight, which takes place on a still, sunny day in June. After mating, the queen is fertilized for life. She loses her wings and seeks out a place to lay her eggs, often returning to the old nest, but sometimes beginning a new colony nearby.

larvae, and also enlarge the nest, excavating galleries in the soil and building the great mound of plant debris which keeps the weather out. This is a never-ending task; the worker ants spend much of their lives repairing the damage caused by wind, rain and unwelcome visitors.

Meanwhile the queen remains in her chamber, laying eggs. She will lay many thousands each

season, hibernating in winter, and may live as long as 15 years. By the time she dies she will have outlived several generations of workers, and they in turn will have reared hundreds of daughter queens to take on her role in the nest and in the surrounding woodland.

KEEPING IN TOUCH
(below) The workers' sense of cooperation is reinforced by communication: information is exchanged by rubbing heads and antennae.

The Woodcock

The secretive woodcock, with its striking camouflage, can be almost invisible when nestled in the woodland undergrowth; in flight, however, its distinctive outline is easily recognized.

As the last rays of the setting sun fade from the trees and most woodland birds fall quiet, a reptilian croaking echoes through the woods, followed by a sneezing *tsi-wick*. Suddenly, the dark silhouette of a plump bird appears in the dim light, its wings beating in slow, measured strokes and its long bill pointing obliquely down. This is the display flight or 'roding' of the male woodcock.

During the spring and early summer, the male woodcock patrols the woods at dawn and dusk, roding in the air until it attracts a mate. The rest of the year, however, both male and female woodcock are almost silent, skulking secretively in the shadows, hidden by the woodland undergrowth.

WOODLAND WADER

Although it lives far from water the woodcock is actually a wader, related to the snipe, curlew and sandpiper. But its ancestors left the wetlands to take up residence in the woods and fields long ago. Only its exceptionally long beak betrays its origins – at over 3″ (8cm), it is nearly a quarter as long as the woodcock's body.

With this long beak, it often feeds in a similar way to other waders. The tip is so flexible and sensitive that the woodcock can detect its prey buried deep in soft earth. Once food is detected, the woodcock appears to suck it up – but to get a firm grip on large, slippery worms (its favourite food) the woodcock may have to burrow in deeper, and then haul the worm out and possibly tear it into pieces to eat. Besides delving into the ground with its beak, however, woodcock often turn over leaf litter, foraging slowly for beetle larvae.

The woodcock is a voracious eater, and every day it eats almost its own body weight in food. All summer long the woodcock forages and delves on the soft woodland floor, concentrating on damp patches rich in invertebrates.

As it feeds, the woodcock is almost invisible, for its russet and buff mottled plumage blends imperceptibly into the fallen leaves and dappled shade. The disguise is completed by the thick black bars across the head which clearly distinguish it from similar species.

Equally distinctive are the woodcock's large, beady eyes, set high on its head. These enable it to see in all directions even when probing for food. The eyes are well suited to the woodcock's life style, but mean that parts of the skull are curiously inverted so that the ear openings are below the level of the eyes and to the fore.

The female woodcock has her hidden nest in

a ferny brake in the lea of a fallen trunk. In a depression lined with leaves and a few feathers she lays four smooth pale buff eggs with chestnut splotches. These she broods for 22 days, sitting so still and so perfectly camouflaged that only a fleeting sunbeam on her huge dark eye betrays her presence.

INVISIBLE BROOD

The young are a light buff colour with chestnut mottlings on the back and, like the adults, blend in perfectly with their surroundings. From their first day, they are able to move away from the nest, although they do not become independent for five or six weeks. At the first hint of danger, they scatter and remain frozen until the danger has passed. Sometimes, the female removes the

A LEAFY NEST
(above) Woodcock make their nests in a patch of hollow ground lined with dry leaves, twigs and feathers, often near the base of a tree trunk. Four eggs are laid on average and these take about 22 days to hatch. Young woodcocks are born with pale brown, mottled down. Their eyes open soon after birth and they are capable of feeding themselves, although the mother keeps a close eye on them until they are fully independent.

RODING
(left) At dusk or at dawn from early March – the start of the breeding season – the male woodcock performs a striking display flight called roding. He patrols his territory, beating his wings in slow, owl-like strokes and uttering two distinctive calls – a deep croak followed by a sneeze-like sound, to attract a mate.

IN FLIGHT the woodcock is distinguished by its long, downward-pointing bill, tawny mottled plumage and dark bars across its head.

BINOCULAR VISION

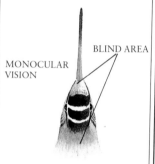

MONOCULAR VISION

BLIND AREA

THE EYES are set high on the sides of its head giving it 360° vision. This enables it to be ever on the lookout for danger.

young to a safer site, and witnesses claim to have seen a woodcock flying with the young clasped between its legs or carried singly in the bill, although this is still a matter of some debate.

Woodcock are known to have bred in every county in the British Isles. Their distribution is rather uneven and, perhaps because they favour dry woodland in summer, they are rarely found at this time of year in the moist south-west of England and Ireland. They clearly need woodland to breed, but even in relatively dry well-wooded parts of the country, such as south Sussex and north Essex, they are strangely absent.

Estimates of woodcock numbers vary widely between 36,000 and 92,000 breeding birds, but the woodcock population seems to be on the increase, especially in young conifer plantations. In November, numbers swell considerably as the birds flee the severe winter of the northern forests. By day they lie low in the woods, flying out at night to nearby farmland to search for food.

Yet though the southern woods in winter are less cold, they are far from safe for the woodcock for it is a popular game bird and the winter woods resound with the clamour of the hunt. Beaters and their dogs crash through the undergrowth, whooping and trilling and bashing the trunks with their sticks. The woodcock, quietly unnoticed before the line of the drive, suddenly breaks out of cover. No longer does it fly with the measured pace of the roding male, but flickers and shimmies like lightning off between the trees. If the bird gets away, it drops deftly back into cover amongst the brown leaves, safe for another summer.

STRIKING CAMOUFLAGE
(right) The woodcock's tawny speckled plumage blends in so effectively with the forest undergrowth that it can be extremely difficult to spot. This camouflage is a highly successful means of defence against predators such as stoats or foxes. Woodcock can also remain completely motionless for hours at a time; only when an enemy gets too close will it take off, all of a sudden, with a flurry of its wings.

THE EGGS Four eggs are laid, each coloured pale buff with chestnut mottling, which makes an effective camouflage.

Green Lanes

Ribbons of open grassy trackway winding through the landscape can be found in almost every county. Some are little more than simple footpaths snaking over bleak moors, others are wide green swathes between farmed fields, edged by tall trees or hedges; but all are green lanes – pathways across the countryside which were once main highways and arteries of communication and trade in times long gone by. Now largely unused except by ramblers and walkers, the turf might once have resounded to the plodding hooves of driven cattle or to the feet of marauding tribal war-bands.

NORTHERN HIGHLANDS
(Stone Walls)

SOUTHERN LOWLANDS
(Hedges)

ANCIENT TRACK

LINE OF ROMAN ROAD
(Now Footpath)

DROVE ROAD

DROVERS INN

LINE OF ROMAN ROAD
(Now Tarmac)

SQUATTERS HOUSE
(c. 1850)

FIELD ENCROACHMENT

ENCLOSURE ROADS
(Some lengths TARMACKED, the rest STILL GREEN)

NEW HEDGES

ORIGINAL LINE OF DROVE

G reen lanes can be found in virtually every county: some are very ancient indeed, but they can belong to almost any century and, as such, are one of the keys which can help unlock the secrets of our land.

THE RIDGEWAY

The oldest green lanes follow the lines of prehistoric routes. A prime example is the Ridgeway, which on today's maps runs for 85 miles from Ivinghoe Beacon, Bucks, along the scarp of the chalk downs, past the famous Uffington White Horse, to end near the stone circles at Avebury in Wiltshire. Its original length was even greater – running from the flint mines in Norfolk down across the chalk to end by the sea in Dorset. The Ridgeway today is a long distance green footpath hemmed in by fenced fields on either side. Originally it would have been a broader, braided route following the higher, drier ground.

Ancient peoples used the route – warbands, migrating families and their cattle and the first pedlars carrying flint or bronze axes to barter. Like other old routes, the Ridgeway never went out of busy use until quite recently.

Of similar antiquity is the Peddar's (Pedlar's) Way in Norfolk and the Icknield Way, which crosses Cambridgeshire and Hertfordshire. Both were improved by the Romans, and although much of the Icknield Way has been incorporated into modern roads, the Peddar's Way remains a green lane for most of its length.

These ancient trackways sired a web of somewhat similar routes which also remained busy with traffic until recent times. These were the long-distance drove roads. The roads carried cattle, sheep and pigs from the countryside to the towns, or to the great stock fairs, such as that held on Midsummer Common, Cambridge. In the absence of better transport the livestock had to walk to market and only with the advent of the railways did the drove roads really begin to decline. The Welsh Road, for example, ran from the Welsh borders to Buckinghamshire. A stretch of another route survives as Sewstern Lane on the border of Leicestershire and Lincolnshire.

NEW SETTLEMENTS

Many fine drove roads cross the Cheviots – they became important when the Act of Union (1707) put a stop to cross-border cattle raiding and opened up new markets for Scottish beef and mutton. The cattle even travelled as far south as London. Where these drove roads converged, at Elsdon, Northumberland, for example, a village grew up – with a large green for the animals, a pound for the stray stock and a drover's inn, all of which still remain.

Animals apart, people needed to travel too, and although the Romans left a grid of well-

HIGHWAYS AND BYWAYS
(left) The British countryside is criss-crossed by a complex network of routeways, the earliest dating from prehistoric times. The oldest tracks may appear only as cropmarks, although some still survive as long-distance paths. Other green lanes may be the remnants of a Roman road or a drove road – sometimes no more than a series of furrows, sometimes a wide walled or hedged passage designed for large numbers of animals. Subsequent building and agricultural developments have changed the course of many cross-country routes; new straight roads resulted from field enclosure, and like earlier tracks survive as a reminder of travel in bygone days.

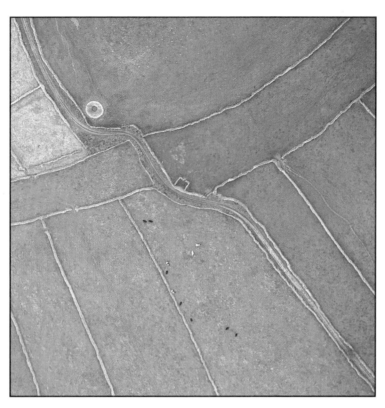

UPLAND AND LOWLAND LANES
(above) Hundreds of miles of drove roads snake their way through our upland landscape, where they are characteristically flanked by drystone walls. The hedges which edge the enclosure track (below) are typical of lowland lanes.

made roads, these fell into disrepair on their departure and soon became impassable and unmarked. In later centuries what roads existed were so pot-holed and muddy that only in a few drier southern counties were carts comparatively common. When that intrepid traveller Celia Fiennes visited Kendal, in the Lake District, around the end of the 18th century all she found were small tumbrils the size of wheelbarrows. Nevertheless, groceries and even chairs were traded south from Kendal at a cost of 1d a pound weight freighting charge, mainly by the age-old means of pack animals.

Roads were not regarded as structures but as common strips of land on which no one could build their house, sow their crops or stack their manure. Upkeep of the roads, if it was thought necessary at all, was usually confined to digging a trench nearby and throwing the earth from it into the hollows and depressions in the road surface. Not surprisingly, most roads were quagmires for much of the year.

THE COMING OF THE COACH

Coach transport really began to force the changes though, going hand-in-hand with road improvement across the new, regulated landscape created by the field enclosure movement. At the same time, many straight new roads were constructed – 40 feet wide and ditched at each side. Toll houses (turnpikes) built along their routes exacted a fee for the privilege of using them. Eventually stage coaches were rattling along the turnpike roads at unprecedented pace.

The days of the rambling, muddy track as the main routes across the land were now numbered and from hereon it was but a short step to the tarmac of today.

Nature Walk

Pub signs often commemorate old droving days, others give false clues. Look for:

DROVERS' INNS, which grew up along the drove roads, often in extremely remote areas. Many still survive.

MARKET TAVERNS, which may have originated to serve local farmers, or drovers who sold on their animals to be fattened up for market.

ANIMAL SIGNS, like The Lamb and The Bull, usually have very different origins. In many parts of Britain The Lamb is a reminder of a prosperous wool trade, whilst elsewhere it may represent the Holy Lamb, recalling the Crusades. And although The Bull is often situated in a market square, it probably refers not to the market ring, but to the bull ring, and to the popular sport of bull-baiting.

Life on the Lane

Unspoiled by tarmac and traffic, the green lane harbours flowers and grasses exiled from the surrounding farmland, along with their attendant insects and spiders.

Like lengthy strips of green meadow, the ancient drove roads persist as broad, grassy lanes across hill and dale. Passing over different soils and through different types of countryside, they may have the characteristics, the plants and animals of chalk grassland, of acid moorland or of damp sheltered lowlands.

On dry, limestone soils, the grasses of the lane are often spangled with flowers that are rare elsewhere, because grasslands have been 'improved' with fertilizer. White umbels of burnet saxifrage, dark blue knobs of devil's bit scabious and, perhaps, the grey and pink spires of downy woundwort mingle with the froth of grass flowers. Beneath them are yellow ranks of cowslips and the red and green globular flower heads of salad burnet. Here and there is the opulent purple gleam of a pasque flower, the bright pinky-purple flower spikes of pyramidal orchids, and the velvety delicacy of bee orchids. Hugging the ground are the tiny gentian-blue flowers of milkwort, the white stars of wild strawberry, and the yellow clusters of horse-shoe vetch and bird's-foot trefoil. Many of these plants are adapted to the dry conditions of chalk grassland, and extend roots deep into fissures in the limestone that underlies the soil. The roots of salad burnet descend 20″ (50cm), and those of horseshoe vetch up to 36″ (90cm).

MYRIAD INSECTS

The flowers and grasses are alive with insects in the sunshine. Grasshoppers chirrup and jump away from your feet as you walk. Bumblebees buzz around the flowers, and flies and beetles wander over the flattened umbels of burnet saxifrage. Small picture-winged flies circle around each other on thistle heads, dipping and twisting their conspicuously black-patterned wings. What looks like a black and yellow solitary wasp turns out, on closer examination, to be a two-winged fly. It is a conopid, flies that not only mimic wasps, but also parasitize them, as well as bees. With stealth and accuracy, they attach their eggs to the host in flight – no mean feat – and, after penetration, the fly larva

HARES BOXING
The 'boxing matches' and extravagant leaps and chases of 'mad March hares' are one of spring's most spectacular sights. Surprisingly, this courtship and territorial behaviour has not yet been fully documented or explained. Sadly, brown hares appear to be declining in England and Wales.

WILDLIFE OF THE GREEN LANE

The plants and animals of the green lane reflect the countryside across which the lane passes. To the left of the picture are species of acid, upland soils; to the right, species of chalk, downland soils. Wherever a spring forms muddy pools, species more usually associated with ponds occur: the pied wagtail, midges and pond skater, for instance. The trees and hedges of downland are a favourite haunt of the hole-nesting little owl, whereas the wheatear favours a niche among stones. The butterflies home in on food plants for their caterpillars: the southerly marbled white lays her eggs on grasses; the northerly large heath lays hers on plants of acid soils.

KEY TO FEATURES AND SPECIES

1 Curlew
2 Heather
3 Sheep
4 Brown argus
5 Common green grasshopper
6 Melancholy thistle
7 Meadow pipit
8 Pasture
9 Little owl
10 Horse fly
11 Wheatear's nest
12 Hare

13 Midges
14 Quaking grass
15 Meadow foxtail
16 Large heath
17 Bracken
18 Pied wagtail
19 Meadow brown
20 Meadow grasshopper
21 Burnet saxifrage
22 Devil's bit scabious
23 Black slug

24 Stream crossing lane
25 Dung flies
26 Bird's foot trefoil
27 Marbled white
28 Ghost moth
29 Common frog
30 Pond skater
31 Dor beetles

GHOST MOTH
(left) This unassuming night-flying species comes into its own as dusk falls. The males gather together and their pale shapes can be seen swinging, wraith-like, to and fro above the grass. This unusual display, during which males are said to release a goat-like scent, is designed to attract females. It can be seen in June and July.

WILD STRAWBERRY
(right) The delicate flowers of this wayside plant appear from April and the edible fruits ripen from June to August.

develops inside the host's abdomen, attached to one of the larger tracheal trunks or breathing tubes.

Where the green lane dips down into a valley, it becomes damper and more overgrown. It is bordered by ancient hedges where brambles and clematis twine through the guelder rose and hawthorn. A farmer uses the lush green expanse as pasture for his cattle, and insects that feed on dung are common. Long-legged yellow dung flies rise from cow-pats at your approach, and a curiously long-snouted hoverfly, *Rhingia campestris*, is feeding from the nectaries deep in the tubular flowers of ground ivy. *Rhingia* is an almost globular, orange-bodied fly, with the sucking mouthparts mounted on a prominent rostrum. It lays its eggs on grass or other plants that overhang cow-pats, and when the larvae hatch, they drop onto the dung, on which they feed and within which they live.

Cattle attract blood-sucking flies, and as you walk, you too are continually irritated by large horse-flies humming around your head. It is only the females that suck blood, from incisions made by their dagger-shaped mouthparts; males visit flowers to feed on nectar. Some of the smaller species of horse-fly are handsome creatures, with patterned wings and iridescent eyes that gleam and change as they catch the light, like watered silk.

A whole range of butterflies and moths have caterpillars that feed on grass, and are plentiful along the green lane. The butterflies are much in evidence in the sunshine, feeding at flowers and basking on leaves. Orange large skippers flit from thistle to thistle, and a silver-spotted skipper, somewhat similar but with silvery-white spots on the underside of the greener hind wings, is resting on a leaf with hind wings held horizontal and the fore wings half open. Their caterpillars use silk to construct shelters from grass blades, those of the large skipper making a single leaf into a tube, those of the silver-

spotted spinning several leaves together. Drab meadow browns flap in and out of the shade of the hedge, and bright orange small heaths bask on grass flowers, to take off at the slightest disturbance.

Also to be seen is the brown argus, a small butterfly with a band of red-orange blotches near the edge of its brown wings. This belongs to the same family as the blues, as is evident when it closes its wings to show their undersides, patterned with tiny, white-edged, black spots.

UNUSUAL SPIDERS

Many spiders have spun their webs over and between the grass stems. Little hammock webs, the sort that glisten in the morning sun when etched with dew, have been spun by diminutive money spiders, many of them black with red legs. The males have bizarre turrets and domes on their heads, said to wedge open the female's jaws during the risky (for the male) business of mating.

A female nursery-web spider has constructed a gossamer scaffolding between several grass stems, within which she hangs her egg sac just before the young emerge. Much more impressive, not to say alarming, is the glossy, brown purse-web spider with massive forward-projecting jaws. She spins a silken tube at ground level, within which she lurks, piercing unsuspecting prey through the wall of the tube, then pulling them in.

Gaudy black and red burnet moths rest on ragwort leaves, taking off almost ponderously when disturbed. They are unusual for moths, in being both brightly coloured and day-flying. Slender-winged pyralids, grass moths, flutter as you push through the grass, then alight again and seem to disappear, so closely do they resemble a rolled, dead grass blade. Examine chewed grass leaves carefully, and you may find the brown caterpillar of a straw underwing

YOUNG CUCKOO
(below) This fledgling cuckoo has swamped the ground-nest of the meadow pipit which has reared it — and still it waits to be fed by the smaller adult pipit. Cuckoos lay 77% of their eggs in the nests of meadow pipits, reed warblers and dunnocks. The females parasitize nests of the species that raised them, and the eggs of meadow pipit-cuckoos and reed warbler-cuckoos closely resemble those of their hosts. Natural selection has led to egg mimicry — many birds abandon a nest containing a strange-looking egg. Oddly, cuckoo eggs do not match the blue eggs of dunnocks.

MARBLED WHITE
BUTTERFLIES
MATING
*(right) This elegant
species can be seen
from June to August
in English counties
south of Durham and
in South Wales. The
female (on the right) is
larger and browner
than her mate.
Marbled whites
belong to the same
family as the meadow
brown and small
heath, and, like them,
have caterpillars
which feed on grass
and overwinter,
before pupating.*

or of a cloud-bordered brindle, and if you pull up the grass, you may discover the caterpillar of a flounced rustic moth feeding on the roots.

In the fading light, a hare races across the green lane, closely pursued by another. A long, musical, mewing call betrays the presence of a little owl, which has been perching motionless for much of the afternoon on a fence post, hardly visible unless you catch the glint of its large, yellow eyes. A grey, long-tailed, hawk-like bird swoops across the lane, alights in the hedge, and gives a bubbling chuckle. Her mate answers from across the valley – 'cuckoo'. Earlier in the day, the female cuckoo laid an egg in the nest of a meadow pipit deep in the tangle of grasses at the edge of the lane.

ACID-LOVING PLANTS

The plants growing amongst the grasses in green lanes in the north on acid soils are rather different from those of the southern chalklands. Bracken and heather spread in from the open moor and crowd out the grass. The greenish-

HOVERFLY IN FLIGHT
*(inset below) This fly –
Syrphus luniger – is one of
more than 230 species of
hoverfly which can be found
in Britain. The males hover
while awaiting females. Both
sexes visit flowers for nectar
or pollen. The flower in the
picture is storksbill.*

MELANCHOLY THISTLES
*(right) The flower heads of
these thistles droop at first –
hence their name.
Melancholy thistles grow
commonly in Scotland,
northern England and Wales,
adding a splash of bright
colour to damp meadows
and banks. They flower from
June to August.*

red, sparse flower spikes of sheep's sorrel and the white-felted leaves and red-purple flowers of melancholy thistle mingle with the grass flowers. Towering over them all are elegant foxgloves: 'fox' is a corruption of 'folks', implying that they belong to the fairies, and *gleow* is the Anglo-Saxon name for a musical instrument incorporating a row of bells. So foxglove is another way of saying fairy-bells. Meadow pipits frequent the green lane here too, but there is another common bird, which flits across the open grass with a flash of white rump – a wheatear. The name we use is a modified and censored version of the old, and vulgar, name that described its white rump.

Plate 3.

Hedge Parsley

Greater Burnet Saxifrage

Restharrow

GREATER BURNET SAXIFRAGE (*Pimpinella major*) A 16-40″ (40-100cm) perennial of lanes and banks, found growing amongst grasses. It prefers basic soils but is local in most places, except the North, where it is rather rare. Flowers from June-August.

HEDGE PARSLEY (*Torilis japonica*) A plant of grassy places, banks and hedges. Widespread and common except in the far North. White lacy flowers appear in July, dominating roadsides after the rough chervil is over. A 2-40″ (5-100cm) annual, it is stiffly hairy.

RESTHARROW (*Ononis repens*) Tough, wiry and trailing, it earned its name as it was reputed to halt the plough. A woody perennial of rough grassland on poor soils, with 1-2′ (30-60cm) trailing stems and summer flowers. Widespread but scattered; most common on chalk.

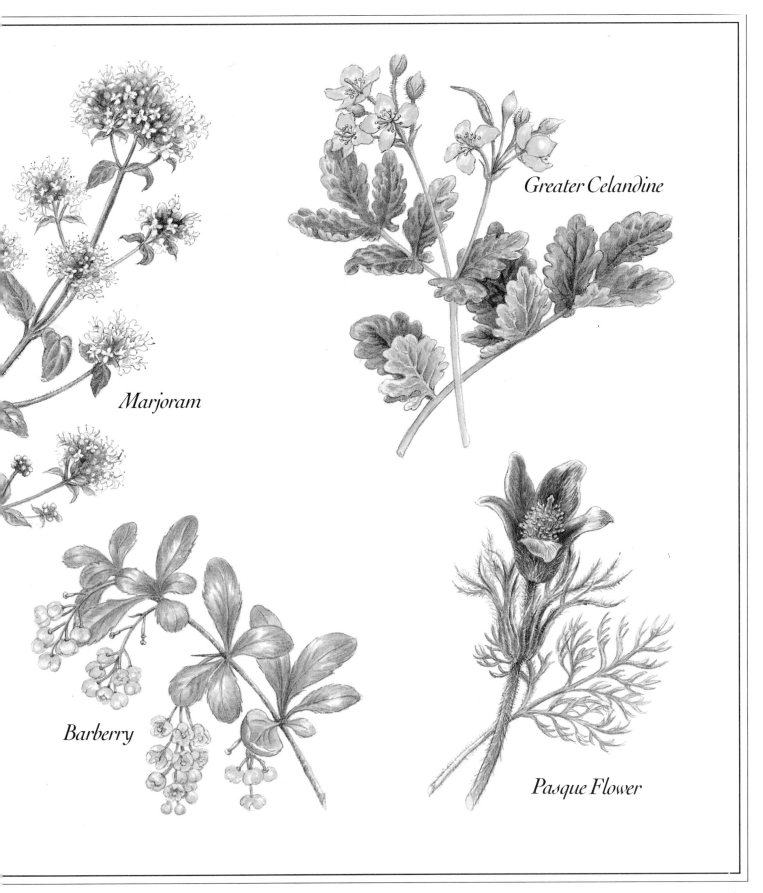

Marjoram

Greater Celandine

Barberry

Pasque Flower

MARJORAM (*Origanum vulgare*) One of the delicately scented herbs of our disappearing downlands; found locally in grassy, chalky places, especially upon banks; rarer in the North. The heads of little flowers are borne in June and July on a 9-15″ (23-38cm) stem.

BARBERRY (*Berberis vulgaris*) A 3-8′ (90-240cm) shrub of hedges and scrub; probably a native and widely planted. The early summer flowers are followed by red fruit, which were candied or made into jelly. The yellow inner bark was given to people with jaundice.

GREATER CELANDINE (*Chelidonium majus*) Perhaps native, but long since grown in gardens as a medicinal herb. A 1-3′ (30-90cm) perennial, commonest in the South, growing on banks and walls and by hedges. Bears flowers through summer. The sap is bright orange.

PASQUE FLOWER (*Pulsatilla vulgaris*) One of our most beautiful flowers, bringing its vibrant purple blooms to chalky downs and banks around Easter time – Pasque is Old French for Easter. A rare perennial not endemic in England. The flower stalks reach 12″ (30cm).

Caterpillar

Plumed Prominent

Brown-tail

Caterpillar

Straw Underwing

BROWN-TAIL (*Euproctis chrysorrhoea*) Most familiar are the hairy larvae, wintering and feeding communally in silk tents, and sometimes devastating hawthorns and other bushes and trees. The adults fly in late summer. Most frequent in the South and East.

PLUMED PROMINENT (*Ptilophora plumigera*) Found in a few chalky places in the South. Takes its name from the elegant antennae of the male. The eggs, laid on field maple and sycamore, hatch in spring. Larvae pupate in summer, adults fly November-December.

STRAW UNDERWING (*Thalpophila matura*) A fairly common moth, with very distinctive hind wings. It is on the wing in July and August, laying eggs on the various grasses which are its food plants. Overwinters as a larva, then feeds up and pupates the following spring.

Ghost Moth

Flounced Rustic

Clouded-bordered Brindle

Caterpillar

CLOUDED-BORDERED
BRINDLE (*Apamea crenata*) Flies
from May until July and is common
in most places. Eggs are laid on
grass heads; the larvae feed on the
grasses, overwinter, then pupate
during spring. Both adults and
larvae are variable in colour.

GHOST MOTH (*Hepialus humuli*)
Widespread and fairly common in
grassy places during summer, when
the males hover and fly back and
forth in groups – probably a
courtship display. The larvae feed
on roots, overwintering, perhaps
twice, before pupating in May.

FLOUNCED RUSTIC (*Luperina
testacea*) A very variable moth in its
forewing colouring. Generally
common – most frequent in England
and Wales – on the wing in August
and September. Larvae feed on grass
roots before and after overwintering, then pupate in summer.

The Song & Mistle Thrush

Thrushes are best known for the brilliance and clarity of their song,
heard ringing from the trees on fine winter days and –
in the case of the mistle thrush – even in stormy weather.

Both thrushes are widespread in Britain. There may be three and a half million nesting pairs of song thrushes, of which under a quarter leave Britain for France and Spain in winter. At this time, however, many migrant song thrushes arrive here from northern Europe, bringing the numbers up to between six or ten million birds.

Though equally widespread, the mistle thrush is much more thinly scattered with perhaps only half a million or so birds remaining here in winter. Many of the young birds migrate to southern Europe while adult thrushes simply leave northern Britain for the South and the Irish population does not migrate at all. Numbers of visitors from the Continent are low.

FAVOURED HABITATS

Song thrushes are familiar garden birds, but live equally happily in a wood with thick undergrowth, or in a dense hedge beside a grassy pasture where they can hop about in search of worms. The mistle thrush is far less frequent in the average garden. It really prefers larger more open areas such as parkland with big, old trees (city parks, woods and orchards). It may also breed in bushy places on the edges of moors and visit treeless hills in search of berries in the autumn. Unlike the song thrush, it forms flocks after breeding, and these roam farmland and wild, hilly and remote countryside.

As a dull and dreary midwinter afternoon slowly dissolves into a damp, windswept evening, a row of tall, leafless ash trees begins to sway. Perched high in one of the branches, fully exposed to the wind and silhouetted against what little light is left in the sky, is a mistle thrush, singing its heart out. Despite the inclemency of the weather, and fast approaching night, the mistle thrush's song is loud, wild and exuberant. Fluty, full-throated notes ring out in a challenge to the weather to do its worst and have justly earned the bird its popular name of 'stormcock'.

All thrushes are magnificent songsters. The notes of the song thrush tend to be more strident and less mellow in tone than those of the mistle thrush, but few birds achieve such clarity and brilliance in their song. It is the repetition of little tunes, phrases and individual notes that best characterizes the song thrush. It too will serenade throughout the winter, but rarely with quite the vehemence of the mistle thrush singing in the face of a howling gale.

SONG THRUSH
(above) The aptly-named song thrush is a common sight in our gardens, singing its clear flute-like notes from a high perch on fine days. Its song is perhaps the most easy to recognize of all garden birds by the vigour and repetition of its notes and phrases.

MISTLE THRUSH
(right) The largest of the thrushes, the mistle thrush is rather less widespread than the song thrush, preferring more open areas such as parks, and building its nest high in a tree. A bold and aggressive bird, it is fearless when defending its nest or feeding place, and will even tackle birds larger than itself.

SNAIL SMASHING
(left) In colder weather when worms are hard to find, snails become an important source of food for the song thrush. Holding the snail in its bill, the thrush smashes the shell repeatedly against a hard object like a large stone or post – using it as an anvil – until the soft flesh can be drawn out and eaten. Favourite sites soon become littered with the tell-tale remains of discarded snail shells.

The mistle thrush is the larger of the two species, at 10½ inches (27cm), with a relatively smaller, rounder head and longer wings and tail. It is greyer, its wing feathers have paler, more streaky edgings and the underside is more evenly covered with large, round black blobs. A song thrush is smaller, usually 9 inches (23cm), browner and more evenly coloured above, with a delicate yellow-buff chest fading to white underneath, sporting V-shaped spots of brown and black. The birds can also be distinguished in flight. The song thrush keeps low, flies fast and disappears quickly into a hedge, perhaps showing a flash of bright buff under the wing. The mistle thrush gains a greater height, bounding along in deep, sweeping undulations, flashing patches of white under its long, pointed wings and showing pale edges to its tail.

Mistle thrushes breed early, making a large nest of grass and lumps of earth, often quite easily visible on a large branch, well before the tree has come into leaf. Four eggs, cream or bluish with brown blotches and spots, are laid in March or April, hatching after 13 days of incubation by the hen. The cock bird then joins in feeding the chicks, which fly after about two weeks. The young mistle thrushes are paler and yellower than the adults, with crescent- or drop-shaped spots of black and white on their underparts. Mistle thrushes feed on berries, slugs, earthworms and snails.

Song thrushes are rather more secretive in their nesting habits, choosing a site in a thick bush or among dark green ivy where the nest will be well concealed. The nest is characterized by a lining of smooth, bare 'mud' – often a mixture of rotten wood or dung and saliva. In this unpromising cup are laid possibly the most beautiful of all bird's eggs, with clear sky blue shells dotted with spots of intense, inky black. The hen incubates them for two weeks and the chicks fly after a further two weeks.

UNUSUAL HABIT

One of the best-known features of song thrush behaviour is their method of eating snails, for they are particularly adept at snail-smashing. They choose a suitable stone, or hard wooden post as an anvil and, with swinging motions of the head, smash the snail to bits until the soft flesh can be drawn out and swallowed. Often the loud, hollow smacking of shell on stone can be heard from some distance away and provides as clear a clue as the pile of shattered shells, to the presence of this inventive bird.

Where snails are less easy to find and worms are plentiful – in warmer weather, for example – song thrushes will live quite happily on worms, fruit and berries.

IN FLIGHT the song thrush has brown spotted underparts and yellow-orange patches on the underwing; the spots on the mistle thrush are larger and the underwing is white.

MISTLE

SONG

THE EGGS of the song thrush are bright blue and speckled while the mistle thrush's are pale buff and blotched.

The Harbour

Man has been a coastal seafarer for hundreds, perhaps thousands, of years. And by taking advantage of naturally sheltered inlets or by building barriers and breakwaters, he has exacted a living from the sea safe from its stormy wrath. Over the years these natural and man-made harbours have helped shape the coastal landscape by attracting settlements to the water's edge. In time some of these expanded enormously, becoming centres of international trade. Others, though, have remained quiet, sleepy backwaters where life goes on much as it has for centuries.

Harbours have an important place in the history of Britain. Here in the past was handled the very stuff which made Britain a prosperous, powerful nation. Silk from the Orient and raw cotton from America, tea from India and ores from Africa were unloaded, while bales of finished cloth, pig iron, fine china, guns, boats, and machinery were shipped out to the rest of the world.

But the harbours were not only busy with foreign trade. Long before the building of an efficient road system inland, much freight went from one part of Britain to another by sea. There is no record of the total, but its sheer size is hinted at by a disaster figure. In 1872 no less than 2000 vessels were wrecked or lost in storms – and this was but a fraction of the boats sailing around the coast, harbour to harbour.

SAFE HAVENS

On the rocky west coast, boats have been sheltered since time immemorial in the many coves which form natural harbours. If large enough, these havens could feed a small cluster of houses by fishing, and it was easy on such rocky coastlines to build out rough breakwaters to add to the natural protection of the cliffs. This is the kind of harbour typical of Cornwall

NATURAL HAVEN
(right) The rugged and unapproachable coastline of north Cornwall is broken only by the safe haven of Boscastle harbour – a naturally sheltered inlet whose steep cliffs of slate formed the basis of the trade for which the harbour was constructed. The village of slate cottages clusters round the twisting creek.

PORTS AND HARBOURS
(below) Harbours of different kinds are built to suit different situations, from the great modern man-made container ports such as Dover (top), to havens capitalizing on natural features, such as coves and estuaries. In time some harbours silt up stranding the town inland, as has happened at Rye, Orford and Bridport.

and much of south-west England. At the heart of it is a wharf – the landing place for the boats and the focus of harbour life. In some cases this is rather like a village green, surrounded by a huddle of huts and fishermen's houses. Sometimes this wide wharf remains, but in other places such as Mevagissey, it has long since been built over. Though popular with generations of holidaymakers, these harbours retain little of their original busy working atmosphere.

On the south and east coasts a different kind of harbour is more typical. This is usually set at the mouth of a river which is often narrowed by a pair of breakwaters. Here, too, a variety of small fishing craft may be seen, and perhaps buildings that reflect past signs of the industry, like fish cellars and net lofts.

On this more open coast, ports, such as Orford in Sussex, often meet a surprising fate. At the time of Henry II, Orford was a thriving harbour, but then the river began to extend the shingle spit at its mouth and created a channel parallel to the coast which cut Orford off from the sea. Today, this spit stretches so far out towards the sea that a boat leaving its moorings has to travel five miles to the open sea. Not surprisingly, Orford's importance as a port subsequently declined.

Great Yarmouth was once threatened with much the same fate; however in the 16th century

SCOTTISH FISHING PORT
(right) Stonehaven, south of Aberdeen provides safe anchorage for fishing boats sheltering from fierce east winds and sea mists or 'haars'.

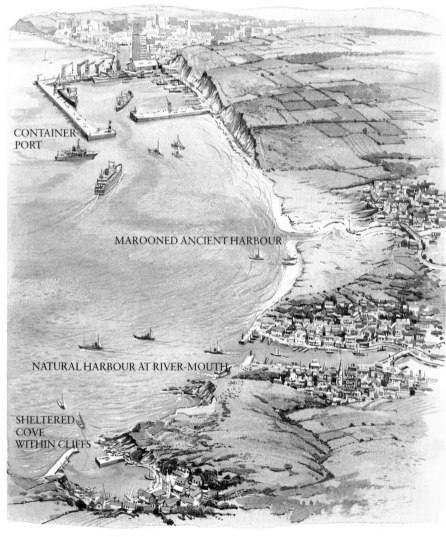

CONTAINER PORT

MAROONED ANCIENT HARBOUR

NATURAL HARBOUR AT RIVER-MOUTH

SHELTERED COVE WITHIN CLIFFS

a clear basin was dug out, for the seventh time, by hundreds of men, women and children. So well was the job done that the harbour remained clear and the town is still an important port.

Dover, one of our classic harbours, overlooked by a Roman 'pharos' or lighthouse and a massive castle atop the famous White Cliffs, was at first a smallish place, but grew in size as trade with Europe increased. Today not much remains of its old world charm, and its huge man-made breakwaters make it one of the largest harbours of the world, serving container vessels as well as cross-channel ferries carrying 5 million passengers a year.

Aberdeen, Hull and Lowestoft are also important ports, still heavily involved with fishing. Here are harboured the middle water trawlers which fish the grounds up to Iceland, and the steel stern boats which follow the herring shoals. Supply vessels run to the offshore oil rigs – a sign of the times. By and large, however, air traffic has usurped the crown of the sea trade.

Small harbours are fascinating places – their life and atmosphere seem to embody the very romance of the sea. For the naturalist too they hold great interest. Rarely inland are we able to get so close to so many truly wild species as we can at the water's edge.

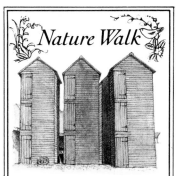

Nature Walk

NET LOFTS Tall, thin huts built with clapboard were once used to store and dry fishing nets.

FLAGS These give signals to boat owners regarding the weather at sea. One flag shows a wind speed of 17-27 knots.

HARBOUR CHAIN During the Napoleonic Wars, some harbours were spanned by a defensive chain.

NAVIGATION TOWERS These mark the main deep water channels in and out of the harbour.

Along the Quay

**Combining several micro-habitats all in one, the harbour
is home to a range of flowers, seaweeds, molluscs, invertebrates and birds,
while the bountiful sea draws crustaceans and fish in at full tide.**

Nestled by the solid stone quay, barnacled fishing boats gently ride their moorings, sheltered from the sea's full force by the seaweed-hung jetty. An angler casts a line towards a shoal of mackerel; a loud *kee-yow* echoes from a herring gull on a cottage roof; and two lesser black-backed gulls wrestle in flight over a small plaice.

The man-made harbour combines features of the headland, the rocky shore, the sandy beach and the open sea. The lichens and flowering plants of the headland cliffs thrive on harbour walls and buildings. Gulls nest among the chimney pots. Each new high tide brings with it crabs, shrimps, prawns and fish in search of food. Various free-floating creatures, notably the common jellyfish, are simply carried in by the sea. This jellyfish's sting is so weak that it rarely affects humans, but other species – the lion's mane jellyfish, for instance – can inflict a painful sting.

The stone, concrete or wooden jetty attracts many species usually found on rocky shores. Seaweeds find a fast anchorage and among them live porcelain crabs, barnacles, mussels,

whelks and winkles. Below the low water mark are species which prefer to remain submerged: colourful anemones, dead man's fingers (a soft coral) and minute colonial animals, such as sea squirts and sea mats, which encrust the jetty or may grow on seaweed. Wooden pilings may be riddled with the tunnels of the gribble and shipworm which can cause serious structural damage.

At low tide a small area of sheltered beach is often uncovered. Many harbours have a mix of mud and sand which is ideal for deposit-feeding burrowing invertebrates, although some harbours (especially in estuaries) are too muddy.

IN THE MUD AND SAND

Even a rich muddy-sand harbour floor appears somewhat lifeless at low tide. The animals are beneath the surface. Most leave no trace of their presence, but there are exceptions. A pattern of short shallow grooves radiating from a central hole indicates the location of a peppery furrow shell. This bivalve mollusc will be buried up to 4″ (10cm) below the sand, with two tubes (siphons) running up to the surface. The long inhalent siphon moves over the sand, sucking

WALL PLANTS
*These plants are growing
on an old stone wall
near the sea, but might
equally be found on
a derelict building
or in a sheltered spot
on the sea cliffs.
In addition to lichens
and mosses, there
are ivy, navelwort
(with circular leaves),
common polypody fern
(bottom left) and sea
spleenwort fern (bottom
centre).*

LIFE IN THE SHELTERED HARBOUR

At low tide the zones of lichens and seaweeds can be seen. At the top are yellowy lichens, then blackish ones and below them the white of barnacles. The seaweeds range from green at the top, down to brown and red, and are most numerous on the inner wall. The shoreline attracts waders and the rock pipit to feed on the invertebrates in the uncovered sand and seaweed. Terns and cormorants dive for fish both in the harbour and offshore, while gulls scavenge for scraps. Seals follow fish shoals in with the tide or come to beg fish scraps from friendly fishermen. Most of the harbour birds nest nearby. The turnstone, though, nests in the Arctic, but is widely seen from August to May. The cormorant, herring gull, rock pipit and fulmar nest on the cliffs, while common terns may join the lesser black-backed gulls in the sand dunes or perhaps alongside oystercatchers on sandy, rocky or pebbly shores. The harbour plants grow on rocks, cliffs or stone walls.

KEY TO THE SPECIES

1 Immature lesser black-backed gull
2 Lesser black-backed gull
3 Fulmar
4 Common scoters
5 Porpoises
6 Lichens
7 Wrack seaweeds
8 Enteromorpha seaweeds
9 Grey seal
10 Common tern
11 Cormorants
12 Turnstones
13 Herring gull
14 Starfish
15 Thrift
16 Oystercatchers
17 Edible crab
18 Wallflower
19 Rock pipit
20 Buckshorn plantain
21 Cuttlefish shell
22 Common mussel
23 Dog whelks
24 Rock samphire
25 Red valerian
26 Polypody fern

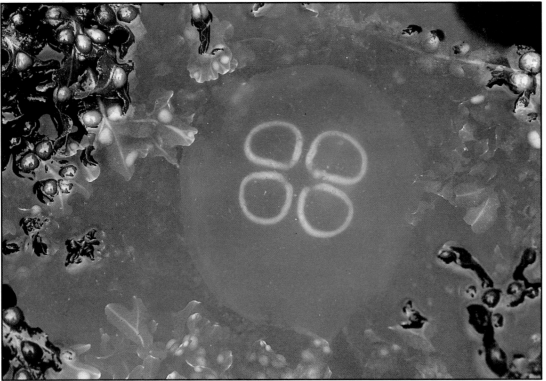

COMMON JELLYFISH
The four pale violet circles – the jellyfish's reproductive organs – account for its alternative name of moon jellyfish. By contracting its umbrella-shaped body it can move up and down in the water but is swept across the sea at the mercy of the currents. Swarms often drift into harbours or bays on the tide. The bluish, transparent bell can be up to 12" across and is fringed with stinging tentacles which stun the small fish and swimming crustaceans on which it feeds. Some young fish – such as horse mackerel, whiting and haddock – seem immune to the stings and often shelter under the bell where they are protected from the larger fish which prey on them.

up fine particles (just like the hose on a vacuum cleaner) and leaving grooves where it has rested. Sucked down within the shell, food particles are strained off by the gills, leaving the water to be expelled up the shorter exhalent siphon. Other bivalves frequently found buried in muddy sand include the Baltic tellin and sand gaper, both of which feed through siphons.

Worm casts and nearby depressions in the sand are signs of lugworms. Much sought after by anglers, these remain hidden in U-shaped burrows below the surface. Common ragworms, on the other hand, are active scavengers and hunters, crawling through or over the muddy sand in search of crustaceans. Red ribbon worms may lurk under stones, while the pinkish cat-worm and the plump, brown peanut worm stay buried and unseen at low tide.

On hard structures, seaweeds are usually more abundant within the shelter of the harbour

than outside. It is easy to assume that these familiar plants of rocky shores – flat wrack, knotted wrack and so on – 'prefer' sheltered conditions or 'need' protection from the waves. This is not so.

Seaweeds only grow where they are able to germinate and are not eaten. The main grazer of young seaweeds in Britain is the common limpet, which thrives under fairly exposed conditions. With fewer limpets present, more seaweeds (and, therefore, the animals that live among them) survive in shelter.

Abundant seaweeds inhibit the settlement of acorn barnacles. This is one reason why (in Britain) these are usually most common on the outer wall. Distantly related to the goose barnacles, which occasionally reach western shores on driftwood (our winters are too cold for them to breed), acorn barnacles have a free-swimming larval stage. The mobile larvae ensure that these

BLACK-BACKED GULLS
(below) The lesser black-backed gull is similar in size to the herring gull but has yellow legs; its darker back and wings vary from dark grey to black. The larger and heavier great black-backed gull is blacker above and always has pink legs.

GREAT BLACK-BACKED GULL

SEAWEED ZONATION
Channelled wrack grows at the top, then spiral wrack and, lower down, knotted wrack.

LESSER BLACK-BACKED GULL

sedentary crustaceans can be found on any hard surface within the harbour – including boat hulls.

The major predator of acorn barnacles is a carnivorous snail, the common dog whelk. With no free-swimming stage in its life cycle, this whelk is confined to permanent structures and is never seen on boats. Dog whelks also attack mussels by boring a neat round hole through the shell, injecting a paralysing agent and digestive enzymes into the mussels' bodies, then, perhaps two days later, sucking out 'mussel soup' through the hole. Attacks on barnacles follow a similar procedure except that adult dog whelks can inject their narcotic without having first to bore a hole.

HARBOUR WASTE

Man is a wasteful animal and for centuries has discarded his rubbish into the sea. Barnacles and seaweeds attach themselves to hard objects thrown into muddy harbours – but it is the edible items of human refuse, such as scraps and offal from fishing boats and domestic waste, that attract the scavengers.

Under loose stones, you will probably find shore crabs. The few you see at low tide give no indication of the veritable army of their fellows that will march into the harbour with the rising tide, to snatch anything visible and depart again on the ebb.

The shoreward migration of crabs is matched

WING DRYING
Cormorants dive for fish and their plumage soon becomes waterlogged, so they spend long periods hanging their wings out to dry. They are often to be seen perched on buoys or rocks around the harbour.

by a similar movement of shrimps, prawns and fish, all scavenging for food. Among other species, plaice, cod, pollack, mackerel and conger may all come in, though one or two conger eels may be resident in underwater hide-aways.

The calmer waters of the harbour may make it easier for cormorants to see the flatfish they hunt – and there are plenty of places on which to stand and dry their wings afterwards.

Along the tideline, small waders (including turnstones, dunlin and sanderling) scuttle along snatching up stranded items of food. Unless the harbour is very muddy, there are usually more waders feeding inside than out – the pickings are richer there. You may have to get up early to see waders, but not so the gulls.

Increasingly, herring gulls are abandoning their traditional cliff-ledge nesting sites for roof-tops. Surprisingly the more oceanic kittiwake is following suit, choosing window ledges of warehouses and other high buildings. The reason is obvious – decreased commuting between home and food supply – but it will be interesting to see how long the locals tolerate the combination of early morning call and distinctive odour, once the novelty has worn off.

RED VALERIAN
(above) This plant with fragrant flowers grows strongly on walls, rocks, steep banks and cliffs, often close to the sea. Commonest in the South, it is absent from much of Scotland and Northern Ireland. The flowers may be pink or white.

SHOAL OF POOR COD
(right) Growing up to 9″ (23cm) long, these fish are generally found offshore, but shoals may come into the harbour on the high tide.

Thyme-leaved Sandwor

Alexanders

Ray's Knotgrass

Rock Sea-lavender

Wild Carrot

ALEXANDERS *(Smyrnium olusatrum)* This stately edible plant grows up to 6' (1.75m) tall, and often shades out smaller plants. It colonizes coastal wasteland areas and hedgebanks. The yellow flowers are borne from April to June and produce ridged black seeds.

RAY'S KNOTGRASS *(Polygonum oxyspermum)* Found on sand or fine shingle above high tide, this is a rare plant of south, west and Irish coasts. It has tough prostrate stems 4-40″ (10-100cm) long, and bears small pink flowers between July and October.

ROCK SEA-LAVENDER *(Limonium binervosum)* A spreading perennial which forms loose mats on sea-cliffs or stabilized shingle. It is most common on the south-west coasts of England, Wales and Ireland. The erect flower-stems may reach 20″ (50cm) between July and September.

THYME-LEAVED SANDWORT *(Arenaria serpyllifolia)* A spreading semi-erect annual or biennial, 1-10″ (2.5-25cm) tall, which grows from tiny seeds on walls, cliffs and bare ground. The small flowers are borne at the end of the straggling stems between June and August.

Wild Cabbage

Fennel

Wild Leek

WILD CARROT *(Daucus carota)* This 12-36″ (30-90cm) biennial with finely-cut fern-like leaves grows on grassy cliffs and fields of the south and west coast, especially on chalky, light soils. The flower heads can be cream or purplish, and are produced between June and August.

WILD CABBAGE *(Brassica oleracea)* Cultivated cabbages and cauliflowers have all descended from this coarse sea-cliff biennial. 12-24″ (30-60cm) tall, it is locally common in southern England and Wales on chalky rocks. The glaucous leaves are waxy to resist drying.

FENNEL *(Foeniculum vulgare)* A tall, 24-52″ (60-130cm), pleasant smelling perennial, fennel only grows in the southern half of Britain. Found on seaside wasteland and along lanes, it has fine feathery leaves and heads of tiny flowers between July and October.

WILD LEEK *(Allium ampeloprasum)* A very rare native bulb of rocky coasts and coastal wasteland in the south-west, the wild leek has tall 24-80″ (60-200cm) stems, and flat leaves with rough margins. A round head of flowers is produced in July or August.

Plate 4

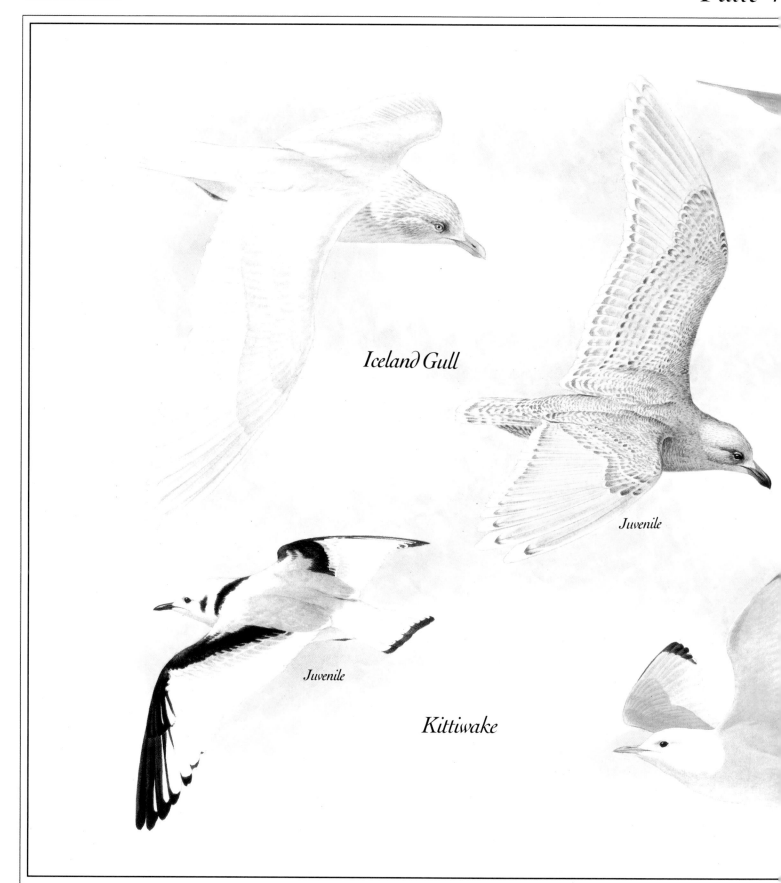

Iceland Gull

Juvenile

Juvenile

Kittiwake

ICELAND GULL (*Larus glaucoides*)
Similar to the glaucous gull, the
(22″ 56cm), Iceland gull is smaller
and lighter, and it has longer wings
and a smaller head and bill in
proportion to its body. Infrequent
visitors to northern shores, they
feed on fish, carrion and rubbish.

KITTIWAKE (*Rissa tridactyla*)
A bird of the open sea, the 16″
(41cm) kittiwake only comes on
land to breed. Nests – cups of grass
stuck to the rock with seaweed and
guano – are made close together on
narrow cliff ledges and two blotched
eggs are laid. The chicks are reared

by both parents for six weeks until
they can fly. Juveniles have
additional black wing and collar
markings. The name kittiwake is a
phonetic approximation to the
bird's loud call. The diet consists of
fish and crustaceans scooped up
from the water.

Glaucous Gull

Juvenile

GLAUCOUS GULL *(Larus hyperboreus)* A large 27" (70cm) gull, which takes three years to mature, growing its adult plumage in its second year. Similar in size, it differs from the great black-backed gull by having blue-grey plumage. The glaucous gull is an uncommon winter visitor from the Arctic, which favours coasts and harbours, where it competes aggressively with other gulls for food – fish, crustaceans, other birds and carrion. Less noisy than many gulls, it utters a range of barks and shrieks. The young have buff speckled plumage.

The Herring Gull

Gliding over the harbour on strong, five-foot wings,
the herring gull is ever watchful, biding its time and waiting
for man to provide its next meal.

Drifting high over the harbour on the warm summer air, the herring gull is in its element. A supremely confident flier, it can float gently for hours with barely a wingbeat to disturb the peace. Even an irritating insect is easily dealt with by a deft flick of the leg.

Suddenly, the low chug of a returning fishing boat breaks the silence and the gull is off, wheeling and squealing, ever-eager to seize on the easy pickings the boat may provide. The herring gull is a true scavenger, with an apparently indiscriminate appetite, and it has learned to make the most of food provided, however inadvertently, by man. Indeed, the herring gull now seems as much at home on the rubbish dump as at sea.

As our cities grow and we discard ever more rubbish, the adaptable herring gull has been swift to take advantage of the new opportunities for food. Inland sightings of gulls used to be rare – associated with stormy weather at sea – but in recent years gulls are seen inland more and more throughout the winter, on reservoirs, playing fields and even on city centre rooftops. Only in the spring will most of these gulls return to their haunts by the sea to feed on fish, molluscs, smaller birds and their eggs – though even here they are happy to eat whatever is available.

The herring gull is a big, strong, aggressive bird – almost two feet long, with a wing span of nearly five feet – and these qualities, as well as its supreme adaptability, has helped it to win out over other species as man has cut into its natural food sources and living space. Puffins returning to their nests with a beakful of fish may often lose their catch to a bullying herring gull. Ducks and terns, meanwhile, are sometimes physically evicted from their breeding grounds by gulls.

Gulls often squabble amongst themselves, too, and the territorial fights of mating males can be especially ferocious, although blood is

BORN SURVIVORS

Big and strong, with an iron digestion, the herring gull is one of nature's survivors. While many birds have suffered badly from man's increasing impact on the environment, the herring gull has positively thrived, making the most of our throwaway society to become amongst the most common of all British birds. Long one of the most familiar of all seaside sights and sounds, the gull is now discovering new haunts, often far from the sea. On a damp winter's day, gulls can often be seen, sitting together in twos and threes, miles inland.

VULNERABLE CHICKS
Laid from mid April onwards, gull eggs must be incubated for about a month before they can hatch. Once hatched, however, they are extremely vulnerable to both predation and cold – only one of these three chicks will survive the first month to leave the nest and learn to fly (after about 40 days).

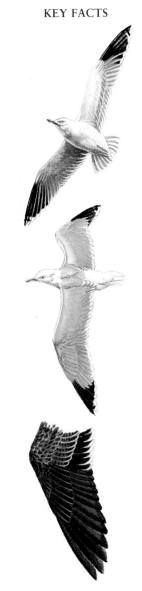

IN FLIGHT adults show white plumage underneath, with black and white wingtips, but are slate grey from above. Juveniles are mottled brown and white (wing above).

rarely drawn. Once they have mated, however, herring gulls form strong family bonds, aided by their highly developed visual and vocal signals. Gulls seem to recognize each other by the coloured circles round their eyes – researchers painting different shades around the eyes have spoiled many otherwise happy matches.

Mating begins early in the spring and although the male is in his fine new breeding plumage, it is the female who takes the initiative. The male simply waits hopefully in a neutral courtship area until an attracted female wheels in and flutters her feathers in front of him. If he is not interested, he rather callously drives her off. Otherwise, he allows her to nuzzle him and peck softly at his beak. At last, he regurgitates – a sign of mutual attraction – and they can mate.

YOUNG GULLS

A cliff ledge or seashore rock have traditionally provided the sites for the gull's simple grass-lined nest but, increasingly, herring gulls are nesting on rooftops and chimneys or on reed beds on reservoirs. The eggs arrive from April onwards, usually three in a clutch, and they are largely incubated by the female while the male keeps her fed by disgorging food from his stomach. Four weeks later, the little brown chicks hatch and start to clamour for food, pecking the red spot on their parents' bills until they regurgitate.

Young herring gull chicks are extremely vulnerable, and barely a third live through the first month. Sometimes foxes and other mammals take the chicks. Sometimes it is other herring gulls. And sometimes it is simply the cold and wet. Of those that survive the first month and learn to fly, perhaps a fifth will die in the first year, forced by older birds to poor feeding sites near the edge of the colony.

Once mature, however, the herring gull's strength and adaptibility ensure that few suffer an early demise – most will live at least 12 years and many over 20. Indeed, gulls are so hardy that conservation authorities often take their eggs to keep numbers down in order to protect ducks and terns. Despite such measures, however, they have continued to multiply and as long as we continue to throw away food their future seems assured.

SEASIDE SCAVENGERS
(below) Juveniles and a mature herring gull swoop on summer scraps.

EGGS are laid three in a single clutch, but a second clutch of one or two eggs may be laid later if the first clutch is lost.

The Rockpool

Rockpools abound along our coast wherever the sea has torn at cliffs which back the shore. Here, the incoming tide creeps over the strewn rocks, filling every crevice, and sometimes splash-filling rock pockets far above the tide-line with spray from the breaking waves. With the sea's retreat, myriad sparkling pools are left, some great, some small, cupped in the rock, to await refreshment on the sea's return. By this eternal cycle, seascapes in miniature take shape within rockpools and many become natural aquarium homes for a wealth of marine life.

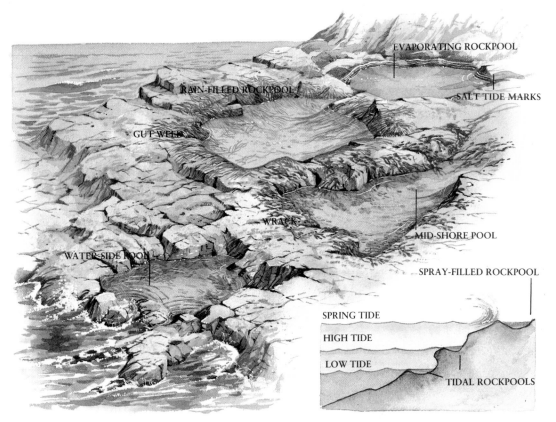

EVAPORATING ROCKPOOL

RAIN-FILLED ROCKPOOL

SALT TIDE MARKS

GUT WEED

WRACK

MID-SHORE POOL

WATER-SIDE POOL

SPRAY-FILLED ROCKPOOL

SPRING TIDE

HIGH TIDE

LOW TIDE

TIDAL ROCKPOOLS

CROWDED CREVICE
(right) A pool the size of this Cornish rockpool will often dry out between tides, and only the most adaptable creatures and plants can live here. Even so, it contains two different species of sea anemone, various algae, limpets and acorn barnacles within its diminutive confines.

INTERTIDAL POOLS
(below) As the sea retreats across the sand at low tide, it leaves a wake of shallow rockpools on this gently shelving beach at Newton Links, Northumberland. The spartan environment provides a home for hardy intertidal lichens.

SHORE ZONES
(above) Rockpools vary with their height above the lowest tide. The highest pools (apart from splash pools) are inundated only by the twice-monthly spring tides but, in between, they often evaporate, leaving only salt rings to mark their shrinking size. Conditions in these pools are extreme: they are heated by the sun, dried by the wind and diluted by the rain – and in winter they may become so cold that they actually freeze. Midshore pools, however, are inundated and uncovered by every tide. Conditions here change with every tide, but are far less extreme, and these pools harbour a profusion of marine life adapted to the variable conditions. Below the normal low tide mark lie pools revealed only by the lowest tides, – most of the time they are part of the sea.

Wherever the coast is rocky, the twice daily falling of the tide leaves glittering rockpools along the shore. Some are little more than puddles, where splashes flung high by breaking waves have accumulated in a dip in the rock. Others are great lagoons, cool and deep, where all kinds of mysterious creatures lurk in the shadows beneath the fronding seaweed. Rockpools form wherever there is a basin in the rock that can trap water as the sea drops away on the ebb tide.

Often, these basins are gouged out by the sea itself, as the unremitting waves pound again and again at a weak point in the rock – perhaps where there is a joint or fault in the rock, or where there is a vein of softer material. Others may occur where rocks at the cliff's foot – brought down by frost and rain and crashing waves – tumble close together on the foreshore, creating little pockets that trap the falling tide.

JOINTS AND FISSURES

Large pools occur most readily where the coastal rock beds lie flat, or slope gradually towards the sea, and where the rock is strongly jointed. Here, sea water may be trapped in great fissures on the rocky platform cut by the waves, or dammed up behind beds of rock rising towards the sea. At Flamborough Head in Yorkshire, the sea has carved a broad swathe across the gently sloping beds of chalk and, each time the tide falls, row upon row of shining pools are left in its wake.

At Flamborough, the pools are broad and shallow. Elsewhere, often where the rock is steeply inclined, the pools may be deep and

narrow. There are pools like this on the north coast of Cornwall where tattered layers of Devonian and carboniferous rock have spilled towards the sea like dominoes, leaving fissures where the sea has worn into the bedding planes.

The most typical formation of this coast is the combe – a deep, steep-sided valley, sometimes tumbling out abruptly on to the shore, usually carrying a stream with it. Where combes drop over low cliffs to the beach, they shed boulders and blocks of split rock. Stream and seawater

Scrambling over slippery rocks and peering into limpid pools may reveal signs of life, such as:

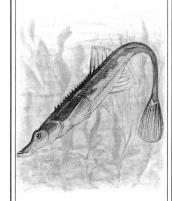

SEA LEMONS, quietly grazing marine organisms. 3″ (8cm) long, this warty sea slug with tentacles and feathery gills produces long ribbons of eggs.

SEA URCHIN SKELETONS or 'tests' up to 8″ (20cm) across, with white tubercles where the spines used to be and lines where the tube feet projected.

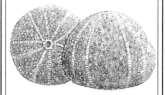

15-SPINED STICKLEBACKS, slender 6″ (15cm) salt water fish, whose mottled coloration forms an effective disguise in the rockpool weed.

combine to carve deep pools among these rocks – often brightly stained with metals from the soil and water. Where combes meet the beach in shallow fans, rockpools are more accessible and are haunted by hopeful lobster-seekers.

A few of the largest pools around the coast were formed by the collapse of sea-caves. Near St Dogmaels in Pembrokeshire, for instance, is Pwll-y-Wrach, the Witches' Cauldron, where the roof of an ancient sea cave has fallen in to leave a vast, dark pool between looming cliffs.

Most rockpools are neither as spectacular nor as sinister as the Witches' Cauldron, but they all share the same ever-changing marginal world between the limits of the tide – there are a few pools up beyond the highest tide, in the splash zone, filled by spray from the breaking waves and by rain, but these are generally small.

Each pool is subjected to a twice-daily routine of dousing and draining. As the tide retreats, the pools drain slowly in its wake. On steeper shores, the pools may descend like the basins of a fountain and, long after the tide has ebbed, the water may continue to trickle, gurgle and drip down over the rocks. After a while, though, all is still in the upper pools and, on hot days, the water begins to warm up in the sunshine and evaporate in the coastal breeze. (On the coldest winter days, the water in the pools may occasionally freeze over, despite the high salt content.) A few hours later, though, the first cool swirl of water in the lower pools heralds the returning tide, and soon all the pools have disappeared again, drowned beneath the rising tide – only to be born again when the tide ebbs.

Pools in the upper shore zone are filled only by the highest spring tides, and tend to be fairly small. Pools in the lower shore zone are large, but are uncovered only at the lowest neap tides. It is the pools in the middle zone, covered and uncovered by every tide that are usually the most fascinating.

The British fascination for exploring rockpools began with the eminent Victorian naturalist Philip Henry Gosse. Gosse's delightful writing about rockpools, and his enthusiastic guided tours of the foreshore near his home in Ilfracombe, helped open the eyes of his fellow countrymen and women to the wonders of these natural seashore aquaria. Soon all kinds of respectable Victorians were donning their rubber boots and making expeditions to the foreshore.

Since then, millions of people have happily scrabbled over rocks slippery with seaweed and rough with barnacles to delve and peer into rockpools, and many have fond childhood memories of the hours spent scrutinizing a miniature sea-world glimpsed through clear, warm water.

In the Rockpool

Rockpools are rich enclaves of marine life, enlivened by bright seaweeds, fast-moving shoreline fish and colourful, though often well camouflaged, anemones, crabs and starfish.

Rockpools are the jewels of the rocky shore. In each one thousands of tiny creatures – some permanent residents, some washed in on the tides – live and interact. There are new discoveries to be made beneath every rock and behind every curtain of seaweed.

The warm, salty pools of the upper shore are fringed with streamers of the green seaweed *Enteromorpha intestinalis* – sometimes called gut weed – and thin films of blue-green algae darken the sides of the rocks. Among the *Enteromorpha*, feathery green fronds of *Cladophora rupestris* sway sinuously as breezes ripple the water. Sandhoppers wriggle through the seaweed, and crabs hide in the crevices and under boulders. The rockpool offers them a safe haven from the prying eyes of gulls.

It is the middle and lower shore pools, refreshed by each tide, that are the real treasure troves. Among the wavy sheets of green sea lettuce and the iridescent purples and brown of carragheen there are fish and crustaceans, worms and sea snails, and thousands of tiny mites too small to see.

Yet it is easy to peer eagerly into a pink-fringed pool and see very little life. One reason for its apparent absence is your shadow cast on the water. Many rockpool inhabitants flee from overhead shadows. This natural instinct saves them from seabird (and human) predators.

Prawns jerk backwards under the weeds, and anemones and fanworms draw in their tentacles. Many animals simply prefer to stay in the cool shelter of the weeds or under rocks near the bottom of the pool. Others are there, but overlooked – successfully camouflaged.

UNDERWATER COLOURS

Some of the pools are lined with coral weed, a red seaweed which forms lime-crusted tufts like miniature petrified forests just below the surface. Another pink alga forms delicate encrustations over the rocky sides and bottom of the pool, as if painted on. It is indeed a form of rock, incorporating lime into its tissues. White squiggles on the rocks look like bird droppings but are actually the hard cases of serpulid worms. These worms spread feathery tentacles into the water to sieve tiny particles of food.

There are other living colours lining these pools. Orange, red and green sponges coat the rocks, filtering the water through tiny pores in their walls. The sea lemon, with its flattened pale body, looks for all the world like a patch of lichen as it grazes on the sponges. And a spattering of tiny stars are the siphons of a transparent colony of sea squirts. These feed like the sponges, drawing water across an internal filter system.

Shrimps and prawns blend with their background, detectable only when they move. Prawns

PURPLE SANDPIPER
A bird very much associated with rocky shores, the purple sandpiper is a winter visitor from the high Arctic. From October it can be seen picking among seaweed by the pools, searching out molluscs, sandhoppers and other crustaceans. They are surprisingly tame birds, perhaps because they nest far from human disturbance.

BIRD'S-EYE VIEW OF A ROCKPOOL

Many of the creatures here are at home both in and out of the water – a necessary attribute for animals that live in the pools higher up the shore. The shrimps, prawns and fish, though, generally live on the lower shore where they are always submerged. The snakelocks anemone, unlike the beadlet anemone, does not occur out of water as it cannot completely withdraw its tentacles.

One predator of the anemones is the sea slug which, far from being deterred by the anemone's stinging cells, digests them and uses them in its own defence. The starfish has the muscular strength to open closed mussels.

KEY TO THE SPECIES

1 Acorn barnacles
2 Common whelk
3 Bladder wrack
4 Shore crab carapace
5 Shore crab
6 Common limpet
7 Common winkle
8 Common shrimp
9 Dahlia anemone
10 Common mussels
11 Common starfish

12 Rough winkle
13 Beadlet anemone
14 Common prawn
15 Coral weed
16 Chameleon prawn
17 Sea lettuce
18 Rock goby
19 Fifteen-spined stickleback
20 Lithophyllum seaweed
21 Breadcrumb sponge

22 Snakelocks anemone
23 Shanny
24 Thick topshell
25 Hermit crab
26 'Parasitic' anemone
27 Common grey sea slug
28 Purple topshell
29 Painted topshell
30 Cowrie shell

BREADCRUMB SPONGE
(below) Not a plant but
an animal, the breadcrumb
sponge encrusts rocks on
the lower and middle
shore. It can be found
both in and out of rock
pools. Its natural colour
is yellow but where the
light is good, green algae
live in the sponge and impart
their colour.

COASTAL OTTER
(above) Though normally
associated with fresh water,
otters thrive on the coast.
Indeed, they are most likely
to be seen on Scotland's west
coast and on the Hebridean
islands. Rockpools form a
ready larder of captive food.
Crabs can be dug out from
under seaweed, molluscs will
be picked off the rocks, and
fish – such as this scorpion
fish – have no escape.

COAT-OF-MAIL SHELL
(below) Also known as
chitons, these molluscs have
articulated armour-plating,
rather like a woodlouse.
Indeed, like woodlice, they
curl up into a ball when
dislodged. They graze algae
off the rocks with a hard,
rasping tongue.

have dark spots of pigment, which can change
size so that the body pattern matches the background. The little chameleon prawn can even
change colour to match the seaweeds it is living
on. In deeper pools shoals of transparent opos-
sum shrimps dart through the water like small
ghosts. The waters of rockpools teem with
thousands of tiny crustaceans, which find trans-
parency a successful camouflage in the bright
surface water.

Some of the crabs match their background by
literally covering themselves with it. They fix
pieces of seaweed and other debris to their
shells by impaling them on the stiff hairs of their
shells.

Hermit crabs are always an exciting find, and
quite common on most rocky shores. They live
in discarded mollusc shells, which provide protection from both predators and the waves.
They select shells into which they can completely
retract their bodies, closing the opening with a
specially enlarged claw.

Starfish glide across the floor of the pool and
over the surrounding rocks at high tide, flattening themselves in sheltered crevices at low tide.

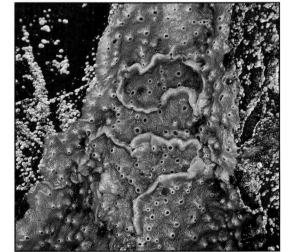

HERMIT CRAB

Nestling in an empty whelk shell, this hermit crab carries around a number of 'parasitic' anemones. These help to camouflage the crab and may be joined by hydroids, sponges and even sea squirts growing on the shell. Hermit crabs may go to great lengths to persuade an anemone to adopt them. Some crabs even pick up the anemone in their claws and place it on their shells. The hermit crab is said to gain protection by the presence of the anemone with its stinging tentacles. The anemone is thought to scavenge pieces of food dropped by the crab.

BLENNY CAUGHT BY A BEADLET ANEMONE

(below) This unwary fish has been harpooned by stinging cells shot out from the anemone's tentacles. When its struggles are over the blenny will be ingested through the mouth in the centre of the tentacles. When not covered by water, the beadlet anemone withdraws its tentacles, closes its mouth and rests like a shiny blob on the rocks, protected against drying out by a slimy mucus.

Sea urchins are conspicuous in the deeper pools of the lower shore. With their armoury of spines they have no need of camouflage.

There are plenty of fish in these pools. Most have a mottled appearance to blend with the brown seaweed fronds. Blennies, particularly, are common. Little gobies usually live on the bottom of the pool under stones or in the sand. Their pelvic fins are fused to form a sucker on the underside, which helps them stay in place when the tide floods the pool.

Other fish are shaped to take advantage of shelter. The eel-like rockling can insinuate itself into crevices, and the butterfish flattens itself under rocks. In deeper pools near the low tide mark, shelter is more abundant and camouflage less important. Here, colourful wrasses hunt for crustaceans.

BRIGHT ANEMONES

After the seaweeds, the sea anemones are the main source of colour in these pools. Their stinging tentacles effectively deter most predators. Like the seaweeds, different species of anemones are found at different levels of the shore. The commonest is the beadlet anemone, found in pools throughout the middle and lower shore, and even out of water on nearby rocks. The larger snakelocks anemone trails its purple-tipped, snake-like green tentacles near the surface of the water.

Other species of shore-dwelling anemone are so well camouflaged that only the slight waving of tentacles gives away their presence. The dahlia anemone's tentacles are mottled, which breaks up their outline. With this camouflage, its prey is more likely to venture within reach.

In deeper pools near the low water mark live plumose anemones, with their feathery white, yellow or pink tentacles. They are filter feeders, trapping tiny particles of debris and microscopic water creatures on sticky mucus sheets coating the tentacles. Clusters of jewel anemones glow among the rocks, often in large numbers, and solitary white cup corals cling to overhanging rocks.

In these shady pools you can find many creatures typical of the coastal sea bed. Many offshore animals lay their eggs in rockpools, and their young flourish in the warmth and safety there until old enough to take their chance in the swirling water beyond. Other rockpool inhabitants, like the starfish and sea urchins, mussels and sea snails, have the opposite strategy. They produce microscopic swimming larvae which drift with the coastal plankton to new homes along the shore.

The intertidal zone is the meeting place between the sea and dry land, between sedentary bottom-dwelling creatures and swimming marine animals. And it is in the rockpool that they mingle most intimately and allow us to glimpse their mysterious world.

PURPLE-TIPPED SEA URCHINS

These attractive urchins are found both in rock pools on the lower shore and in the sea.

Plumose Anemone

Beadlet Anemone

Dahlia Anemone

Jewel Anemone

BEADLET ANEMONE *(Actinia equina)* When the tide recedes these fully retractile anemones are commonly left as blobs of red or green jelly on exposed rocks. Submerged, about 200 crowded tentacles crown a ring of blue dots on a 3″ (7cm) column.

DAHLIA ANEMONE *(Urticina felina)* Common on sheltered rocks, it is short and squat, the column being only 2″ (5cm) high but up to 5″ (13cm) wide. Very varied in colour and pattern. When the dahlia-like tentacles are retracted, it is disguised by debris sticking to the column.

PLUMOSE ANEMONE *(Metridium senile)* A smooth, shiny column 2-5″ (5-13cm) tall has a distinct collar below the crowded head of fine, feathery tentacles. Colour is varied, perhaps orange, white or brown. Common on low shore, beneath rocks and piers.

JEWEL ANEMONE *(Corynactis viridis)* Often brightly coloured, th tiny, ½″ (12mm) high polyp is mor closely related to corals. Three ring of knob-tipped tentacles surround conical mouth. Locally abundant on sheltered rocks at and below lo tide on south and western coasts.

Snakelocks Anemone

Parasitic Anemone

SNAKELOCKS ANEMONE
(Anemonia sulcata) Living in
sunny, sheltered rockpools on the
lower shores of the west and south-
west coasts, this is a short, rather
spreading 1½″ (4cm) anemone. The
6 rows of about 200 2-6″ (5-15cm)
sticky tentacles are non-retractile.

PARASITIC ANEMONE *(Calliactis
parasitica)* This thick, ridged 4″
(10cm) anemone has a beneficial
alliance with hermit crabs. Living
on the crab's 'adopted' whelk shell,
it gains food fragments, protecting
the crab with stinging tentacles.
Uncommon except on south coast.

Sea Lettuce

Coral Weed

Purple Laver

SEA LETTUCE *(Ulva lactuca)*
Abundant on most shores, a bright
green seaweed that grows profusely
near sewage and freshwater outlets.
Seen in summer, the flimsy, smooth
fronds (leaves) are 4-8″ (10-20cm)
long, with reproductive spores
developing at the margins.

CORAL WEED *(Corallina
officinalis)* Rising from a chalky
holdfast, stiff red sprays form tufts
to 5″ (12cm) high, each made up of
calcified bead-like segments with
branches and branchlets in regular,
opposite pairs. Common in pools
and amongst rocks on mid-shore.

PURPLE LAVER *(Porphyra
umbilicalis)* This rose-purple seaweed, up to 8″ (20cm) long, has thin,
gelatinous fronds fixed to rocks by
a holdfast. Widespread, it occurs at
most shore levels. It can survive
when exposed high up the shore but
dries to a blackened sheet.

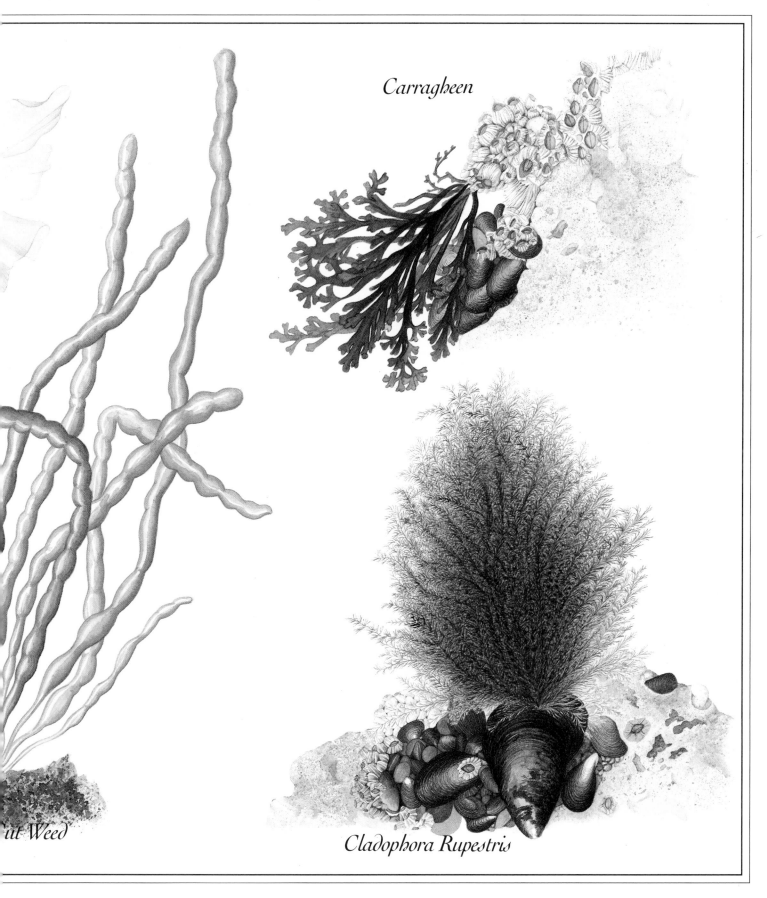

Carragheen

Cladophora Rupestris

ut Weed

GUT WEED *(Enteromorpha intestinalis)* Fronds are intestine-like hollow tubes filled with air, reaching 12″ (30cm). Usually fixed to rocks or stones, this green seaweed is particularly abundant spring–summer in high level pools and near freshwater outflows.

CARRAGHEEN/IRISH MOSS *(Chondrus crispus)* A common, variable red seaweed of mid–low rocky shores all round Britain. Fan-like fronds to 9″ (22cm) spread from a stalk that clings to rocks with a holdfast. It is tallest and thickest near low water mark.

CLADOPHORA RUPESTRIS Though found throughout the year, the wiry, dark green clumps are mostly seen in summer, growing on rocks, mid–low shores and pools, sheltering beneath brown seaweeds. The 3-5″ (7-12cm) tufts consist of many coarse, branched filaments.

The Corkwing Wrasse

Darting like little jewels, corkwing wrasse bring a welcome
splash of colour to the weed-fringed edges of the rockpool
during the spring and summer months.

Approached stealthily on a sunny summer's
day, a large, deep rockpool may yield an
unexpectedly colourful surprise. For in
and around the dark seaweed curtain draping
the pool may lurk one or two corkwing wrasse,
whose almost tropical bright green and blue
colouring may be seen flashing in the bright
sunshine. Also known as Baillon's wrasse, conner
or sea partridge, these spectacular little fish come
inshore from deeper water to spend summer
breeding in the shallows around our rocky coasts,
and sometimes become trapped in rockpools.

Of the seven species of wrasse that frequent
Britain's waters, corkwings are the most common and are found around the east coast of
Ireland and most of the English coast, particularly in the South. Like other wrasse the corkwing is deep-bodied, with a snub nose and the
protruding thick-lipped mouth that characterizes the family. In fact, the family name,
Labridae, derives from the Latin word *labrum*,
meaning lip.

Gregarious fish, corkwings haunt weed-
fringed rocks and eel-grass beds in small groups

ROCKPOOL COLOUR
*Deep in the gloom of the
rockpool the shy corkwing
wrasse brings a burst of
tropical colour as it emerges
from the safety of a rock
crevice to feed. The vibrant
blue and green head stripes
of the male clearly
distinguish him from the
similarly coloured but
stripeless female.*

EFFECTIVE CAMOUFLAGE
Changing his colour to match his surroundings, the male corkwing (left) blends perfectly with the seaweed-encrusted rocks of his pool home. Deep-bodied fish with large scales on the head and sharp spines on the front of the dorsal fin, corkwings have a distinctive black spot just in front of the tail. They use their thick pouting lips to tweezer shellfish from their hold on the rocks. These are then quickly and noisily ground up by the sharp, chisel-like teeth at the front of the jaws and strong knobbly teeth in the throat.

of up to half a dozen individuals. They like the deeper pools, where the rock crevices and coarse seaweeds provide hiding places from which they emerge now and then to feed.

The corkwing swims by 'rowing' its pectoral fins, just behind the gills, rapidly to and fro and waving and twisting the back and anal fins, using the tail as a rudder. If it senses danger it can put on an impressive burst of speed, undulating its muscular body to produce a powerful sweep of the tail. Most of the time, however, the fins are used to make extremely precise manoeuvres – up, down, forwards and backwards – among the seaweed and into holes and crevices in the rocks where this little fish obtains its food.

During the day the corkwing wrasse uses its prominent lips like delicate tweezers to pluck tiny crabs and barnacles from the rocks and seaweeds. It makes short work of molluscs and crustaceans by crushing them in its powerful toothed jaws and swallowing the lot, flesh and shell fragments together. Young corkwing wrasse may 'clean' other species of fish, removing parasites and fragments of dead skin, like a tropical relative of theirs – the striped cleaner wrasse.

At night the corkwing wrasse rests sleeping on its side. It may shelter in rock crevices, bury itself in the sand or sleep – eyes wide open – on a frond of kelp.

DUTIFUL FATHER

When spring arrives, breeding male corkwings undergo a colour change, becoming a brighter blue, and adorned with blue stripes on the lower sides of head and belly. They start to stake out their territories, aggressively chasing away other males from their chosen patch.

Each male then builds up to 14 nests, made by using his prominent lips to weave several layers of seaweed into loose balls. These are usually wedged firmly in spaces between rocks, and are all built at the same time – the male

flitting from one to the other.

When nest-building is over, the male parades proudly in front of one of his nests, fanning the water with his pectoral fins, in an attempt to attract a female. Eventually, a ripe female may lay her large, bead-like eggs at the entrance to his nest, and the male fertilizes them and pushes them rather haphazardly into the nest. He is then kept busy guarding its precious contents from predators, chiefly other fish.

The mating and egg laying process is repeated several times at different nests, then the male chases the female away. He remains a dutiful father, however, protecting the young as soon as they hatch – a difficult task as they face many dangers. As well as being eaten by many fish, they may fall prey to large dahlia anemones, whose pretty but deadly poisonous tentacles entice many a baby wrasse into a fatal embrace.

CUCKOO WRASSE
The most colourful of all British wrasse is the cuckoo wrasse. Here, a stunning male parades his metallic blue and orange colours in front of the handsome red female. During the display his head suddenly blanches for a few seconds, the colour just as quickly re-appearing. If the female is ready she will follow him to the hollowed 'nest' he has excavated on the rockpool bottom, to deposit her eggs. All the eggs develop into female fish, some of which then change sex after 7 to 13 years.

The Starfish

The starfish is a masterpiece of purposeful adaptation,
stalking its helpless victims with unerring accuracy and
feeding on them in a most unusual way.

One of the sea's most unmistakable creatures, distinguished by its simple shape, the common starfish is a highly specialized eating machine. And there is more to this simple creature than at first meets the eye.

One of several species of starfish which live around our shores, the common, or red, starfish is the most abundant. It is variable in colour, though usually yellowish, rather than red and may also be purple or orange, yellow-brown or red-brown. Each of its five (sometimes four or six) fat tapering arms connects to a central disc which contains the mouth, stomach and, on the top surface, the anus.

FLEXIBLE SKELETON

Beneath the surface of the starfish's hard skin is a supple skeleton made of small limy plates that allows the creature to flex its arms and which grows as it matures. The growth rate depends on the amount of food available, and in ideal deepwater conditions, it may reach 20" (50cm)

PEST OF THE MUSSEL BED
(above) Found throughout British waters, the starfish is especially abundant on mussel and oyster beds.

WELL ARMED
(right) The starfish can shed its arms if they get trapped, and can regenerate entirely from a single limb containing a piece of central disc.

across. Those found in rockpools are usually much smaller, around 5" (12cm). It can survive months of starvation, during which time growth stops altogether, and it has another remarkable survival mechanism – a complete new starfish can grow from a single arm with a part of the central disc. A starfish will readily cast off an arm that gets trapped, and about 10 per cent of the creatures have misshapen limbs in the process of regeneration. Projecting through the skin from some of the skeletal plates are white, protective spines: those which line the top of

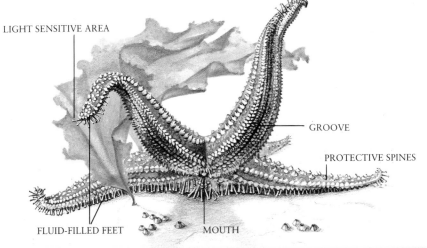

LIGHT SENSITIVE AREA

GROOVE

PROTECTIVE SPINES

FLUID-FILLED FEET

MOUTH

THE SIMPLE LIFE
(left) The starfish lives to eat, and its rudimentary senses of sight and smell are used almost entirely to locate prey. A truly marine animal, it cannot survive long out of water.

TUG OF WAR
(below) To open oyster and mussel shells, the starfish exerts steady suction with its multiple tube feet, gradually forcing a tiny opening. It then inserts its stomach into the shell to consume the contents.

ending in a sucker. When the sac contracts, water is forced into the tube-foot and prevented from flowing back by a valve. The tube foot extends, grips the rock with its sucker, and edges the starfish forward. As the sac relaxes, water returns to it, and the cylinder shortens. On soft sand and mud, the suckers are useless and the starfish has to use its tube feet as legs.

Any of the five arms may take the lead when the starfish moves – they are all perfectly co-ordinated. The starfish does not have a brain, but there is a nerve ring around its mouth from which radial nerve cords go down each arm.

CREEPING CARNIVORE

With such a laborious method of locomotion, achieving speeds of only 2-3″ (5-7cm) per minute, it comes as a surprise to learn that the starfish is an entirely carnivorous animal. Its prey, however, is stationary – sedentary mussels and oysters, and the occasional scallop – so no predatory chase is necessary.

To reach the edible parts of its armoured victim, the starfish humps its body over the mollusc, attaches its tube feet to the two shells, and pulls. A battle of endurance ensues – the mussel closes its valves tightly, but the starfish uses its many tube feet in relays, so when some tire, others are brought into play. Eventually, the mussel becomes exhausted and lets its valves gape a little. A pin-sized gap is enough for the starfish. It turns the lower part of its stomach inside out through its mouth, and inserts the film-like wall into its victim. The starfish has no teeth with which to break down its food, but secretes digestive juices from the stomach wall straight on to its victim, and then absorbs the resulting soup into its stomach, leaving a clean empty shell behind.

The life expectancy of the common starfish is five to six years, and it is sexually mature after the first year; the sexes are separate, though indistinguishable. There are two reproductive organs in each arm which open directly to the sea through tiny pores which shed millions of sperm and eggs straight into the sea each spring. Larvae hatch from randomly fertilized eggs, and drift with other plankton. Few survive the hazards of early development, but those that do will have drifted far from the rockpool in which they started life.

each arm are rigid, giving the starfish an abrasive upper surface; the spines on the underside are flexible and can be closed protectively over the grooves. Some spines top and bottom have tiny pincer-like attachments which keep the surface of the starfish meticulously clean, seizing and crushing any sand grains, shell fragments or bits of seaweed clinging to the animal. This is necessary to keep the skin gills clear – these project all over the starfish's back from between the limy plates, and regulate the intake of oxygen, and the diffusion of carbon dioxide.

The starfish has a mantle of sensory cells that are sensitive to touch – stimulation of any part of the animal evokes a response from the entire body.

Between the spines on the underside are hundreds of tube feet which enable the animal to glide over the bottom of a rockpool without moving its arms. On a hard surface these feet work by hydraulic pressure. Each one has a balloon-like sac attached to a hollow cylinder

Index

Entries and page references in **bold** type refer to main feature articles; page references in *italic* type refer to illustrations